THIRD EDITION

AFRICAN AMERICANS AND THE AMERICAN POLITICAL SYSTEM

Lucius J. Barker
Stanford University

Mack H. Jones
Prairie View A & M University

Prentice Hall, Englewood Cliffs, New Jersey 07632

Library of Congress Cataloging-in-Publication Data

Barker, Lucius Jefferson. [date]
African Americans and the American political system / Lucius J. Barker and Mack H. Jones.
p. cm.
Rev. ed. of: Black Americans and the political system. 2nd ed. 1982.
Includes bibliographical references and index.
ISBN 0-13-084575-2
1. Afro-Americans Politics and government. 2. United States—Politics and government—1945-1989. 3. United States—Politics and government—1989- I. Jones, Mack H. II. Barker, Lucius Jefferson, [date] Black Americans and the political system. III. Title
E185.615.B33 1994
323.1'196073 dc20 93-38022

Acquisitions editor: *Charlyce Jones Owen*
Editorial/production supervision and interior design: *Joanne Riker*
Cover design: *Miguel Ortiz*
Photo research: *Page Poore-Kidder*
Production coordinator: *Mary Ann Gloriande*
Editorial assistant: *Nicole Signoretti*

Previously published under the title:
Black Americans and the Political System, Second Edition

A Paramount Communications Company
Englewood Cliffs, New Jersey 07632

Printed in the United States of America

10 9 8 7 6 5 4 3 2 1

ISBN 0-13-084575-2

Prentice-Hall International (UK) Limited, London
Prentice-Hall of Australia Pty. Limited, Sydney
Prentice-Hall Canada Inc., Toronto
Prentice-Hall Hispanoamericana, S.A., Mexico
Prentice-Hall of India Private Limited, New Delhi
Prentice-Hall of Japan, Inc., Tokyo
Simon & Schuster Asia Pte. Ltd., Singapore
Editora Prentice-Hall do Brasil, Ltda., Rio de Janeiro

TO

MAUDE, TRACEY, & HEIDI

AND

BARBARA, LUMUMBA,
TAYARI, BOMANI,
MAXINE, MARCIA, & WILLIE MAE

CONTENTS

CHAPTER 2
THE NATURE OF THE PROBLEM 30

CHAPTER 3
THE NATURE OF THE SYSTEM 50

CHAPTER 4
THE QUEST FOR POLITICAL RESOURCES 69

CHAPTER 5 THE SUPREME COURT AND THE POLITICS OF UNCERTAINTY 93

CHAPTER 6 COURT, JUDGES, AND THE INTERACTION OF THE LAW AND POLITICS 131

CHAPTER 7 CHANGE THROUGH POLITICS: INTERESTS GROUPS 173

PREFACE

Black Americans and the Political System, Second Edition, was published in 1980 and after a 13-year hiatus, our publishers have prevailed upon us to do what we would have done anyway—publish a third edition. While one of the co-authors has changed, the central objective that guides this volume has not—that is, how black people fare in the American political system.

But there has been a noticeable change since 1980 in the commitment and pace of black progress. Indeed, if anything, the situation facing blacks as we enter the 1990s is actually deteriorating, shattering progress and hopes engendered by the 1954 *Brown* decision, the Civil Rights Movement, the Civil Rights Act of 1964, and the Voting Rights Act of 1965. Yesterday's achievements of the Warren Court and the Kennedy-Johnson administrations have been chipped away and overturned by the more recent Burger-Rehnquist courts and the Reagan-Bush administrations.

The symbols of change of the 1950s and the 1960s are simply not being converted into the substance of change envisioned. On the one hand, those symbols (such as black elected officials) in large measure tend to obscure the continuing hardships and plight that blacks experience in everyday life. But on the other hand, those symbols are being replaced by other symbols indicating that the position of blacks in American society remains as uncertain as ever.

Two recent dramatic occurrences demonstrate the point. First, President Bush's appointment in 1991 of black conservative Judge Clarence Thomas to replace Justice Thurgood Marshall, widely heralded as "Mr. Civil Rights," confirmed even more that the once strong support blacks had received from the federal government was indeed a thing of the past. Second, the Rodney King verdict and the resulting Los Angeles violence, and violence across the country, brought frightening memories of urban violence of the 1960s, shockingly revealing the continued gross inequities and maltreatment that black Americans still face in today's America. Viewed in broad perspective, these two highly visible signs remind us all of the deep difficulties and barriers involved in overcoming the racial "problem." They likewise challenge all

Americans to focus once more, and place on their agendas, the question of how blacks fare in this country. That is the challenge and burden of this volume.

The story of how African Americans fare in the political system is both fascinating and frustrating. It continues to provide one of the most penetrating vantage points from which to view the nature and operation of the political system. Indeed, the experience of blacks in American politics allows us to relate the constitutional theory and structure of our political institutions and processes to their everyday operation and practice. We can see most vividly, for example, how and in what ways the structures and functions of the Congress, the Presidency, the Supreme Court, and the bureaucracy affect the aspirations of blacks and other minorities. In a similar vein, we can view the roles that interest groups and political parties perform in the political system as they relate to blacks. The insights that are unearthed in an analysis of this nature are quite fascinating, revealing the intricate nature and functioning of the political system in ways that might otherwise be obscured.

But we also find the endeavor frustrating. Given the nature and operation of the political system, it is still debatable whether we can bring about the kind of changes necessary so that blacks and the minorities can enjoy the full benefits and responsibilities of American society. As we define it in Chapter 2, the "problem" that blacks face in this country has many dimensions. Some aspects of the "problem" are quite visible, open, and tangible. They involve very concrete deprivations relating to the socioeconomic status of African Americans. To be sure, certain positive legal actions and some progress have come about in this regard, almost always, however, in response to crisis situations, such as the Los Angeles riots following the Rodney King verdict. In any case, there have been continuing and growing manifestations that "enough" has been done for blacks. These include adverse Supreme Court decisions, conservative policies and practices of the Reagan-Bush administrations, and open and visible resurgence of racist behavior and attitudes on college campuses and in election campaigns.

There are other aspects of the "problem," however, that are more elusive, intangible, and intractable. We refer here to institutional racism—practices, arrangements, and rules of institutions that act so as to collectively advantage some and disadvantage others. Many institutions (both public and private) operate in certain ways so as to seriously disadvantage blacks in contexts where "race" per se is never mentioned. In their book *Institutional Racism in America*, for example, Prewitt and Knowles suggest that institutions "reward by providing career opportunities for some people and foreclosing them for others." (p. 8) "They reward," the authors continue, "by the way social goods and services are distributed—by deciding who receives training and skills, medical care, formal education, political influence, moral support and self-respect, productive employment, fair treatment by the law, decent housing, self-confidence, and the promise of a secure future for self and children." As we ponder how African Americans fare today, it is clear that "institutional racism" remains a continuing and viable obstacle to black progress in both public and private arenas and in all sectors of our politics and society.

Hence, despite the quite notable progress that has been made since the 1950s and 1960s, as we moved into the 1980s, and now 1990s visible signs abound indicating that such progress has been blunted and indeed may be going in reverse. Thus, it remains more uncertain than ever whether we as a nation can maintain, or more aptly *regain,* the reserve and determination necessary to overcome the "problem." The situation, of course, is perennially complicated by international developments that cause priorities and commitments to be constantly shifted and rearranged in order to meet what are considered the most pressing or "most important problems" at the time.

Clearly these developments include resource allocations that might be needed with respect to such matters as the newly developing democracies in Eastern Europe, and particularly matters that involve the lessening of the cold war and the increasing needs required to deal effectively with the demise and restructuring of what was once a powerful Soviet Union, now the Commonwealth of Independent States. As a result, the attention and resources necessary to deal with pressing domestic problems are viewed by some as more needed to deal with these other needs and considerations. Overall then, as often in the past, it remains the case today that intervening events and developments both at home and abroad—ranging from personnel changes following elections to rearrangement of priorities occasioned by threats to peace and by war itself (such as the 1990 Persian Gulf war)—serve to threaten progress in overcoming "the problem" and the continuing debilitating effects of racism in this country. But as the Los Angeles riots following the Rodney King verdict in 1992 explosively indicate, domestic problems can also pose serious threats to peace and security and much *closer* to where we live and work everyday. Clearly such situations require the attention and concern of all Americans.

Thus, just as in the first edition, our major purpose remains an attempt to describe and analyze America's racial "problem" in terms of the dynamics and operation of the political system. And we have tried to do more than merely update changes that have occurred over time. We continue to make real efforts to suggest the meaning and implications of these changes for African Americans, for whites and all Americans, and for the political system generally.

For example, we discuss in various contexts: (1) the nature and limits of electoral politics in dealing with "the problem"; (2) the opportunities and constraints that shape the role of black elected and appointed officials; (3) the political and social implications of demographic trends; (4) the changing functions and problems facing civil rights groups; (5) the persistent and changing nature of the "problem" facing African Americans; and (6) factors that influence and shape the response to the "problem" by institutions in both public and private sectors of our socio-economic order (such as, Congress, the President, Supreme Court, interest groups, commerce and business, and the communications and information industry.) In a concluding chapter we, as authors and as Black Americans, "speak out" on particular topics and developments that hold important and long-range implications for our overall politics and society.

A few other comments. Just as in our earlier editions, we continue to provide some special features. For example, at the end of each chapter we provide several Topics or Questions that hopefully will stimulate thought and discussion about matters dealt with in the respective chapters. These topics should prove useful in small or large group settings, or as assignments for written papers. Additionally, we also include at the end of each chapter a selected bibliography for those who might wish to do additional reading. And, as mentioned earlier, a special feature of this volume (Chapter 11) offers interpretations and perspectives on various topics and issues that are designed to stimulate discussion and debate.

We wish to acknowledge a number of persons who have helped us along the way. In addition to those mentioned in the earlier second edition, we wish to thank those selected by our publishers to review this third edition: Professors Robert C. Smith, San Francisco State University; Michael W. Combs, University of Nebraska–Lincoln; and Lewis A. Randolph, Ohio University. We also wish to thank those who provided other invaluable assistance with this edition including Jeremy Buchman, graduate research assistant at Stanford and Carole Neuenhoff, for secretarial assistance at Prairie View A & M University.

CHAPTER 1

BLACK AMERICA AND THE POLITICAL SYSTEM: THE POLITICS OF UNCERTAINTY

While I applaud the judgment of the Court that a University may consider race in its admissions process, it is more than a little ironic that, after several hundred years of class-based discrimination against Negroes, the court is unwilling to hold that a class-based remedy for that discrimination is permissible. In declining to so hold, today's judgment ignores the fact that for several hundred years Negroes have been discriminated against, not as individuals, but rather solely because of the color of their skins. It is unnecessary in 20th century America to have individual Negroes demonstrate that they have been victims of racial discrimination; the racism of our society has been so pervasive that none, regardless of wealth or position, has managed to escape its impact. The experience of Negroes in America has been different in kind, not just in degree, from that of other ethnic groups, it is not merely the history of slavery alone but also that a whole people were marked as inferior by the law. And that mark has endured. The dream of America as the great melting pot has not been realized for the Negro; because of his skin color he never even made it into the pot.

Justice Thurgood Marshall, Dissenting Opinion,
University of California Regents v. *Bakke* (1978).

The question posed by this case is whether the Constitution prohibits a union and a local school board from developing a collective bargaining agreement that apportions layoffs between two racially determined groups as a means of preserving the effects of an affirmative hiring policy, the constitutionality of which is unchallenged.

Under Justice Powell's approach, the community of Jackson, having painfully watched the hard-won benefits of its integration efforts vanish as a result of massive layoffs, would be informed today, simply, that preferential layoff protection is never permissible because hiring policies serve the same purpose at a lesser cost. As a matter of logic as well as fact, a hiring policy achieves no purpose at all if it is eviscerated by layoffs. Powell's position is untenable.

Justice Thurgood Marshall, Dissenting Opinion
Wygant v. *Jackson Board of Education* (1986)

INTRODUCTION

The two excerpts from dissenting opinions of Supreme Court Justice Thurgood Marshall, which appear as epigraphs to this chapter, illustrate vividly the ambivalence of the United States in confronting the race problem as both a moral and an economic question. In the 1978 *University of California* v. *Alan Bakke* case, considered by many to be the most important civil rights case to reach the Supreme court since the 1954 landmark school desegregation case,[1] by a 5-4 vote the justices came to two major conclusions. First the court decided that Alan Bakke, a white applicant, must be admitted to the University of California-Davis Medical School since that institution's special admissions program was so inflexibly structured as to be biased against whites. Second, the Court concluded that it was not unlawful under a carefully structured and flexible affirmative action plan to consider race as a "plus" in establishing admissions criteria.

In the *Wygant* case, eight years after Bakke, the court held that although race may be taken into account in hiring to achieve racial balance, maintaining racial balance cannot be used to apportion layoffs if it has adverse effects on whites as individuals. And in 1989 the Court went a step further when it ruled in a Richmond, Virginia, case involving minority set-aside contracts that race conscious numerical remedies are suspect and therefore can be used only to address specifically identified instances of discrimination but not historical patterns of racial discrimination.[2]

Overall, the *Bakke, Wygant* and *Richmond* cases reflect the continuing efforts of American policy makers to deal with the race problem without acknowledging that certain societal elements materially benefit from racial discrimination and even more importantly without accepting the fact that the continuing inequities cannot be eliminated without material cost to whites, individually and collectively.

We appear to be unable or unwilling to cope with present realities in order to overcome the sordid legacy of the past. But our "roots" persist. The problem of race and color will not fade away in clouds of legal formalities and patriotic symbols. The use of clever slogans such as "deracialization," "children at risk," or "the declining significance of race" diminish neither the racial character or urgency of the problem. It must be faced squarely and forthrightly. The civil rights movement and subsequent events vividly evidence a determination among African Americans to share fully and equally in the benefits and responsibilities of the American society. And the fact that much observable progress has been made does not lessen this continuing determination. If anything, such progress increases the impatience with the pains and vestiges of race discrimination that remain. Of course, the persistence of such problems makes it that much more difficult to espouse such values as "freedom" and "equality" in convincing and meaningful terms.

In addition, it is hard to overlook or ignore the plight of those who constitute the largest minority in the country as African Americans do. African Americans make up about 12 percent or 29,986,000 of the approximately 248,709,000 people in the United States. During the 1960s the black population increased by almost four million, and from 1970 to 1990 the increase was about five million. While the population growth rate has thus slowed, the rate of increase among blacks (and other minorities) continues to be more than among whites. Between 1980 and 1990 the black population increase was 13 percent compared to 6 percent for whites.

Our discussion thus far suggests that this problem persists in part because of several factors. First, there is the determination and drive of blacks to share fully and equally in American society. Second, there is the stark realization by many persons, both whites and blacks, that America's evolving and continuing commitment to such values as liberty and equality demands action to overcome such problems. And, finally, there is the plain fact that in a democracy the sheer size of the black population makes it not only hypocritical but very impractical to ignore such problems. Consequently, how we deal with the problem of race and color takes on both moral and political importance.

But for many Americans, the matter of race and color is no longer among the nation's "most important problems." To be sure, issues tend to be somewhat cyclical in American politics and seldom command prime attention over a long period. However, regardless of the issue, the matter of race is never far below the surface. For example, a closer look at many of the most important problems in the 1990s, such as unemployment, energy, and health care, reveals all too clearly that our inability to deal with these problems can reap untold and disproportionate hardships on blacks and other minorities. And the fact that these problems affect all Americans should not lead us to overlook their extra impact on those who already suffer deprivations because of race and poverty.

In a related vein, however, there is a growing tendency to define what are basically racial problems in nonracial terms.[3] For example, the fact that a disproportionate number of blacks as compared to whites remain unemployed or underemployed is increasingly defined as a class instead of a race phenomenon.[4] Put another way, it is often argued that if blacks have the job prerequisites in terms of education and training then they can compete successfully with whites and will not suffer from race discrimination. Thus, the problem is said to be more a matter of class instead of race. This, of course, begs the question of why these requisites are so low among one race of people and it also fails to explain why the return on these requisites, education for example, is significantly lower for blacks than for whites. Indeed in 1980 the median income for black males with four years of college and working full time was $17,861, considerably less than the $26,139 for white males with four years of college and even less than the median income of $19,857 of white male high school graduates.[5]

Or take another example. The school desegregation controversy is now widely defined and discussed in terms of "quality education." It is suggested that "quality education" rather than "racial integration" should be the primary goal. Obviously, this is a laudable goal, and it is very appealing and attractive to a great many persons, white and black. But we suggest that blacks should question this attempt to define the school desegregation controversy in "nonracial" terms. We need to examine more closely the political and policy implications of what is involved. The point is that defining the school desegregation controversy in terms of "quality education" could perpetuate inferior schools in predominantly black communities. History has shown that blacks have invariably not received the kinds of resources (i.e., money, professional staff) necessary to achieve and maintain quality public education. Differential and unequal treatment based solely on race and color has been so deeply ingrained in the nation's laws and traditions that one should be wary of mechanisms that permit continued isolation (and differential treatment) of blacks from the American mainstream.

Overall then, it is clever to define the desegregation controversy in terms of "quality education," since defining the issue in this way stimulates support from a number of blacks, who believe, justifiably in some cases and wistfully in others, that "our" schools are as good as or better than "theirs." The banner of "quality education" also stimulates racial pride—for example, blacks do not need whites to have a "quality" school. And this, too, is undoubtedly the case. But, as Justice Marshall put it so well in his *Bakke* dissent, we cannot ignore the fact "that for several hundred years Negroes have been discriminated against, not as individuals, but rather solely because of the color of their skins." Aside from its other values, public school desegregation makes it difficult to discriminate against blacks "solely because of the color of their skins." Consequently, while not eschewing the laudable goal of "quality education," blacks should constantly be alert lest this "nonracial" term be used as a cover to return to a "separate but equal" era where "separate" was very separate and "equal" was very unequal.

We are, of course, keenly aware that how issues are defined might be matters of strategy that could cut both ways. But, on balance, we believe that—at least in examples such as those above—the main objective of those advocating "nonracial" explanations of black deprivation is to divert attention from the fact that race remains a real problem. We suggest that such attempts at issue definition (or redefinition) will not, however, permit us to circumvent or to ignore for long that the problem of race is still very evident in American life. As Justice Blackmun put it in his *Bakke* dissent: "In order to get beyond racism, we must first take account of race. There is no other way." It is hoped that we will heed Justice Blackmun's advice and continue to come to grips with the problem of racism.

There are a number of things we need to explore in this chapter as we focus on this continuing problem. In a political system in which population and votes contribute to political power, a sizable minority can have considerable weight. But before we can assess the influence of blacks as such a minority in this political system, we need to know more about African Americans: the distribution of the black population; their socioeconomic status; the political and social characteristics of the black "community"; the kinds and dimensions of problems that blacks continue to face; and the political behavior and participation of the black electorate. We also need to know more about white Americans, particularly their attitudes toward blacks and the race problem. We also must give attention to the values, structures, and dynamics of the political system and how these relate to the capacity and capability of the system to deal with problems of race and color. In general, we think it is particularly important to understand the past experience of blacks in the political system. What that experience can suggest to us about the present and future status of blacks, and indeed of the political system itself, is one of the principal reasons for this volume.

But before addressing any of these questions it may be useful to explore briefly the frames of reference used in the study of black politics because the framework employed can determine the meaning or interpretation we give to our experiences.

In the remainder of this chapter we (1) discuss several frames of reference used to study African American politics in the United States; (2) review briefly the history of the African American political struggle; and (3) discuss the importance of the size and distribution of the African American population as a political resource.

FRAMES OF REFERENCE AND AFRICAN AMERICAN POLITICS

African American politics, like all other forms of social activity, can be understood only in the context of a particular approach or frame of reference. A frame of reference is a set of general assumptions about the nature of the subject or experience being investigated, what concepts or categories of analysis are the most useful for understanding it, what level of analysis should be adopted, and what questions should be explored to develop the most useful understanding of that which is being investigated.

Frames of reference serve dual functions in social inquiry: as lenses and as blinders. As lenses they provide the basis for giving a particular meaning to experience; as blinders they may render the investigator unaware of competing perceptions and interpretations of that same reality. To reinforce the point, a decision to accept certain assumptions as a point of departure is at the same time a decision to reject others. For example, the scholar who begins with the assumption that there is an inexorable process through which disadvantaged groups are gradually integrated into the American political, social, and economic systems as equals is at the same time a decision to reject the counterview that the struggle for inclusion should be viewed as a conflict between one group seeking to maintain its dominant position and another seeking to overturn the hierarchy. Similarly a decision that certain concepts have greater empirical utility for understanding reality is a decision that other concepts and the explanations which might be constructed using them are less useful. Thus to accept pluralism, assimilation, accommodation, and related concepts as orienting devices for studying African American politics precludes the use of concepts such as class, class struggle, and the like. A frame of reference tells what to look for. In that sense it illuminates. On the other hand it draws our attention away from other developments and causes us to remain oblivious to other interpretations of reality. In that sense the frame of reference acts as a blinder.

In recent years there has been considerable discussion about the most useful frame of reference for understanding African American political life in the United States.[6] For example, the pluralist, melting-pot model has been challenged on the grounds of both descriptive adequacy and prescriptive utility; that is, its adequacy in describing exactly what transpires in the politics of black America and its usefulness in stimulating critical thinking regarding what can or should be done to transform the inequitable conditions under which blacks live. Below we will discuss the pluralist model since it is the most commonly used, and three alternatives which have challenged its hegemony.

PLURALIST, MELTING-POT, RACE RELATIONS CYCLE MODEL

The pluralist model depicts the United States as a society which moves predeterminedly toward a state of equilibrium characterized by countervailing forces which insure that no one group predominates and all groups get something substantial. The model views the United States as a series of ethnic communities which over time are melted into an integrated nation. The model assumes that new groups are at first considered outsiders and are relegated to a subordinate status, but that over time they will become more and more Americanized and in the process strengthen their competitive position until they are ultimately accepted as equal ingredients in the American nation. The histories of Irish Catholics and European Jews are often cited as empirical examples which validate this theory. It is only a matter of time, the model infers, before African Americans like European ethnic groups, become an equal partner in a new equilibrium.

However, inasmuch as African Americans were part of American society long before several of the ethnic groups which had already achieved parity in American society, it was necessary to make special modifications in the pluralist, melting-pot model to make it "fit" the African American experience. The race relations cycle of Robert Park and the citizenship political development cycle of Talcott Parsons offered such modifications.[7]

Park argued that when the cultures of people of different races came into contact their relations went through four distinct stages: contact, conflict, accommodation, and assimilation. According to this theory, after the initial stage of conflict, the weaker group would accommodate itself to the dictates of the stronger one and this accommodation would eventually make possible the cultural transformation of the weaker group and ultimately its assimilation into the dominant culture.

This process of assimilation was said to be a function of certain laws of human development and therefore irreversible, although the process might be delayed by certain accidents of history. In due course, according to the logic of Park, the "race problem" would be solved through assimilation.

Park's race relations cycle was offered as a general theory to explain the pattern of sociocultural relationships which developed following the contact of racially different cultures. By contrast, Parsons was more concerned with the pattern of political relations which ensued. He hypothesized that, based upon the experiences of European ethnic groups in America, the African American struggle for inclusion would go through three fairly distinct stages before full equality was realized. The first stage would involve a struggle for basic legal rights, and it would be followed by agitation for full and effective political participation which would be won and consolidated. Finally, the subordinate group would shift its efforts toward acquiring the economic and social resources sufficient to permit the group to function on an equal footing with other groups.[8]

Park's race relations and Parsons's citizenship-development cycles are both based upon the assumption that there is a gradual and almost automatic process through which subordinate racial groups gradually achieve equal status. Scholars who employ the race relations or citizenship-development cycle models assume that the African American political experience in the United States is analogous to that of one European immigrant group or another and use the experience of the latter as a benchmark in assessing the presumed position of African Americans along the predetermined path toward assimilation and equality.

Critics of this approach assert that history provides prima facie evidence that the African American political struggle for inclusion has been fundamentally different from that of European immigrant groups and that consequently these pluralist models are inappropriate devices for describing the dynamics of black politics. Moreover, critics continue, the cycle models with their telelogical focus, assumption of automatic change, and tacit support for gradualism reduce the prospects for analyses which might yield more promising prescriptions for fundamental change.

THE COLONIAL MODEL

During the decades of the 1960s and 1970s when the intensified struggle for African American advancement was met in many quarters with equally intense white resistance, the idea of automatic racial progress and the appropriateness of political strategies linked to such notions came under attack. Scholars began to search for a frame of reference which on the one hand would give a more satisfactory description and explanation of the then contemporary developments and on the other hand would lead to more convincing prescriptions for effective remedial action. The colonial model as a frame of reference evolved in this context.

Proponents of the colonial model argue that it captures the essence of the economic, cultural, and political dimensions of the African American predicament and that it is therefore especially useful for developing a comprehensive understanding of black politics. Essentially the colonial model suggests that the relationship between African Americans and the holders of state power in the United States is similar to that which exists between the colonized and the colonial master. Focusing on the spatially separate African American communities of the urban North and the heavy concentrations of African Americans in the southern Black Belt, the colonial model views African Americans as a unit apart, an internal colony, which is systematically exploited by white society. Blacks are viewed as a separate nation which exports cheap labor and imports finished goods from the broader community.[9] The sharp and enduring differences between blacks and whites on various indicators of socioeconomic well-being such as income, employment, and health care are depicted as the result of the exploitative colonial relationship.

As powerless colonial subjects, blacks are viewed as being unable to influence positively the decisions which determine the conditions under which they live, even when blacks occupy authoritative positions. This apparent paradox is explained by the idea of neocolonialism. The real holders of power, neocolonialism asserts, are those who control pivotal economic resources both within and external to the black community, and it is they who determine the direction of important political decisions even when they are made ostensibly by black political authorities.

Just as classic colonizers disrupted and undermined the cultural autonomy of the colonized and imposed upon them the culture of the colonizers, the same is said to be the case with the internal black colony. The black community is pictured as the object of cultural imperialism dating back to slavery and continuing with the appropriation and commodification of black cultural forms during the present epoch. The ability of the black colony to mobilize its resources and particularly its human resources for effective political struggle is undermined by the destruction of its cultural base.[10]

THE DOMINANT-SUBORDINATE GROUP MODEL[11]

The dominant-subordinate group model is an extension of "power theory" which conceptualizes politics as but an extension of the unending universal struggle for power and black politics in the United States as a local manifestation of the same. What distinguishes the black-white struggle in the United States from other local manifestations of this ubiquitous power struggle, the model infers, is the use of the ideology of white supremacy and the related notion of black inferiority to justify the dominant position of whites and to defend the various institutions and practices which sustain white domination.

Drawing on these assumptions in an earlier work[12] one of the authors argues that the key to understanding black politics in America is the realization that those in superordinate positions invariably act in such a manner as to preserve their position of dominance and that, therefore, whites in the United States act toward blacks in such a manner as to maintain white hegemony. Thus rather than conceptualizing black politics as a process through which black people, propelled by some unseen hand, move inexorably to a position of equal status, it is more appropriate to conceptualize it as a power struggle between two groups, one bent on maintaining its position of dominance and the other struggling for liberation.

Historically, dominant groups have used several basic political strategies to maintain their position of dominance. These include (1) assimilation, (2) legal protection of minority rights, (3) pluralism, (4) population transfer, (5) continued subjugation, and (6) extermination. On the other hand, subordinate or oppressed groups have attempted to use the first four strategies along with a fifth—reversal of status through revolutionary activity—to alleviate their oppressed conditions. At any point in time there will be identifiable forces within the dominant community advocating the use of any one or any combination of the six strategies as the optimum method for maintaining control while, conversely, within the subordinate community there will always be groups advocating the use of any one or any combination of the five counterstrategies as the optimum means for alleviating their oppressed condition.

Generally speaking, factions within the respective communities seek, first of all, to solicit intracommunity support for their position and then to influence elements in the formal political structure such that a faction's position becomes national, state, or local policy. For example, the National Association for the Advancement of Colored People (NAACP) seeks, first of all, to convince the black community that integration is the proper strategy for political advancement and then to have its position adopted as national policy.

Thus black politics has four distinct dimensions: (1) a struggle within the white community regarding the optimum means for maintaining white control with minimum systemic stress and strain; (2) a struggle within the black community over the optimum strategy for liberation; (3) conflict and collaboration between and among black and white factions; and (4) struggle within formal governmental structures over authoritative policy decisions. These four struggles occur simultaneously and interdependently. Black politics is their sum. It must be noted, however, that these struggles cannot be neatly separated from all other power struggles going on simultaneously in society, and that therefore developments in the realm of black politics are often influenced, disproportionately, by other conflicts.

The dominant-subordinate group model makes several contributions to our efforts to conceptualize black politics. By highlighting the role of the white supremacist ideology in justifying the white position of dominance, it provides a better basis for studying and understanding the intractability and the enduring character of the American race problem than those other approaches which assume a certain preordained evolution toward a predetermined end. It also provides the basis for a more insightful understanding of internal conflicts within each of the communities and of the alliances which develop between black and white factions.

The dominant-subordinate group model, however, is not without its shortcomings. The most glaring one is its failure to provide a basis for identifying and understanding the material basis, the economic elements of the black problem. The assumption that the white community acts in a manner to maintain its position of dominance conveys the impression that white dominance is an unqualified end in and of itself, and in the process the model begs the fundamental question; dominance toward what end and in whose discrete interest.

HARRIS'S ALTERNATIVE FORMULATION[13]

The alternative formulation advanced by Donald Harris, a Stanford economist, was not developed as a frame of reference for black politics per se but rather as a critique of the colonial model as a conceptual scheme for understanding the economic conditions of black America. Nevertheless it is a useful device for describing and interpreting the material base of black politics and for understanding how the two—economics and politics—converge.

Writing in response to what he perceived to be both the descriptive inadequacy and prescriptive limitations of the colonial model, Harris argues that although there are superficial similarities between the history and conditions of African Americans and conventional colonial subjects, the similarities are more apparent than real, and that, moreover, the prescription which naturally evolves out of the colonial model—political independence and a separate nation state—is neither a logical nor feasible strategy for African Americans.

Harris's alternate formulation begins with the assumption that the spatial separation of blacks in racially segregated neighborhoods does not mean that blacks exist as a unit apart. Blacks are not a separate economic entity that interacts with a broader and separate American economy of which it is not an integral part, as is the case in a classic colonial relationship. Rather Harris views African Americans as an integral part of the American political economy and suggests that the persistence of the unequal economic status of blacks is to be explained by examining (1) the basic structure of the American economy, (2) the essential laws of American capitalist development conditioned by the racist ideology of white supremacy, and (3) by understanding how the three—the structure, the laws, and the racist ideology—come together to determine the position of blacks in the economy.

The key to understanding the enduring unequal economic conditions of blacks, according to this model, is to be aware of the fact that the American economy is divided into two distinct sectors, the corporate and petty capitalist sectors. The corporate capitalist sector provides a reasonably adequate material life for those workers employed in it. The return to workers in the petty capitalist sector is much less adequate. In addition to the two sectors, and existing in a dialectical relationship to them, is a sizable and fluctuating number of potential workers who are unable to find work in either sector. The existence of these two sectors and the nature of the intersectoral flows between them are said to be functions of the laws of American economic development. The distribution of black workers within these sectors, particularly the disproportionate clustering of blacks in the least rewarding sector of the economy, is said to be the result of the laws of American economic development conditioned by racism. Racism, institutional and personal, insures that blacks remain in subordinate positions.

The corporate capitalist sector is comprised of large capital intensive enterprises which pay relatively high wages to its largely unionized workers and even higher salaries to its managers. The petty capitalist sector is made up of relatively small, often poorly capitalized, labor-intensive firms with a low paid preponderantly nonunionized work force. The fact that black workers are employed disproportionately in the petty capitalist sector and in the lower job categories of the corporate capitalist sector, according to this model, explains much of the differential in black-white income figures.

Moreover the extreme deprivation of inner-city blacks both as workers and consumers, which the colonial model explains as the result of superexploitation, is explained by the alternative formulation as the result of the laws governing the relationship between the corporate and petty capitalist sectors. The model assumes that there is always tension between the two sectors because of the dominant corporate capitalist sector's constant drive to expand. When technological breakthroughs and other general economic conditions make it feasible to do so, it expands into areas heretofore exploited by petty capitalists. Thus the most profitable areas in the petty capitalist sector are constantly being gobbled up by the corporate sector, leaving the petty capitalist to struggle in an increasingly marginal environment. To stay afloat as employers, petty capitalists must get more out of their workers while minimizing labor costs, and similarly, to survive as merchants, they must get maximum return from sales. Thus, according to the model, the low wages and unsafe, repressive working conditions which are increasingly commonplace as one descends the scale in the corporate capitalist sector and which exist in varying degrees throughout the petty capitalist sector are explained at least partially by intersectoral dynamics. The same explanation is said to hold for the shoddy practices of inner-city merchants, landlords, and financial institutions. Racism and the sociocultural structures, institutions, and practices spawned in its ideological wake, the model argues, are important factors in rationing access to the two sectors and in determining the racial composition of the group of workers unable to find places in either sector. But the volume of low paying jobs, repressive working conditions, and endemic unemployment are functions of the nature of the economic system and not merely the consequence of racism.

To the extent that the American culture, like all others, is the product of an evolutionary process, present-day institutions are necessarily and definitionally extensions of their historical antecedents as conditioned by societal values and changing material conditions. Thus the model assumes that the educational, social, political, and cultural institutions which have evolved are parts of a social whole that routinely recreates and sustains conditions which ensure white access to favored positions and relegates blacks to the least desired ones. The alternative formulation, of course, does not deny that in many instances racism and racist practices may supersede the laws of capitalist development in explaining the inequitable position of blacks in the American economy. Such would be the case when better qualified blacks are denied job interviews or refused bank loans.

Turning to the implications of Harris's alternative formulation for understanding black politics, it suggests that the struggle against racism in employment is a struggle for equalizing unemployment among the races. It infers that to the extent that African American politics is first and foremost a struggle to end the general deprivation of African Americans *it is in part a struggle to equalize the distribution of deprivation throughout the society*. Thus the reduction of blacks unemployment would mean a commensurate increase in white unemployment.

The chief virtue and contribution of Harris's alternative formulation toward understanding black politics is that it brings to the fore the material basis of black politics. This approach sensitizes the observer of the need to understand the discrete interests involved and rescues the subject from ethereal discussions of moral dilemmas and psychological domination. It also places it in a more empirically grounded context. While it probably cannot stand alone as a frame of reference for black politics, it is certainly a valuable supplement.

In our view no single one of the frames of reference discussed above can be said to be the correct one. Each of them calls attention to certain important aspects of the black political experience, but some may be more useful than others. Throughout this text we will make use of these and other frames of reference as it may seem appropriate. In the next section we will use the dominant-subordinate group model in our discussion of the historical background of contemporary black politics.

A BIT OF HISTORY: THE POLITICS OF UNCERTAINTY

The black political struggle for inclusion has been at once a struggle to overcome constitutional and statutory barriers to black political participation as well as a campaign to transform the American political culture which legitimizes and sustains exclusionary institutions and practices. The ultimate objective of black politics, therefore, is to create the conditions under which African Americans might enjoy material, cultural, and social equality with their white compatriots. In that sense, black politics, like all other politics, is a means toward an end. In the end, it is the end that matters.

Passage of the several civil rights acts of the 1960s, culminating with the adoption of the Voting Rights Act of 1965 and the Housing Act three years later, signal, more or less, the triumph of efforts to overcome legal barriers to black participation and economic access. Three decades later, however, the material, social, and cultural conditions under which African Americans live remain markedly different and *unequal* to those of whites. Indeed there is considerable evidence which suggests that the material inequality between black and white Americans is actually growing. This paradoxical situation provides the setting within which contemporary black politics unfolds. The following brief survey of the history of black politics will help us understand how this paradoxical situation came to be.

THE BEGINNING, 1619-1865[14]

Even though there is some evidence that African Americans may have come to what is now the United States as early as the sixteenth century, the unbroken black presence began when some 20 Africans landed in Jamestown, Virginia, in 1619. Contrary to popular opinion and in spite of the fact that the African slave trade had been going on for more than a century, apparently the first blacks who came to the United States in 1619 did not come as slaves but as indentured servants and for the first two decades their legal status was the same as their fellow white servants. The change of their status from indentured servant to slave occurred over several decades in the various colonies and the rise and refinement of the ideology of white supremacy to justify black slavery followed a similar progression.

Indeed prior to the Civil War, communities of free blacks existed side by side with slavery. When the United States was launched as a republic in 1790 there were 59,000 free blacks, 27,000 in the North and 32,000 in the South.[15] Although initially given the right to vote in most states, free blacks were almost completely disfranchised by the 1840s. The various states also imposed other legal restrictions on free blacks such as limiting their mobility by requiring them to carry passes and by imposing severe limitations on occupations in which they might engage.

Prior to 1857, albeit in piecemeal fashion, the national government signaled its acceptance of the rising ideology of white supremacy.

According to a prominent historian;

> Reflecting the popular concept of the United States as a white man's country early Congressional legislation excluded Negroes from certain federal rights and privileges and sanctioned a number of territorial and state restrictions. In 1790 Congress limited naturalizations to white aliens; in 1792 it organized militia and restricted enrollment to able bodied white male citizens; in 1810 it excluded Negroes from carrying the United States mail . . . on the basis of such legislation, it would appear that Congress had resolved to treat Negroes neither as citizens nor aliens.[16]

But in 1857, the Supreme Court, in the *Dred Scott* decision quoted at length below, embraced without reservation the dominant ideology of white supremacy and the related view that blacks had no rights which whites were bound to respect. The Court said:[17]

> The question is simply this: can a negro, whose ancestors were imported into this country and sold as slaves, become a member of the political community formed and brought into existence by the Constitution of the United States, and as such become entitled to all the rights, and privileges, and immunities, guaranteed by the instrument to the citizen.
>
> The only matter in issue before the court, therefore, is, whether the descendants of such slaves, when they shall be emancipated, or who are born of parents who had become free before their birth, are citizens of a state in the sense in which the word "citizen" is used in the Constitution of the United States.
>
> We think they are not, and that they are not included, and were not intended to be included, under the word "citizens" in the Constitution and can, therefore, claim none of the rights and privileges which that instrument provides for and

> secures to citizens of the United States. On the contrary, they were at that time considered as a subordinate and inferior class of beings, who had been subjugated by the dominant race, and whether emancipated or not, yet remained subject to their authority, and had no rights or privileges but such as those who held the power and the government might choose to grant them....
>
> In the opinion of the court, the legislation and histories of the time, and the language used in the Declaration of Independence, show that neither the class of persons who had been imported as slaves, nor their descendants, whether they had become free or not, were then acknowledged as a part of the people, nor intended to be included in the general words used in that memorable instrument.
>
> It is difficult at this day to realize the state of public opinion in relation to that unfortunate race, which prevailed in the civilized and enlightened portions of the world at the time of the Declaration of Independence, and when the Constitution of the United States was framed and adopted. But the public history of every European nation displays it, in a manner too plain to be mistaken.
>
> They had for more than a century before been regarded as being of an inferior order; and altogether unfit to associate with the white race, either in social or political relations; and so far inferior, that they had no rights which the white man was bound to respect; and that the negro might justly and lawfully be reduced to slavery for his benefit. He was bought and sold, and treated as an ordinary article of merchandise and traffic, whenever a profit could be made by it. This opinion was at that time fixed and universal in the civilized portion of the white race. It was regarded as an axiom in morals as well as in politics, which no one thought of disputing, or supposed to be open to dispute; and men in every grade and position in society daily and habitually acted upon it in their private pursuits, as well as in matters of public concern, without doubting for a moment the correctness of this opinion....
>
> The language of the Declaration of Independence is equally conclusive. . . . The general words . . . would seem to embrace the whole human family, and if they were used in a similar instrument at this day, would be so understood. But it is too clear for dispute, that the enslaved African race were not intended to be included, and formed no part of the people.

Chief Justice Taney's opinion in *Dred Scott* was and remains the most clear and candid statement of, and defense for, the ideology of white supremacy to become a part of the American public record.

With such attitudes prevailing it is not surprising that during this period the dominant political strategy among blacks was to secure legal protection for free blacks and emancipation of the slaves. As the *Dred Scott* case demonstrated, continued subjugation was the dominant but not exclusive policy in the white community. Strands of legal protection and population transfer were clearly evident. White support for policies other than continued subjugation however was essentially a northern phenomenon supported primarily by church-based societies.

Population transfer as a strategy for dealing with the black political presence received support from diverse quarters, including prominent whites such as Thomas Jefferson and President James Monroe. These forces, led by the American Colonization Society, advocated emigration of blacks to Africa. Although many blacks opposed emigration of free blacks because they felt that it would only prolong slavery, there was black support for population transfer schemes including persons such as Paul Cuffie and Bishop Turner. The issue was debated in the black convention movement and in the black press. Several modest population transfer schemes were actually implemented. Some transferred blacks to Africa and others began black settlements in what was then the Western frontier.

EMANCIPATION, RECONSTRUCTION, AND NULLIFICATION, 1866-1883

The defeat of the South in the Civil War and the resultant emancipation of the slaves ushered in an era in which legal protection and continued subjugation became the primary strategies for maintaining white dominance, while legal protection and assimilation[18] became dominant policy orientations among blacks. Legal protectionists prevailed during the 1860s and 1870s and succeeded in having the Constitution amended and statutes passed which established legal protection against slavery, bestowed citizenship upon blacks, affirmed the right to vote, insured access to all public accommodations, and guaranteed due process and equal protection of the laws to blacks. Statutes also provided federal guarantees of protection from terror and intimidation from whatever source in the exercise of these rights. Thus by 1875 the legal status of blacks was technically equal to that of whites.

However, as is widely understood, legal victories are merely reflective of the balance of political forces at a given historical moment. Whether such victories can be consolidated, sustained, and become consensual elements of the society's cultural fabric is determined by the evolution of the competing forces. In this case the evolution of forces mitigated against black interests. In effect, the Republicans made a deal with white southern Democrats in order to keep the presidency. Following the compromise of 1877, in which the proponents of legal protection capitulated to the advocates of continued subjugation, the political fortunes of blacks declined precipitously. The Supreme Court by 1883 had nullified the principal sections of the civil rights laws designed to protect black rights and to shield them from intimidation and terror. Consequently black political participation as voters and officeholders was severely constrained and blacks were rapidly reduced to a state of penury and powerlessness.

TERROR, LYNCHING, AND REIMPOSITION OF WHITE SUPREMACY, 1884-1914

From 1884 to the first decades of the twentieth century, continued subjugation through terror remained, a fortiori, the major policy among whites, especially in the South. Violence and the threat of violence were used to intimidate and

For almost a century lynching and other acts of terror were used to intimidate and repress African Americans. Congress refused to make lynching a federal crime. The photo above is from a 1930 lynching in Marion, Indiana. *(UPI/Bettmann Newsphotos)*

dissuade blacks from political activism. Lynchings including ritualized burning at the stake were routine events not only in the South but also as far north and west as Oklahoma, Indiana, Illinois, Ohio, and even Wyoming.[19] Burnings and hangings were spectacles, announced in advance, attended by whites including women and children, and covered on assignment by newspaper reporters in a manner not unlike contemporary coverage of sporting events.[20]

Many blacks, quite understandably under the circumstances, withdrew from political activity altogether. Among those who continued to struggle politically, fighting for legal protection remained the dominant tendency, but advocates of assimilation and population transfer were also active. The white use of terror however accomplished its purpose. Blacks won no major political victories during this period. By 1901 the last black congressman had left office and the state and local governing bodies were rapidly reclaiming their lily-white complexion. Nevertheless, black political struggle did go on. Much of the political infrastructure upon which future black political activity would rest was built during these years. The celebrated debate between Booker T. Washington and W.E.B. DuBois over the appropriate strategy for black advancement occurred and both the NAACP and the National Urban League were founded during this period.

THE STRUGGLE FOR THE VOTE, 1915-1944

This period marked the beginning of the end of legal exclusion of blacks in the South and the end of defacto exclusion in the North. In 1915[21] the courts outlawed the infamous grandfather clause used to "legally" prevent blacks from voting.[22] However, through a series of disingenuous ploys that came to be known as the white primary, the Southern states were able to defeat the intent of the *Guinn* decision and continue to curb black political participation. Following the strategy of legal protection, blacks mounted campaigns to have such practices declared unconstitutional. However, each victory in court was met with enactment of another exclusionary device in 1927,[23] 1932,[24] and 1935.[25] Not until 1944 in the *Allwright*[26] decision was the white primary effectively declared unconstitutional.

In the North, the migration of blacks from the South increased the black population such that it became an important political force. Black voters in Chicago were able to send Oscar DePriest to the U.S. Congress in 1921, and elsewhere black voters were able to help defeat several senatorial candidates who seemed hostile to black interests. As a result of growing black electoral strength, the northern wing of the Democratic party under the leadership of Franklin Roosevelt began to court black voters by advocating legal protection of black rights. At the same time, protest activities, including picketing, sit-ins, and consumer boycotts, precursors of the civil rights campaigns of the 1960s, were carried out to bring about integration in the urban centers of the North.

THE STRUGGLE FOR RACIAL INTEGRATION, 1945-1965

Following the death of the white primary in 1944, black political activity increased significantly. Assimilation/integration became the dominant policy orientation among both black and white factions. The seminal *Brown* v. *Board of Education* ruling in 1954 which repudiated the separate but equal doctrine buoyed the proponents of integration and served as the midwife of the incipient civil rights movement.

Proponents of assimilation/integration, after considerable struggle to overcome those committed to continued subjugation, persuaded Congress to pass several laws, culminating in the Voting Rights Act of 1965, which when taken together repudiated all forms of segregation and discrimination and committed the country, at least formally, to the full integration of African Americans in American society.

However, the intense opposition by many white interests to integrationism and the noticeable lag in the pace of material advances in comparison to the legal victories led some to challenge the effectiveness of integration as the major policy orientation. As a result, groups supporting pluralism, nationalism, and revolution as optimum strategies all began to compete for and win adherents within the black community. For example, the Student Nonviolent Coordinating Committee (SNCC), which began as an integrationist organization and played a major role in ending state-sponsored segregation and voting rights discrimination, adopted a nationalist-pluralist orientation. The Congress on Racial Equality (CORE) that had played a leading role in the fight to end segregation in public accommodation soon followed.

THE STRUGGLE FOR ECONOMIC EMPOWERMENT, 1966-1986

The century-long struggle for political access was based upon the premise that unfettered political participation would lead to social and economic equality. The significant increase in black political participation, particularly as elected officials, during the 1970s and 1980s, set the stage for testing this premise. Economic empowerment was the focal point of black political activity.

Black politics during this period, which is commonly referred to as the era of Black Power, was conditioned by both nationalist and integrationist sentiments. Nationalist ideas were employed to lobby for public policies designed to help create a black entrepreneurial class and to exhort black consumers to support black businesses. On the other hand, integrationism was used to support the assimilation of black entrepreneurs into the American corporate elite.

Specifically, political pressures were brought to bear upon both government and private corporations to induce them to adopt affirmative action programs for hiring and promoting black workers and to increase their transactions with black-owned firms. Governments were asked to set aside designated percentages of the contracts for goods and services for black enterprises. Private companies were urged to award more franchises to black entrepreneurs.

This quest for economic empowerment through political pressure threatened the self-interest of some whites and was interpreted by many of them as a movement to secure preferential treatment for black Americans. As a consequence, the national consensus that had developed during the latter stages of the civil rights movement began to disintegrate.

Affirmative action and other race-specific programs were characterized by some as reverse discrimination. Consequently (as discussed in Chapter 2), the American electorate began to turn away from issues supported by black leadership. By 1980, the black political agenda had become isolated from the American political mainstream. This was most evident in the presidential elections of 1980, 1984, and 1988 when blacks were the only major constituency which supported the nominee of the Democratic party.

In 1992, however, blacks were on the winning side when the Democratic nominee, Bill Clinton, was elected president with approximately 39 percent of the white vote and 82 percent of the black vote. Perhaps understandably, yet ironically, black political leadership in the 1992 campaign tacitly agreed not to raise race specific issues in order to help the Democratic nominee.

IMPORTANCE OF POPULATION SIZE AND STRATEGIC DISTRIBUTION

Armed with an understanding of how frames of reference condition what we come to know and with at least a cursory understanding of the several frames of reference used to interpret black political life and informed by the brief discussion of the history of black political activity in the United States, we may complete our introductory discussion with an analysis of the black population as a political resource.

In the United States political system the wealth controlled by a group and the size and distribution of its population are perhaps its two most important sources of potential political power. Since blacks control little wealth, population strength becomes their major source of potential political power. Thus a brief comment on the social-political profile of the black population is in order.

The special importance of the size of a group's population, of course, lies in the "one person, one vote" principle which undergirds the American electoral process, but there are special features in the electoral system which, under certain circumstances, might render a group potentially more politically powerful than its size alone would justify.[27] The process through which the president is elected is one such feature. It is probably the most important one because of the dominant role of the president and the presidency in the American political scheme.

The winner-take-all system through which the president is elected makes it possible for a group to exert disproportionate influence on the process if its population is strategically located. The president is not chosen by popular vote but by the electoral college in which each state has a number of votes equal to its representation in the House of Representatives and the Senate. The fact that a candidate who gets the most votes in a given state gets all of that state's electoral votes obviously places a premium on winning in those states with large numbers of electoral votes. As a result the potential political power of a group is enhanced if its population is strategically distributed such that it can influence election results in the larger states.

It is also true that from time to time and for various reasons political leaders from certain areas of the country, for example New England, and especially New York, may exert disproportionate influence on the political direction of the country. In such an eventuality, being able to influence the electoral process in those areas could translate into significant political power.

Finally, given the increasing urbanization of the country, the major metropolitan areas within the states are especially important in both state and national politics. Consequently, influence within them may be parlayed into valuable political capital.

Theoretically then, the size and distribution of the black population could give the black community a strategic voice in these areas, and by extension, significant national political influence.

THE BLACK POPULATION: POLITICAL-SOCIAL PROFILE

At the time of the Emancipation Proclamation the black population was heavily Southern and rural. Since that time, responding to the push-pull dynamic of more stringent racial restrictions in the South and growing economic opportunities in the North and West, the black population has become highly urban. It is not only urban but strikingly big city oriented. In 1990 more than 83 percent of the black population lived in metropolitan areas with 56 percent living in central cities of such areas. And as Table 1-1 demonstrates the urbanization of the black population continued unabated from 1950 to 1990 in spite of the general decline of the cities.

Black political potential, as a result of the continued urbanization, has increased noticeably although prospects for converting that potential into real power is another matter. In 1970 there were seven major cities with black population majorities and four of them had black mayors. By 1980 there were 17 such cities and 13 had black mayors.[28] By 1990 all 17 had black mayors. Another 13 major cities had black populations between 45 and 49 percent.

Regionally, with the net out-migration having ended in the early 1980s, more than half of the black population, 53 percent, remains in the South. The Northeast has 15 percent, the North Central, 20 percent, and the West, 8

TABLE 1-1 Percent distribution of population inside and outside metropolitan areas by race, 1950–1990

	1950		1960		1970		1980		1990	
	BLACK	WHITE	BLACK	WHITE	BLACK	WHITE	BLACK	WHITE	BLACK	WHITE
Metropolitan Areas	59	63	68	67	74	68	82	75	83	75
Central Cities	44	35	53	32	58	28	60	27	56	24
Outside Central Cities	15	28	15	35	16	40	22	48	27	51
Outside Metropolitan Areas	41	37	32	33	26	32	18	26	17	25

SOURCE: U.S. Department of Commerce, Bureau of the Census, various publications.

percent. Thus the great potential is in the Southern region where six of the seven states with a black population of 20 percent or more are located. Only the border states of Delaware and Maryland along with Illinois and New York among the non-southern states have black populations of 15 percent or more.

With population size as a principal resource, the black political potential is also greater in the South at the municipal and congressional district levels. By 1986, although only 5 of the 19 major cities with a black voting age population majority (VAP) were in the South, 8 of 13 with a black VAP between 45 and 49 percent were located there, as were 49 of the 72 congressional districts with a black VAP of 20 percent or more.[29] Fourteen of 17 districts in which blacks comprise between 30 and 39 percent and 27 of 33 with a black VAP between 20 and 29 percent are all in the South. However, only 4 of the 16 majority black congressional districts and none of the 5 with a black VAP between 45 and 49 percent are in the South.

To round out the picture, we may note there are 70 electoral votes in the 7 states in which the black population is 20 percent or more of the total and that there are 238 electoral votes in another 12 states in which blacks comprise between 10 and 19 percent of the population. Thus it is clear that the size and distribution of the black population make it a significant potential resource.

However potential power may be converted into actual power only if the means for doing so are also available. In the case of black population strength, presently several factors and trends mitigate against its conversion into significant power. First of all, black electoral strength in the nation's larger cities is offset by the intractable problems and a diminishing resource base in these jurisdictions. As the out-migration of the affluent continues in tandem with the influx of the poor and dispossessed, control of the cities becomes a hollow prize, as much of a liability as an asset in the larger political equation. In 1970, for example, only about 55 percent of the poor blacks lived in metropolitan areas; by 1990 the figure was up to 83 percent. Over half, 56 percent, of the nation's poor blacks now live in central cities of metropolitan areas.

Indeed the growing impoverishment of blacks in the urban centers of the Midwest and Northeast where black political power historically has been highest questions the real impact of electoral participation. It was in the Midwest—Gary, Chicago, Detroit—and in the Northeast—New York, New Jersey—that black congresspersons and the first of a spate of big city black mayors were elected. Yet by 1990 the poverty rate for blacks was higher in the Midwest, 42 percent, than in any other region of the country including the South.[30] The black poverty rate in the Northeast has also climbed dramatically and continues to grow. In 1990 it was 34 percent compared to 37 percent in the South and 30 percent in the West.

Regarding congressional districts, continued intransigence of white authorities along with other factors has mitigated against converting black population strength into real political power. Until 1990, this was especially true in the South where the black political potential is greater. For example, in

1990 only 5 of the 123 congresspersons from the ten states of the Old Confederacy were black. No state had more than one even though blacks were more than 25 percent of the population in five of the ten Southern states and more than 15 percent in eight of them. However, following the 1990 census, blacks were able to use the Voting Rights Act to force Southern legislatures to reapportion in a more racially equitable manner. As a result, the number of black congresspersons from the region increased from five to seventeen with every state except Arkansas having at least one black congressperson and five having two or more.

Nationally, as is the case in majority black cities, black population strength as a political resource is undermined by the prevailing dire economic conditions. For example, in 1990 six of the nation's ten districts with the highest poverty ratio were represented by a black congressperson. Further undermining black political potential is the fact that all ten congressional districts with the highest concentration of blacks suffered substantial population decline, an average of 22 percent, between 1970 and 1980.

Finally, the growing conservatism of whites in recent presidential elections has depreciated the strategic importance of black population strength as a political resource. As a minority, black population strength is more readily converted into political power when there is a split among white factions and black voters can combine their numbers with one of the white factions *to insure victory of the candidate more supportive of black interest*. This has always been a key element in black political strategies. However, since 1968, even though blacks have given no less than 82 percent of their vote to the presidential candidate perceived by them to be more supportive of black interests, the candidate favored by them has been successful only twice.

The fact of the matter is that there has been a conservative shift in white voting behavior and growing racial polarization in presidential elections dating back to the 1968 presidential campaign of Alabama Governor George Wallace, who, at that time, was known only for his ardent support for racial segregation. Appealing to diverse interests thought to be discontented with what was pictured as the profligate American welfare state, the Wallace movement captured national attention and 13.5 percent of the popular vote, a surprisingly high figure for a third party candidate. Together the two more conservative candidates in the 1968 election, Wallace and Nixon, received 62 percent of the white vote. Black voters gave Hubert Humphrey, the liberal Democrat, 85 percent of their vote.

Since 1968, this pattern has intensified. Blacks have given no less than 82 percent of their votes to the candidate thought to be more supportive of their interests, but except for 1976 and 1992 its candidate has been soundly beaten in every election. The 1976 election was something of an anomaly because the successful Jimmy Carter campaign benefitted both from the political fallout of the Watergate affair and Carter's ability to appeal to southern whites as a native son. With the exception of the anomalous 1976 election, from 1968 to 1992 there was an unbroken progression of white voters toward the more conservative end of the political spectrum with the increasing isolation of blacks around the center being the result. Under these circumstances, black voters had little chance of identifying whites with whom they might coalesce to form majorities to pursue mutually beneficial ends. Thus, the strategic distribution of the black population has been robbed of its political significance.

In 1992, the candidate favored by black voters, Bill Clinton, was elected president but he received only 39 percent of the white vote. Moreover, as mentioned earlier, Clinton and his black allies deliberately de-emphasized issues and policies of special interest to blacks.

Some have argued that this increasing isolation of blacks could and indeed should be ended by blacks following their white compatriots toward political conservatism. However, to date, black voters by and large appear to be unimpressed by this counsel to end their isolation by supporting candidates and programs they believe inimical to black interests.

Conclusion

We have seen quite clearly that the status of African Americans in American society has largely been determined, as Chief Justice Taney said in *Dred Scott*, by the "indelible marks" of race and color. And for the most part these are the same "indelible marks" that continue to shape the everyday life of blacks in this country. We have also seen that there is a material base to the race problem. We have observed that certain material inequities are routinely generated by the American political economy and that the indelible marks of race and color and the institutions built around them serve to visit a disproportionately large share of these inequities among African Americans.

Although the interconnected nature of racism and the material imperatives of American society explain much of the black predicament, we have noted that there is a more "purely" racial dimension as well. This is reflected in the indignities and harassment which blacks, regardless of their material possessions, experience simply because of their race. For example, whites have no worry about whether they can buy a house where they choose, or will be identified as a potential shoplifter by a clerk or security guard merely because of their race. Such worries, however, are constantly with African Americans and are important elements in their perceptions of American society.

We have also seen that blacks have been involved in an unending political struggle to transform their unhappy circumstances and that this struggle has borne considerable fruit in spite of sustained efforts of white factions of considerable means to maintain white domination and black subjugation. By the end of the 1960s all legal barriers to black political participation and access to pivotal economic institutions had been removed. Nevertheless the overall well-being of the black community remained substantially less satisfying than that of whites.

The history of black political participation is not at all encouraging. There have, of course been some notable advances. But basically blacks still do not realistically enjoy the same opportunities, rights, and privileges as white Americans do. To be sure, there continue to be attempts in both the public and private sectors to address this general problem. Overall, however, there remain a certainty and an uncertainty about the life chances of blacks in this country. The certainty is that blacks, in widely disproportionate numbers, are at the lower ends of just about every important segment of American life. The uncertainty is whether or not we can generate "the will" to overcome this certainty within the existing political-social order.

Topics for Discussion

1. The authors state that "how to achieve racial justice with harmony remains our most critical and potentially explosive internal problem." Do you agree with this assessment? Why or why not?

2. The Harris alternative framework suggests that the economic debilities which afflict African Americans, that is, unemployment, low incomes, poverty, and substandard housing are systemic and that racism insures that blacks receive more than their fair share of them. Assuming that Harris is correct, does this mean that the struggle to reduce the level of black unemployment and poverty is at the same time a movement to increase the level of these debilities among whites?

3. Since the early 1970s African Americans have shifted from "protests to politics" in attempts to achieve their policy objectives. However, even though blacks have made substantial gains in the political arena, the gap in socioeconomic well-being between blacks and whites remains substantial. What inference would you draw from this regarding the efficacy of political participation as a strategy for black advancement?

4. The U.S. Supreme Court has been instrumental in the denial and procurement of rights for African Americans. For instance, during slavery and Reconstruction, the Court sanctioned policies which intensified black subordination. The Warren Court, on the other hand, was instrumental in eliminating racial segregation. The current Rehnquist Court has diluted the impact of policies adopted during the civil rights era of the 1960s and 1970s. How do you assess the overall impact of the Supreme Court on the struggle for racial justice?

Suggested Readings

Bardolph, Richard. *The Civil Rights Record: Black American and the Law, 1849-1970.* New York: Thomas Y. Crowell Company, 1970.
An extensive collection of documents with respect to African Americans' changing legal status.

Beard, Charles A. *An Economic Interpretation of the Constitution of the United States*. New York: Macmillan Company, 1954.
A work concerning the constitutional history of the nation with emphasis on the economic basis of the Constitution.

Bell, Derrick A. *Race, Racism and Law*. Boston: Little, Brown, 1973.
A collection of cases and materials that portray the racism in American law.

Bell, Derrick A. "The Racial Imperative in American Law," in Robert Haws, ed., *The Age of Segregation: Race Relations in the South, 1890-1945*. Jackson, MI: University Press of Mississippi, 1978.
A study of the role which the American legal system played in ensuring that the rights of African Americans would be denied in the antebellum South.

Bennett, Lerone. *Black Power U.S.A.: The Human Side of Reconstruction, 1867-1877*. Chicago: Johnson Publisher and Co., 1967.
A humanistic interpretation of Reconstruction.

Bennett, Lerone. *The Challenge of Blackness*. Chicago: Johnson Publishing Co., 1972.
A collection of essays on and about the struggle by African Americans to attain political and cultural power in the United States.

Berlin, Ira. *Slaves without Masters, The Free Negro in the Antebellum South*. New York: The New Press, 1974.
An excellent discussion of social and political status of free blacks in the antebellum South.

DuBois, W. E. B. *Black Reconstruction*. New York: Harcourt Brace Jovanovich, 1935.
A forceful essay devoted to analyzing the role of blacks in the attempt to reconstruct democracy in America, 1860-1880.

Franklin, John Hope. *From Slavery to Freedom: A History of Negro Americans*. 5th ed. New York: Alfred A. Knopf, 1978.
The seminal study on the history of African Americans in the United States which analyzes slavery, Reconstruction, the New Deal, the civil rights movement, and the present.

Franklin, John Hope. *Reconstruction after the Civil War*. Chicago: University of Chicago Press, 1961.
A penetrating discussion of the plight of blacks immediately following the Civil War.

Frazier, E. Franklin. *The Negro in the United States*. New York: Macmillan Company, 1957.
An assessment of the status of blacks in America.

Hamilton, Charles. *The Black Experience in American Politics*. New York: Capricorn Books, 1973.
Readings that analyze the plight of blacks in America.

Harrington, Michael. *The Other America*, rev. ed. Baltimore, MD: Penquin Books, 1970.
A seminal work on the problems of being poor in America.

Henderson, Lenneal J., Jr., ed. *Black Political Life in the United States*. San Francisco: Chandler Publishing Co., 1973.
Articles that deal with various aspects of black political experiences. Includes a detailed bibliographical essay by editor.

Higginbotham, A. Leon, Jr. *In the Matter of Color: Race and the American Legal Process. The Colonial Period*, Vol. 1. New York: Oxford University Press, 1978.
An analysis of race and the legal process from 1619 to the Declaration of Independence and the American Revolution (1776).

Jaynes, Gerald and Robin Williams, eds. *A Common Destiny, Blacks and American Society*. Washington, DC: National Academy Press, 1989.

A collection of thoroughly researched articles on the socioeconomic, cultural, and political status of African Americans.

Jennings, James, ed. *Race Politics and Economic Development*. London: Verso Press, 1992.
A collection of critical essays on the economic oppression of the black urban population.

Jones, Franklin and Michael Adams. *Readings in American Political Issues*. Dubuque, IA: Kendall/Hunt, 1987.
A wide ranging collection of readings covering political beliefs, political participation, political institutions, and public policy.

Kilson, Martin. "Political Change in the Negro Ghetto, 1900-1940s," in Natan I. Huggins, Martin Kilson, and Daniel M. Fox, eds., *Key Issues in the Afro-American Experience*. New York: Harcourt Brace Jovanovich, 1971.
This work, like those in the entire volume, examines the changing status of African Americans.

Logan, Rayford W. *The Betrayal of the Negro*. New York: Collier Books, 1965.
A comprehensive analysis of the status of blacks in America between 1877 and 1901.

Meier, August, and Elliot Rudwick, eds. *Along the Color Line: Explorations in the Black Experience*. Urbana, IL: University of Illinois Press, 1976.
Essays on black leadership, nationalism, power, and nonviolent protest.

Myrdal, Gunnar. *An American Dilemma*. New York: Harper & Row, 1964.
A classic study analyzing the status of blacks in America.

McPherson, James M., Laurence B. Holland, James M. Banner, Jr., Nancy J. Weiss, and Michael D. Bell. *Blacks in America: Bibliographical Essays*. Garden City, NY: Doubleday & Co., 1972.
Detailed bibliographical essays organized around important topics and periods in black history. A useful tool for research and history.

Rainwater, Lee. *Behind the Ghetto Walls*. Chicago: Aldine Publishing Co., 1970.
An examination of the dynamics of the socioeconomic inequality of the American political system with emphasis on the ghetto.

Rose, Harold. *A Spatial Behavioral Perspective*. New York: McGraw-Hill, 1971.
An examination of America's urban black communities from a geographic perspective.

Sloan, Irving, Jr., comp. and ed. *The Blacks in America: 1492-1977*, 4th rev. ed. Dobbs Ferry, NY: Oceana Publications, 1977.
Essays on the varied experiences of blacks in America.

Taeuber, Karl E., and Alma F. Taeuber. *Negroes in Cities: Residential Segregation and Neighborhood Change*. Chicago: Aldine Publishing Co., 1965.
A penetrating comparative analysis of the pattern as well as the process of residential segregation over time.

Walters, Ronald W. *Black Presidential Politics in America*. New York: State University of New York Press, 1988.
An imaginative discussion of the strategic use of presidential politics in the struggle of racial justice.

Notes

1. *Brown* v. *Board of Education of Topeka*, 349 U.S. 483 (1954). These affirmative action cases are discussed in detail in Chapter 5.
2. *Richmond* v. *Croson*, 448 U.S. 469 (1989).

3. See Frank J. Sorauf, *Party Politics in America*, 3rd ed. (Boston: Little, Brown, 1961) Chapter 8.
4. Ibid., p. 54.
5. Denys Vaughn-Cooke, "The Economic State of Black America—Is There A Recovery?" in *The State of Black America 1984* (New York: National Urban League, Inc., 1984), p. 13.
6. See for example, Chandler Davison, *Biracial Politics* (Baton Rouge: Louisiana State University Press, 1972), especially Chapters 1-4. Also Mack H. Jones, "A Frame of Reference for Black Politics," in *Black Political Life in the United States: A First as the Pendulum*, Lenneal Henderson, Jr., ed. (San Francisco: Chandler, 1972), pp. 7-20.
7. The following discussion of Park and Parson draws heavily on Stanford M. Lyman, *The Black American in Sociological Thought: A Failure of Perspective* (New York: Capricorn, 1972), especially Chapters 2 and 4.
8. Talcott Parsons, "Full Citizenship for the Negro American," in *The Negro American*, Talcott Parsons and Kenneth Clark, eds. (Boston: Houghton Mifflin, 1966), especially pp. 716-744.
9. See William E. Tabb, *The Political Economy of the Black Ghetto* (New York: Norton, 1970); Robert Allen, *Black Awakening in Capitalist America, an Analytic History* (New York: Doubleday, 1969); and Ronald Bailey, "Economics Aspects of the Black Internal Colony," *Review of Black Political Economy* (Summer 1973).
10. See Harold Cruse, "Revolutionary Nationalism and the Afro-American," in *Rebellion or Revolution* (New York: William Morrow, 1968), pp. 74-96.
11. When first developed, the model was labeled the Dominant-submissive group model. Since that time the author has concluded that the term "subordinate" is more appropriate than "submissive." See Jones, *Frame of Reference*.
12. The following discussion is reprinted with slight modification from Mack H. Jones, "Black Politics from Civil Rights to Benign Neglect," in *Negotiating the Mainstream, A Survey of the Afro-American Experience*, Harry A. Johnson, ed. (Chicago: American Library Association, 1978), pp. 164-195.
13. See Donald Harris, "Black Ghetto as Internal Colony: A Theoretical Critique and Alternative Formulation," *The Review of Black Political Economy* (Summer 1972), pp. 3-33.
14. This historical overview draws extensively from Jones, "Black Politics," pp. 164-195.
15. Figures computed from Table 1 in Hanes Walton, *Black Politics, a Theoretical and Structural Analysis* (New York: J.B. Lippincott Co., 1972), p. 52.
16. Leon Litwack, *North of Slavery* (Chicago: University of Chicago Press, 1961), p. 31.
17. *Dred Scott* v. *Sandford*, 60 U.S. 393 19 Howard 393 (1857). Of course federal courts prior to *Dred Scott* had rendered pro-slavery decisions. See for example, Derrick Bell, "The Racial Interpretation of American Law" in *The Age of Race Relations in the South 1890-1945*, Robert Haws, ed. (Jackson, MS: University of Mississippi Press, 1968).
18. Given the cultural taboo on interracial marriage, no white faction and perhaps no black faction either can be said to have advocated complete assimilation as a strategy for solving the race problem. Perhaps integrationism may be a more appropriate term.

19. See Ralph Ginzberg, *100 Years of Lynching* (New York: Lancer, 1962), especially, pp. 253-270.
20. Ibid., p. 46. The author reproduces a newspaper clipping which describes the chagrin of newspaper reporters when those who had scheduled a lynching granted a reprieve to a victim in order to allow him to have a farewell interview with his family. The scheduled change made it difficult for reporters to meet their deadlines.
21. *Guinn* v. *United States*, 238 U.S. 349 (1915).
22. States adopted constitutional provisions which established stringent property, literacy, or other qualifications as prerequisites for voter registration, but excluded those whose ancestors could have qualified to vote prior to 1865. This allowed the "legal" exclusion of blacks while most whites who could not pass the literacy test retained their eligibility.
23. *Nixon* v. *Herndon*, 273 U.S. 536 (1927).
24. *Nixon* v. *Condon*, 286 U.S. 73 (1932).
25. *Grovey* v. *Townsend*, 295 U.S. 45 (1935).
26. *Smith* v. *Allwright*, 321 U.S. 649 (1944).
27. For elaboration of this point, see Dianne Pinderhughes, "The Black Vote—The Sleeping Giant," in *The State of Black America 1984*, pp. 69-93.
28. James D. McGhee, "The Changing Demographics of Black America," in *The State of Black America 1983* (New York: National Urban League, 1983), pp. 27-28.
29. Data on congressional districts were extracted from *The JCPS Congressional District Fact Book*, 2nd ed., Linda Williams, ed. (Washington, DC: Joint Center for Political Studies, 1986).
30. Figures on regional poverty rates are taken from David Swinton, "Economic Status of Blacks 1985," in *The State of Black America 1985* (New York: National Urban League, 1985), pp. 135-199.

CHAPTER 2

THE NATURE OF THE PROBLEM

Economic realities dominate life within Black America, but to many white Americans the struggle of blacks is over, and nothing further needs to be done. They see that blacks vote now with little impediment, they have jobs they never held before, they hold elective offices, they can go to the best schools, and they are free to patronize the hotel or restaurant of their choice.

But what is apparent on the surface fails to reveal what is underneath . Within Black America a third of its people are at or below the poverty line and have a fifty percent chance of growing up underprivileged, undereducated and underemployed. A third of its adults who want to work can't find it, and two out of three of its teenagers are in the same boat. Its average income is 58 percent of that of white America.

John E. Jacobs, The State of Black America, 1988
(New York: National Urban League, 1988), p. iii.

In this chapter we explore two important dimensions of the black predicament in the United States, the unequal socioeconomic conditions of African Americans and the divergent perceptions of blacks and whites of this reality. This will sharpen our understanding of the setting within which black politics unfolds.

Unemployed workers respond to a job announcement. Unemployment is a routine outcome of the economic process, but black unemployment is almost always twice as high as the white rate. *(AP/Wide World Photos)*

African Americans, like other disadvantaged groups, have always viewed political participation as a means through which full equality in the social, economic, and cultural life of the country could be obtained. Accordingly, when the civil rights movement of the 1960s succeeded in eliminating legal restrictions on black political participation, it did not mean that the black political struggle was over. Rather it meant that the struggle to use political participation to transform the unequal social, economic, and cultural status of blacks had just begun.

Throughout the history of the United States blacks have lagged behind white Americans on practically every accepted measure of socioeconomic well-being. This had been and continues to be true of all categories of African Americans, male and female, young and old, urban and rural, married and single, and in every geographical region of the country.

To be sure, there has been considerable improvement over the years. Blacks are decidedly better off than they were a few decades ago. Blacks have shared in the overall economic growth and development of the country, but the gap between black and white well-being has remained more or less constant. In fact recent evidence suggests that the gap may in fact be widening.

However, current perceptions of the socioeconomic conditions of African Americans and therefore of the conditions which black politics must address are not necessarily consistent with reality. Indeed the perceptions of this reality by blacks and whites differ markedly.

According to poll results, discussed later in this chapter, many whites apparently believe that conditions supportive of black equality have been realized and that consequently further government action to promote black advancement is neither necessary nor constitutionally appropriate. Many blacks, on the other hand, take a diametrically opposed view.

Before discussing further these differing perceptions of reality, we will first attempt to describe that reality as it is reflected in socioeconomic statistics compiled primarily by the national government.

UNEQUAL SOCIOECONOMIC CONDITIONS—WEALTH AND INCOME

In market economies such as the United States, wealth and income are reliable indicators of socioeconomic well-being. The type and amount of income which one receives indicates one's potential role in the political and economic system. The several types of income are listed on Table 2-1.

Property income reflects ownership of wealth in the form of liquid assets, real or personal property. Those with significant property income will likely have substantial wealth and consequently they will possess the potential for greater political power.

Income from wages and salaries, on the other hand, means that the individual is a supplier of labor. Except for those with especially high salaries, this source of income does not reflect disproportionate political strength.

Self-employment has the potential for generating political power and farm self-employment income represents potential political power because it is directly related to ownership of land.

Transfer income, which includes among other things social security payments, private retirement pensions, unemployment compensation, and welfare payments, is second only to wages and salaries as a source of income. A considerable proportion of transfer income is distributed by government to persons experiencing financial difficulty. Thus it reflects the absence of wealth and the political potential associated with it.

Both black and white families receive the same types of income, but the proportions of their incomes that come from the different sources vary significantly. Those sources of income associated with political power are more prominent among whites than among blacks.

From Table 2-1 we see that the preponderant source of income for both black and white families is wages and salaries, but blacks receive slightly more of their income from this source than whites. Since 1969, however, the propor-

TABLE 2-1 Types of income received by families by race, selected years, 1969–1983 (percentage distribution)

TYPE OF INCOME		1969	1974	1979	1983	1990
EARNINGS						
Wages and Salaries	Black	85.4	81.7	80.8	79.6	79.6
	White	79.8	78.0	75.9	74.7	72.3
Non-Farm self-employment	Black	3.0	2.0	2.3	1.8	2.5
	White	7.7	6.7	6.6	6.1	6.1
Farm self-employment	Black	0.4	0.2	(b)	(b)	(b)
	White	1.5	1.5	1.2	0.6	0.5
OTHER THAN EARNINGS						
Property Income[a]	Black	0.6	0.6	0.9	1.4	2.0
	White	4.0	4.2	5.5	6.4	7.9
Transfers and all other[b] Income	Black	10.6	15.4	16.2	17.5	15.0
	White	6.8	9.6	10.5	12.2	13.4
Public assistance, welfare	Black	4.2	6.0	5.1	4.7	3.3
	White	0.4	0.7	0.6	0.6	0.5

[a] Includes dividends, interest, net rented income, income from estates or trusts, and net royalties.
[b] Includes social security or railroad retirement income, public assistance or welfare payments, supplemental security income, retirement and annuities, veterans payments, unemployment.
SOURCE: Bureau of the Census, Current Population Series, P-60, *Money Income of Families and Persons in the U.S.*, various years.
1990 figures taken from David Swinton, "The Ecomonic Status of African Americans: Limited Ownership and Persistent Inequality," in *The State of Black America 1992* (New York: National Urban League, 1992), p. 92.

tion of total family income derived from wages and salaries has declined for both groups.

The other two types of earned income—farm and non-farm self-employment—are also declining as a proportion of family income for both black and white families. Among black families, farm self-employment income is virtually nonexistent and non-farm self-employment accounts for less than two percent of family income.

Both of the non-earning categories—property and transfer income—have increased as a proportion of family income since 1969. However, the proportion of black income coming from property income remains insignificant. The per capita black property income was $181 in 1990 compared to $1207 for whites.[1] The proportion of white families reporting some property income was more than twice that of blacks and on average white recipients of property income received more than four times the amount received by blacks.

Transfer income,which is often associated with economic deprivation, but not exclusively so, provides a high proportion of the income of black families and the proportion of black families receiving income from this source is slightly higher than that for white families. In 1990, 48 percent of black families and 38 percent of white families, received government transfer income.[2] Twelve percent of black family income compared to nine percent of white family income came from government transfer payments in 1990. Public assistance or welfare, which is only one of several types of transfer income, accounts for 3.3 percent of black family income, but only about one-half of one percent of the income of white families.

Despite the fact that higher proportions of blacks receive transfer income and the fact that a greater proportion of black income derives from transfers, blacks in 1990 received smaller mean (i.e., the average amount received per recipient) transfer income, $4,832, than whites whose mean figure was $6,505.[3] The fact that white families receive a disproportionate large share of non-public assistance transfer payments such as private pensions, annuities, and so forth, explains this seemingly paradoxical situation.

In summary, those sources of income which reflect potential political power—property and self-employment income—are disproportionately high among white families and those which reflect limited political potential—welfare and other transfers—are more important sources of black family income.

MEDIAN FAMILY INCOME

The disparity between black and white family income has been both persistent and strikingly consistent since the 1940s. During the four decades since the

FIGURE 2-1
Median Black Family Income as a Percent of Median White Family Income, 1967–1990. SOURCE: Current Population Reports, Series P-60, *Money Income of families and persons in the U.S. 1990*

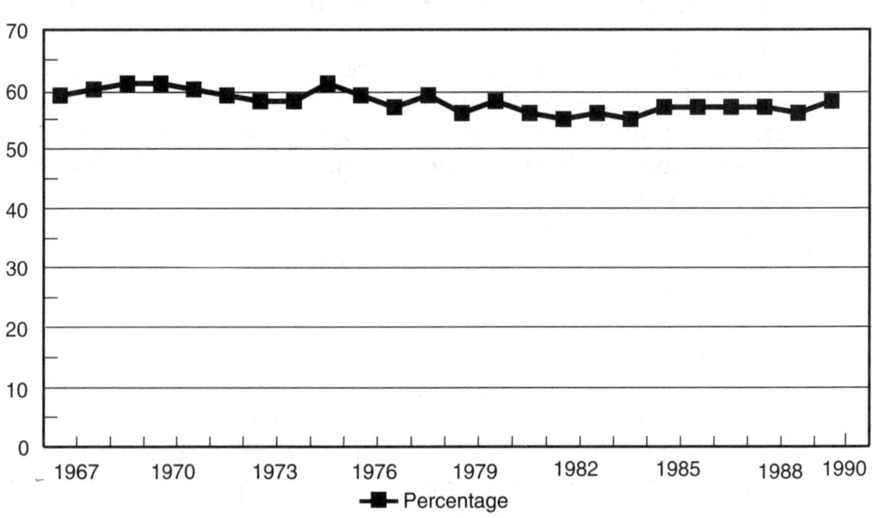

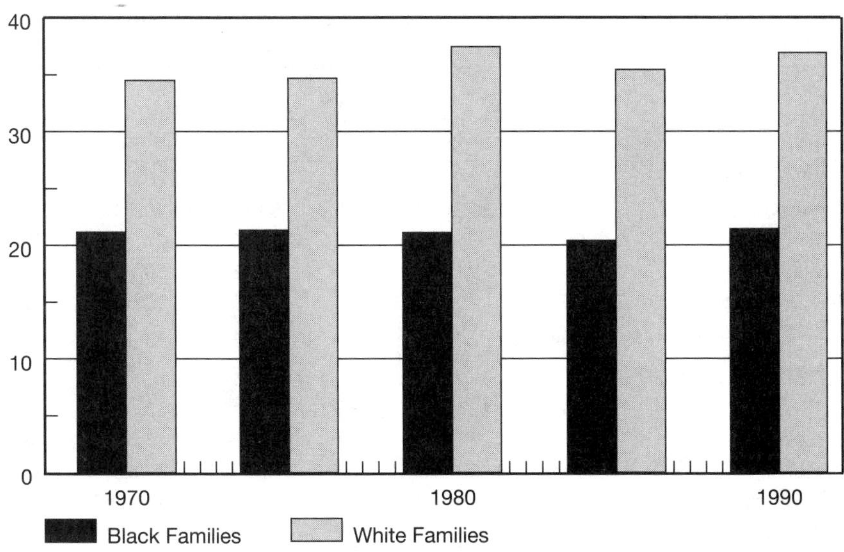

FIGURE 2-2
Median income in constant (1990) dollars for families by race, 1970-1990.
SOURCE: Current Population Reports, Series p-60, *Money Income of Families and Persons in the U.S.* 1990
(In Thousands)

end of World War II, as Figure 2-1 shows, a period of sustained economic growth punctuated by periods of both expansion and recession, the median income of black families has fluctuated around 50 to 60 percent of the median for white families.

In 1950 the median income for black families was equal to 53 percent of the median for white families. Ten years later it was virtually the same, 53.8 percent of the white median. As Figure 2-1 shows, during the Vietnam War era black family income rose to around 60 percent of the median of white families, reaching a high of 62 percent in 1975. However, as the war-induced economic boom receded so did black family income. By 1982 it had fallen to about 55 percent of the median of white families, which was the lowest ratio since 1960. The 1990 median income of black families of $21,423 was only 58 percent of the $36,915 median for white families.

It is also instructive to note that in constant dollars the median income of black families actually declined by $39 between 1972 and 1990.

In recent years some analysts have suggested that the disproportionately large number of households headed by single black women explains the sizable gap between black and white median family incomes. However, the issue appears to be much more complex.

It is true as demonstrated by Table 2-2 that the difference in median income of black and white married couples is less than that of the overall black

TABLE 2-2 Medium family income in 1984 and 1990 by race, number of earners and type of family

	1984		BLACK/ WHITE RATIO	1990		BLACK/ WHITE RATIO
	BLACK	WHITE		BLACK	WHITE	
TYPE OF FAMILY						
Married Couples	$23,418	$35,058	.78	$33,784	$40,331	.84
Wife Works	28,775	35,176	.82	40,038	47,247	.85
Wife Not Working	14,502	24,246	.60	20,333	30,781	.66
Male Householder	15,724	25,110	.62	21,848	30,570	.71
Female Householder	8,648	15,134	.57	12,125	19,528	.62
NUMBER OF EARNERS						
Total	$15,537	$27,752	.56	$21,423	$36,915	.58
No Earners	5,277	12,941	.41	6,305	17,369	.36
One Earner	11,809	22,050	.54	16,308	27,670	.59
Two Earners	25,334	32,260	.79	34,050	43,036	.79
Three Earners	32,984	40,374	.82	43,813	54,632	.80
Four or More	38,143	51,309	.74	59,983	67,753	.89

SOURCE: Bureau of the Census, *Current Population Series*, P-60, *Money Income and Poverty Status of Families and Persons in the United States.*, Various years.

and white populations. However, in 1990 black married couples had considerably less income than their white counterparts. The median for black couples was $33,784 compared to $40,331 for whites. Adding to the complexity, families headed by white women had a median income of $19,528 compared to $12,158 for black female-headed household. Moreover, the median income of households headed by white women was only slightly less than the median of those headed by single black men and those of black couples with the wife not working outside the home.

Finally it should be noted that the disparity between black and white family incomes is not simply a regional problem.

As Table 2-3 shows the out-migration of blacks from impoverished areas of the South over the last 30 years together with the economic decline of the cities of the Northeast and Midwest has eliminated the heretofore significant

TABLE 2-3 Median family income in 1984 and 1990 by race and region of country

	1984		BLACK/ WHITE RATIO	1990		BLACK/ WHITE RATIO
	Black	White		BLACK	WHITE	
Northeast	$16,326	$29,705	.55	$20,674	$34,387	.60
North Central	14,367	27,683	.52	17,204	31,054	.55
South	14,863	26,054	.57	17,662	29,162	.61
West	19,209	28,509	.67	23,984	31,794	.75

SOURCE: Bureau of the Census, *Current Population Report*, Series P-60, *Money Income and Poverty Status of Families and Persons in the United States*, various years.

regional differences in the ratio of black to white incomes. The median income for black families in 1990 was actually lowest in the Midwest and black income as a percent of white income was actually lower in the Northeast and Midwest regions than in the South.

INCOME AND PUBLIC SECTOR EMPLOYMENT

Both blacks and whites who work for government on average have higher earnings than workers in the private sector. This is so at least partially because a higher proportion of the public work force than private sector workers are professionals. However, the difference between the earnings of blacks who work for government and those employed in the private sector is much greater than that which prevails for white workers.

The average earnings of black male government employees in 1983 was $15,174 compared to $11,794 for those in the private sector, a difference of 29 percent.[4] The margin for the white male public sector worker was only 8 percent. For black women the average public sector earning was $11,819 compared to $8,789 for the private sector.

Within the federal work force the public to private sector earnings gap was greater than for government workers in general. The average earnings of black males working for the federal government in 1983 was $19,324, a margin of 64 percent above average private sector earnings. Black women employed by the national government earned $13,988, or 59 percent above the private sector average. The margins for white men and women employed by the national government were 31 and 63 percent respectively.

Not only do blacks receive proportionately higher wages in the public sector, but they also hold a higher proportion of public sector jobs, particularly within the federal work force. In 1983 blacks comprised only 9.5 percent of all workers but they held 15 percent of all federal jobs. Public sector jobs, which include jobs with federal, state, and local governmental units, accounted for 24 percent of all jobs held by blacks but only 15 percent of those held by whites.

LABOR FORCE PARTICIPATION

The labor force participation rate is the proportion of the working age population actually working or actively seeking a job. The labor force includes the employed and the unemployed, but it does not include those who are not looking for jobs even if they want one.

Historically blacks were more likely than whites to be in the labor force. For example in 1900, 65 percent of blacks aged 14 and over compared to 52 percent of whites were in the labor force.[5] During recent times black and white labor force participation rates have been roughly equal with black men having slightly lower rates and black women having higher rates than their white counterparts.

Since 1970 the makeup of the American labor force has changed considerably as women have entered in greater numbers and the proportion of males has declined. During these same years the position of blacks in the labor force has deteriorated. Black male participation rates have declined more sharply than those of white men while the increase in the rates for black women has lagged behind that of white women.

As Figure 2-3 shows, the labor force participation rate for black men dropped from 81 percent in 1962 to 71 percent in 1988. The decline for white males was much less dramatic, from 82 percent in 1962 to 77 percent in 1988. Black women increased their participation rate from 48 percent in 1962 to 58 percent in 1988. The rate for white females, however, went up from 37 to 58 percent.

The declining fortunes of blacks in the labor force are the result of fundamental structural changes in the American economy. The decline of heavy industries of the Midwest and Northeast and the closing of lumber mills and other industrial plants of the South have curtailed employment opportunities for all workers, but especially for black males. Many experienced black workers have dropped out of the labor force after losing their jobs because the skills they possessed cannot be used in growth areas of the economy. Increasing numbers of black youth who have really never held a job face a similar problem. Often they too do not have marketable skills. The skill deficiency of

FIGURE 2-3

Labor force participation rates by race and gender, 1960-1988, persons 16 years and older. SOURCE: Bureau of Labor Statistics *Handbook of Labor Statistics* (various years)

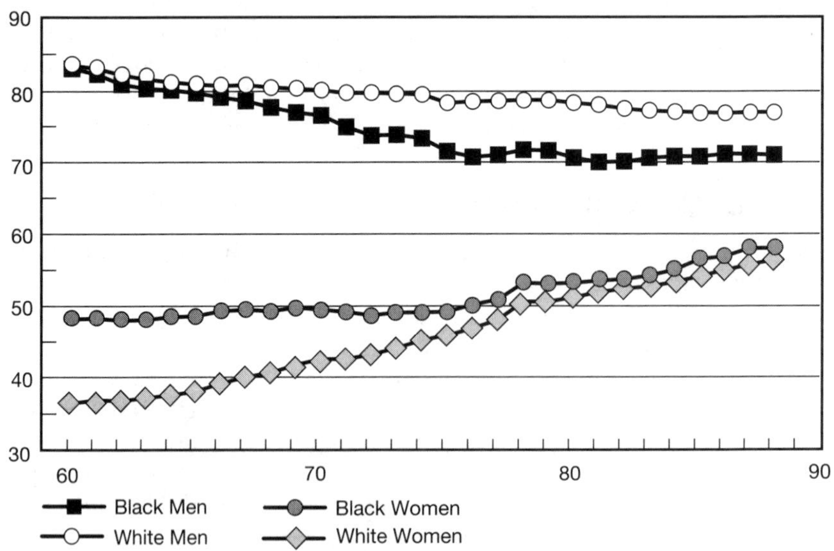

those workers is compounded by the fact that the economy is not creating new jobs as fast as the labor force is growing. A disproportionate share of the job shortage is falling on black workers.

EMPLOYMENT AND UNEMPLOYMENT

The unemployment rate is the percentage of those in the labor force who are unable to find work. In the modern era, black unemployment has been consistently and substantially higher than that of whites. In 1955, the black rate doubled the white rate for the first time. Since then, as is evident from Figure 2-4, black unemployment has been at least twice that of whites in every year except three, 1970, 1971, and 1975. From 1975 to 1988, the average annual unemployment rate for both black men and women was 14.6 percent compared to 6.1 percent for white men and 6.6 percent for white women.

The employment ratio, which focuses on those who have jobs rather than those who are unable to find them, is the percent of the working age population that is employed either part time or full time. Thus while the unemployment rate is the proportion of the labor force without jobs, the employment ratio is the percent of the population with jobs. Those who drop out of the labor force, that is, stop looking for jobs, are not included in the unemployed, but since they are still in the population they are considered when calculating the employment

FIGURE 2-4
Unemployment rates by race and gender 1960-1990.
SOURCE: Bureau of Labor Statistics *Handbook of Labor Statistics* (various years)

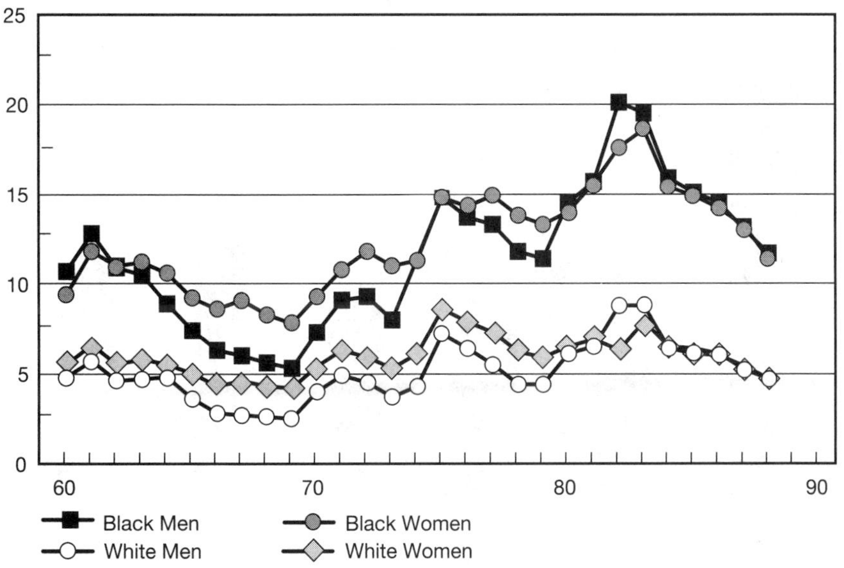

ratio. Taken together, the employment ratio and the unemployment rate yield a better understanding of how a group is faring in the work force.

Because black male unemployment has been increasing and their labor force participation has been declining, the percent of black men with jobs, the employment ratio, has been falling faster than the unemployment rate has been increasing. The employment ratio for black men has also been falling faster than the labor force participation rate. Between 1962 and 1988 the employment ratio for black men went down from 72 percent to 67 percent. The employment ratio for white males dropped only half as much as that of black men, from 78 percent to 75 percent.

For black women whose labor force participation rate increased, the employment ratio went up from 42 percent in 1962 to 54 percent in 1988. The increase for white women, however, was much greater than that of black women, from 36 percent to 54 percent. Thus by 1984 a significantly higher proportion of the working age population of whites than blacks had jobs. Blacks are being pushed from the ranks of the gainfully employed at an alarming rate.

POVERTY

The national government has developed a formula to determine the amount of cash income necessary for families to maintain a certain quality of life. Under the formula, the poverty threshold, which varies according to the

FIGURE 2-5

Percent of families in poverty by race, selected years 1959-1989. SOURCE: Bureau of the Census *Current Population Reports*, Series P-60, *Characteristics of the Population Below the Poverty Level* (various years)

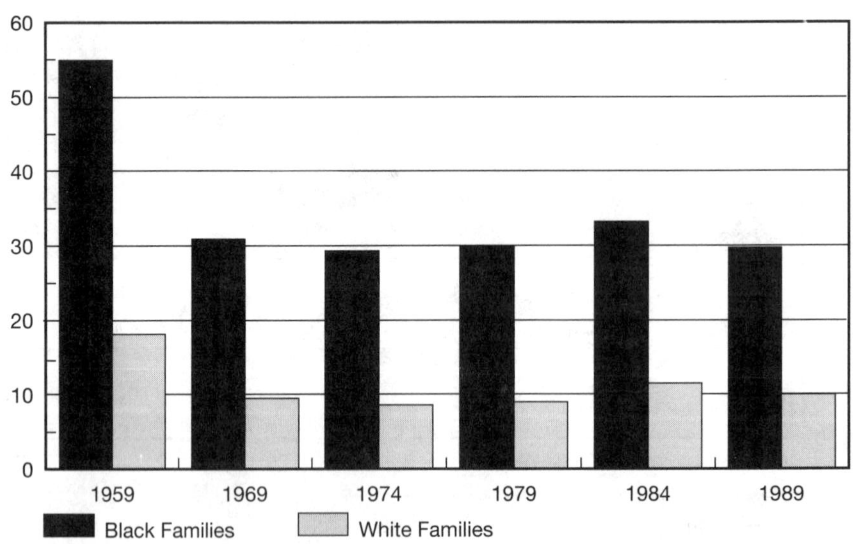

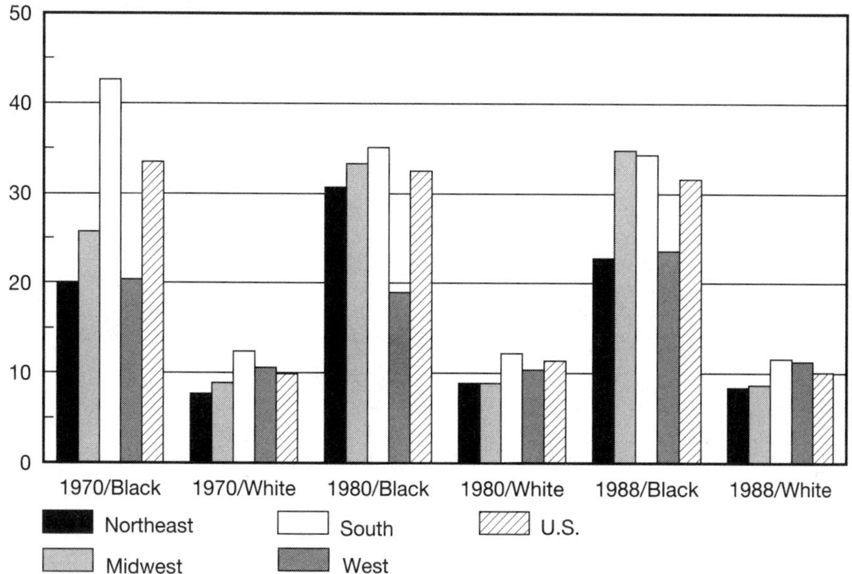

FIGURE 2-6

Poverty rates by race and region 1970, 1980, and 1988. SOURCE: U.S. Department of Commerce, Bureau of the Census, *Money Income and Poverty Status* (various years), Current Population Reports Series P-60 (various years)

family size and location, is an amount equal to three times "an economy food plan." In 1990 the poverty threshold for an urban family of four was $13,359.

Since the government began measuring poverty in 1959, the proportion of black families living in poverty has declined dramatically, from 48 percent to 32 percent in 1990. However, the ratio of black-to-white poverty has shown no improvement. Throughout this 30 year period the proportion of black families classified as poor has fluctuated between three and four times the rate for whites.

As Figure 2-6 and Table 2-4 (on page 42) show, black families are disproportionately poor in every region of the country and the ratio of black to white poverty is largely unaffected by educational attainment. The poverty rate among black college graduates has also fluctuated around three times the poverty rate of their white cohorts.

The constancy and persistence of the ratio of black-to-white poverty suggest that both the factors which cause poverty in general and those which account for the difference in black and white poverty rates are basic features of the American economic system.

BLACK BUSINESS OWNERSHIP

Historically the low level of black business ownership has been cited as both a cause and an effect of the unequal position of blacks in American life.

TABLE 2-4 Poverty status in the U.S. in 1990. Persons 25-34 years old by race, gender, and educational attainment

	BLACK	WHITE	BLACK/WHITE RATIO
Did Not Complete High School			
Both Sexes	50.1	30.2	1.6
Male	31.5	22,8	1.4
Female	63.7	38.5	1.6
Completed High School - No College			
Both Sexes	27.4	9.8	2.8
Male	16.7	7.0	2.4
Female	38.2	12.6	3.0
Completed College			
Both Sexes	10.6	2.7	3.9
Male	13.8	3.0	4.6
Female	7.9	2.5	3.2

Source: Bureau of the Census, *Current Population Reports*, Series P-60, *Poverty in the U.S.*, 1990, Table 11.

Consequently strategies for black advancement have almost always been linked to efforts to increase black business ownership. Such efforts became national policy in the 1960s under the slogan of "black capitalism." Beginning in 1968 the national government inaugurated a series of programs designed to encourage the development of new black-owned firms and to strengthen and sustain existing ones. These programs offered assistance in a variety of ways. Some offered technical and financial assistance to black entrepreneurs. Others specified that certain proportions of federal contracts were to be set aside for minority-owned firms Some state and local governments adopted similar programs. Many of the nations large philanthropic foundations and major corporations joined in efforts to promote black business development. In spite of such efforts, however, black business ownership remains minuscule. As Table 2-5 shows, although the number of black-owned firms has continued to increase, the significance of black-owned firms in the economy is actually declining.

In 1987, the last year for which data are available, black firms comprised about three percent of all firms and accounted for one percent of all business revenues. The preponderance of black-owned firms had no paid employees and those with paid employees had only about three employees each.

Gross receipts (not to be confused with profits), that is the total revenue taken in by a firm and from which all operating costs must be paid, remain exceedingly modest. Average gross receipts for all black-owned firms was approximately $47,000[6] in 1982 compared to a national average of $146,700.[7]

TABLE 2-5 Selected characteristics of black-owned businesses in the United States 1982-1987

	1982	1987
Number of Firms	308,260	424,165
Number of Firms with paid employees	37,841	353,350
Average Number of Employees in Firm with Paid Employees	4	3.1
Average Gross Receipts All Firms	836,624	46,592
Average Gross Receipts of of Firm with Paid Employees	176,937	199,540
Average Gross Receipts of Firms Without Paid Employees	16,991	15,940

SOURCE: Bureau of the Census, *Survey of Minority-Owned Business Enterprises-Black*, MB 87-1, July 1990.

BLACKS AND WHITES DO NOT SEE THE SAME REALITY

Efforts to use the political process to eliminate black inequality would certainly be enhanced by biracial consensus on the nature and cause of the black predicament and an agreement on the range of appropriate policy choices. Unfortunately for the country, no such consensus exists. Although neither community is monolithic, the perceptions and attitudes of black and white Americans differ markedly on these matters.

Polls show that blacks continue to believe that racial discrimination is the major cause of black inequality while whites assign greater weight to the behavior of blacks themselves. As Campbell and Schuman put it:

> While admitting the presence of discrimination, white people show a strong tendency to blame the disadvantaged circumstances of Negro life on Negroes themselves. Although they do not subscribe to genetic theories of racial inferiority they find much to criticize in the attitudes and behavior patterns they see as characteristic of Negroes and apparently feel that it is within the power of Negroes to improve their own situation.[8]

But blacks, on the other hand, see a different reality. As one reporter observed:

> To be a black American in 1985 is to be trapped in a no man's land. The trap is to listen to whites happily tell you that the battle against racism has been won, the world is colorblind, you can compete and make it on your own.
>
> The reality, to black eyes, however, is to know that while life is better than 20 years ago, you still are treated, seen and identified on the basis of your color.[9]

Results from a 1986 *ABC News/Washington Post* poll firmly support the above characterization of black and white perceptions. As is evident from Table 2-6, more than two-thirds of black respondents believed that racial

TABLE 2-6 Blacks' and whites' explanation of racial inequality in 1981 and 1989 (percentages*)

	1981		1989	
	BLACK	WHITES	BLACK	WHITES
Mainly due to discrimination				
Yes	67	38	69	46
No	27	58	29	52
Because blacks have less inborn ability				
Yes	25	23	24	14
No	69	74	76	84
Because blacks don't have chance for education it takes to rise out of poverty				
Yes	72	53	67	63
No	25	44	31	36
Because blacks don't have sufficient will power or motivation				
Yes	47	58	44	43
No	47	36	54	54
Because whites don't want them to get ahead				
Yes	74	46	75	43
No	20	47	20	52
There is discrimination but many of the problems are brought on blacks by themselves.				
Yes	50	73	52	56
No	40	19	42	35

*Percentages do not total 100 because "no response" and "don't know" answers are omitted.
SOURCE: Adapted from Table 5-3 in Lee Sigelman and Susan Welch, *Black Americans' Views of Racial Inequality*, New York: Cambridge University Press, 1991, p. 91.

discrimination was the primary cause of black inequality. Perhaps even more foreboding, more than three-fourths of blacks surveyed agreed with the assertion that whites do not want blacks to get ahead. Conversely 38 percent of whites, a sizable minority, agreed that black inequality was mainly due to racial discrimination but only 18 percent thought that whites did not want blacks to get ahead.

The sharp perceptual differences between blacks and whites are also reflected in their responses to questions about the presence of discrimination in various aspects of American life. In the five areas listed in Table 2-7, a preponderant majority of whites in 1981 and 1989 believed that there was no discrimination in the three job-related categories nor in education or housing, but a majority of blacks in 1989 believed that there was discrimination in the job market and in housing.

Differences in the perceptions of blacks and whites also extend to their views of the major issues facing the country and their assessment of existing policies and circumstances. During the 1984 presidential campaign a Joint Center for Political Studies-Gallup poll[10] found that 48 percent of whites were satisfied and 43 percent were dissatisfied with the "way things were going,"

TABLE 2-7 Black and white perception of discrimination against blacks, 1981 and 1989 (percentages*)

	1981		1989	
	BLACKS	WHITES	BLACKS	WHITES
Getting a quality education				
Discriminated	27	6	37	11
Not discriminated	68	90	61	87
Getting decent housing				
Discriminated	42	16	52	20
Not discriminated	53	78	47	76
Getting unskilled labor jobs[b]				
Discriminated	41	10	3	
Not discriminated	50	83		
Getting skilled labor jobs				
Discriminated	56	19	53	15
Not discriminated	36	72	44	79
Getting managerial jobs				
Discriminated	57	22	61	23
Not discriminated	31	64	36	71

[a]Do not total 100 because "don't know" and "no response" omitted.
[b]Not asked in 1989.
SOURCES: Polling data from national surveys. Adapted from Table 3-3 in Lee Sigelman and Susan Welch. *Black Americans' Views of Racial Inequality*, (New York: Cambridge University Press, 1991) p. 57.

but 79 percent of blacks said they were dissatisfied and only 14 percent reported being satisfied.

The same survey revealed that 68 percent of whites thought that the situation "had gotten better for blacks" over the past five years and only four percent of whites thought the conditions of blacks had gotten worse. Among blacks themselves 30 percent said that things had gotten worse and 37 percent agreed that things had gotten better.

Perhaps even more indicative of the perceptual gap between the two groups are their responses to the question, "Do you think most white people want to see blacks get a better break, or do they want to keep blacks down?" Forty percent of the black respondents felt that whites wanted to keep blacks down while 23 percent disagreed. The white response was just the opposite with 43 percent viewing white intentions in a positive light.

Finally 38 percent of blacks but only 6 percent of white respondents listed "civil rights of minorities" as a major public policy issue.

Given the information discussed above, there can be little doubt that blacks and whites see a different reality. However, as mentioned earlier, neither community is monolithic. In both communities there are opinion groups of varying size which agree with the majority opinion of the other community. That is to say, on many issues significant numbers of whites agree with the majority of blacks and vice versa.

For example, even though a preponderance of blacks cite racial discrimination as the primary cause of black inequality, there is considerable support among black respondents for arguments that the behavior of blacks themselves are major contributing factors to black inequality. Some 45 percent of blacks agreed with whites that blacks do not have sufficient will power and motivation to pull themselves out of poverty. Forty-seven percent believe that blacks would be as well off as whites "if they would try harder," and 80 percent of blacks agreed that blacks who are well off financially do not do as much as they should to help other blacks.

Similarly, although whites are less inclined to perceive discrimination, a sizable minority of white respondents agreed that black inequality was due mainly to discrimination. A majority of whites agreed with the proposition that blacks "don't have a chance" to get the education it takes to rise out of poverty. Finally, 37 percent of whites disagreed with the argument that blacks lacked the motivation and will power to pull themselves out of poverty.

In the long run the level of agreement and the range of shared perceptions among blacks and whites may be more important than perceptual differences because if a consensus is ever developed it will likely grow out of these areas of initial agreement.

Conclusion

The examination of socioeconomic data presented in this chapter demonstrates conclusively that the gap between the well-being of blacks and whites remains a reality. Moreover, since 1959 the gap has remained virtually unchanged. About this there can be no dispute. However, much dispute remains about the meaning of this information. What does it tell us about the nature and causes of black inequality? What does it imply about the most promising public policy options for promoting black equality?

There is no agreement on the answers to these questions in either the scholarly literature or the popular media. In our view, the data suggest that black inequality is systemic and that its elimination will require fundamental changes in the political and economic systems. Why do we hold this view?

During the quarter century covered in this chapter, the American economic system experienced unprecedented economic growth and expansion. This period also witnessed an intense and largely successful campaign to end all government-sanctioned racial discrimination. Most societally significant overt racially discriminatory practices by private individuals and groups were also eliminated. Yet in spite of these developments, the gap between black and white well-being persisted. It persisted in every area of the country and for every category of educational attainment. Overall, the size of the gap was more or less constant. Black unemployment was consistently twice that of whites, black median income stagnated between 50 and 60 percent of the white median, and the black poverty rate hovered around three times the white poverty rate.

All of this suggests to us that consistent with the tenets of Harris's alternative framework continuing black inequality is the result of certain dynamics of the American economic and political systems. That is to say, it appears to us that when the basic institutions of American society—institutions such as our schools, financial institutions, corporations, labor unions, welfare agencies—are functioning according to legal stipulations and consistent with our cultural expectations they, willy-nilly, routinely create and reinforce conditions of black inequality. If we are correct, the elimination of black inequality will require fundamental changes in the American political and economic systems.

Topics for Discussion

1. "The Nature of the problem of blacks in the American political system is more than socioeconomic inequality. There is an attitudinal dimension that is of equal importance but it is somewhat more difficult to grasp." Discuss the meaning and significance of this comment, and in doing so give particular attention to data that offer evidence on the "attitudinal dimension" of the problem.

2. How can we explain the fact that over the past 25 years the gap between blacks and whites on most indicators of socioeconomic well-being has remained more or less the same even though black political participation has increased dramatically? To what extent do the frames of reference discussed in Chapter 1 help us understand this paradox?

3. What resources are needed to overcome these inequities? Who has control of them? How can they be brought to bear on the problem?

4. "The struggle to reduce poverty and deprivation among black Americans is, willy-nilly, a struggle to increase these debilities among whites." Evaluate this assertion. For the purpose of discussion, assume that it is valid and discuss its implications for the prospect of solving the race problem.

5. Polling data presented in this chapter show that blacks and whites do not see the same reality. In your view, what accounts for these differences? How can this perceptual gap be overcome?

Suggested Readings

Bullock, Charles S., and Harrell R. Rodgers, Jr., eds. *Black Political Attitudes: Implications for Political Support.* Chicago: Rand-McNally, 1972.
Investigations of the political beliefs, attitudes, and stereotypes of blacks; political socialization of black children; and policy outputs and black political influence.

Bullock, Charles, III, and Harrell R. Rodgers. *Racial Equality in America: In search of an Unfulfilled Goal.* Pacific Palisades, CA: Goodyear Publishing Co., 1975.
An analysis of the factors contributing to the continued state of racial inequality in the United States.

Bullock, Charles, III, and Harrell R. Rodgers. *Racism and Inequality: The Policy Alternatives.* San Francisco: W.H. Freeman, 1975.
Discusses the public policies and options available to deal with racial inequality in the United States.

Dye, Thomas. *The Politics of Inequality.* Indianapolis, IN: Bobbs-Merrill, 1971.
Deals with the social and political inequities of the American political system.

Glasgow, Douglas G. *The Black Underclass.* San Francisco: Jossey Bass, 1980.
An empathetic analysis written from the perspective of inner city youth.

Harlan, Louis R. *Separate but Unequal.* New York: Atheneum, 1969.
A study of public school campaigns and southern racism from 1901 to 1915.

Jones, Barbara A.P., ed. *New Perspectives on Unemployment.* New Brunswick, NJ: Transaction, 1984.
Collection of ideologically diverse critiques of alternative explanations of unemployment.

National Urban League. *The State of Black America.* Washington, DC: National Urban League, January 1992.
A group of essays focusing on the current status of blacks in various areas, for example, economic, education, health, and political participation.

Newman, Dorothy, et al. *Protest, Politics and Prosperity: Black Americans and White Institutions, 1940-1975.* New York: Pantheon Books, 1978.
A critical analysis of historical developments in social and economic institutions with respect to the status of blacks over time(1940-1975) in various issue areas, for example, employment and equal employment opportunity, housing and fair housing legislation, health care delivery, and job requirements and education.

Sigelman, Lee and Susan Welch, *Black Americans' Views of Racial Inequality.* New York: Cambridge University Press, 1991.
A comprehensive analysis of the views of African Americans on racial inequality with some comparison of black and white attitudes.

Sniderman, Paul and Michael Gray. *Race and Inequality, A Study in American Values.* Chatham, NJ: Chatham House, 1985.

Sowell, Thomas. *Economics of Politics and Race.* New York: Quill, 1983.
An ambitious effort to place race and politics in an international perspective.

Wilson, William J. *The Declining Significance of Race: Blacks and Changing American Institutions.* Chicago: University of Chicago Press, 1978.
An argument that race is becoming less important in American society.

Notes

1. David Swinton, "The Economic Status of African Americans' Limited Ownership and Persistent Inequality," in *Economic Status of Black America. (New York: National Urban League, 1992), p. 95.*
2. U.S. Bureau of Census, *Current Population Reports,* Series P-60, no. 174, *Money Income of Households, Families, and Persons in the United States 1990. (Washington DC: Government Printing Office, 1991).*
3. Swinton, *Economic Status,* p. 93.
4. The figures in this discussion of the role of the public sector in black employment are drawn from Andrew Brimmer, "The Future of Blacks in the Public Sector," *Black Enterprise* (November 1985), p. 39.
5. John Reid, "Black America in the 1980s," *Population Bulletin* 37, no. 4 (December 1982), p. 26.

6. U.S. Bureau of the Census, *1987 Survey of Minority Owned Business Enterprises, Black*, MB 87-1 (Washington, DC: Government Printing Office, 1990).
7. Ibid. Table 2, p. 29.
8. Angus Cambell and Howard Schuman, *Racial Attitudes in Fifteen American Cities* (Ann Arbor, MI: Institution of Social Research, University of Michigan, 1968), p. 25.
9. Jack Williams, "So You Think Blacks are Better Off Today than 20 Years Ago?" *Washington Post National Weekly Edition* (April 15, 1985). Quoted in Thomas Cavanagh, *Inside Black America* (Washington, DC: Joint Research Center for Political Studies, 1985) p. 3.
10. Thomas Cavanagh, *Inside Black America*, pp. 2-6.

CHAPTER 3

THE NATURE OF THE SYSTEM

When we talk about black politics we are not talking about ordinary politics. And we are not talking about ordinary politics because the American political system has not created a single social community in which the reciprocal rules of politics would apply. Conventional politics cannot solve this problem, because conventional politics is part of the problem. It is part of the problem because the political system is the major bulwark of racism in America. It is part of the problem in the sense that the political system is structured to repel fundamental social and economic change.

We hear a great deal about the deficiencies, real or imagined, of certain black leaders, but not enough attention, it seems to me is paid to the framework within which they operate. That framework prevents radical growth and innovation—as it was designed to prevent radical growth and innovation.

Mervyn M. Dymally, "The Black Outsider and the American Political System"*

INTRODUCTION

Why do blacks and others talk about the "system," or the "establishment"? What are the values of the system and what are its basic features? What are its biases? How do blacks view the system? How are they affected by the system's values, features, and structures? These and related questions comprise the focus of this chapter. Our immediate purpose here is to get an overall view of the system, the political philosophy which conditions it, its values, its features, and its nature. To these we now turn.

POLITICAL PHILOSOPHY AND AMERICAN POLITICS

Understanding the political philosophy of a people is one key to understanding their political system because every political system originates in the context of a political philosophy and, in turn, the political philosophy shapes the growth and development of the political system.

In the United States as in other Western democracies, liberalism is the dominant political philosophy. The struggle for racial justice in the United States has been, on the one hand, a struggle to force the country to fulfill the political promise of the liberal philosophy and a critique of its economic limitations on the other. In this section we discuss the nature and function of political philosophy and demonstrate how the liberal philosophy has conditioned the black struggle in the United States.

Political philosophy is comprised of coherent sets of assumptions about the nature of political reality and political ideals to be pursued.[1] It includes theories about human nature, the origins of government, the relationship between individuals and government and between government and society. Political philosophies also identify practices, institutions and historical agencies through which the desired future should be pursued and they include ethical standards for judging both individuals and institutions. Thus, political philosophies stipulate both means and ends and provide evaluative criteria.

Political philosophies are not the products of idle theorizing. Rather they originate within the context of ongoing debates about the nature of political reality and struggle over societal goals and the most efficacious means for achieving them.

Ordinarily political philosophies arise as challenges to the status quo and provide the basis for a different interpretation of reality and ideological support for an alternative course of human development.

For example, the liberal philosophy of the Enlightenment provided the ideological justification for replacing the old feudal-mercantile order with the liberal state. And in turn, Marxism as a political philosophy made the case for socialism as the successor to the liberal state.

Political philosophies are also both instrumental and symbolic. The institutions, agencies, and practices stipulated by them are instrumental devices through which proponents of the new order can replace their predecessors. The rights of man, popular suffrage, and representative government, for example, were instrumental devices which allowed the rising property classes of the eighteenth and nineteenth centuries to replace the old dominant classes.

Political philosophies are symbolic because both the goals and agencies and institutions proposed by the philosophy become potent symbols around which the entire political process evolves. Goals such as freedom and equality and agencies such as representative government, universal suffrage, and free enterprise, though instrumental in their origin, become ideological precepts and potent political symbols which can be used to condition political behavior and in turn establish the boundaries of legitimate political discourse and debate.

Once the boundaries of legitimacy are established, all contending factions, both those who wish to conserve and those who wish to transform the present system are expected to embrace the goals implied in the dominant philosophy. Both are expected to pursue their objectives through agencies and institutions sanctioned by the philosophy. Thus, the agencies and institutions articulated by the dominant philosophy are projected as devices for both conservation and transformation.

The quotation from Congressman Mervyn Dymally which introduced this chapter reflects his awareness of this contradiction. He suggests that the "rules" within which American politics is played are structured to prevent the kind of changes which might eliminate black inequality. Yet blacks are obliged to defer to these rules.

The following discussion of some of the important assumptions of liberalism, the dominant philosophy which guides American political practice, will further clarify this contention.

In the course of our discussion, we will distinguish between the liberal philosophy and liberalism, the "L" word used as a pejorative label for liberalism in political campaigns. As mentioned earlier, the liberal philosophy arose in Europe as a reaction to the authoritarian and restrictive practices of the feudal and mercantile periods. With emphasis on the rights of property holders, the inviolability of individual rights, and its celebration of the emancipatory character of the market economy the liberal philosophy provided the ideological justification and the structural outline for the rise of the modern capitalist state.

The liberal philosophy provided the ideas and ideals for transforming the old order into a more just and egalitarian system in which the productive capacities of individuals and society could be maximized. Individualism, freedom and equality were among its basic values and goals. Popular suffrage, representative government, political parties, free market institutions, and derivative structures were agencies through which the liberal society was to be realized.

To a considerable extent, the liberal philosophy lived up to its promise. Freed from theocratic domination and mercantilist restrictions, the rising property classes of Europe and subsequently the United States created societies with unmatched political freedom and material plenty for some.

By the turn of the twentieth century, the new order, the modern liberal state, had been firmly established in the United States although its promise of egalitarian development was far from reality. Moreover, the Great Depression of the 1930s demonstrated that the agencies of transformation originally prescribed by liberal philosophy were incapable of obviating the new problems which arose as the liberal state matured.

The new problems included, among other things, unregulated, rapacious predatory business practices, endemic unemployment, exploited and unprotected work force, subsubstandard housing and health care, and continuing racial segregation and exploitation. New agencies, institutions, and practices had to be grafted upon existing ones to address these problems. These new agencies, for the most part, involved some form of government intervention. And, as the problem of the mature liberal state became more and more intractable and government interventionist activities proliferated, the role of government in addressing social and economic problems became the primary cleavage in American political thought. Those less supportive of government intervention are identified as conservatives and more supportive ones retain the liberal label. Both, however, are adherents of the liberal philosophy and both are committed to the preservation of liberal society. They differ on the best means for doing so. In contemporary American political parlance, the "L" word (liberal) is used to refer to those who support greater government intervention to solve social and economic problems.

This schism among the adherents of liberal philosophy in the United States regarding the role of government in solving social and economic problems has special implications for the struggle for racial equality and economic justice because most black strategists have assumed that government intervention is a necessary though not sufficient prerequisite for black advancement. This assumption has of necessity placed blacks as a more or less permanent fixture on the left side of the dominate societal cleavage. And in turn it has robbed blacks of potential political power which could exist under more favorable circumstances. That is to say, if whites were more or less evenly divided, blacks could tilt the system toward interventionist practices.

There are two other elements in liberal philosophy which have special implications for the struggle which we wish to discuss. One is the principle of inequality and immobility of income and wealth and the other is the portrayal of economic deprivation as a necessary stimulant for economic growth and development. Both of these have had negative effects on the struggle for black advancement. Liberal philosophy offers equality as both a value and a goal, but inequality and immobility of income are culturally sanctioned features of the American political culture. By inequality and immobility of income, we mean that a rather small segment of the population receives a disproportionately large share of the national income and that the pattern of inequality remains more or less constant. Kolko[2] for example, has shown that when the population is divided into tenths, the top one-tenth receives an amount equal to the share received by the bottom five-tenths and that this pattern has existed throughout this century. Recent reports suggest that changes in this pattern are unlikely in the foreseeable future.[3]

Regarding the nature and causes of material deprivation, liberal philosophy argues that individual rights and responsibilities are paramount and that government's primary responsibility is to create and safeguard conditions under which individual fulfillment can be pursued. To create such conditions, the philosophy infers, market forces should be allowed to function unhampered by arbitrary intervention. Such a course of action, it is said, would ensure wise and efficient allocation of resources and in the process provide an adequate standard of living for all who are willing to work.

But according to some liberal philosophers, both historical and contemporary, the masses must be goaded or cajoled into productive labor. As Townsend argued in the late nineteenth century,

> Hunger will tame the fiercest animals, it will teach decency and civility, obedience and subjection to the most perverse. In general, it is only hunger which can spear and goad them [the poor] on to labor.[4]

Thus, liberal philosophy condones drastic income inequality but depicts poverty and deprivation as the result of individual or group failure. The special significance of these two related aspects of liberal philosophy lies in the way in which they structure perceptions of black deprivation and condition public discussions of appropriate policy responses.

Due to reasons discussed elsewhere in this book, blacks cluster disproportionately in the bottom tenths of the national income pyramid. The systemic forces which account for the inequality and immobility of income in the broader population make it difficult for blacks to advance as a group. An interlocking set of social customs, economic institutions, political practices, and legal conventions, all conditioned by the ideology of white supremacy, produce conditions which sustain the deprived state of African Americans.

However, inasmuch as liberal philosophy portrays deprivation as a largely self-inflicted debility, public policy discussions focus more on reforming black individuals and groups than on reforming the system itself. We see this in the unending stream of welfare and education reform schemes designed to treat the symptoms rather than their systemic causes.

There are other political values which condition our understanding of the problem. They too are conditioned by the liberal philosophy. To them we now turn.

AMERICAN POLITICAL VALUES AND "THE PROBLEM"

INDIVIDUALISM, EQUALITY, AND FREEDOM

Individualism, equality, and freedom are values that are interwoven in the American political fabric. But the definition, scope, and application of these values remain illusive and subject to intense controversy. The Declaration of

Independence provides one of the earliest and most vivid expressions of these concepts in the American experience. In it Thomas Jefferson wrote that "all men are created equal and are endowed by their Creator with certain inalienable rights . . . and among these are life, liberty, and the pursuit of happiness." Government, according to Jefferson, was instituted to secure these ends. Whenever any government destroys them—that is life, liberty, or property—it is the right of the people to throw off such governments and to institute others that will secure these ends.

Here we get the basic thrust for the notions of individualism: the importance and worth of each individual and the view that individuals have certain "rights" with which no state government should interfere. Indeed, it is the very purpose of government to protect these rights. This emphasis upon the importance and worth of the individual is certainly one of the main currents throughout the history of liberal-democratic thought. Similarly, we get the notion of equality, a noble concept but a difficult one to harness. As it has evolved in the American experience, we may view equality as having three parts: political, legal, and social.

Political equality is perhaps best expressed, at least in more recent times, through the "one person, one vote" principle. Each person's vote in public affairs—elections—should count the same as that of any other person. By *legal equality* is meant that no person is above the law; all are subject to the law. Put another way, every individual is equal under the law. All people have the right to life, liberty, and property. This means, in terms of social equality, that individuals should not be treated badly because of their station in life or the circumstances of their birth. Each person should enjoy an equal chance to succeed in life and develop to full potential within the limits of the human and material resources available to them.

This, in turn, requires that all individuals should have maximum freedom to do what they choose to chart their lives and to determine their own interest as they see fit without external interference, especially from government. To exercise such self-determination in pursuit of their chosen interests or goals is the essence of *freedom*. This means that the individual has certain rights and freedoms upon which government should not intrude. In short, government has *limits*. It is in our understanding of individual freedom that we begin to see the central features of American politics.

Government, of course, is not the only corporate body which may interfere with the exercise of individual freedom. Large corporations, professional associations, and the like, because of their control over material resources and access to channels of impersonal communications, may effectively alter the range of choices available to individuals. Indeed they may influence the individual's perception of what the possible choices can be.[5] The individual has at least a formal political relationship with government. But with other corporate bodies there may be no formal relationship at all for many of the affected parties and thus no avenues for redressing grievances.

These basic political values, however, were not originally meant to apply to blacks. This was true of Jefferson's Declaration of Independence as well as other early American documents, including the Constitution. That this was the case was forcefully shown by Chief Justice Taney in the *Dred Scott* decision. However, these values did not begin with Jefferson; nor of course, did they end with him. Indeed, putting these basic values in liberal-democratic theory into practice is quite another matter. Intense controversy continues over the definition, scope, and application of these values. For one thing, in particular circumstances these values may and do collide and conflict with each other. Individualism, for example, may conflict with what many might think is necessary to safeguard the "public interest" or to promote the "general welfare."

As the history of African Americans in this country clearly shows, the denial of these basic values can diminish both the material and psychological well-being of a people and lead to persistent frustrations. And such frustrations may lead to disruptive behavior which can affect the individual as well as society. In part, this is a consequence of the interrelationship among the three values. Take equality, for example. Political, social, and legal equality are so closely related that it is difficult, if not impossible, to enjoy one type of equality if denied the other types. Or put another way, to deny equality in one area affects the realization of equality in other areas. Many blacks, because of socioeconomic inequities, do not enjoy political or legal equality and vice versa.

Of course, some may hold that the American concept of equality is not as encompassing as outlined above. It is plausible to suggest that the central thread running through the development of the idea of equality in America is something that may be called "equality of opportunity." But, as exemplified in *Regents* v. *Bakke*, there is considerable disagreement over the meaning of this phrase. Many view "equality of opportunity" in a very formal, legal manner. They point to the civil rights laws of the 1950s and 1960s to support their position. Past history aside, they argue, the fact is that now (since the passage of these laws) there is "equality of opportunity" and this concept should be accepted and applied equally to *all* persons. Indeed, the differences of interpretation have apparently cost blacks the support of some of their traditional allies. But our view is that as thus construed, "equality of opportunity" has become a fashionable way by which many white liberals and others, whether they mean to or not, continue the status quo in American society. Sufficient attention must be given to overcoming the "accumulated disadvantages"—incurred in over 200 years of massive deprivation authorized in law and actualized in practice—before the *formal* "equality of opportunity" as articulated in recent court decisions and civil rights laws takes on real meaning. The doctrine does indeed ring hollow when it is so often used to rationalize vacuous notions like "reverse discrimination." Or as an explanation when blacks and other minorities are denied jobs and other advantages because they are not "qualified." The data presented in Chapter 2 and throughout the volume clearly suggest that the wide disparities between blacks and whites in the socioeconomic realm are due to a combination of racial discrimination and certain basic features of the American economy rather than to "individual differences." They suggest to us that perhaps equal opportunity should be considered a means for achieving the ultimate goal of equal outcomes.

MAJORITY RULE AND MINORITY RIGHTS

In a sense, the concept of minority rights is reflected in our discussion of individualism. But we compare it here with majority rule to indicate how Americans hold to two values that seem to be contradictory. The idea that political decisions should be made by majority rule (or at least by pluralities) is based on the premise that individuals enjoy political equality, that is, that one person's vote should count as much as the next. Thus, there is a strong preference that decisions of the majority (or plurality) should prevail over any minority or smaller group of individuals. Having majority rule work as a way of making decisions rests as much on acquiescence of the minority as it does on the sheer weight of numbers of the majority. But, as we have indicated, Americans hold to both majority rule and minority rights. Therefore, there is a built-in tension between the two values. This tension involves not only the *process* of making decisions but also the *content* of the decision. For majority rule to be accepted as legitimate and for it to prevail without coercion it must respect and have the respect of minorities.

Majority rule is perhaps an ideal way of making public decisions in a homogeneous political community in which there is a high consensus on values and a widely accepted agreement on what to disagree about. In the absence of fundamental antagonisms, parties to a dispute are willing to accept the outcome of majority decisions because they have no reason to fear that the outcome will severely threaten survival of their way of life. And equally as important, they can be confident that in other future conflicts their side has a good chance of being part of the prevailing majority.

In the United States, unfortunately, the race question has always been a fundamental antagonism, particularly between blacks and whites. Substantial factions from each community are inclined to view an unfavorable outcome as a threat to its way of life. Under such circumstances, majority rule decisions are often met with defiance by one side or the other. Such tensions are inherent when there is a commitment to both majority rule and minority rights.

LEGALISM

We have heard many times the expression that America has a "government of laws and not of men." The phrase symbolizes the legalistic mold of the American political system. The chief symbol of this American attachment to legalism is the written Constitution which is the fundamental law. From the town or city council to the county board, to the state and national governments, the citizen is overwhelmed with legalism. It flows from laws enacted by legislative bodies, with orders of executives, and with rules and regulations coming from many bureaucratic structures. In this sort of situation, the symbols assume an importance of their own, aside from actual impact of particular laws on individuals. This strong attachment to the idea of written law is accompanied by the view that it is not only practical but also *desirable* to have such regulations. This idea is so widespread in American thinking that it goes beyond government policies and actions and extends into private life and organizations. Consequently, it is not unusual for a new organization or club to argue about "bylaws" which will govern the group's activities.

To be sure, the attachment to legal forms is important to the functions of the political system. The law is used to shape major directions or change in social policy. And it is called into play in distributing benefits and costs and policies and programs to various groups. But laws, no matter how well written, are neither self-enforcing nor self-interpreting. Moreover, the law is not always what the statute says it is. Frequently one can find gaps or room to maneuver within the legal boundaries. It is this characteristic of American law, the unwritten law, which can be as important to individual citizens as that which is written. In any event, this preoccupation with law and legalism gives importance to those who are trained in law. It gives lawyers generally a dominant role in politics and government far beyond their sheer numbers. It also points up the importance of courts as policy-making arenas in allocating benefits and values in the political system. This subject is explored more fully in Chapter 5.

The excessive attention which Americans often give to the law and legalism sometimes obscures a fundamental point about the law and the American political system, namely, that the law, to a great extent, is but a reflection of the resolution of conflicts between contending factions for material advantage. When bills are passed or rulings are made by courts and regulatory bodies, there are winners and losers. Invariably the winners attempt to make their victory permanent by incorporating its terms into the permanent law. The losers seek to minimize their loss by influencing the interpretation and implementation of the law as best they can.

When the law is viewed in this fashion the expression that the United States is a government of laws and not of men takes on different meaning. It means merely that it is a system in which contemporary conflicts are regulated and moderated by the community-sanctioned resolution of past conflicts between competing interverts.

CONFLICT *BUT* COMPROMISE

Given their heterogeneous population mix, Americans have come to expect conflict. But we have also come to expect that conflict can be managed.

Conflicts cover many issues in American life. They may be drawn along a number of lines: racial, ethnic, social, economic, political, or, more likely, over a combination of these. And as we shall discuss later, some of this conflict is built into the system itself. In any event, the racial conflict (or problem) cuts across all these lines. It promotes sharp divisions and provokes strong emotions from the parties involved. To many Americans, mainly white Americans, it is a conflict (to some just another conflict) that not only has to be managed by the system, but one that can also be managed through restraint and reason. Essentially this means that both sides must give a little and compromise their differences. This willingness to compromise is perhaps the most important characteristic of American politics. Neither side can expect the other side to give in completely; the *American* way is the *middle* way. To hold fast to your position, no matter what the cause, is viewed as hostile, unsportsmanlike, uncooperative. However, all legitimate positions must fall within the prevailing consensus on what to disagree about. Positions which do not are considered extremist and therefore illegitimate.

Identification of what constitutes the middle way, however, is contingent upon prior understanding of what are the outermost boundaries of legitimate debate and conflict in American politics. The boundaries were established initially by the Federalists and anti-Federalists when the Republic was founded in 1789. Both accepted the white supremacist ideology. Their major differences centered around the role of the government in the economy. This cleavage, though modified by circumstances of history, remains the primary point of debate in American politics.

When the country was founded, political participation was limited to property-holding white men, and the differences, which became the dominant cleavage in American politics, reflected the interests of and divisions within the propertied classes. These classes, then, established the prevailing boundaries and determined the rules of the political game.

Over the years, of course, the American political process became democratized as non-property-holding white men, black men, and later women were eventually given the franchise. However, as Schattschneider pointed out some time ago[6] new participants entering the political system were obliged to accept the existing boundaries and to pursue their interests within the constraints and according to the rules imposed by them. These conditions for admission as participants in the American political system undermined the effectiveness of black political participation as a strategy for black advancement because, as mentioned earlier, the existing rules of the game create and reinforce the conditions which are responsible for black inequality.

FEATURES OF THE SYSTEM

The political values we just discussed are so tied to the nature of American politics that it is difficult to say whether such values have more influence on the system or vice versa. What we can say is that both the values and the features of the system reinforce one another. For example, the idea that the people are sovereign, that they are supreme, is firmly implanted in the Constitution and its amendments. This supremacy is voiced by the people through regular and periodic elections in selecting a representative government. The people, however, retain sovereignty. Through a written constitution they limit what the representatives, as governors, can do. This is the idea of limited government. It finds expression in the Constitution through such provisions as the delegated powers of the Congress and the Bill of Rights. The Bill of Rights, for example, is designed to limit governments from intruding upon the rights of the individual. But, as with many features of American government, when we go below the surface a number of factors emerge. The problem of defining the people (and hence making the concept of popular sovereignty work) has been a continuing one for democratic governments generally and American government in particular. The problem is one of inclusion and exclusion. Blacks, women, 18-year-olds, as well as malapportioned urban residents, readily come to mind. And while all of these groups are now formally included as part of the people, their actual inclusion may be another matter. For, as African Americans well know, constitutional-legal inclusion does not necessarily guarantee inclusion in practice.

Let us explore this idea a bit further. Elections are a main way to translate popular sovereignty into working, *representative government*. But this raises a number of questions. For example, what are the dynamics of American elections? What are the structures of election? What consequences flow from these structures, such as single-member districts or the frequency of election? Who is advantaged by these structures? Who is disadvantaged? In the single-member district, for instance, the winner takes all. This means that the majority (even if a coalition of minorities) rules and the minority loses. But elections, as we know, afford a way of managing conflict, quieting issues, and promoting compromises.

In any event, the election winner is pictured as representing all constituents, even though the winner may not be a particular group or faction. And the official may indeed try very hard to reflect the views of all constituents up to the point that it tends to jeopardize chances for reelection. But can an official *really* represent the group if the official is not of that group? This, of course, raises an age-old question about representation. We repeat it here only to emphasize its continuing importance to blacks and others insofar as it pertains to the structure of elections and the nature of representative government.

Of course, other constitutional-legal features such as federalism and separation of powers also shape our political landscape. With respect to federalism, the Constitution provides for a division of powers and authority between a central government and states. This division of powers certainly has consequences for how we deal with problems and how we manage conflict. For one thing, it means that the number of forums to deal with conflict is 51 rather than 1 as would be the case of a single central government. This increase in the number of forums to deal with conflict often brings about an *increase* in conflict itself. And, of course, some people see benefits in using states as experimental political laboratories. Others see the need for unified action, for a single national policy. The point here is that federalism is not without its advantages and disadvantages in given situations. Federalism, for example, permitted southern states to "handle" the racial problem as they saw fit; this worked to the advantage of whites but to the serious disadvantage of blacks. In any event, federalism like so much of the political system often requires negotiations, bargaining, and compromise among various controlling interests in state and national government.

The Constitution also incorporates the doctrine of *separation of powers*. Under this doctrine, the authority of the national government is divided among three branches: legislative, executive, and judicial. The functions are allocated accordingly: The legislature makes laws, the executive enforces laws, and the judiciary interprets laws. But the lines of separation are not this neatly drawn. Indeed, under another arrangement—*checks and balances*—the Constitution also gives each branch some say in how the other branches carry on their functions. For example, Congress can pass legislation, but the president may veto it. However, the legislation can still become law if Congress can muster enough votes (two-thirds of both houses) to repass it over the president's veto. And, of course, the Supreme Court can invalidate laws passed by Congress, even those approved by the president. But the Constitution provides the Supreme Court with neither the "sword nor the purse" to enforce rulings. It must depend on the president and others to do so. Thus, while the Constitution provides for three independent branches, at the same time it so intermingles their authority as to make it necessary for the branches to be *interdependent* rather than *independent* of each other. In short, one purpose of the separation of powers and the checks and balances is to keep government officials from becoming too powerful.

These constitutional features are also designed to prevent any group, even a majority, from a complete domination of government at any one time. The Constitution provides that officials of the three branches are to be selected for different terms of office and by different constituencies. For example, all members of the House of Representatives are elected every two years from essentially local constituencies, the congressional districts. Presumably, they represent different interests from the Senators who are elected statewide for six-year terms with one-third elected every two years. The president is elected by the entire nation via the electoral college for a four-year term with the entire nation as his constituency. And members of the federal judiciary, including the Supreme Court, are appointed by the president with the approval of the Senate. They hold office for life and are not subject to popular election. Overall then, the manner in which the Constitution provides for the selection and tenure of public officials poses formidable barriers to the complete domination of government by any group or interest at a given time. As Parenti has noted, they also insulate government from mass sentiment.[7]

Just as with federalism, the actual operation of the separation of powers and checks and balances fosters both conflict and cooperation. Different constituencies and overlapping terms of office tend to cause conflict. But the fact that the three branches share in each other's powers—as, for example the president and Congress do in law making—tends to compel cooperation and compromise. In short, federalism, separation of powers, and checks and balances reflect the diversity of interests in American politics. They also *institutionalize* and *preserve* the *prevailing* rather than *aspiring* interests. They promote *incremental and marginal change* rather than *decisive and fundamental change*. And no matter what their virtues, these features of American politics pose built-in disadvantages to the kind of decisive, fundamental change needed to deal with problems facing African Americans and other minorities.

The two-party system also stands out as a striking feature of American politics. Our parties have developed as the political system has developed and vice versa. Indeed, so interwoven are political parties within the political system that many Americans perhaps assume that such organizations are expressly provided for in the Constitution. They are not. Understandably, then, the two-party system both influences and promotes the dominant political values of the system. Consider, for example, that the role of parties in forming majorities leads to an attempt to get diverse interests and individuals to work together and to the necessity of conflict management through moderation and compromise. As Sorauf put it:

> At the most fundamental level the American parties, and those of the other democracies, serve democracy by reaffirming and promoting its basic values. The very activities of the two gigantic and diversified American parties promote a commitment to the values of compromise, moderation, and the pursuit of limited goals. They also encourage the political activity and participation that a democracy depends on. And they reinforce the basic democratic rules of the game: the methods and procedures of orderly criticism and opposition, change by the regular electoral processes, and deference to the will of the majority.[8]

Political parties certainly reinforce the basic values of American politics. These organizations operate on and promote the assumption that *all* problems can be settled and settled *peacefully within* the political system. That parties are large and diversified organizations also means that they handle problems so as to promote the values of "compromise, moderation, and the pursuit of limited goals." As such, our party system serves to reinforce the type of "incremental and marginal change" that is so characteristic of American politics. At the same time the political parties serve as barriers to fundamental change.

By running for the presidential nomination of the Democratic Party in 1984 and 1988 the Reverend Jesse Jackson attempted to make the system more accountable to African Americans *(AP/Wide World Photos)*

ON ELITES AND POLITICAL PARTICIPATION

African Americans, perhaps more than other citizens, have reason to show more concern for elites and "the tyranny of the majority." They are, despite increased participation and importance in the political process, almost a "permanent minority" in American politics. Many blacks continue to be the victims of discriminatory practices against them as individuals and as a group. The existence of such practices in broad segments of white society almost makes a discussion of elites unnecessary. Similarly, the notions of majority rule and agreement on values combine with the elite presence to make up a political system which African Americans view as inevitably hostile to their interests. From the perspective of the black minority, the middle-class, "politically actives," "amateur democrats," as well as the upper class, constitute an establishment. Because the consensus on American values depends heavily on the actions and attitudes of such groups, the black minority tends to regard them as essentially the same with respect to black concerns.

In the late 1950s social scientists such as Floyd Hunter and C. Wright Mills produced books which seemed to show that there existed what has come to be known as the *"power elite"* in most American communities. These elites were said to exercise much influence on the shaping of public policy. Seldom were the members of these elite groups elected officials. Their activities were frequently out of the public view. The work of these two scholars touched off an academic debate which continues to the present.[9]

In this chapter we do not directly enter the power elite debate. However we do take the position that at both the national and local levels certain individuals because of their institutional affiliation and positions exercise greater political power than others and that blacks are woefully underrepresented in such positions.

Thomas Dye[10] has attempted to identify a "national institutional elite" by identifying what he calls the major national institutions and the positions of authority within each of them. He divides American society into 12 sectors: (1) industrial corporations, (2) utilities, (3) banking, (4) insurance, (5) investments, (6) mass media, (7) law, (8) education, (9) foundations, (10) civic and cultural organizations, (11) government, (12) military. Using admittedly subjective criteria, Dye determines which firms or units within each sector are "major institutions" and which positions within these institutions are positions of authority.

Dye's system revealed 7,314 positions of authority occupied by 5,778 different individuals. Only 20 of them were black.[11] He concluded that "no blacks have ever been presidents of a major industrial corporation, bank, utility, insurance company, investment firm, communication network, prestigious university, or top civic cultural organization."[12]

Dye's system for identifying the elite is open to question.[13] However, any other system would in all probability yield similar results. No matter what criteria are used, only a few blacks are among the power elite. Moreover, the process of institutional elite recruitment is such that those who ultimately reach such institutional position, be they black or white, will likely share the dominant institutional outlook.

Conclusion

The American political system is grounded in the liberal philosophy of the Enlightenment which offered individualism, equality, and freedom as major values and which championed representative government, popular suffrage, and free market economic institutions as historical agencies through which the goals of a more just and egalitarian society could be realized.

The system which eventually evolved in the United States has been one of unprecedented material advancement and widespread political participation. African Americans, however, have not shared equally in the material development of the country. Nor have they been equal political participants. This is so because certain other values embedded in liberal philosophy and reinforced by the ideology of white supremacy gave rise to an interlocking set of economic, political, and cultural forms which create and sustain conditions of black inequality.

Liberal philosophy accepts income inequality and immobility as part of the natural order of things. For well-known historical reasons, blacks have always been represented disproportionately among the impoverished of America. The institutions and practices which routinely function to sustain income inequality and income immobility in general also sustain black inequality.

Topics for Discussion

1. The text states that "it is plausible to suggest that the central thread running through the development of the idea of equality in American is something that may be called 'equality of opportunity.'" But the text goes on to state that "there is much disagreement over the meaning of the term, that is, 'equality of opportunity.'" What is the nature of this disagreement? How might it relate to the controversy over the current problems that disproportionately affect blacks? Discuss.

2. Liberal democracy seeks to insure equal opportunity for all and protection of minority rights while egalitarian democracy is committed to equal outcomes. Can racial inequalities in America be eliminated so long as the United States remains committed to liberal democracy?

3. The political value system in America contains values that appear (at certain times at least) to be contradictory. For example, some of the connotations of "individualism" (and "minority rights") seem contradictory or in opposition to the value of "majority rule." Discuss how these values—individualism (minority rights) and majority rule—work to the advantage and disadvantage of blacks and other minorities in their struggle for equality.

4. It has been suggested that certain features of the American political system (e.g., separation of powers, two-party system) pose built-in disadvantages to the kind of *decisive, fundamental change* needed to deal with problems facing blacks and other minorities. Do you agree with this view? Are there situations in which these features might work to the *advantage* of blacks and minorities? Discuss.

5. "Constant unemployment and poverty are enduring systemic features of the U.S. economic system. Institutional racism allocates these debilities disproportionately among black Americans." Evaluate this assertion and discuss its implications for efforts to achieve racial equality.

Suggested Readings

Bachrach, Peter. *The Theory of Democratic Elitism.* Boston: Little, Brown, 1967.
A critique of the democratic creed in America.

Commager, Henry S. *Majority Rule and Minority Rights.* New York: Peter Smith, 1950.
Looks at democracy, judicial review, and how they affect majority rule and rights of minority.

Cruse, Harold. *Plural but Equal.* New York: William Morrow, 1987.
A critical examination of the position of blacks and the performance of black leadership in America's Plural society.

Dahl, Robert A.*Pluralist Democracy in the United States: Conflict and Consent.* Chicago: Rand McNally & Co., 1967.
An analysis of the American political system by one of the leading exponents of pluralism.

Dahl, Robert A. *Who Governs? Democracy and Power in an American City.* New Haven CT: Yale University Press, 1961.
A description of decision making in New Haven, Connecticut, exemplifies how pluralist democracy operates in that city.

Domhoff, G. William. *Who really Governs? New Haven and Community Power Reexamined.* New Brunswick, NJ: Transaction Books, 1978.
Examines critically the notion of pluralism and the idea of community power.

Dye, Thomas R., and Harmon Zeigler. *The Irony of Democracy: An Uncommon Introduction to American Politics,* 4th ed. Belmont, CA: Wadsworth Publishing Co., 1978.
Examines the American political system as an "elitist" democracy and challenges the prevailing pluralistic-democratic view of the American political system.

Dye, Thomas. *Who's Running America? Institutional Leadership in the United States.* Englewood Cliffs, NJ: Prentice Hall, 1976.
A theoretical and empirical analysis of the leadership class in the United States.

Fresia, Jerry. *Toward an American Revolution.* Boston: South End Press, 1988.
Analysis of the nondemocratic forces which influenced the drafting of the U.S. Constitution.

Hartz, Louis. *The Liberal Tradition in America: An Interpretation of American Political Thought since the American Revolution.* 1955.

Holden, Matthew, Jr. *The White Man's Burden.* New York: Chandler Publishing Co., 1973.
An examination of the possibilities of the American republic to reconcile racial conflict.

Kariel, Henry S. *The Decline of American Pluralism.* Stanford, CA: Stanford University Press, 1961.
A critique and challenge to pluralism in the American political system.

Kelso, William Alton. *American Democratic Theory: Pluralism and Its Critics.* Westport, CT: Greenwood Press, 1978.
Critically analyzes pluralism as a democratic theory.

Knowles, Louis L., and Kenneth Prewitt, eds. *Institutional Racism in America.* Englewood Cliffs, NJ: Prentice Hall, 1969.
A collection of essays and articles that argue that racism is ingrained in the structuralized institutional fiber of the United States.

Levitan, Sar A., et al. *Still a Dream.* Cambridge, MA: Harvard University Press, 1975.
A thoughtful analysis of the changing status of black Americans from 1960 to 1975.

Marable, Manning. *How Capitalism Underdeveloped Black America.* Boston: South End Press, 1983.
An ambitious effort to show that black inequality is a function of the dynamics of United States capitalist development.

Mills, C. Wright. *The Marxists.* New York: Dell, 1962.
Provides a conceptual framework for analyzing political philosophies and succinct description of both the liberal and Marxist political philosophies.

Mills, C. Wright. *The Power Elite.* New York: Oxford University Press, 1956.
A study of the dominance of "power elite" in the American social system.

Newman, William M. *American Pluralism: A Study of Minority Groups and Social Theory.* New York: Harper & Row, 1973.
Pluralism examined in the context of the attempts by minority groups to participate effectively in American society.

Parenti, Michael. *Democracy for the Few.* 2nd ed. New York: St. Martin's Press, 1977.
Focuses on the theme that the American political system functions to serve the interests of corporate wealth at the expense of the majority of the people.

Polsby, Nelson W. *Community Power and Political Theory.* New Haven, CT: Yale University Press, 1966.
A review from a pluralist perspective of the literature on community power structures and policy making in local communities in hope of developing a theory on power distribution in America.

Notes

* Mervyn M. Dymally, ed., *The Black Politician: His Struggle for Power* (Belmont, CA: Wadsworth, Inc., 1971), p. 120. Reprinted by permission of the publisher, Duxbury Press.

1. This discussion of the nature of political philosophy is adapted from C. Wright Mills, *The Marxist* (New York: Dell, 1962), pp. 11-29.
2. Gabriel Kolko, *Wealth and Power in America* (New York: Praeger, 1962), pp. 14-20.
3. See David Swinton, "The Economic State of Black America in the 1980s," in *The Economic State of Black America 1990* Janet Ewart, ed., (New York: National Urban League, 1990), pp. 31-32.
4. William Townsend, *Dissertation on the Poor Laws,* cited in Paul Therkildsen, *Public Assistance and American Values* (Albuquerque: University of New Mexico, 1964), p. 9.
5. For further explication, see Michael Parenti, *Inventing Reality, The Politics of the Mass Media* (New York: St. Martin's Press, 1986).
6. E.E. Schattschneider, *The Semisovereign People* (New York: Holt, Rinehart and Winston, 1964).
7. See Michael Parenti, *Democracy for the Few* (New York: St. Martin's Press, 1987).
8. See Frank J. Sorauf, *Party Politics in America,* 3rd. ed. (Boston: Little Brown, 1976), Chapter 8.
9. For the original statements of these views, see Floyd Hunter et al., *Community Power Structure* (Chapel Hill: University of North Carolina Press, 1953); and C. Wright Mills, *The Power Elite* (New York: Oxford University Press, 1956). Perhaps the most notable critiques of the positions set forth in these works are contained in Robert A. Dahl, *Who Governs* (New Haven, CT: Yale University Press, 1960) and Nelson W. Polsby, *Community Power and Political Theory* (New Haven, CT: Yale University Press, 1963). The writings of Peter Bachrach and Morton Baratz provide a contrasting interpretation to those presented by Dahl and Polsby; the reader should carefully examine the arguments put forth in their essay "The Two Faces of Power," *American Political Science Review* (1962), pp. 947-52.
10. Thomas Dye, *Who's Running America,* 5th ed. (Englewood Cliffs, NJ: Prentice Hall, 1990).
11. Ibid., p. 197.

12. Ibid., p. 199.
13. Dye's system defines institutional elites as (1) those occupying positions of authority in companies controlling over half of the nation's total corporate assets; (2) those occupying formal positions of authority in the major civilian and military bureaucracies of the national government; (3) those occupying positions of authority in the mass media, prestigious law firms, major philanthropic foundations, the leading universities, and the recognized national civic and cultural organizations.

CHAPTER 4

THE QUEST FOR POLITICAL RESOURCES

In allocating income, wealth, status, knowledge, occupation, organizational position, popularity, and a variety of other values every society also allocates resources with which an actor can influence the behavior of other actors in at least some circumstances. . . . Extreme inequalities in the distribution of such key values as income, wealth, status, knowledge and military prowess are equivalent to extreme inequalities in political resources.

Robert A. Dahl, *Polyarchy*[*]

Those who seek change through politics must have the power to persuade or force other political actors to respond in a manner supportive of the desired change. To bring about such a response the group must have not only the resources necessary to influence the target group but also the means for converting the resources into actual power by bringing them to bear upon those whose behavior must be influenced.

In democratic societies such as the United States, economic wealth, favorable population distribution, voting and holding public office are all potential sources of power. Each of these can be used to political advantage by those who possess them providing they have the means for converting them into actual power. The politics of African Americans has been a constant struggle to acquire such resources and convert them into actual power.

In previous chapters we discussed economic wealth and black population distribution as political resources. In this chapter the focus is on voting and holding office as political resources. We will examine two case studies of recent efforts of blacks to convert these resources into actual political power. One case study will examine efforts of blacks in the rural South to achieve empowerment through electoral participation. The second case study will analyze efforts to create a national black political organization to enhance black political empowerment. This chapter also discusses efforts to achieve black empowerment through presidential politics and the rise of black conservatives and their efforts toward resource mobilization.

VOTING AS A LIMITED RESOURCE

Securing the right to vote dominated the black political agenda from Emancipation until the 1960s. Passage of the Voting Rights Act in 1965 brought the quest for the vote to a successful conclusion[1] and pushed the struggle for black political empowerment to a new level as converting black voting strength into political power became the focal point of the black movement.

TABLE 4-1 Reported voter registration and turnout, total population and blacks, 1966-1984

	VOTER REGISTRATION					
	TOTAL POPULATION			BLACKS		
	PEOPLE OF VOTING AGE (THOUSANDS)	PEOPLE REGISTERED (THOUSANDS)	REGISTRATION RATE (%)	PEOPLE OF VOTING AGE (THOUSANDS)	PEOPLE REGISTERED (THOUSANDS)	REGISTRATION RATE (%)
1966	112,800	79,295	70.3	10,533	6,345	60.3
1968	116,535	86,574	74.3	10,935	7,238	66.2
1970	120,701	82,181	68.1	11,472	6,971	60.8
1972	136,203	98,480	72.3	13,493	8,837	65.5
1974	141,299	87,889	62.2	14,175	7,778	54.9
1976	146,548	97,761	66.7	14,927	8,725	58.5
1978	151,646	94,883	62.6	15,636	8,921	57.1
1980	157,085	105,035	66.9	16,423	9,849	60.0
1982	165,483	105,966	64.1	17,624	10,422	59.1
1984	169,963	116,106	68.3	18,432	12,223	66.3
1988	178,098	118,589	67.0	19,692	12,700	64.0

SOURCES: Data for 1966-1984 taken from Thomas E. Cavanagh, *Inside Black America, The Message of the Black Vote in 1984 Election* p. 21. The 1988 data computed from U.S. Bureau of Census, Current Population

In order to convert voting strength into actual political power a group must be able to maximize voter registration and voter turnout, develop institutional structures for recruiting supportive candidates for public office, and mobilize support for such candidates. Once supportive candidates have been elected the group must develop a system to hold them accountable to the group.

Thus neither the election of black officeholders nor being the swing vote which determines which white candidate will be elected is prima facie evidence that the black vote has been converted into black political power. The acid test of political power is the extent to which those who are elected with black support are able to secure passage of public policies supportive of black interests.

To date, blacks have made considerable progress in stimulating voter registration and electing blacks to political office but their impact on policy outcomes, however, has been much less pronounced.

Table 4-1 shows the considerable progress that blacks have made in stimulating voter registration. Although black registration continues to lag behind the national rate, since 1965 the gap has been narrowed significantly. Black registration trailed the rate for the total population by ten percentage points in 1966, but by 1984 the difference was only two percentage points. Some attribute much of the recent increase in black voter registration to enthusiasm spawned by Jesse Jackson's candidacy for the presidency.

TABLE 4-1 Continued

	VOTER TURNOUT		
	TOTAL VOTERS (THOUSANDS)	BLACK VOTERS (THOUSANDS)	BLACK VOTERS A % OF TOTAL VOTE
1966	62,518	4,398	7.0
1968	78,964	6,300	8.0
1970	65,888	4,992	7.6
1972	85,766	7,032	8.2
1974	63,164	4,786	7.6
1976	86,698	7,273	8.4
1978	69,587	5,812	8.4
1980	93,066	8,287	8.9
1982	80,310	7,581	9.4
1984	101,878	10,293	10.1
1988	102,224	10,144	10.0

Reports, *Voting and Registration in the Election of November 1988* (Washington, D.C.: U.S. Government Printing Office 1989), p. 20.

Black voters as a percent of total voters also increased significantly, from seven percent in 1966 to ten percent in 1988. Moreover, black voters as a percent of all voters compared favorably with their percent of the total voting age population which was ten percent.[2]

The voter registration and voter turnout figures reported in Table 4-1, it should be noted, are national estimates. They do not convey the considerable variations which exist throughout the country and among different age groups. These variations can have serious consequences for efforts to convert the vote into political power. For example, in some jurisdictions in which the black vote may be the potential swing vote, registration may be low, and as a result the potential to determine the outcome of close elections may not be realized. In others where blacks constitute preponderant majorities, black registration may be unusually high. There are other electoral districts in which blacks are a majority of the voting age population but a much smaller fraction of the total registered voters.

The absence of a national clearing house for voter registration and voter turnout figures makes impossible a more refined discussion of this issue. It is safe to conclude, however, that black voter registration has increased substantially since 1965, but that registration levels remain depressed in some jurisdictions.

The process through which voting is operationalized as political power depends, among other things, upon the nature of the electoral environment. If the group is a majority in the electoral district, it can elect a representative of its own choosing. If it is not, its members must forge coalitions with others to elect candidates and pursue its interest.

Since 1965 blacks have made measurable progress in electing black candidates to public office, especially from electoral units in which they are in the majority. Relatively few black officeholders, however, have been elected from majority white electoral districts.

There were some 7,490 black elected officials in 1991 compared to 1,469 in 1970.[3] However, blacks still constituted only 1.2 percent of all elected officials. The preponderant majority of them, 92 percent, were elected in county and municipal jurisdictions. In 1988 throughout the United States there were only four blacks who held statewide elected positions including Douglas Wilder who was elected governor of Virginia that year. Although the number of black officials at county and municipal levels is impressive when compared to those at the state and national levels, black representation is far from being proportionate to black voting strength. In many of the predominantly black counties and municipalities of the South, for example, black representation remains low. Of 22 majority black counties in Mississippi, blacks comprised a majority on the county governing authority in only 5 of them in 1986. Similarly blacks controlled only 1 of 20 such governing boards in Georgia. None of the 12 majority black counties in South Carolina had a majority black governing board in 1982.

BLACK ELECTED OFFICIALS AND POLITICAL EMPOWERMENT AT THE LOCAL LEVEL

Recent studies have shown that while black elected officials have provided their constituents with benefits in housing, employment, education, health care, police protection, and other areas,[4] they have not been able to alter substantially the priorities of the governing bodies on which they serve.[5] Consequently their primary contributions have been limited to ensuring a more racially equitable distribution of public goods and services within existing priorities, but as we have already argued black well-being is compromised by the existing priorities.

The limited impact of black elected officials may be explained by a variety of factors, some of which are general and systemic while others may be peculiar to a given community The lack of disciplined, independent black political organizations is a general and systemic problem which mitigates against black empowerment in practically every community although it is more pronounced in some communities than in others. In some cases the small number of black officials and the absence of viable coalition partners explain their lack of effectiveness. Finally, in some jurisdictions the intransigence of the entrenched white oligarchy, particularly in the rural South, is the primary impediment to black empowerment.

Thus the dynamics of the struggle for empowerment through electoral activity is, to an extent, unique to time and place. Accordingly there can be no general model of the process of empowerment. Rather our general understanding must come through case studies over a variety of situations chosen for their theoretical relevance. Major American cities with black mayors and the majority black counties of the rural South provide ideal settings for studying the dynamics of the struggle for black empowerment. Inasmuch as numerous case studies dealing with black mayors and black empowerment are readily available elsewhere,[6] we will focus on majority black counties of the rural South.

In these counties, because the prospects for achieving power is high, the populations are relatively small, and the overall system correspondingly less complex and more manageable, blacks are more inclined to wage a sustained struggle for control rather than simply for increased access. On the other hand, because control of county government in the rural South is a major economic resource, the entrenched white elite is likely to be equally intense in its opposition to black empowerment. The clash of these opposing forces, then, provides a good setting for observing the dynamics of the struggle for black political empowerment.

One such area is the "black belt" counties of southwest Alabama. The struggle by blacks to gain control in this region has been unrelenting for more than a quarter of a century. The opposition of the white elites has been equally as spirited. In their efforts to prevail both sides have sought support from both national and state political actors. Consequently the struggle in the Alabama black belt, though local in scope, has national significance.

MOBILIZATION AND EMPOWERMENT IN THE ALABAMA BLACK BELT

The Alabama black belt is composed of ten contiguous rural counties in southwest Alabama. Blacks are a majority of the population in eight of the counties, and approximately 42 percent in the other two. Some 58 percent of the region's 200,000 inhabitants and 53 percent of the registered voters are black.[7]

The contemporary struggle for empowerment in the Alabama black belt goes back to the voter registration campaigns of the early 1960s which captured national and international attention. The region was a staging ground for much of the political mobilization and agitation which culminated with passage of the Voting Rights Act. The Student Nonviolent Coordinating Committee (SNCC), a civil rights organization which played a major role in overturning the racial caste system of the rural south, was active in Lowndes and surrounding counties. Martin Luther King, Jr. and the Southern Christian Leadership Congress Conference conducted campaigns in Greene County. The infamous murders of Jimmie Lee Jackson, a black voter registration worker, and two white sympathizers, the Reverend James Reeb and Viola Liuzzo, all occurred in the Alabama black belt.

The area was also the scene of the famed Selma to Montgomery march and the bloody confrontation on the Edmund Pettis Bridge. It was the unrelenting opposition of white officials in this area to black voter registration which led to passage of the 1965 Voting Rights Act. The latter gave the national government discretionary authority to register black voters when local registrars refused to cooperate. And subsequently federal officials did in fact register black voters in nine of the ten Alabama counties.

Twenty years later black electoral success in the Alabama black belt was more substantial than in many other areas of the country. The success, however, was the product of two decades of intense struggle for empowerment.

There were virtually no registered black voters and no black officials in the area in 1965. By 1985 blacks controlled five of the region's ten county governing bodies and five of eleven area school boards. Nine of the 42 municipalities in the region were directed by blacks and three black sheriffs, one state senator and three state representatives had been elected in this ten-county region.

The magnitude of the electoral success of the struggle for empowerment in the Alabama black belt is put in sharp relief when it is compared with that in the 79 predominantly black counties in nine other southern states. In those counties blacks control the county governing

ALABAMA BLACKBELT COUNTIES

board in less than one-third of them while another third have no black representation at all.

Black electoral success in the Alabama black belt did not come overnight. Greene county came under black control in 1970, but breakthroughs did not occur in the other counties for more than a decade. Indeed, as of 1986 black representation remained minimal in three of the counties. The county seat, which is usually the financial and commercial center in the rural South, remained under white control in each county.

The dominant white elites used a variety of tactics, both legal and extralegal to thwart black efforts, and both black and white factions solicited involvement of outside interests in their efforts to prevail.

The first concerted push for black empowerment occurred in Greene county in 1966. Blacks ran a full slate of candidates for county offices, but in spite of an overwhelming black voting majority, only one black candidate was elected.

Two years later, following a more intense voter registration and voter education campaign, blacks nominated a set of candidates under the banner of a newly formed independent black political party. However the white county probate judge defied a decision of the U.S. Supreme Court and refused to place the names of the black candidates on the ballot and the government remained all white.

Ultimately the federal courts voided the results of the 1968 election and ordered the county to hold a special election in 1969. It was in the 1969 election that blacks gained control of the county governing board.

TABLE 4-2 Population and distribution of black elected officials in Alabama black belt, 1974 and 1986*

COUNTY	1980 POPULATION		TOTAL NUMBER OF ELECTED OFFICIALS	NUMBER OF BLACK ELECTED OFFICIALS	
	TOTAL	%BLACK		1974	1986
Choctaw	16,839	43	14	0	3
Dallas	53,981	54	13	0	1
Hale	15,604	63	14	0	2
Lowndes	13,253	75	15	5	9
Marengo	25,047	53	13	0	4
Perry	15,012	60	13	1	8
Pickens	21,481	42	13	0	0
Greene	11,021	78	14	13	14
Sumter	16,908	69	14	2	9
Wilcox	14,735	68	14	0	13

*Includes county governing board, probate judges, circuit clerks, school board members, tax assessors, and tax collectors.

SOURCE: Field interviews by the authors

(United Press International Telephoto)

The next year blacks were elected as probate judge and tax assessor, giving them control of all county offices.

Following the success in Greene county, black civic leagues in other counties embarked upon similar efforts. However, they faced intense opposition from local whites who engaged in legal subterfuge and economic and political intimidation to discourage black voter registration.[8] Some counties permitted registration only at the county court house during normal working hours. Although state law authorized the use of deputy registrars to make registration more convenient, several counties refused to do so.[9]

When black registration became sufficient to challenge white dominance, various strategies were pursued to reduce the power of the black vote. Following the election of two black commissioners in Wilcox county in 1980, the Alabama legislature, under the local courtesy rule,[10] passed bills requiring voters in four black belt counties to "reidentify" themselves or be purged from the rolls. In effect, the bills allowed the counties to clear registration rolls because all registered voters had to appear in person to reidentify themselves or their names would be dropped from the rolls. Black leaders argued that this was a thinly disguised effort to undercut black voter registration. The justice department ultimately rejected reidentification bills for two of the counties.

Whites also used racially biased annexation and incorporation schemes to prevent black empowerment. In some counties, heretofore unincorporated areas were incorporated within racially gerrymandered boundaries to insure white majorities. Other municipalities simply annexed white areas to create majority white towns. These discriminatory changes in electoral procedures were not submitted to the Justice Department for review in violation of the Voting Rights Act.

Black belt whites also used their state and national political connections to maintain their dominant position. One example was their campaign to destroy the Federation of Southern Cooperatives, a black-controlled, economic self-help organization which was located in Sumter County and which was a major independent resource for blacks throughout the black belt. The federation provided educational and technical assistance to 130 cooperatives of low-income and mostly black farmers in 14 states. With a well-trained and politically astute staff, a modern training facility with sophisticated publishing capabilities, and a budget of several million dollars funded primarily by federal grants and gifts from foundations, the federation's communication and mobilizing capabilities exceeded those of most other institutions in the region. For blacks in rural Alabama it was an unprecedented resource. To local whites it was a threat to their privileged position.

The federation was technically a nonprofit and therefore nonpolitical organization, but persons associated with it were active in regional politics. The educational and technical assistance available through the federation reduced the vulnerability of local blacks to economic and political intimidation from whites.

This was apparent in 1978 when a former staff member of the federation led a boycott of the Sumter County school system in opposition to policies of white officials who continued to run the public school even after their children were transferred to the white segregated academy.

Persons identified with the federation were also identified with a group of black residents who outmaneuvered a group of local white businessmen, which included the mayor of the county seat, and bought a valuable stretch of river front property. The land purchase was especially significant because the land was along the Tombigbee River which was to become part of the Tennessee-Tombigbee Waterway, a billion dollar federal public works project to connect the Midwest to the Gulf of Mexico. For local blacks to compete with the dominant white interests in such a venture was unusual and for blacks to prevail was almost unthinkable.

In 1979, shortly after the school boycott and a few months before introduction of the reidentification bills, a meeting was called by white leaders to develop a strategy to deal with the threat posed by the federation. At the meeting which was attended by several county officials, representatives from the offices of both United States senators and reportedly the local U.S. congressman, a decision was reached to ask the General Accounting Office, the investigating arm of the U.S. Congress, to investigate charges that the federation had misused federal funds.[11] Local whites said that there was evidence that such funds had been misused. Federation officials saw the request for the audit as political harassment.

The General Accounting Office, after a preliminary audit, reported to the Alabama congressman that it found no evidence of malfeasance.[12] A few months later, however, the federation became the subject of a federal grand jury investigation. The focus of the investigation was never disclosed publicly, but according to those questioned by the FBI agents, the latter were seeking evidence that the federation had misused federal funds.

The grand jury subpoenaed practically all of the federation's records dealing with federally funded programs and questioned more than 200 people living in five states.[13] After almost two years of investigating, the U.S. attorney ended the investigation without seeking an indictment against any of the officers of the federation.

However, while the federation was being investigated by the federal grand jury, its financial status declined considerably. Contributions from government and philanthropic foundations fell from $2.5 million to $500,000 annually. This resulted in staff layoffs and a general decline in the strength of the federation. Officials of the federation accused federal officials of conspiring with local whites to destroy it.

According to black activists, there were other instances of collusion between local whites and federal officials to stymie black empowerment. Specifically, blacks charged that a series of federal voter fraud charges against black political activists in Greene and Perry County in 1985 were politically inspired acts of intimidation. The government charged that black leaders misused the absentee ballot process to favor their candidate.

Traditionally, in rural Alabama significant numbers of people vote absentee.[14] These include workers who commute to jobs outside their voting district and the sick and elderly for whom traveling to the polls may be an ordeal. Maximizing one's share of absentee ballots is an important concern of most political campaigns. Political activists attempt to identify their supporters and arrange for absentee ballots to be sent to them and for the completed ballot to be returned to county election officials. Absentee ballots often provide the winning margin in close elections.[15]

The 1985 cases grew out of federal grand jury investigations in the five black belt counties which are controlled by blacks. The cases were made pursuant to a U.S. Department of Justice policy, devised in 1984, to investigate political participants who seek out the elderly, socially disadvantaged, or illiterate "for the purpose of subjugating their electoral will."[16]

Eight black political leaders and one sympathetic white in Perry and Greene Counties were indicted on a total of 215 criminal charges of altering, falsely witnessing, and mailing absentee ballots.

All three Perry county defendants were acquitted on all charges. One Greene county defendant was convicted on 4 of 37 charges and two other defendants, in a plea bargain, pleaded guilty to 1 misdemeanor each.

During the course of the investigations, however, scores of black political activists were subpoenaed to appear before grand juries. Hundreds of elderly blacks who had voted absentee were questioned by FBI agents and many of them were called upon to travel to distant places and testify as witnesses in various trials.

Black leaders believe that these tactics intimidated many of the elderly and that as a result they would be less inclined to vote in the future.

The struggle for black empowerment and white opposition to it also surfaced in the reapportionment process following the 1980 census. State legislative districts were drawn in a manner which blacks in the black belt felt was discriminatory. Ultimately the federal courts imposed a redistricting plan which made possible the election of black legislators. In 1983 one senator and three state representatives were elected from the region. Following the 1990 census a majority black congressional district which included black belt counties was created.

The election of black legislators represented a significant increase in black political empowerment. Blacks could now use the local courtesy principle to advance their interest through the Alabama legislature. For example, the newly elected black legislators used their position to have the state legislature authorize counties in their districts to switch from at-large to district elections and thereby increase the chances for black electoral success.

White resistance, however, continued unabated. After more than a decade in which black candidates invariably defeated their white opponents in runoff elections, Greene County whites adopted a new strategy. Rather than nominate whites who were destined to lose, they decided to develop alliances with certain blacks in order to try to defeat those black incumbents who had led the movement for empowerment and whom whites thought were too radical.[17] Under the at-large system a preponderant majority of white votes combined with a minority of the black vote would be enough to win an election.

The strategy worked in 1984. The slate of black candidates endorsed by the white-dominated coalition won the elections. As a result, for the first time since 1970 control of county government was in the hands of those supported by the dominant white oligarchy.

However, in response the black legislative delegation lobbied successfully to change the election of county commissioners and school board members from the at-large to a district system. Under the new system white influence would be limited to the one district in which they were the majority.

In the 1986 elections held under the district system, those blacks who had won with white support in the previous election were defeated.

In summary, the case study of the Alabama black belt counties demonstrates that the quest for black empowerment will be opposed by those whose material interests are threatened and that both economic and political, legal and extralegal means will be used to retard black empowerment. A well organized movement with strong, capable leadership is essential for black electoral success, and as noted earlier, electoral success is only the beginning of black empowerment.

NATIONAL ORGANIZING AS A POLITICAL RESOURCE

One key instrument through which political potential may be converted into actual power is an ideologically informed, disciplined political organization which can develop an issue agenda, convert the issue positions into policy options, and mobilize support for those options. The need for such a national organizational base has not escaped black political leaders, but efforts to develop such organizations have yielded only limited results.

Such attempts date back to the 1840s when free blacks called conventions to develop strategies to protect their interests. During the contemporary era, the Gary Convention of 1972, named after the Indiana city in which it was held, was the most significant attempt to build such a national black political organization.

The Gary Convention was called by a number of prominent black elected officials, civil rights leaders, and others to develop a strategy for mobilizing black political power nationally. The 3,000 delegates from 44 states[18] who attended the convention represented a cross section of black America.

Deliberations at the convention revolved around an "Outline for a Black Agenda," a document that had been prepared by a task force of black intellectuals and other designated persons prior to the convention. The preamble asserted that "the American system does not work for the masses of our people and it cannot be made to work without radical fundamental change."

The agenda enumerated 30 objectives designed to "eliminate racism and exploitation from American life" and stressed the need for blacks to organize to realize them. Delegates authorized the establishment of a continuing national structure, to be called the National Black Assembly, and state assemblies to mobilize resources and maximize black political strength. National black political conventions were to be held quadrennially to coincide with U.S. presidential elections.

In sum, the national organization envisaged by the conventioneers of the Gary Convention would comprise state assemblies which, in turn, would have regional subdivisions. Participation would be open to elected officials; representatives of religious, civil rights, and other organizations; and private individuals. There would also be a national assembly in which states and major black organizations would be represented. This would be a comprehensive organization through which all elements in the black community could find expression.

The National Black Political Assembly authorized by the Gary Declaration was formed but almost instantly it was torn asunder by ideological, strategic, and tactical differences and it soon ceased to function.[19]

Perhaps more so than any other event in the recent history of black political struggle, the Gary experiment demonstrated that both black leadership and the rank and file are aware of the need for an independent comprehensive national black political organization. The rapid demise of the National Black Assembly, on the other hand, dramatized that good intentions notwithstanding, there are systemic factors which make the development of such organizations difficult if not possible. An examination of the factors that led to the speedy demise of the National Black Political Assembly will clarify this point.

Driven by the slogan "unity without uniformity," the black agenda adopted at Gary was little more than a transitory compromise between largely incompatible tendencies: between nationalist and integrationist; between those who advocated an independent black political party and those committed to working within the conventional two party system; and between those committed to revolutionary ideals and those seeking reformist solutions.

These diverse and sometimes contradictory interests were able to unite behind a common declaration. However, as efforts were made to go beyond the declaration and begin building structures through which the objectives were to be pursued, serious schisms surfaced among the different groups. For example, certain elements were unwilling to participate if persons identified with opposing ideologies occupied prominent positions in the assembly.

In addition to ideological differences, the way in which various black groups and their leaders are integrated into the overall American political system made it difficult for them to pursue certain provisions of the agenda without compromising their effectiveness within the system. For example, members of the Congressional Black Caucus, who were prime sponsors of the Gary Convention, felt compelled to disassociate themselves from certain provisions of the foreign policy section of the document which were perceived by some to tilt toward the Arabs in the Arab-Israeli dispute. Had they not done so, they risked losing support among their Jewish constituency which is an important source of financial support for many black politicians.

The fact that most of the elected officials, particularly the nationally prominent ones, were active members of the Democratic party left them unenthusiastic about the idea of forming an independent black political party. Similarly, the NAACP, a leading organization in the reformist integrationist movement, took exception to the separatist tone of the Gary Declaration and denounced it as being revolutionary rather than reformist.[20] To be associated with separatist revolutionary efforts would have undermined the effectiveness of the NAACP.

On the other hand, the more radical community-based organizations such as the Congress of African people were unencumbered by ties with mainstream American institutions and groups. For them the National Black Political Assembly was an instrument to be used in the struggle for revolutionary transformation.

Under such circumstances the demise of the National Black Political Assembly was predictable. The diverse groups which came together at Gary might have found numerous opportunities to work together on an ad hoc basis, but being part of a united front with a common corporate identity was an entirely different matter. Within such an organization individual organizational identities give way to the identity of the new collective. Each constituent unit of the collective inherits the enemies of each of the other constituents. The negative assessments which detractors may make of any one of the constituent organizations may be extended to any or all of them.

The leadership of the constituent groups, under such circumstances, may view the cost of membership in such a united front as prohibitive. Membership in the united front, they may reason, does not strengthen their ability to deal with forces external to the black community, at least in the short run, and it undermines their traditional base of support.

Seen in this way, the forces and circumstances which give rise to the need for disciplined, independent black political organizations are the same ones which make the survival of such organizations problematical.

In the absence of such a national organization, efforts toward national black political empowerment continued to evolve around the politics of presidential elections. This is the subject of the next section.

PRESIDENTIAL POLITICS AND RESOURCE MOBILIZATION

The presidency is the centerpiece of the American political process and it has been at this level in the political process that blacks have exercised their greatest political influence. The winner-take-all feature of the presidential election system and the strategic location of black voters in populous eastern and midwestern states give blacks potential power in presidential politics which exceed their numbers.

During the 1960s black leadership used this potential to enlist the moral authority and the political muscle of the presidency in the struggle for empowerment. As a result black representation in the federal bureaucracy, the court system, and regulatory agencies increased considerably. Many private corporations and state and local governments followed the lead of the national government in creating new opportunities for African Americans.

However, as noted in Chapter 2, the black vote is becoming increasingly marginalized in presidential politics. From 1968 to 1984 the candidate favored by black voters lost every election except the anomalous 1976 election.[21] In no election since 1968 has the candidate favored by blacks received a majority of the white vote. President Reagan in 1980 and 1984 received 55 percent and 67 percent, respectively, of the white vote while almost 90 percent of the black vote went to his Democratic opponent on both occasions. And as mentioned earlier, even though the candidate favored by blacks was elected in 1992, he received only 39 percent of the white vote.

Thus there appears to be a realignment of white voters in presidential elections. The shift of white southerners from the Democratic to Republican party is the most dramatic element in this realignment. Should this pattern continue, the ability of blacks to use the presidency as a political resource would be diminished, and that could have a negative multiplier effect on the overall movement.

The growing marginalization of the black vote in presidential politics has given rise to three related and somewhat paradoxical responses which may have long-term consequences for the evolution of black politics in the United States. First of all, black voters view the Republican party as being increasingly hostile. A 1986 national poll revealed that 72 percent of black respondents felt that leaders of the Republican party did not care about their problems; 42 percent felt that Republican leaders were getting worse and more than half, 56 percent, perceived the President to be a racist.[22]

At the same time, the Democratic party, apparently fearful of becoming a minority party composed of minority groups, began to retreat from those programs which made it attractive to black voters. But in the absence of a more attractive alternative, black voters remain as unenthusiastic partners in a relationship gone sour, as was evident in 1984 and 1988 in the wake of Jesse Jackson's unsuccessful presidential campaigns. Even though many black voters were unhappy with the manner in which party leaders reacted to Jackson, they still gave overwhelming support to the Democratic party.

To complete the paradox, a small but growing number of nationally prominent black thinkers in the early 1980s began urging blacks to end their increasing marginalization by joining white voters in their shift to conservatism and the Republican party.

We examine their arguments next.

IDEOLOGY AND RESOURCE MOBILIZATION—THE NEW BLACK CONSERVATISM[23]

The views of the new black conservatives, like those of other groups, are not monolithic. Nevertheless we can identify certain positions which constitute the core of their creed. What distinguishes them from the more traditional black leaders and thinkers is their belief that rather than being a positive force, government and government-sponsored social welfare programs are primary impediments to black progress. Like their white counterparts, black conservatives are generally opposed to the interventionist state. They deride social welfare programs and claim that government and government-created dependence are among the major problems confronting African Americans.

The ideological presuppositions of the black conservatives generate a perception of the black predicament which is radically different from that espoused by the traditional black leadership.

Economist Walter Williams, a leading black conservative, argues that it is not racial bigotry but the "rules of the game" that account for many of the problems faced by blacks.[24] A second economist, Thomas Sowell, claims that government has been responsible for suppressing black advancement and that the "great achievement of the civil rights organizations has been getting government off the back of blacks."[25]

Harvard economist Glenn Loury received national attention in 1984 when he argued in several prestigious journals that inasmuch as the civil rights movement was virtually complete it was necessary to look beyond racism to explain the problems of the black poor. The explanation, he argued, is to be found in the values, social norms, and attitudes of the poor blacks themselves.[26]

Loury accused conventional black leadership and the black middle class from which it comes of refusing to confront the "enemy within." Instead the black leadership, he claimed, use the plight of the black poor to justify state interventionist programs which benefit the black middle class.

According to Loury, the problem of the black poor is really a moral one beyond the reach of effective government action. Primary responsibility for uplifting the black poor, in his view, lies with the black middle class. Pleas by the latter for government intervention to meliorate the problems of the black poor are characterized by Loury as inappropriate appeals to others for deliverance.

In our view, the argument that the problems of the black poor are the result of government intervention is contradicted by both popular perception and available evidence. No data are available which establish a correlation between state intervention and black deprivation. However, the reverse seems to be the case. The multiplicity of state interventionist transfer payment programs, of which welfare is only one, were all adopted to remedy widely recognized problems in the American political economy. Programs such as Aid to Families with Dependent Children (AFDC), Medicare, Medicaid, and housing assistance were approved by Congress only after the need was demonstrated through extensive public debate.

Moreover the fact that in 1990 such a large proportion of all Americans receive some form of federal transfer payments, 29 percent of whites and 33 percent of blacks,[27] challenges the notion that such programs are a primary cause of the problems of the black poor.

The claim that government has been a party to the suppression of blacks is true. But it is also true that it was intervention by the national government in response to the militant black protest of the 1960s which eliminated state-sanctioned segregation and discrimination in the South. This set in motion an interdependent and inseparable series of developments which led to the inclusion of African Americans in institutions and positions in both the public and private sectors which had been previously closed to them.

The argument of the black conservatives that the problems of the black poor are essentially functions of the "enemy within," that is, the presumed pathological culture of the black poor and that the persistence of black poverty is a reflection of the moral failure of black leadership and the black middle class, is perhaps the most popular tenet of the conservative creed. This argument dovetails quite nicely with the long-standing white supremacist notion that the unequal position of blacks is due neither to racism nor systemic economic conditions but to the inappropriate behavior of blacks themselves. This explanation absolves the broader society of any guilt in causing the problem and excuses them from any responsibility for resolving it.

How the creed of the new black conservatives differs from that of the more conventional black leadership and the implications of these differences for the struggle for racial equality can be clarified further by examining their policy recommendations.

POLICY RECOMMENDATIONS OF THE BLACK CONSERVATIVES

Educational reform and enhanced labor force participation are two major concerns of black conservatives. They argue that substandard schools and the educational deficiencies which result from them account for much of the economic inequality experienced by blacks. Current federal education programs, in their view, are at least part of the problem. As a solution, conservatives advocate the development of free market educational systems stimulated by preferential tax laws and direct assistance to needy students.

Publicly financed vouchers would be given to eligible low-income students to attend schools of their choice. Voucher holders, according to the conservative thesis, would gravitate toward schools of demonstrated quality. As a result, substandard schools would be forced to improve their quality or go out of business.

But there are those who suggest that such free market education might have consequences far beyond those imagined by black conservatives. For example, one possible outcome of such an educational system would be the siphoning off of the better prepared black youngsters into a few prestigious secondary schools while the learning environment of the bulk of black youth remained unchanged. Black graduates of such selective secondary schools would be the most objectively qualified to enter the equally selective major universities. Upon graduation from college this privileged group would be in line to receive the most prestigious and rewarding positions open to blacks. And, as far as they might be concerned, their privileged position would be the result of merit. Conversely and by inference, the subordinate positions occupied by their compatriots who were left behind in inner-city schools would also be explained by racially neutral meritocratic factors.

Consequently, both privilege and deprivation would be seen as the result of individual effort. The view that the poor are responsible for their plight would be reinforced.

Furthermore, black leadership and those who staff and administer the social, economic, cultural, and educational institutions which manage the disadvantaged black communities would be chosen disproportionately from this privileged group. Having spent their crucial formative years in institutions in which they were the only black or one of a few, many might be inclined to accept the interpretation of the black predicament which prevails in such institutions. Consequently as professionals and leaders they would bring to their work perceptions of the black poor which differed little from those of their white counterparts. Such black professionals would serve more as buffers facilitating the continued domination of the poor than as agents for transformation. This would heighten class contradictions within the black community and diminish further the prospects for black unity and hence, for black empowerment as well.

A second policy recommendation of the black conservatives is the imposition of a subminimum wage to enhance the position of blacks, particularly black youth in the labor force. Minimum wage legislation, conservatives argue, overprices labor and as a consequence eliminates many jobs which could be held by black teenagers and other unskilled workers.

Experience gained through such jobs, the argument runs, would lead to better paying positions in the future. This new pool of experienced workers with marketable skills would create its own demand and have a long-term beneficial impact by reducing the number of unemployable youth and the chronic social problems which are said to result from their presence.

Critics of the black conservatives charge that there is little evidence that a subminimum wage would have such a positive impact.[28] Under the present law, they point out, 63 percent of all trade and 85 percent of service establishments can already legally pay young people a subminimum wage.[29] A 1970 Labor Department study showed that of 4,615 firms authorized to hire full-time students at a subminimum wage "over half used less than their authorization or did not use them at all."[30] Studies of workers who are illegally paid subminimum wages reveal that white workers hired under such conditions are likely to be teenagers but that blacks working for subminimum wages tend to be adults and primary wage earners in the family.

All of this suggests to some critics that the introduction of a subminimum wage would reduce the return to labor below the acceptable minimum while doing little to promote black advancement.

Overall, though black conservatives remain a small minority within the black community, their views are increasingly well received by important policy makers at the state and national levels. The appointment of Judge Clarence Thomas to the Supreme Court is an example of this trend. Clearly this development has important implications for the quest for resources and black politics generally.

Conclusion

Of the several potential sources of power, favorable population distribution, voting, and holding public office appear to be the most promising ones for black empowerment. Considerable progress has been made in increasing black voter registration and electing blacks to public office. Black voters have determined the outcome of many important elections. Nevertheless, voting and holding office are limited resources and their limited potential has not been fully realized due to the absence of disciplined independent black political organizations.

However to say that it is the absence of a disciplined independent organizational base which accounts for the limited payoffs from electoral politics may be to engage in circular reasoning because the same forces that account for the inequitable position of blacks in America also account for the circumstances which mitigate against the development of disciplined, independent black political organizations.

Let us elaborate. Enhancing the economic strength of the black community and thereby lessening its vulnerability to outside forces has always been viewed as a prerequisite for black political empowerment. However, efforts to create a viable black entrepreneurial class, if they are to be successful, almost always require supportive action by government and the mainstream business community. For this reason both the black economic and political elite are reluctant to be identified with independent black organizations perceived by whites to be threatening. Moreover as the black elite pursues its objectives of economic empowerment, it becomes functionally integrated into the existing system such that its own well-being is linked to the response of the very mainstream institutions which a disciplined black organization would confront.

Of course other less vulnerable forces in the black community could attempt to develop such organizations. However, such efforts would threaten the hegemony of the existing black leadership and for that reason might be opposed by the latter. Moreover the established black leadership would likely cite their positive and functional relationship within mainstream institutions to reinforce their claim to be effective leaders and to undermine the appeal of any would-be challengers.

The black leadership which emerges under such circumstances is inclined neither to build independent disciplined organizations nor to challenge the fundamental assumptions and practices of the existing order.

Topics of Discussion

1. Identify what you believe are one or two of the major problems facing African Americans. Now identify the resources required to solve or ameliorate them. Who controls the resources and how likely are they to use them to solve the problem in question? Discuss thoroughly and justify your position.

2. List four or five potential sources of black political power and discuss how each may be converted into real power. What are the prospects for doing so?

3. Examine critically the arguments of black conservatives such as Glen Loury, Thomas Sowell, and Walter Williams. What do they see as the causes of black inequality and what resources are required to end it?

4. Even though the two-party system has not solved the problem of black inequality, most blacks have refused to join efforts to establish an independent black political party. What would be the advantages and disadvantages of such a party?

Suggested Readings

Bachrach, Peter, and Morton S. Barztz. *Power and Poverty: Theory and Practice.* New York: Oxford University Press, 1970.
An analysis of political power, authority, influence and force in the policy-making process.

Barker, Lucius, ed. "Black Electoral Politics," *National Political Science Review* 2 (1990).
Features a symposium on big-city black mayors.

Crotty, William J. *Political Reform and the American Experiment.* New York: Thomas Y. Crowell Company, 1977.
A study of how the reforms in the American electoral system, especially changes in enfranchisement rules and voter registration, have affected the American political system.

Edelman, Murray. *The Symbolic uses of Politics.*Chicago: University of Illinois Press, 1967.
An examination of the impact of symbolic action on both spectators and players in the political game.

Fuster, Lorn, ed. *The Voting Rights Act.* New York: Praeger, 1985.
A collection of articles on the implementation of the Voting Rights Act.

Howard, John and Robert Smith, eds. *The Annals of the American Academy of Political and Social Science* 439 (September 1978).
A collection of theoretical and empirical articles on black urban politics in the 1960s and 1970s.

Lawson, Steven F. *Black Ballots: Voting Rights in the South, 1944-1969,* New York: Columbia University Press, 1976.
A study of how the legal and political institutions in the United States responded to black efforts to attain the vote in the South in the years following World War II.

Lewinson, Paul. *Race, Class and Party.* New York: Russell, 1965.
A study of black suffrage and white political strategies in the South.

Mitchell, William C. *Why Vote?* Chicago: Markham, 1971.
A counter to the argument that voting is merely a symbolic event.

Morrison, Minion K.C. *Black Political Mobilization.* Albany: State University Press of New York, 1987.
A study of political empowerment in rural Mississippi.

Parker, Frank. *Black Votes Count.* Chapel Hill: University of North Carolina Press, 1991.
An excellent study of the struggle for black empowerment in Mississippi from 1965 to 1988.

Preston, Michael, et al., eds. *The New Black Politics.* New York: Longman, 1982.
A collection of articles on black empowerment in local, state, and national setting.

Rose, Peter I., et al., eds. *Through Different Eyes: Black and White Perspectives on American Race Relations.* New York: Oxford University Press. 1973.
A reader examining the differing perspectives of black and white Americans on race relations.

Simms, Margaret and Malreaux, eds. *Slipping Through the Cracks, The Status of Black Women.* New Brunswick, NJ: Transaction Books, 1986.
A collection of descriptive and analytical articles on the socioeconomic status of black women in the United States.

Woodward, C. Vann. *The Strange Career of Jim Crow.* 3rd rev. ed. New York: Oxford University Press, 1974.
A classic study both of Southern segregation under the "Jim Crow" system and of the extension of these ideas into contemporary society.

Notes

* New Haven, CT: Yale University Press, 1971, p. 82.

1. For an excellent discussion of the struggle for voting rights, see David J. Garrow, *Protest at Selma* (New Haven; Yale University Press, 1978).
2. U.S. Bureau of Census, *Current Population Reports*, Series P-20, *Voting and Registration in the Election of November 1988* (Washington, DC: Government Printing Office, 1989).
3. *Black Elected Officials, A National Roster 1985* (Washington, DC: Joint Center for Political Studies), Table 1, p. 11.
4. See as examples, William Nelson, "Black Mayors as Urban Managers," *The Annals* 439 (September 1978), pp. 53-67; Mack H. Jones, "Black Officeholding and Political Development in the Rural South," *Review of Black Political Economy* 6 (Summer 1976), pp. 375-407; and Huey Perry, "The Impact of Black Political Participation on Municipal Boards and Commissions," *The Review of Black Political Economy* 13 (Winter 1983), pp. 203-218.
5. Mack H. Jones, "Black Political Empowerment in Atlanta," *The Annals* 439 (September 1978), pp. 90-117.
6. See for example, "Symposium: Big City Black Mayors: Have They Made a Difference?" *National Political Science Review* 2, pp. 129-195.
7. Calculations are based upon figures given in Allen Tullos, "Not So Simple Justice," *Southern Changes* 7 (May-June 1985), p. 4.
8. For a discussion of the variety of tactics used by whites in the Alabama Black Belt to thwart black participation, see *Hearings on Extension of the Voting Rights Act* before the Subcommittee on Civil and Constitutional Rights of the Committee on the Judiciary, 97th Cong., First Ses., 1982, pp. 751-68; 1511-1624.
9. Ibid, p. 756.
10. Under local courtesy rules, a bill which applies only to a given legislative district or portions of a district are routinely passed by the full legislature if it has unanimous consent of the district's legislative delegation. This means that the senator or representative of a given county has almost unlimited legislative powers in such matters. White state legislators used this power extensively to frustrate black efforts in majority black counties.
11. See Thomas Bethel, *Sumter County Blues, The Ordeal of the Federation of Southern Cooperatives* (Washington, DC: National Committee in Support of Community Based Organizations, 1982).
12. Ibid, p. 14.
13. Ibid, p. 15.
14. See Allen Tullos, "Crackdown in the Black Belt," *Southern Changes* (March-April 1985), pp. 1-5.
15. See *Hearings on Extension of Voting*, p. 1579. A fact sheet circulated by a defense committee for those charged with absentee voter fraud asserted that in electoral contests between black and white candidates the average margin of victory for black candidates was 200 votes and that the average number of black absentee ballots was around 400. "Fact Sheet on Federal Grand Jury Investigations of Black Leaders in Alabama for Voter Fraud" (Gainesville, AL: Alabama Black Belt Defense Committee, 1985), p. 41.
16. Department of Justice Policy Manual quoted in Allen Tullos, "Not-So-Simple Justice," *Southern Changes* (May-June 1985), p. 4.

17. In a widely circulated letter calling for support the group announced that the key to success was to "support good, responsible blacks and to keep whites out of the race," *Green County Democrat*, Eutaw, Alabama, 13 June 1984, p. 1.
18. For an excellent collection of commentaries on the Gary Convention, see *Unity without Uniformity*, compiled by Senator Mervyan Dymally, California legislature (Sacramento, CA: 1972).
19. See "Dead End or New Beginning? National Black Assembly," *Black World* 25 (October 1975) pp. 2-46; Harold Cruse, "The Little Rock National Black Political Convention," *Black World* 23 (October 1974), pp. 10-17; 82-84; William Strickland, "The Gary Convention and the Crisis of American Politics," *Black World* 21 (October 1972), pp. 18-31.
20. See "NAACP Blasts Preamble," *Post-Tribune*, Gary, Indiana, 11 March 1972, p. 1.
21. The election of Jimmy Carter in 1976 on the heels of the Watergate scandal was thought by some to be more of a reaction to the scandal than an endorsement of Carter's philosophy. The thorough defeat of the latter by Reagan in 1980 lends credence to this supposition.
22. *ABC News/Washington Post* poll.
23. This discussion is drawn on Mack H. Jones, "The Political Thought of the New Black Conservatives: Analysis, Explanation and Interpretation," in Franklin Jones, et al., eds., *Readings in American Political Issues* (Dubuque, IA: Kendall/Hunt, 1987).
24. Walter Williams, *The State Against Blacks* (New York: New Press, 1982), p. xvi.
25. "Thomas Sowell on Meet the Press," *Manhattan Report*, special ed. 1, no. 8 (November 1981), p. 7.
26. Loury's thesis was first published as "A New American Dilemma," *The New Republic* 184 (December 31, 1984). It was published in a slightly different form in four other nationally circulated journals.
27. David Swinton, "The Economic Status of the Black Population," in *The State of Black America 1992* (New York: National Urban League, 1992), p. 92.
28. Robert Hill, "The Economic Status of Black American," *The State of Black America 1981* (New York: National Urban League, 1981), pp. 1-59.
29. Ibid, p. 15.
30. Ibid, p. 18.

CHAPTER 5

THE SUPREME COURT AND THE POLITICS OF UNCERTAINTY

I do not believe that the meaning of the constitution was forever "fixed" at the Philadelphia convention. Nor do I find the wisdom, foresight, and sense of justice exhibited by the Framers particularly profound. To the contrary, the government they devised was defective from the start, requiring several amendments, a civil war, and momentous social transformation to attain the system of constitutional government, and its respect for the individual freedoms and human rights, we hold as fundamental today . . . What is striking is the role legal principles have played throughout America's history in determining the condition of Negroes. They were enslaved by law, emancipated by law. Along the way, new constitutional principles have emerged to meet the challenge of a changing society.

Justice Thurgood Marshall*

Our task in this case, like any other case involving the construction of a statute, is to give effect to the intent of Congress. To divine that intent, we traditionally look first to the words of the statute and, if they are unclear, then to the statute's legislative history. Finding the desired result hopelessly foreclosed by these conventional sources, the Court turns to a third source—the "spirit" of the Act. But close examination of what the Court proffers as the spirit of the Act reveals it as the spirit animating the present majority, not the Eighty-eighth Congress.

Justice William H. Rehnquist**

A PRIME EXAMPLE

Few can forget the fierce and widely publicized controversies that accompanied President Ronald Reagan's nomination in 1987 of Judge Robert Bork to the U.S. Supreme Court. Nor, of course, can we forget the furor and sensationalism that followed President George Bush's nomination in 1991 of Judge Clarence Thomas to the high court. Indeed, at bottom, these nominations illuminated vividly and dramatically the various interests and stakes involved in selecting those who sit on the Court. Though few nominations are as controversial as those over Bork and Thomas, the matter of judicial selection, as we discuss later, represents a prime example of the important role that courts and judges play in American politics and society.

In the end, of course, the decisions rendered by judges on major policy issues of the day represent the most concrete example of the role and influence of courts in politics and policy making. Consider, for example, a 1986 Supreme Court decision with respect to the highly controversial issue of affirmative action. In 1972, as a result of racial tension in the community and its schools, the School Board and Teachers Union of Jackson, Michigan, entered a collective bargaining agreement under which, if it were to become necessary to lay off teachers, those with the most seniority would be retained, except that at no time could minority teachers be laid off at a greater percentage than they represented at the time of such layoffs. This provision was designed to preserve the effects of a hiring policy whose goal had been to increase the percentage of minority teachers in the school system. In accord with the agreement, and when layoffs became necessary, non-minority teachers were laid off while minority teachers with less seniority were retained. The displaced non-minority teachers brought suit in federal district court alleging that their equal protection rights under the Fourteenth Amendment had been violated. But the district court dismissed the teachers' claims and held that such racial preferences were permissible in an attempt to remedy societal discrimination by providing role models for minority students. The Court of Appeals affirmed. But in 1986 in *Wygant* v. *Jackson Board of Education*, the Supreme Court struck down the agreement as violative of the equal protection clause in that it allowed the school board to dismiss white teachers with more seniority and retain black teachers who had less seniority.

While the immediate issue in *Wygant* was the validity of the collective bargaining agreement, it is instructive to view the case in broader terms. Some saw the case as a vivid example of the increasing practice of "reverse discrimination," whereby whites are and would be denied benefits (e.g., jobs, promotions) because of their race. Others saw the case as a crucial test which could determine whether affirmative action programs, designed to overcome centuries of racial oppression, would or could remain in effect. Still others viewed the issue differently. But essentially what was before the Court in 1986, just as in the widely publicized *Bakke* case in 1978, was a major policy battle between two sharply contending forces: (1) those who wanted the Court to support the Jackson Board of Education program as consistent with affirmative action goals and principles and (2) those who wanted the Court to strike down the program as an example of "reverse discrimination" violative of the equal protection clause.

Overall, and when viewed in perspective, the *Wygant* decision did little to clarify the continuing policy debate over "affirmative action" versus "reverse discrimination." If anything, the decision represents a prime example of how the "politics of uncertainty" continues to haunt the fundamental political and social status of African Americans. And as we discuss later, *Wygant* may also be seen as part of a more general change in the tone and substance of civil rights decisions that seems to have differentiated the Warren Court from the Burger Court, and now the Burger Court from the Rehnquist Court.

Additionally, and in a broader context, the *Wygant* case also represents a prime example of the situation that Alexis de Tocqueville observed long ago. Sooner or later major political issues are translated into legal issues. This observation is certainly supported by the involvement of courts in racial problems. And this involvement has been anything but neutral, that is, above politics. Indeed, because of the American belief in the "majesty of the law," courts and other participants in the legal process play a crucial role in determining who gets what, when, and how.[1]

This importance of courts and judges in the political process was made clear early in the nation's history in the classic case of *Marbury* v. *Madison*. Chief Justice John Marshall's 1803 decision went a long way toward establishing the principle of judicial review: the authority of courts to declare legislative acts (e.g., acts of Congress) unconstitutional. Marshall made it clear that whether or not an act of Congress conflicts with the Constitution is in the final analysis a matter for the Court to decide. "It is emphatically the province and duty of the judicial department," said Marshall, "to say what the law is."

While there is no specific basis or authority in the Constitution for the Court's power to declare acts of Congress unconstitutional, the force of Marshall's argument in *Marbury* v. *Madison* is now fully imbedded in our constitutional system. Moreover, that power not only refers to actions of the national government but to actions of state and local governments as well. In short, it is the special province of courts and judges to authoritatively decide conflicts over constitutional interpretation. And such decisions are anything but neutral, above the policy struggle. Thus, it is hardly surprising that conflicting interests frequently turn to the Court for support. When, for example, the Supreme Court decided in *Plessy* v. *Ferguson* (1896) that "separate but equal" facilities were constitutional, it strongly supported the segregation policies of southern whites. It was a major setback to civil rights for African Americans. But when the Court decided in *Brown* v. *Board of Education* (1954) that "separate but equal" was unconstitutional, it strengthened the rising civil rights movement and dealt a severe blow to segregationists. In the 1978 *Bakke* case, and the 1986 *Wygant* decision, the Court rendered decisions that gave some constitutional support to the major contending interests. Such decisions on major political issues tend to assure continued controversy and added opportunities for court involvement.

STATUTORY INTERPRETATION

Thus far we have focused on the highly visible role of the Court in interpreting the Constitution. This emphasis is quite understandable since the "interpretation of the Constitution . . . is the highest and most difficult responsibility that American judges are called on to perform."[2] Nonetheless, we should mention here that a major part of the workload of courts in America consists of cases dealing with statutory interpretation as opposed to constitutional interpretation. Statutory interpretation refers to the work of courts in applying and enforcing laws (statutes), such as those enacted by Congress. Constitutional interpretation refers to the role of courts in applying and enforcing various provisions of the Constitution.

In deciding conflicts concerning statutory law, the role of courts can become crucial in determining who wins or who loses as a result of specific legislative enactments. For example, in *Grove City College* v. *Bell* the Court interpreted Title IX of the 1972 Education Amendments so as to blunt its use as an effective weapon in monitoring federal grants to institutions that discriminated against persons on account of sex. The Court held that Title IX prevents such discrimination in particular programs or activities receiving federal grants but not in the institution as a whole. This severely limited the scope of Title IX.[3] And in the 1984 *Stotts* decision in Memphis the Supreme Court interpreted Title VII of the Civil Rights Act of 1964 so as to disallow attempts by lower courts under a consent decree to safeguard jobs of recently hired black workers against bona fide seniority claims of white workers who had been employed longer. To some extent, then, what a statute means is what the courts say it means. And the language inevitably found in statutes, which more or less reflects compromises needed to enact such legislation, obviously means that "the opportunities for the exercise of judicial discretion in statutory interpretation are both frequent and wide."[4]

When we combine the traditional function of courts in statutory interpretations with that of judicial review, we begin to see more clearly the enormous importance of courts and judges in the political process. We begin to see more clearly the influence of courts in determining who gets what, when, and how. This influence is undoubtedly enhanced by the strong attachment Americans have to doing things "legally" and "according to law." Under our system of government, courts exercise a crucial role in determining what is "legal" and "according to law." Accordingly, courts are the focal point of the legal process. However, we should not overlook the fundamental role of other participants in that process, especially that of the lawyers.

Lawyers make up the legal profession from which judges come. They are the principal gatekeepers to the courts and to the legal process in general. Their special training gives them the knowledge needed to negotiate the details of the process on behalf of their clients. The legal process is indeed controlled by lawyers. Such control is stabilized by the strong influence and representation of lawyers in government as well as in the private sector. Again, it was de Tocqueville who observed that if he had to describe where the aristocracy lies in America it would be in the lofty role and deference accorded lawyers. De Tocqueville's observation is even more valid today. Lawyers and the public alike acknowledge the importance of lawyers and the legal profession. This is remarkably consistent with de Tocqueville.[5] Unfortunately, since there are so few black lawyers,[6] it is also consistent with the very limited role and influence that blacks have not only in the legal system but also in the political process generally.

COURTS AND JUDGES

Judges, like legislators, are also engaged in the business of allocating resources, making rewards, and imposing deprivations. The fact that a judge is so involved, as Peltason puts it, is "not a matter of choice but of function."[7] "Judicial participation," continues Peltason, "does not grow out of the judge's personality or philosophy but out of his position."[8] Thus, it is their position with authority to render decisions to support certain interests and not support others that leads us to describe judges no less than legislators as participants in the political process. Consequently, courts, the institutional structures in which judges operate, become important forums in managing and resolving conflict in the governing system.

To be sure, certain factors that tend to remove or insulate courts and judges from politics can sometimes obscure their crucial role in American politics. Consider our attachment to the belief in a "government of laws and not of men [individuals]." Consider, moreover, that courts stand as constant reminders of these attachments and are to rule according to law. While general public opinion and special interests may influence other decision makers, the judge's influence is believed to come from the law and what the law requires.

Consider also the methods of selecting judges; these methods, which increasingly emphasize their expertise in the law and their judicial temperament, are based upon the judges' accountability to no one save the law and their own consciences. In addition, consider the formal and informal expectations (norms) concerning how judges are to act, behave, and carry on their high duties. Moreover, these jurists must show impartiality and neutrality. Above all, judges are to be above politics. Admittedly, these and other factors do shape judicial behavior and how courts function. They also shape our perceptions of courts and judges and how we think they should carry out their responsibilities. All this, however, does not change the crucial and often determining roles that courts perform in the business of governing. Indeed, rather than lessening their functions, these perceptions and expectations strengthen the judicial hand.

We are not attempting here to equate the functions of courts with legislatures, or judges with elected politicians. Rather, we suggest that courts, through proper judicial procedures, also make decisions that determine who gets what, when, and how. However, decision making in the judicial forum—unlike the legislature, for example—does not supposedly turn on numbers, wealth, or social standing. Rather it turns on the law. And though much of the law is itself influenced by these very factors (for example, wealth and social standing),[9] once enacted it may be subject to judicial interpretations which might or might not support interests that led to its original enactment. In any event, the structure of courts is such that they do not necessarily respond to the same interests as do other political institutions, such as legislatures. This element of discretion and the authority of his or her decisions place the judge in a position of power and influence in the American government system. How one gains such a position and what manner of person becomes a judge are of obvious importance to those interested in the allocation of values.

COURTS AND JUDICIAL SELECTION

Three main criteria stand out in the selection of federal judges. These "selection variables" are competence, party affiliation, and ideological considerations.[10] The latter two factors are primarily political. Thus, they will be determined largely by political officials, such as the president, United States senators, and state and local party officials. The potential nominee is almost always (90 percent of the time) a member of the president's party. In addition, the kinds of support he or she has given the party, as well as the "right" ideological positions on important policy issues, define more accurately the best nominee for a federal judgeship. However, the competence part, having to do with the legal ability, experience, and judicial nature of the nominee, are primarily "legal" matters to be determined through institutionalized legal channels such as the American Bar Association (ABA) Committee on Federal Judiciary. The role and influence of these key participants in the selection process vary widely depending upon a number of factors, for example, the particular judgeship to be filled (Supreme Court, court of appeals, district court) and the political context in which the appointment is being made.

The president makes all appointments to federal court judgeships, but the president's appointments must be confirmed by the Senate. While appointments to lower federal courts are very important, it is the appointments to the United States Supreme Court that are most visible and command public attention. This means that the stakes are very high in terms of who serves on that Court. Given the authority and prestige of the Supreme Court and since vacancies occur only occasionally, it is obvious that the president savors the authority and opportunity in making such appointments. While certain other considerations such as race, religion, ethnic affiliation, gender, and geographic balance may enter, a president will perhaps be most concerned about the ideological and policy dispositions of potential nominees. Indeed, decisions of the Supreme Court have nationwide implication. They can do much to promote, frustrate, or negate presidential policies and programs. But by the same token, other participants in the selection process—both official and unofficial—attach added importance to Supreme Court nominations for the same reasons.

Consequently, senators and other public officials, the ABA and leaders of the bar, organized interest groups and concerned citizens will all use the full range of their influence to make certain the "right" person is selected. All it takes is a "controversial" appointment to bring the dynamics of selecting a Supreme Court justice into full focus. And there are some well-publicized examples. The story of one such appointment, that of Judge G. Harrold Carswell, is brilliantly told by Richard Harris in his description of the unsuccessful attempt of President Nixon to appoint Carswell to the Court.[11] The Carswell episode, it will be recalled, followed the earlier unsuccessful Nixon effort to place Judge Clement Haynsworth on the Court. Of course, the 1987 attempt of President Reagan to appoint and elevate federal appellate judge Robert Bork to the Supreme Court engendered one of the most bitter, divisive, and engulfing confirmation battles in history. Kevin Lyles's case study of the Bork nomination in the next chapter and the accompanying commentary on the highly controversial Clarence Thomas nomination portray vividly the dynamics and dimensions involved in judicial selection battle.

What kinds of judges have come out of this judicial selection process? The overwhelming majority of federal judges are white, Anglo-Saxon, Protestant males. The few who come from other racial (black), ethnic, and religious backgrounds (Jewish, Catholic) were mainly appointed by Democratic presidents. Clearly of course, President Bush's appointment of black conservative Judge Clarence Thomas to the Supreme Court indicates how, on occasion, Republicans, too, might select judges from these groups. In general, however, the proclivity of Democrats to appoint such persons may be explained in part by the attachment that economically disadvantaged and ethnic groups have to the Democratic party. In addition to being White Anglo-Saxon Protestants (WASPs), federal judges generally have been "politically active"; that is, they have been actively involved in politics prior to their appointment. Appointments to the Supreme Court, however, have gone in large measure both to those who have held important political or legal office (for example, United States senator or attorney general) or to those who have achieved prominence in the legal profession (for example, in the ABA or in prestigious law schools).

This discussion about courts and judicial selection leads to a major conclusion: Those who are selected as federal judges mostly represent the dominant political interests at any given time. Hence those who are disadvantaged in "political" arenas will find, as far as representation is concerned, that they are similarly disadvantaged in the judicial forum. It should come as no surprise then that black representation, as well as representation of women and Hispanics in the third branch at all levels (national, state, and local) is very small. While tradition, structures, and insulation of the judicial office serve to hide these selection biases, their visibility becomes all too clear when one takes a closer look at the facts. In the late 1970s, for example, of about 500 judges on the federal district courts and courts of appeals, the Justice Department estimated that before the appointment of new judges pursuant to the Omnibus Judgeship Act (see below), there were 23 blacks, 11 women, and 7 Hispanics on these courts.[12] And, of course, the only two blacks to serve on the U.S. Supreme Court were Thurgood Marshall, appointed in 1967 by President Johnson, and Clarence Thomas, appointed in 1991 by President Bush. Yet, there are some other developments that could affect the number of minorities in the third branch, including the creation and addition of new courts and judgeships.

In 1978, for example, Congress passed the Omnibus Judgeship Act which established 117 new federal district judgeships and 35 additional seats on the courts of appeals.[13] As an outgrowth of the new legislation, President Carter issued two executive orders providing for standards and guidelines for the merit selection of federal district judges and for the establishment of a Circuit Judge Nominating Commission for the selection of judges to the courts of appeals. The commission was designed to operate through panels in each circuit which would be composed of lawyers, nonlawyers, persons of both sexes, and minority group members. The Carter administration had hoped that merit selection would increase the number of women and blacks in the federal judiciary.

It is somewhat ironic, but not surprising, that preliminary results of "merit selection" indicate the continued domination of white male nominees for judgeships. The use of criteria, such as long years of "prior legal experience," tend to limit possible minority nominees who have just recently entered the legal profession in any substantial numbers.[14] Indeed, even with the merit plans in operation, it was estimated in early 1979 that of 77 persons recommended for 54 judgeships under the 1978 legislation, only 5 were blacks (including 2 women), 3 were Hispanic males, and 3 were white women. Thus, the nominees still overwhelmingly tend to be white males. Yet by October 1979, there were some encouraging signs. As of that time, of the 109 nominations which President Carter had made under the new act, 16 had been white women, 14 had been blacks (including 4 black women), and 4 had been Hispanics. And of the 80 confirmed nominations, there were 13 white women, 8 blacks (including 2 black women), and 2 Hispanic men.[15] That these 23 appointments increased the representation of women and minorities on the federal bench by 56 percent (from 41 to 64) lends evidence to the continued sparsity of their numbers.

A CHANGING FEDERAL JUDICIARY: THE REHNQUIST COURT AND THE REAGAN-BUSH LEGACY

While many of President Carter's judicial appointments were undoubtedly "liberal," those of President Reagan and President Bush were of a clear conservative mold and not expected to further the interests of blacks and other minorities. In all, during the 1980s Reagan had the opportunity to fill almost 45 percent of the existing 900 federal judgeships, including the appointment of three new justices to the Supreme Court (O'Connor, Scalia, Kennedy). He also, of course, elevated Justice Rehnquist to the position of chief justice to replace Chief Justice Burger. Although particular appointments might not turn out as expected, by and large those selected as federal judges reflect fairly well the overall views and positions of the president, and in view of their lifetime tenure, will continue to do so long after the president leaves office. Should this pattern prevail, it seems unlikely, at least in the next ten years or so, that blacks and other minorities will find strong support for their interests in the federal judiciary.

This support certainly cannot be expected to come from black and minority judges whose numbers remain small. By and large, appointments to the federal judiciary reflect the relative strength of various interests among those who make up the president's constituency, or those whose support the president would like to cultivate. As a result, we would expect and have seen more black and minority judicial appointments coming under Carter than under Reagan or Bush. Even so, the number of such judges remains woefully sparse especially when viewed in relation to their proportions in the population. In the federal courts, for example, between 1960 and 1989 a total of 50 African Americans were appointed, and 28 of these were Carter appointees; as of 1988 there were 14 African Americans on courts of appeals; and as of 1992, there have been 2 African Americans on the Supreme Court (Thurgood Marshall, who retired in 1990, and Clarence Thomas who was appointed in 1991.) While the number of African American judges fluctuates over time, some idea of their relation to the total number of judges may be gleaned from the fact that as of 1991, the total of authorized judgeships on district courts was 649; on the courts

Marshall and the Rehnquist Court: Shown in a formal picture with the Rehnquist Court, Justice Thurgood Marshall found that though his views were generally in line with the more liberal Warren Court, they were increasingly at odds with the more conservative Burger and Rehnquist Courts. *(Copyright National Geographic Society)*

of appeals 179 judgeships; and of course the number of justices on the Supreme Court is 9. Overall, and as we begin the 1990s, the fact that there are still so few black judges is yet another example of the disproportionate representation and influence of blacks in the American political system. But the election of President Clinton in 1992 might well indicate a return to the inclination of the Carter administration to appoint more women, blacks, and minorities to the bench. Early indications suggest that President Clinton, not unlike his predecessors, will have ample opportunities to make judicial appointments to both the Supreme Court and lower federal courts as well. This, of course, was exemplified in early 1993 when Clinton appointed Judge Ruth Bader Ginsburg to the Supreme Court to replace retiring Justice Byron White.

At this point, we should reemphasize that courts play far too important a role to perpetuate the romanticized notion that the judiciary is "above" or "beyond" politics. Courts are a part, although a differentiated and specialized part, of the political system. For, as stated earlier, "[Courts] are in the political process . . . not as a matter of choice but as a matter of function."[16] Those judges who do not wish to become involved (self-restrainers) are supporting certain interests as much as those judges (judicial activists) who do become involved. And this involvement, of course, concerns applying and enforcing statutes. Overall, the participation of courts in both constitutional and statutory interpretation has increased the visibility of the judiciary in politics. As a consequence, courts are of vital political importance to blacks and other minorities. Indeed, as we shall observe in more detail, courts can play important and sometimes crucial roles in the formulation of public policies, including policies relevant to blacks and other minorities.

COURTS, POLICY MAKING, AND CIVIL RIGHTS

Earlier in this chapter we discussed the role of law and courts in the political system. The uniqueness of that role is highlighted by the authority of American courts to exercise judicial review. How courts exercise their authority and for what ends inevitably brings them into the business of policy making. It also brings them into the thick of political controversy. The history of the Supreme Court in dealing with racial problems clearly shows these various factors. Particularly, it clarifies the role of the Court in the political system and the nature and limitations of the judiciary in forming public policy.

Prior to the Civil Rights Act of 1964 the political branches had done almost nothing to deal with the problem facing blacks in America. The Civil Rights Act of 1957—the first such legislation passed by Congress since Reconstruction—and the later Civil Rights Act of 1960 were little more than sympathetic gestures toward civil rights interests. It was not until the passage of the 1964 act that the political branches at last began to come to grips with the problem. But, as we shall see, the 1964 act did not just come about. Dire circumstances and enormous resources created the environment conducive to its passage. A crucial element in this environment was the strong support given blacks by the Warren Court, highlighted by the famous *Brown* decision of 1954. Indeed, the Warren Court did not shy away from the problem of race; unlike previous Courts, it met and directly addressed issues that had long been brushed aside and stymied in the political process.

Courts in many ways are the forums of last resort, especially for those who are politically disadvantaged. The resources needed to achieve desired objectives through the judicial process are much more attainable and available to minorities than those needed to prevail in the political process. It stands to reason then that blacks who were (and are) certainly disadvantaged in the political system have for some time resorted to the judiciary rather than to the political branches to protect their interests. These efforts were primarily the work of the NAACP and later the NAACP Legal Defense staff. Here was a small group of lawyers whose only armor included the good will and help of a large lay organization (NAACP); a modest amount of money coming mainly from voluntary contributions; courageous litigants with good causes; and most important, the keen intellect and endless devotion of the legal staff itself which made good cases out of good causes. The successes achieved by the NAACP, although limited, give some hope to those who believe that the problem can be resolved through the system.

Yet, as we shall see, the records of the Burger Court and now the Rehnquist Court suggest that judicial victories, like political victories, are time bound and thus subject to change. The fact is, for example, that in some areas the Burger Court seems to have read the Constitution differently from the Warren Court, illustrating anew that the meaning of the Constitution (and law) is not fixed and unchanging. That law and the courts stand as barriers to the tyranny of the majority is not at all certain. In fact, time and again we are reminded of the reverse—that law and courts are indeed instruments of majority rule. If judges interpret the law contrary to persistent majorities, sooner or later the judges (and the law) will change.

Whether this should be the case in a democratic government—as the government of the United States is described—is not of concern here. What does matter is that African Americans and others who place their hopes and trust in courts should be aware that the nature of law and the judiciary is anything but static. Though blacks were greatly encouraged by the actions of the Warren Court, a sober reminder is that the Supreme Court of earlier years had much to do with legitimating and perpetuating the very racial inequities with which both the Warren Court and other branches of the national government had to deal. But, as we shall see, such progress made in these areas has once again been put in jeopardy by certain subsequent actions of the Burger-Rehnquist Courts and by the Reagan-Bush administrations. Let us take a brief look at history.

CONSTITUTIONALIZING RACISM: ITS BIRTH AND DECLINE

Decisions of the Supreme Court did much to constitutionalize and legitimize racism. They helped create a climate conducive to fostering rather than eliminating racial segregation. In the civil rights cases (1883), for example, the Court effectively rebuffed attempts of the Reconstruction Congress to get rid of some of the badges and incidents of slavery. In 1875 Congress passed the first public accommodations statute in history. It forbade racial segregation in various places of accommodation open to the public, for example, hotels, inns, and theaters. But the Supreme Court ruled that neither the Thirteenth nor the Fourteenth Amendment provided constitutional support for the congressional action. A significant holding of the Court in that case was that the Fourteenth Amendment applied to "state" action and not to "private" action (that is, to action by individuals). Privately owned accommodations could discriminate among their customers without fear of constitutional restrictions. This state-private action distinction of the civil rights cases has not been wholly abandoned. But its effect has been largely overcome by the 1964 Civil Rights

Act and by subsequent decisions of the Warren Court. Nonetheless, the decision in the civil rights cases in 1883 reflected the waning of Reconstruction policies in the South and the return of white control/black subordination in that region.

An even more ominous decision was made by the Court in *Plessy* v. *Ferguson* (1896). In this case, the Court upheld a Louisiana statute that required racial segregation of passengers on trains as a valid exercise of state police power. Specifically, the Court held that segregation of the races was not the discrimination proscribed by the equal protection clause of the Fourteenth Amendment. In short, classification by race was not arbitrary and without reason and was within the state's authority. States, under this formula, could provide separate facilities for the races if they were equal. Here then, the Court sanctioned "separate but equal." In so doing, in effect, it constitutionalized racism. To be sure, state laws and practices certainly treated blacks separately, but not at all equally. The *Plessy* decision, in effect, legitimated racial segregation not only in transportation but also in every aspect of life including education, voting, public accommodations, employment, and so on.

Take education, for example. Just three years after *Plessy*, the Court upheld the actions of a Georgia county school board in maintaining a high school for whites but discontinuing a high school for blacks because of financial difficulties (*Cumming* v. *Board of Education*, 1899). The Court reasoned that the black high school was discontinued temporarily for economic reasons and did not indicate that the school board was discriminating because of race. In this way, the Court skirted the constitutional issue of segregation. But once again blacks (and minorities) suffered because of the state authorities' (and now the Supreme Court's) decision. Similarly, the Court avoided the racial segregation issue in two other school cases. In *Berea College* v. *Kentucky*, (1908) though Berea is a private college, the Court sustained a Kentucky law that required segregation of blacks and whites in both public and private institutions as a valid regulation by the state of corporate charters. In the second case, *Gong Lum* v. *Rice*, (1927), the Court upheld Mississippi's exclusion of Asian Americans from white public schools. This Court action upheld Mississippi segregation laws generally and gave them constitutional legitimacy.

Some change in the Supreme Court stance toward racial segregation in public education began to surface in 1938 in a Missouri law school case (*Missouri ex. rel. Gaines* v. *Canada*). Missouri maintained a law school for whites but refused to accept blacks. Missouri did, however, offer blacks scholarships to attend law schools outside the state. This "out-of-state scholarship" arrangement became one of the many avenues used by southern states to foster racial segregation. However, the Court ruled that where the state did maintain certain educational opportunities for whites, it must furnish such opportunities to all of its residents "upon the basis of an equality of right." More importantly, the Court gave notice that it would begin to scrutinize more closely the "equal" part of the "separate but equal" doctrine (*Pearson* v.

Murray, 1936). But Missouri and five southern states (Texas, Louisiana, Florida, North Carolina, and South Carolina) responded to the Court decision in *Gaines* by establishing separate law schools for blacks. This action quite naturally led to legal challenges as to the standard of equality required by the "equal protection clause" of the Fourteenth Amendment.

The Texas law school case (*Sweatt* v. *Painter*, 1950) provided the opportunity for the Supreme Court to explain the meaning of the "equal protection" provided by the "separate but equal" formula. While not overturning "separate but equal," the Court ruled that the legal education Texas had offered to blacks was not equal to that provided by the state to whites. And most importantly, the Court defined equality in such a way as to signal the end of "separate but equal." In terms of faculty, curriculum, size of student body, and scope of the library, the University of Texas law school was superior to the law school for blacks. Chief Justice Vinson, who spoke for the Court, reasoned that

> What is more important, the University of Texas Law School possesses to a far greater degree those qualities which are incapable of objective measurement but which make for greatness in a law school. Such qualities, to name but a few, include reputation of the faculty, experience of the administration, position and influence of the alumni, standing in the community, traditions and prestige. It is difficult to believe that one who had a free choice between the law schools would consider the question close.

That the "separate but equal" doctrine was being subjected to a more rigid test was also evidenced by another 1950 Supreme Court decision, *McLaurin* v. *Oklahoma*. The Court ruled that the Fourteenth Amendment (equal protection) required that black students (in this instance McLaurin) be accorded the same treatment as other students. In general, *Sweatt* and *McLaurin*, though at the professional and graduate school level, signaled the declining support of the Supreme Court for racial segregation. And, as we shall see later, while the Court finally declared "separate but equal" unconstitutional, it can never be forgotten that the Court (and the judiciary generally) supported and furthered racial segregation in education.

Political participation by blacks in voting provides another example of how decisions of the Supreme Court legitimated racism in America. It was not until 1944, for example, that the Court finally declared the white primary unconstitutional as a deprivation of rights secured by the Fifteenth Amendment (*Smith* v. *Allwright*). Though the focus of the litigation was in Texas, the white primary was one of the chief methods used by southern states to prevent blacks from voting and from participating in politics generally. Many other devices were used to disfranchise blacks including the "grandfather clause," the poll tax, and literacy tests. The grandfather clause was declared unconstitutional in 1915, but the poll tax and literacy tests were not overcome until the 1960s through the combined efforts of the Court and Congress. In addition, less formal devices were used to stifle black voting through physical intimidation and violence and ranged from loss of jobs to loss of life.

The "white primary" was as simple as it was effective. Since the Democratic party was the dominant party in the South and since the winner of that primary was inevitably the winner of the general election, the way to prevent blacks from having any real effect on the election of southern officeholders was to prevent them from joining the Democratic party and hence voting in that party's primary election. But in 1944, the Supreme Court overruled one of its earlier decisions and held that the primary was not the "private" affair of the Democratic party. The Court ruled that the party (and its primary) was so enmeshed in and supported by state law and state election machinery that it had become an agent of the state. Consequently, if the party engaged in racial discrimination, its actions amounted to "state action" forbidden by the Fifteenth Amendment.

Blacks suffered inequities and deprivations as a result of discrimination in other areas as well. In addition to education and politics, the plight of blacks and other minorities in their efforts to obtain jobs and housing and to gain service in places of public accommodations was similarly stymied by laws and legal action. As we shall see later, it was only after the 1954 *Brown* decision and well into the 1960s before the national government began to address the quality of life for blacks and other minorities in these areas. But even these actions, as we shall also see, have still not secured equality of treatment and opportunity for blacks in this country. Nonetheless, just as in the past, the Supreme Court (and the judiciary generally) continues to play an important role.

The importance of the Court's role for policy outcomes is demonstrated by the generally favorable position of the Warren Court toward racial problems and the much more uncertain positions of the Burger and Rehnquist Courts toward such problems. In the remainder of this chapter the role and implications of Court participation in dealing with racial policy will be examined.

THE WARREN COURT AND RACIAL DISCRIMINATION

The school segregation cases (*Brown* v. *Board of Education*, 1954) set the tone that the Warren Court was to follow in matters relating to racial segregation. The tone was one of "great policy pronouncement" followed by less grandiose and certainly less definite decisions to implement such policies. For example, the Court boldly declared that where racial segregation was based upon law, black schools were inherently unequal. In short, racial segregation in public school education was declared unconstitutional. But the Court hedged in 1955 when it made its decision to implement the 1954 policy. The force of the Court's decision was blunted both by its remanding (sending back) cases to federal district courts and by the flexibility given those courts to implement school desegregation "with all deliberate speed." In later decisions the Warren Court had to deal bit by bit with a variety of schemes and strategies designed to circumvent the decision. But the Court slowly did so, eventually finding most of these schemes unconstitutional. Moreover, the Court applied the principle of its 1954 *Brown* decision to other areas that involved public facilities.

Then in the 1960s when the elective political institutions joined the battle, the Court found ways to legitimate the legislative response to civil rights demands. The Civil Rights Act of 1964, for example, was by far the most extensive rights legislation since Reconstruction. It forbade discrimination against persons in places of public accommodation and in employment. The act also provided substantial new weapons to fight against discrimination, including a mandate to cut off federal funds to agencies that practice discrimination. Nonetheless, despite strong constitutional challenges and precedents (especially the civil rights cases of 1883), the Warren Court supported this congressional exercise of legislative authority.

CIVIL RIGHTS IN THE BURGER AND REHNQUIST COURTS

SCHOOL DESEGREGATION: IMPLEMENTING BROWN

Generally, the Burger Court tempered the trend and tone of the Warren Court in combating racial segregation and discrimination. To be certain, particular decisions of the Court supported many policies of the Warren Court. But when these individual decisions are viewed in terms of evolving judicial policy in broad issue areas, it becomes evident that the Court refused to extend or expand such policies. Rather, by imposing more strict evidentiary requirements and through various other strictures, the Court tended to narrow and limit the application of these very doctrines. Take the area of education. The Burger Court was still concerned with the implementation of the 1954 *Brown* ruling which outlawed racial segregation in public schools. In 1969, for example, the Burger Court unanimously held against the attempts of the Justice Department to delay beginning integration plans in certain Mississippi school districts. In so doing the Court stated again the formula established late in the Warren Court era that integration of public schools must begin "at once." Further, in *Swann* v. *Charlotte-Mecklenburg Board of Education* the Court approved busing as a judicial tool for integrating public school districts in which officials had deliberately created or enforced a "dual" system on racial lines. *Swann* granted federal judges wide discretion to establish remedial measures in combating state-enforced segregation. At the same time, however, *Swann* was seen by lower courts as lessening judicial presence in this area, especially if in their view a unitary school system had been achieved. And in *North Carolina* v. *Swann* (1971) the Court declared a state statute unconstitutional in that it limited the discretion of school authorities to overcome the effects of dual educational systems. Such a policy "must give way," said Chief Justice Burger, speaking for a unanimous Court, "when it operates to hinder vindication of federal constitutional guarantees."[17]

In *Keyes* v. *School District No. 1, Denver, Colorado* (1973), the Court began to tackle the tough problems of dealing with racial segregation northern style. But the Court declined to build on or expand the Warren Court's desegregation decisions. It continued to recognize the distinction between *de facto* and *de jure* segregation. However, *Keyes* did put northern school districts on notice that where intentional segregation occurred in particular units within a school district, those units must be desegregated. It also held that the burden of proving that a policy of intentional segregation in that unit did not demonstrate a segregative intent with respect to the entire district rested on the defendant school board. *Keyes* shows important legal support for improving the quality of education for minority school children in northern areas. But one cannot help but note the apparently gradual steps of the Court in judging constitutional rights of black and other minority children. Specifically, the Court's reluctance to abandon the de jure/de facto distinction in determining the constitutional rights of minority school children and the obligations of school districts seriously slowed down meaningful changes of racial balances in the North. Clearly, meaningful changes that could come about in large metropolitan areas might necessitate the use of busing. Earlier, it will be recalled, the Court had approved busing as a permissible tool to effect public school integration. However, it had left the extent to which this "tool" could be used somewhat unclear. In dealing with the city-to-suburbs busing issue, the position of the Burger Court toward busing became clearer. The Court called a halt to the Detroit metropolitan-wide (interdistrict) busing plan.

The thorny issue concerns whether students may be bused across district lines to remedy the segregative effects of central city school districts which are predominantly black. As is well known, the overwhelming black majorities in central cities, which exist because of the flight of whites to suburban areas, make it virtually impossible to effect an integration remedy of a central city school district even if that central city district were found to have purposefully engaged in de jure segregation practices (for example, drawing of attendance zones, location of new school buildings). The black central city school district, hemmed in with a suburban ring of white school districts, is still a familiar pattern in America today. To break this pattern some have suggested a metropolitan-wide solution (interdistrict busing) for what they consider a metropolitan-wide problem (rigid segregation patterns in city and suburban schools).

As would be expected, this multifaceted issue eventually came to the Supreme Court. The first time around, however, in the 1973 Richmond, Virginia, case (*Bradley* v. *School Board*, 412 U.S. 92), the Burger Court left the issue essentially unresolved when the Court divided in a 4-4 deadlock. (Justice Powell did not participate in the case, apparently because of his involvement in the Virginia school situation prior to his appointment to the Supreme Court.) But it was not long before the issue was again before the Supreme Court. And this time, in the 1974 Detroit case (*Milliken* v. *Bradley*), the Burger Court, with Justice Powell joining a five-man majority, made its position clear. A multidistrict remedy, said Chief Justice Burger who spoke for the 5-4 majority, could not be used to solve single-district de jure segregation unless other affected districts had engaged in constitutional violations. Since earlier rulings of the Court had been confined to violations and remedies within a single school district, Burger said that for the first time the Court was asked to decide "the validity of a remedy mandating cross-district or interdistrict consolidation to remedy a condition of segregation found to exist in only one district." In holding against such a remedy, the Chief Justice stated:

> Before the boundaries of separate and autonomous school districts may be set aside by consolidating the separate units for remedial purposes or by imposing a cross-district remedy, it must first be shown that there has been a constitutional violation within one district that produces a significant segregative effect in another district. Specifically it must be shown that racially discriminatory acts of the state or local school district or of a single school district have been a substantial cause of inter-district segregation.

Burger concluded that since the record contained evidence of de jure segregated conditions only in Detroit city schools, the remedy (of the lower courts) was inappropriate. "It is clear, . . ." said Burger, "that the district court, with the approval of the court of appeals, has provided an interdistrict remedy in the face of a record which shows no constitutional violations that would call for equitable relief except within the city of Detroit." However, since "the constitutional right of the Negro respondents in Detroit is to attend a unitary school system in that district," and since that district had engaged in unconstitutional segregation policies, Burger remanded the case for "prompt formulation of a decree directed to eliminating the segregation found to exist in Detroit city schools."

Justices Douglas, White, and Marshall filed dissenting opinions, the latter two being joined by Justice Brennan. Justice Thurgood Marshall, who at one time led the NAACP's attack against segregation, bitterly attacked the Court's decision and called it a "giant step backwards." "The rights at issue in this case," he said, "are too fundamental to be abridged on grounds as superficial as those relied on by the majority today." Marshall continued:

> We deal here with the right of all of our children, whatever their race, to an equal start in life and to an equal opportunity to reach their full potential as citizens. Those children who have been denied that right in the past deserve better than to see fences thrown up to deny them that right in the future. Our Nation, I fear, will be ill-served by the Court's refusal to remedy separate and unequal education, for unless our children begin to learn together, there is little hope that our people will ever learn to live together.

In 1977 the Court took another look at the Detroit situation in *Milliken* v. *Bradley II* (1977) and ruled unanimously that federal courts have the authority to require school officials to employ a variety of remedial and compensatory programs in order to alleviate the effects of illegal racial segregation. This ruling, however, reinforced the Court's view requiring remedies to be fitted to the scope and nature of the discriminatory actions found.

As it has evolved, the position of the Court is that a finding of discrimination for which remedies may be fashioned must be based on particularized findings, on a determination of whether there was a "discriminatory intent." This more stringent requirement was articulated most forcefully by the Court in cases involving racial discrimination in the issue areas of employment and housing. For example, in *Washington* v. *Davis* (1976), blacks charged that testing and selection procedures used by the District of Columbia police department had a racially disproportionate impact against blacks. But the Court held that a mere showing of disproportionate racial impact of the selection procedures is not enough. Rather, where a constitutional claim is raised, aggrieved blacks must show that there was an "intent" to discriminate against blacks. Similarly, in the Arlington Heights housing case (*Village of Arlington Heights, Illinois* v. *Metropolitan Housing Development Corp. (1977)) the Court ruled that merely showing that the "ultimate effect" of a zoning decision of the village board was racially discriminatory was not enough. Rather, the court made it incumbent on developers and proponents of low-income and public housing to shoulder the very strict burden of proving "discriminatory intent"—of showing that the "motivating factor" was purposefully and intentionally to discriminate on the basis of race.*

But though articulated most forcefully in housing and employment cases, this more rigorous criterion was transported and applied to race discrimination cases on education as well. For example, in *Dayton Board of Education* v. *Brinkman* (1977), the Court specifically cited its decision in *Washington* v. *Davis* and said it was not enough to base the remedy of a citywide busing plan on racial discrimination resulting from "cumulative violations" and that more particularized findings of official segregative acts were required before such a remedy could be implemented.

By 1979 the *Dayton* case was once more before the Court for decision.[18] And so was a similar situation from Columbus, Ohio.[19] In *Dayton* the Court held that a systemwide remedy was justified to overcome racial segregation in the public school system. The segregation complained of involved such practices and policies as faculty hiring and assignments, the location and construction of new and expanded school facilities, and the use of optional attendance zones and transfer policies. Justice White, who spoke for a 5-4 majority, first reviewed the history of the case. White stated that though the federal district court "conceded" that Dayton schools were "highly segregated," it ruled that "the Board's failure to alleviate this condition was not actionable absent sufficient evidence that racial separation had been caused by the Board's own purposeful discriminatory conduct."[20] However, the court of appeals reversed and "expressly held that 'at the time of *Brown I*, the defendants were intentionally operating a dual school system in violation of the Equal Protection Clause of the Fourteenth Amendment,'" and that the "'finding of the district court to the contrary is clearly erroneous.'"[21] Justice White said that the district court had "ignored the legal significance of the intentional maintenance of a substantial number of black schools in the system at the time of *Brown I*."[22]

The decision in the *Columbus* case commanded a larger 7-2 Court majority.[23] Unlike *Dayton*, the court of appeals and the Supreme Court majority in *Columbus* upheld the findings and conclusion of the district court. Indeed, Justice White, who also spoke for the majority in *Dayton*, agreed with the trial court's finding that the Columbus schools "were openly and intentionally segregated on the basis of race" at the time of the 1954 *Brown* decision and that the "'Board of Education never actively set out to dismantle this dual system.'"[24]

The dissenting opinions in *Dayton* and *Columbus* warrant special attention not only for what they said about those cases but also what they might suggest for future cases and policy directions of the Court. Justices Rehnquist and Powell dissented in both cases, while Chief Justice Burger and Justice Stewart concurred in *Columbus* but dissented in *Dayton*. The reservations which the four justices had with the court majority focused on (1) the role of deference that should be accorded to the trial judge (the district courts) in school desegregation litigation; (2) the importance of linkages to the present and whether or not dual school systems existed at the time of the 1954 *Brown* decision; and (3) the need to follow appropriate legal standards in the determination of whether or not systemwide remedies are warranted.

Though varying in emphasis, there was a good deal of commonality and overlap in the views of the dissenters, especially among Chief Justice Burger and Justices Rehnquist and Powell. For example, Justice Rehnquist, in dissent joined by Powell, hit particularly hard at the lower courts' attempts to draw linkages, relationships, and inferences between pre-1954 violations and such current segregation as might exist in the school system. Rehnquist said that "the lower courts' methodology would all but eliminate the distinction between *de facto* and *de jure* segregation and render all school systems captives of a remote and ambiguous past." And by so approving this methodology, Rehnquist charged that the Court majority itself

> suggests a radical new approach to desegregation cases in systems without a history of statutorily mandated separation of races: if a district court concludes—employing what in honesty must be characterized as an irrefutable presumption—that there was a "dual" school system at the time of *Brown I* . . it must find post-1954 constitutional violations in school board's failure to take every affirmative step to integrate the system. Put differently, *racial imbalance* [emphasis his] at the time the complaint is filed is sufficient to support a system-wide, racial balance school busing remedy if the district court can find *some* [emphasis his] evidence of discriminatory purpose prior to 1954, without any inquiry into

> the causal relationship between those pre-1954 violations and current segregation in the school system.[25]

Chief Justice Burger especially agreed with this aspect of Rehnquist's opinion and said that "nothing in reason or our previous decisions provides foundation for this novel legal standard."[26] Increased efforts to desegregate schools in the North led some northern congresspersons, not unlike their colleagues from the South, to reassess their support.

Increased efforts to desegregate northern public school systems, particularly through the "funds cutoff" provision of the 1964 Civil Rights Act, led to increased efforts in the Congress to restrict such enforcement. These efforts were supported by members of Congress from the North as well as the South and were intensified after President Nixon's election in 1968 and the *Swann* decision in 1971. Much of this activity was designed to curb busing as a remedy for school desegregation. One rather watered down anti-busing provision was attached to the massive aid-to-education act of 1974. A more stringent provision, passed as a rider to the Commerce, Justice, and State Department 1981 appropriations measure, was vetoed by President Carter who believed it would be a dangerous precedent for Congress to interfere in executive law enforcement responsibilities.

After his election in 1980, however, President Reagan, working through his assistant attorney general for civil rights (W. Bradford Reynolds), developed a "new leniency" in enforcing *Brown*. Compliance litigation was brushed aside for voluntary measures adopted through negotiated consent decrees. These decrees stressed such concepts as the "magnet school" to achieve acceptable racial mix and almost always relegated the view of mandatory busing as a remedy of last resort. And the administration worked to get lower level federal courts to stop existing busing plans but mostly to no avail. (See for example, situations in East Baton Rouge Parish, Louisiana and Nashville, Tennessee.)

Another strategy of anti-busing forces was to use the popular initiative and referendum as methods to restrict busing. These efforts, however, had mixed results in the courts. In a Seattle case, for example [*Washington* v. *Seattle School District No. 1*, 458 U.S. 457 (1982)], the Supreme Court found violative of the equal protection clause a statute that prohibited assignment of pupils to schools outside their neighborhood. Although the statute allowed exceptions for assignment outside the neighborhood for a number of purposes, it singled out racial desegregation as a "prohibited" purpose. As such Justice Harry Blackmun, who spoke for the Court, viewed the statute as contrary to *Hunter* v. *Erikson* since it structured a "decision-making process" where subsequent "state action placed special burdens on racial minorities."

On the same day, however, the Court upheld a state constitutional provision adopted by California voters that limited the power of state courts to mandate busing only in the kinds of situations where federal courts would be required to use such a remedy to overcome a Fourteenth Amendment violation. In effect, the Court found that all California voters had done, unlike Seattle, was to decide that Fourteenth Amendment standards were more appropriate for state courts to apply than the more exacting standards of its own constitution. Justice Powell, who spoke for the 8-1 court majority, agreed with the lower court finding that there was no "discriminatory intent"; rather the measure was adopted to advance "legitimate non-discriminatory objectives."

But the Court did not agree with the Reagan administration's attempt to circumvent *Brown* by allowing the IRS to terminate its long-standing policy of denying tax-exempt status to schools that practice racial discrimination. The administration argued that Congress had not authorized the IRS to enforce such a policy but was rebuffed in the *Bob Jones* case [461 US 574, (1983)] when the Court rejected the efforts of two private schools to prevent the IRS from enforcing its policy of denying such exempt status to schools that practice racial discrimination. Chief Justice Burger, speaking for seven of the eight member majority, declared that racial discrimination policies and practices in education are contrary to "fundamental national policy." But one year later in *Allen* v. *Wright* [104 S. Ct. 3315 (1984)] the Court held that due to lack of standing parents of black children could not sue the IRS for granting exemptions to such schools. This, of course, underscored once more the uncertainty of the law as applied to African Americans.

Of course, for many persons the overriding question about school desegregation is whether federal court supervision should cease once districts have met requirements of *Brown*. In short, some school districts have sought to terminate such supervision arguing that they are now operating unitary school systems that fully comport with Brown. But some civil rights interests believe that without court supervision districts might well revert to policies and practices that could lead to resegregation. In *Pasadena City School Board* v. *Spangler* (1976), Justice Rehnquist speaking for a 6-2 majority stated that school officials in the instant case had complied with the district court's order to obtain racial neutrality with respect to attendance patterns and that the district court could not require school authorities to make year-by-year adjustments of its attendance zones. "Once the affirmative duty to desegregate has been accomplished and racial discrimination through official action is eliminated from the system," said Justice Rehnquist, school officials are not obligated to make annual adjustments in the racial composition of schools caused by demographic changes. It should be noted that three years after the *Pasadena* case, the district court returned complete authority to the school board.

In general, the termination of federal court supervision met with mixed results in various jurisdictions. To be sure, it is reasonable to suggest that the Reagan-Bush "flavored" judiciary, including the Rehnquist Court, seemed inclined to increasingly allow state and local institutions more control over education as well as other matters, for example, abortion. To be sure, after years of federal court supervision, some local school boards sought to remove such scrutiny on the ground that they had fully complied with *Brown* with respect to operating a unitary school system. In 1976 they began to meet with some success. For example, in *Pasadena* Chief Justice Rehnquist stated that the district court, having once implemented a racially neutral attendance pattern in order to remedy the perceived constitutional violations on the part of the defendants . . . had fully performed its function of providing the appropriate remedy for previous racially discriminatory attendance patterns.

Further, in *Board* of *Oklahoma City* v. *Dowell* [111 S.Ct. 630 (1991)] Chief Justice Rehnquist, speaking for the Court majority, emphasized the importance of moving away from federal court supervision of public school desegregation efforts once such schools had attained unitary status. Stating that school desegregation decrees "are not intended to operate in perpetuity," Rehnquist indicated that

> Local control over education of children allows citizens to participate in decision making, and allows innovation so that school programs can fit local needs. . . . Dissolving a desegregation decree after the local authorities have operated in compliance with it for a reasonable period of time properly recognizes that "necessary concern for the important values of local control of public school systems dictates that a federal court's regulatory control of such systems not extend beyond the time required to remedy the effects of past intentional discrimination."

The Chief Justice concluded that "in considering whether the vestiges of *de jure* segregation had been eliminated as far as practical, the District Court should look not only at the student assignments, but to every facet of the school operations–faculty, staff, transportation, extracurricular activities and facilities."

Justice Thurgood Marshall, joined by Justices Blackmun and Stevens, issued a sharp dissent. He charged that the majority had veered away from the "central aim" of the Court's desegregation jurisprudence, the elimination of racially segregated schools, and prevention of their recurrence. He particularly argued that such supervision should not be withdrawn "so long as conditions likely to inflict the stigmatic injury condemned in *Brown I* persist," which he contended would by the majority acceptance of some "one-race schools." Marshall charged that the practical effect of the Court's decision was to allow the return of "many of its elementary schools to their former one race status," which to him "suggests that 13 years of desegregation was enough."

That removing federal court supervision would remain perhaps the crucial issue in the school desegregation controversy became more of a reality when the Court revisited the matter a year later in *Freeman* v. *Pitts*, the DeKalb County, Georgia school case [112 S. Ct. 1430 (1992)]. The decision was rendered by eight justices, with Justice Thomas not participating since he had not been confirmed when the case was heard. All justices agreed that federal court supervision could end once a school district had complied with certain factors. But agreement stopped there as the justices sharply disagreed over the scope and timing of the application of the various factors, specifically over whether court supervision could be terminated in one category (student assignments). There was also sharp disagreement over whether full court supervision should be continued until each facet of the school operations had been desegregated. Justice Kennedy, joined by the Chief Justice and Justices White, Scalia, and Souter, thought that such supervision may be removed in some areas while continuing in others. Justice Scalia would accelerate removal of federal court supervision even more, saying that "plaintiffs alleging Equal Protection violation must prove *intent and causation* [emphasis added] and not merely the existence of racial disparity."

But Justice Blackmun, in an opinion joined by Justices Stevens and O'Connor, strongly cautioned that district courts should make a searching examination to ensure that actions of local school boards themselves had not in any way contributed to continued segregation. "It is not enough," said Justice Blackmun, "for [the school board] to establish that demographics exacerbated the problem; it must prove that its own policies did not contribute." Overall, and though unanimous in their view that at some point federal supervision could be removed, the sharp disagreement over how and when that point would be reached indicates that the controversy over the full implementation of *Brown* is likely to continue for some time to come. However, the complexity and conflictual nature of the issues involved suggest clearly that such matters remain difficult to handle, making it hard to predict with any degree of certainty how particular governmental institutions, especially courts, will rule. Of course, the 1990 Court decision in the Kansas City, Missouri case (*Missouri* v. *Jenkins*) offers a prime example of the complexity of the questions involved in such cases. Here, a bare 5-4 majority ruled that under certain circumstances in a school desegregation case, a district court may well order property tax increases to implement a valid federal court desegregation order. Justice White, plus Justice Stevens and the three liberals on the Court (Brennan, Marshall, and Blackmun) constituted the majority while Chief Justice Rehnquist and Reagan appointees (Scalia, Kennedy, and O'Connor) were in the minority. On the one hand a number of factors—the age of Justice Blackmun, the resignation of Justice Brennan in July 1990 and Justice Marshall in 1991, and then subsequent replacement of them by Justice David Souter and Justice Clarence Thomas—suggest that the Court may not only overrule *Missouri* v. *Jenkins* but might change the tone in school desegregation and civil rights areas as well.

On the other hand, this change in judicial tone and policy may be slowed, even turned around, given the election of President Clinton and the opportunities that might allow him to change the composition of both the Supreme Court and lower federal courts.

AFFIRMATIVE ACTION: EMPLOYMENT PROBLEMS

The Supreme Court has also been confronted with the sensitive and emotion-laden issues embodied in the "affirmative action versus reverse discrimination" controversy. In 1978, of course, the Burger Court decided the *Bakke* case relative to affirmative action programs in state university admissions.[27] The immmediate issue involved in *Bakke* was the validity of the special admissions program as it related to the denial of Bakke's admission to the University of California-Davis medical school. On June 28, 1978, the Court on the one hand supported the affirmative action interest by holding that it is lawful for race to be considered as a factor in a university's admissions process. On the other hand, the Court supported those who were fighting against "reverse discrimination" and "quotas" by holding that the particular Davis program was unlawful and by ordering Bakke's admission to the medical school. Both aspects of the decision were reached by 5-4 votes, with only Justice Powell agreeing to both outcomes. Thus, the Court was sharply divided: there was no majority opinion; instead there were six opinions totaling almost 160 pages.

Justice Powell announced the judgment of the Court and wrote what some refer to as the "prevailing" opinion in the case. There is no doubt that Powell's position did prevail. His vote proved decisive and broke the apparent stalemate between the two equally divided factions on the Court. Essentially, Powell's view was that while race may be considered a "plus" in a university's admissions process, the particular Davis program, in his opinion, was unconstitutional. Powell's view that race constitutionally may be considered as a factor in the university admission process was supported by four justices (Brennan, Marshall, Blackmun, and White). But whereas Powell thought the particular Davis program used race in such a way as to violate constitutional standards, the four other justices thought that the program did not violate the Constitution. However, Powell did find the needed support for this position among his four other colleagues (Chief Justice Burger and Justices Stevens, Stewart, and Rehnquist) who joined in an opinion written by Justice Stevens. The Stevens group agreed with Powell that the particular Davis program was invalid and that Bakke should be admitted to the medical school. But they disagreed with how Powell reached that conclusion. In short, unlike Powell (and the Brennan group of justices), the Stevens group thought that it was unnecessary to reach or decide the constitutional issue involved. The Davis program, in their opinion, violated the intent as well as the "plain language" of the Civil Rights Act of 1964 (Title VI) by excluding Bakke because of his race.

However, the *Bakke* case left a number of issues unanswered. Hence, and not unexpectedly, the issue was once again before the Court in 1979. However, this time the Court faced the issue in the area of employment[28] rather than in education. The Kaiser Aluminum and Chemical Corporation, in a national collective bargaining agreement with the United Steelworkers, instituted a voluntary affirmative action plan to ensure equitable representation in plant craft training programs. Under the plan, 50 percent of the openings in such programs would be reserved for black employees until the percentage of black craft workers in a plant became commensurate with the percentage of blacks in the local labor force. Brian Weber, a white plant worker, brought suit challenging the institution of an affirmative action program at the Kaiser plant in Grammercy, Louisiana, where he worked. Weber charged that the program violated the prohibition of Title VII of the Civil Rights Act of 1964 against racial discrimination in employment since he thought the program unfairly discriminated against him because he was white.

But Justice Brennan, writing for a 5-2 majority, held that "the very statutory words [of Title VII] intended as a spur or catalyst to cause employers and unions to self-examine and to self-evaluate their employment practices and to endeavor to eliminate, so far as possible, the last vestiges of an unfortunate and ignominious page in this country's history, . . . cannot be interpreted as an absolute prohibition against all private, voluntary, race-conscious affirmative action efforts to hasten the elimination of such vestiges."[29] "It would be ironic indeed," said Justice Brennan, "if a law triggered by a Nation's concern over centuries of racial injustice and intended to improve the lot of those who had 'been excluded from the American dream for so long' constituted the first legislative prohibition of all voluntary, private, race-conscious efforts to abolish traditional patterns of racial segregation and hierarchy."[30] However, Chief Justice Burger and Justice Rehnquist dissented. They concluded that "Kaiser's racially discriminatory admission quota is flatly prohibited by the plain language of Title VII."[31]

Overall, in *Weber* the Court decided that Title VII permitted voluntary affirmative action programs by private companies as long as the measures are temporary and do not unnecessarily restrict the rights of innocent persons. One year later in *Fullilove* v. *Klutznick* [448 U.S. 448 (1980)] the Court upheld a congressional law requiring that state and local governments applying for grants under the Public Works Employment Act of 1977 give assurances that at least 10 percent of each grant would be for contracts with minority business enterprises. In upholding the "10 percent set-aside", as the program was called, the Supreme Court stressed the broad remedial powers of Congress to remedy the effects of past racial discrimination. The Court also noted the temporary nature of the program.

But the Reagan administration continued to push its position that under affirmative action each beneficiary must be required to establish that he/she was an actual victim of discrimination. Clearly, full acceptance of this standard would severely limit race-conscious group-based remedies and undermine the use of past and societal discrimination as a rationale for affirmative action. For the Reagan administration the actual victim standard was the appropriate one to be followed in determining the constitutionality of both voluntary and court-imposed affirmative action programs.

In *Firefighters* v. *Stotts* [467 U.S. 561 (1984)] the Burger Court undoubtedly gave some support and hope to those who embraced the position of the Reagan administration. In *Stotts* the Court rejected a federal court order (to effectuate an earlier consent decree) enjoining Memphis from following its seniority system in determining layoffs resulting from budgetary shortfalls, the effect of which would be to layoff whites with more seniority than blacks due to past racial discrimination. However, the Supreme Court held that "Title VII protects bona fide seniority systems, and it is inappropriate to deny an innocent employee the benefits of his seniority in order to provide a remedy in a pattern or practice suit such as this." But in *Firefighters* v. *Cleveland* [106 S. Ct. 3063 (1986)] the Court held that Title VII does not preclude "voluntary adoption (in a consent decree) of race-conscious relief that may benefit non-victims" of discriminatory practices. This view was reaffirmed in *Sheet Metal Workers* v. *EEOC* [106 S. Ct. 3014 (1986)] when the Court, focusing on powers of district courts to fashion affirmative action remedies, indicated that Title VII does not "say that a court may order relief only for the actual victims of past discriminations." The Court thus rejected the view that *Stotts* prevents a lower court from ordering affirmative action remedies that might benefit non-victims. "The purpose of affirmative action," said the Court, "is not to make identified victims whole but rather to dismantle prior patterns of employment discrimination and to prevent discrimination in the future." The Court made it clear that "such relief is provided to the class as a whole rather than to individual members," and that individuals entitled to relief "need not show themselves victims of discrimination."

Two important affirmative action cases gave the Rehnquist Court opportunities to consider affirmative action in both race and gender contexts. In *U.S.* v. *Paradise* [107 S. Ct. 1053 (1987)], black plaintiffs in prolonged litigation with the Alabama Department of Public Safety alleged that the state had followed racially discriminatory practices in its employment policies—hiring, promotions, and so forth. Eventually a federal district court issued a "one-black-for-one-white" promotion order as an interim measure to increase rank and status of blacks in the department. Subsequently, on an equal protection challenge under the Fourteenth Amendment, the Court upheld the district court order saying that the relief was "narrowly tailored" to serve a "compelling governmental interest," thus making it unnecessary to apply the strict scrutiny test. Justice Brennan, who wrote the opinion for the Court majority, said that "the persuasive, systematic and obstinate discriminatory conduct of the Department (of Public Safety) created a profound need and a firm justification for the race-conscious relief ordered by the district court." Justice O'Connor's dissenting opinion, joined by Chief Justice Rehnquist and Justice Scalia, charged that the "one-for-one" order would have failed the strict scrutiny test.

In *Johnson* v. *Transportation Agency* [107 S. Ct. 1442 (1987)] the Court upheld an affirmative action plan which provided that "in making promotions to positions within a traditionally segregated job classification in which women have been significantly underrepresented, the agency is authorized to consider as one factor the sex of a qualified applicant." The case that triggered the Court's position was the promotion by the agency of a female employee who ranked slightly lower on test scores than a male applicant, the latter charging that her promotion was unlawful under Title VII of the 1964 Civil Rights Act. The plan did not set aside a specific number of positions or jobs for minorities or women but did provide for the "consideration of ethnicity or sex as a factor when evaluating qualified candidates for jobs in which members of such groups were poorly represented." Justice Brennan, who spoke for the Court, found it appropriate to consider the sex of applicants for skilled craft jobs when there is found to be a "manifest imbalance." Brennan said that employers should compare "the percentage of minorities or women in the employer's work force with the percentage in the area labor market or general population" and "where the job requires special training . . . , the comparison should be with those in the labor force who possess the relevant qualifications." Brennan took special note that the plan "expressly directed that numerous factors be taken into account in making hiring decisions, including specifically the qualification of female applicants for particular jobs." He also found that the plan did not necessarily trammel on "the rights of male employees" or create "an absolute bar to their advancement." Again, Chief Justice Rehnquist joined Justice Scalia's dissenting opinion, as did Justice White in part.

Johnson is important since it filled much of the gap left open by *Bakke* and *Weber*. Specifically, the Court indicated clearly that public employers may institute affirmative action programs even though there has been no judicial, administrative or legislative determination of discrimination and where there is no proof of prior discrimination on the part of the employer. In short, employers may adopt voluntary affirmative action plans that address the underrepresentation of blacks, women, and minorities "caused not only by their own and society's proven employment discrimination, but also by the effects of unconscious discrimination and internalized sexual and racial stereotypes that discourage women and minorities from seeking certain kinds of employment."[32] But it is clear that the Rehnquist Court plans to subject affirmative action plans to increasing scrutiny, clearly resulting in less judicial support for the issue. This is signaled in several major decisions of the Rehnquist Court. For example, the 1989 decision in *City of Richmond, Virginia* v. *J. A. Croson Co.*, (109 S. Ct. 706) took much of the steam out of the Burger Court's *Fullilove* decision which upheld a federal law designed to enhance the economic position of minority contractors by a "set-aside" provision which required that at least 10 percent of grants awarded under the Public Works Employment Act of 1977 be given to minority contractors. Following *Fullilove*, a number of state and local governments adopted their own "set-aside" programs clearly patterned after the federal plan. The City of Richmond adopted one such plan which provided that, due to manifest past discrimination against minority contractors, 30 percent of future contracts awarded by the city would be set aside for minority contractors. White contractors who contested the plan were joined by the Reagan administration which had launched major attacks on race-based affirmative action plans generally.

In a 6-3 decision the Rehnquist Court dealt such plans a major setback when it held that governmental policies utilizing race-conscious numerical remedies are "suspect" and therefore subject to "strict scrutiny." Justice Sandra Day O'Connor, speaking for the majority, said that this kind of plan can only be constitutionally acceptable by showing a "compelling state interest" in order to redress specific "identified discrimination." By adopting the "strict scrutiny" standard the Court indicated that it would be quite difficult for affirmative action plans of any sort to pass constitutional muster. This point was not lost on Justice Thurgood Marshall, the first African American appointed to the Court. In a strong dissent, Marshall lashed out at the majority for taking "a deliberate and giant step backward in the Court's affirmative action jurisprudence." Rather than employing the Court's most exacting standard of scrutiny (strict scrutiny), which almost always results in findings of unconstitutionality, Marshall would utilize an intermediate standard ("mid-level scrutiny") that would determine whether such plans "serve important governmental objectives" and are "substantially related to the achievement of those objectives." This would allow such plans to be subjected to adequate constitutional scrutiny without denying cities a potentially effective mechanism to overcome obvious patterns and practice of past race-based discrimination. Two other 1989 Rehnquist Court decisions also dealt severe setbacks to affirmative action interests. In *Wards Cove Packing Co.* v. *Atonio* (109 S. Ct. 2115) a developing conservative majority on the Court (White, Rehnquist, O'Connor, Scalia, and Kennedy) rejected challenges of employees of two Alaskan salmon cannery companies alleging discriminatory employment practices in violation of Title VII of the 1964 Civil Rights Act. The "burden-of-proof" requirements articulated by the five-person Court majority make it more difficult for a plaintiff in a disparate impact case to win. In *Wards Cove* the plaintiffs had offered considerable evidence of discrimination in job assignments with minorities disproportionately in lower positions and few of them in higher paying positions. While such evidence convinced the court of appeals of a prima facie case of disparate impact, it did not convince the Rehnquist Court majority. Justice White, who spoke for the majority, said that race-based statistical comparisons were not enough to prove disparate impact. Rather, said White, there must be a showing of disproportionality that looks at the "pool of qualified applicants" or the "qualified population in the labor force." And though employers are required to offer a "business justification" for using the challenged practice, said Justice White, "the ultimate burden of proving that discrimination against a protected group has been caused by a specific employment practice remains with the plaintiff at all times." The dissenters sharply criticized the majority. In a biting dissent, Justice Stevens charged the majority with "turning a blind eye to the meaning and purpose of Title VII." Stevens noted that the majority had misread a 1971 decision of the Court itself (*Griggs* v. *Duke Power Co.*) as well as ignored the practice of federal enforcement agencies, all of which had interpreted Title VII to ban practices that had discriminatory effects as well as those practices that indicated discriminatory intent.

In another major setback to affirmative action, the Court, just one week after *Wards Cove*, spoke through Chief Justice Rehnquist and held in *Martin v. Wilks* that although a "consent decree" [the key tool for implementing affirmative action goals] could settle matters among the immediate parties to a lawsuit, such decrees could not "conclude the right of strangers [in this instance white firefighters in Birmingham, Alabama] to those proceedings." The court decision, in effect, opened up the potentiality of a large number of lawsuits challenging consent decrees that have been concluded over the past two decades in a number of affirmative action contexts. Justice Stevens's sharp dissent recognized with dismay this possibility when he warned that the decision would "subject large employers who seek to comply with the law by remedying past discrimination to a never ending stream of litigation and potential liability."

But such court decisions, as indicated earlier in this chapter, may not necessarily be the last word. This is especially true in matters which turn on statutory interpretation (as affirmative action cases tend to do) where Congress has the opportunity to pass subsequent legislation that might overcome or otherwise circumvent adverse court decisions. In fact, it was these very Rehnquist Court decisions that gave impetus to congressional efforts to overcome adverse effects of these and related court actions. And eventually with rare bipartisan support, at least for the Reagan-Bush years, a coalition of Democrats and Republicans—engineered by moderate Republican Senator John Danforth of Missouri—succeeded in winning support from a reluctant President Bush and divided White House staff for the Civil Rights Act of 1991.

The 1991 statute attempts to reverse the effects of some eight court decisions, including *Wards Cove* and *Wilks*. But given last-minute maneuvers of the White House legal counsel (and others as well) to narrow the interpretation and understanding of the new law, it remains to be seen how effective the Civil Rights Act of 1991 will prove. Policy battles over highly controversial issues are never ending; they are continuous.

VOTING ARRANGEMENTS AND REAPPORTIONMENT

The Burger Court also faced issues related to attempts to dilute the increasing influence of the black vote as a source of political power. These discriminatory efforts included replacing single-member districts with multimember districts and the use of at-large elections; the annexation by central cities of white suburban areas to increase the white vote and to decrease black voting strength; and certain reapportionment actions involving the redrawing or restructuring of particular electoral districts. States covered by the Voting Rights Act of 1965, however, are subject to having such schemes reviewed by federal administrative officials and by federal courts. Specifically, Section 5 of the Voting Rights Act forbids changes that have "the purpose or effect of denying or abridging the right to vote on account of race or color."

In 1971 the Court was asked to rule on the use of a multimember district, at-large election scheme from a state (Indiana) not covered by the Voting Rights Act. Here blacks alleged that the Indiana statutes that established Marion County (Indianapolis) as a multimember district for the election of state senators and representatives deprived them of a realistic opportunity to win elections. Specifically, they charged that the laws diluted their votes in the predominantly black inner-city areas of Indianapolis. A three-judge federal district court agreed with this position. But the Supreme Court overturned the lower court decision by a 6-3 vote (*Whitcomb* v. *Chavis*). Justice White, who wrote for the Court, said there was no suggestion that the multimember district in Marion County or similar districts in the state were "conceived or operated as purposeful devices to further racial or economic discrimination." Justice White maintained that "the failure of the ghetto to have legislative seats in proportion to its population emerges more as a function of losing elections than of built-in bias against poor Negroes." . . . "The mere fact that one interest group or another concerned with the outcome of Marion County elections has found itself outvoted and without legislative seats of its own provides no basis for invoking constitutional remedies where, as here, there is no indication that this segment of the population is being denied access to the political system." Furthermore, reasoned Justice White, to uphold the position of one racial group would make it difficult to reject claims of any other groups—for example, Republicans, Democrats, or organized labor—who find themselves similarly disadvantaged.

But Justice Douglas, joined by Justices Brennan and Marshall, filed a strong dissenting opinion in *Whitcomb*. Justice Douglas supported the position of the district court that "a showing of racial motivation is not necessary when dealing with multi-member districts." Justice Douglas maintained that the test of constitutionality for multi-member districts is where there are "invidious effects." And in this case Douglas thought there were such effects since the result of the plan was to "purposely wash blacks out of the system."

In *White* v. *Regester* (1973) the Court considered whether the election of state legislators from multimember districts in two Texas counties violated the equal protection rights of blacks and Mexican-Americans. After examining the history of the political participation of these groups in the two counties, a long history of official segregation including small number of blacks (only two since Reconstruction) elected from the area, the persistence of white-dominated slate making, and technical rules of the electoral process, the Court concluded that within the context of the multimember scheme, the Texas legislative apportionment plan was invidiously discriminatory in violation of the equal protection clause.

Subsequently, in 1976 the Court approved a city reapportionment plan, this time in a case brought under Section 5 of the 1965 Voting Rights Act. In *Beer* v. *U.S.*, the Court reversed a federal district court ruling and upheld a New Orleans city council reapportionment plan that would increase black representation on a seven-member city council (five single members and two at-large) from none to one. Thus, the Court accepted a plan that seemingly still had a racially discriminatory effect (blacks constituted about 45 percent of the population). But it was important to the Court that the plan did not result in "retrogression," but rather in an improvement of the position of blacks in the exercise of the franchise. However, Justices White, Brennan, and Marshall filed strong dissents. White, for example, thought the Court majority failed to consider the twin realities of residential segregation and bloc voting which if it had, and according to his interpretation of the Voting Rights Act (Section 5), blacks would be legitimately entitled to an opportunity to elect at least three members of the city council. Marshall, in an opinion joined by Justice Brennan, concluded that it could very well be that this case represented a prime example for a plan which betters the electoral position of blacks but which remains "blatantly discriminatory."

In *Richmond* v. *U.S.* (1975), the Court approved a Richmond, Virginia plan which by the annexation of white suburban areas reduced the city's black population from 52 percent to 42 percent. Initially, the city's request for approval of the plan under Section 5 of the Voting Rights Act was denied by the United States attorney general because of what he saw as a dilution of black voting strength. But at the suggestion of the attorney general, and in order to overcome the adverse racial impact of annexation, the city eliminated an at-large election structure and replaced it with a single-member district scheme. Nonetheless, a federal district court (District of Columbia) still found the plan defective under the Voting Rights Act. But by a 5-3 vote, a Supreme Court majority overturned the district court since the subsequent electoral structure "fairly recognizes black political strength."[33] At present, Richmond has a black majority city council.

Still another electoral arrangement scheme was at issue in the 1977 case of the *United Jewish Organizations of Williamsburgh* v. *Carey*. Here the Court interpreted Section 5 of the Voting Rights Act[34] in such a way as to uphold a New York state legislative reapportionment plan to increase black representation. The Hasidic Jewish community argued that the reapportionment plan, which restructured certain districts to produce black majorities, was done at the expense of diluting voting strength of the Hasidic Jews by dividing members of that community into two districts. Though no one opinion commanded majority support, the Court nonetheless by a 7-1 vote did agree that the legislature had the authority to take race into account in its reapportionment scheme. The lone dissenter, Chief Justice Burger, said he was troubled by the semblance of a "racial gerrymander" and by what fragmented representation by race might do to the "American melting pot ideal."

By and large, however, the Court continued to press its more demanding standard requiring proof of purposeful discrimination in challenges to various electoral schemes such as multimember at-large structures. In the much publicized *Mobile* v. *Bolden* (1980) case, for example, it was shown that blacks constituted 40 percent of the city's population but had never been elected to its three-member city commission allegedly due to the at-large election scheme. And the federal district court agreed that the scheme had discriminated against blacks. Nonetheless, the Supreme Court reversed and reiterated the need to prove purposeful discrimination to sustain a Fourteenth or Fifteenth Amendment violation, as well as a violation of the Voting Rights Act.

But this more exacting standard of proof used by the Court in *Mobile,* became a focal point of controversy in the 1982 battle to extend the Voting Rights Act. And in the end the act's supporters were successful in getting Congress to reject the more exacting "intent" standard of *Mobile* and include in Section 2 the less exacting "effects or results" standards for proving a discriminatory violation.

At-large electoral schemes that dilute their vote and inhibit their chances of winning continue to raise the ire of black voters. Perhaps in its most definitive consideration of the issue in *Thornburg* v. *Gingles* [106 S. Ct. 2752 (1986)] the Court held that vote dilution charges emanating from multimember district schemes were actionable under Section 2 of the Voting Rights Act of 1965. The Court said that in such cases the plaintiffs must show that the multidistrict scheme, "under the totality of circumstances," results in "unequal access to the electoral process." Specifically, plaintiffs in such cases must show that the multidistrict mechanism "interacts with social and historical conditions to cause an inequality in the opportunities enjoyed by black and white voters to elect their preferred representatives." Among factors that are critical in showing such claims are (1) lingering effects of past discrimination; (2) the extent of racially polarized voting in the electoral jurisdiction; (3) appeals to racial bias in the election campaign; and (4) patterns of racial bloc voting over extended periods of time. Justice Brennan, who spoke for the Court majority, stated that the finding of illegal vote dilution violative of Section 2 was appropriate when the district court, after considering the "totality of circumstances," found that the above factors "acted in concert with the multimember districting scheme to impair the ability of geographically insular and politically cohesive groups of black voters to participate equally in the political process and to elect candidates of their choice."

THE POOR IN COURT

The Burger Court also rendered decisions in another area that is of importance to blacks—poverty law. In general, these decisions indicate that the Court is not disposed to break new ground in order to expand rights of the poor. Consider, for example, the much publicized 1973 Court decision in *San Antonio Independent School District* v. *Rodriguez*. The Court rejected challenges to the local property tax system that provides a significant part of public school finances in 49 of the 50 states. The contention was that the Texas system of supplementing state aid to school districts by means of property tax levied within the jurisdiction of the individual school district violated the equal protection clause. Speaking for a 5-4 majority, Justice Powell said that the financing system, although not perfect, "abundantly satisfies" the constitutional standard for equal protection since the system "rationally furthers a legitimate state purpose or interest," namely, the maintenance of local control of public education. Justice Powell applied the traditional equal protection standard since "the Texas system does not operate to the peculiar disadvantage of any suspect class," and since education, although an important state service, is not a "fundamental" right because it is not "explicitly or implicitly guaranteed by the Constitution."[35] Justice Marshall, in dissent, charged the majority with a retreat from our historic commitment to equality of educational opportunity and an "unsupportable acquiescence in a system which deprived children in their earliest years of the chance to reach their full potential as citizens."

Rodriguez, while not posed in racial terms, has a direct impact on equality of opportunity for racial minorities, since minorities tend to be concentrated in areas where property values are lower and where consequently, regardless of the willingness in some of these areas to pay a substantial rate of tax for education, less money can be made available for educational services.

But *Rodriguez* has not proven the last word. Indeed, a number of state supreme courts have ruled on the constitutionality of their state's school financing system. While several state supreme courts have found that the school financing system utilized in their state violates educational provisions in the state constitution, many other state supreme courts have found their school financing system constitutional. Among those who found their systems unconstitutional was the Texas Supreme Court.

In *Edgewood Independent School District* v. *Kirby* [77 S.W. 2nd 391, Tex. (1989)], the Texas Supreme Court ruled unanimously that the state school financing system violated the state constitutional provision requiring "the support and maintenance of an efficient system of public free schools." Public schools are supported in Texas through state-provided revenues and revenues raised by the local school districts from ad valorem property taxes. The ability of the school districts to raise their share of school support is hindered by disparities in property wealth among the school districts; the property wealth per student in school districts varies between $14 million and $20 thousand. These disparities are reflected in each school district's spending per student, ranging from $2,112 to $19,333. The Texas Supreme Court rejected the state's claim that the word "efficient" suggests a "simple and inexpensive system," ruling instead that "efficient" connotes a system that is effective or produces results. Since the amount of money spent on a student's education has an impact on the education opportunity available to the student, the Texas Supreme Court held that the "efficiency" requirement mandates the equitable and even distribution of education funds. Rather than prescribe a school financing system, the Texas Supreme Court gave the legislature discretion within time limits to develop such a system of school financing. Subsequent developments in state legislative politics make it clear, however, that the matter will be difficult to resolve.[36]

Overall, it seems clear that the Burger Court did not seem disposed to break new ground in poverty law and in shoring up the constitutional rights of the poor. This disposition of the Burger Court is reflected well in *Lindsey* v. *Norment*, a 1972 case that posed a challenge to Oregon's statutory procedures for evicting tenants who failed to pay rent. The tenants had argued that the Court support the view that the "need for decent shelter" and the "right to retain peaceful possession of one's home" are fundamental interests that require "strict scrutiny." But Justice White rejected the tenants' argument and for a 5-2 Court majority said that though the Court appreciates "the importance of decent, safe, and sanitary housing, . . . the Constitution does not provide judicial remedies for every social and economic ill."

In general, this overall review of judicial policies indicates a change in the tone and substance between decisional outputs of the Warren Court, the Burger Court, and now the Rehnquist Court. These changes illuminate vividly the intimate and continuing interaction between courts, laws, and politics, a matter which is the focus of the next chapter.

Topics for Discussion

1. Do you feel that judicial support is important for the attainment of black policy objectives? Explain your position.

2. As quoted in the epigraph to this chapter, Justice Marshall "fears" that the Court has come "full circle." Do you share his belief? Why or why not? Justify your position.

3. The number of blacks in the legal profession is very small. Blacks comprise less than 3 percent of the legal profession in America. How and in what ways does this shortage of black lawyers work to the disadvantage of blacks in American politics?

4. The records of the Burger and Rehnquist Courts suggest judicial victories, like political victories, are not etched in concrete and are subject to change. Do you agree or disagree? How and in what ways do "judicial" victories differ from "political victories"? Are they related? How?

Suggested Readings

See chapter 6.

Notes

* Remarks of Justice Thurgood Marshall at the Annual Seminar of the San Francisco Patent and Trademark Law Association, Maui, Hawaii, May 6, 1987.

** Dissenting in *United Steelworkers et al.* v. *Weber* (99 S. Ct. 2752-53, 1979).

1. Harold Lasswell, *Politics: Who Gets What, When, How* (Cleveland, OH: Meridian Books, 1958).
2. Walter Murphy and C. Herman Pritchett, *Courts, Judges and Politics*, 2nd ed. (New York: Random House, 1974), p. 442.
3. In 1988, however, Congress passed the Civil Rights Restoration Act to overcome the effects of *Grove City*.
4. Murphy and Pritchett, *Courts, Judges, Politics*, p. 408.
5. Cf. Alexis de Tocqueville, *Democracy in America*, ed. J.P. Mayer and Max Lerner, trans. George Lawrence (New York: Harper & Row, 1966), pp. 242-48.
6. In 1988, out of a total of 757,000 lawyers and judges, only 2.3 percent were black or other minorities. See Bureau of the Census, *Statistical Abstract of the U.S.*, 1990.
7. Jack W. Peltason, *Federal Courts in the Political Process* (New York: Random House, 1955), p. 3.
8. Ibid.
9. See John P. Heinz, Robert W. Getleman, and Morris A. Seeskin, "Legislative Politics and the Criminal Law," *Northwestern Law Review* 64 (1969), pp. 277-358.
10. For discussion of judicial selection and characteristics of members of the Court generally, see Thomas Walker and Lee Epstein, *The Supreme Court of the United States: An Introduction* (New York: St. Martin Press, 1992), Chap. 2.
11. Richard Harris, *Decision* (New York: Dutton, 1971).
12. See Nadine Cohodas, "Merit Selection Diversified Federal Bench," *Congressional Quarterly Weekly Report* 37 (Oct. 27, 1979), p. 2418.
13. See Exec. Order No. 12059, May 11, 1978, 43 Fed. Register 20949; and Exec. Order No. 19097, November 8, 1978, 43 Fed. Register 52455. Also see Charles W. Hucker, "Report Card on Judicial Merit Selection," *Congressional Quarterly Weekly Report* 37 (February 3, 1979), p. 189ff.; and Nadine Cohodas, "Merit Selection Diversifies Federal Bench," *Congressional Quarterly Weekly Report* 37 (October 27, 1979), p. 2418ff.
14. "Report Card," p. 194.
15. See generally, "Merit Selection," p. 2418ff.
16. Peltason, *Federal Courts*, p. 3.
17. 402 U.S. 43 (1971), at 45.
18. *Dayton Board of Education et al.* v. *Brinkman et al.*, 99 S. Ct. 2971 (1979).

19. *Columbus Board of Education et al.* v. *Penick et al.*, 99 S. Ct. 2941 (1979).
20. 99 S. Ct. 2976 (1979).
21. Ibid.
22. Ibid. at 2978.
23. 99 S. Ct. 2941 (1979).
24. Ibid. at 2944.
25. 99 S. Ct. 2954.
26. 99 S. Ct. 2952 (concurring in *Columbus*).
27. *University of California Regents* v. *Bakke*, 438 U.S. 265 (1978).
28. *United Steelworkers* v. *Weber*, 99 S. Ct. 2721 (1979).
29. Ibid.
30. Ibid. at 2740.
31. Ibid.
32. Quoted from Barker and Combs, "Civil Rights and Liberties in the First Term of the Rehnquist Court: The Quest for Doctrine and Votes," *National Political Science Review* 1 (1988), Vol. I pp. 31-57 at pp. 50-51.
33. The Court did, however, remand the case to the district court to consider whether purposeful discrimination was involved. Subsequently, the plan as approved by the district court contained nine wards—four with black majorities; four with white majorities; and one "swing" district with approximately equal numbers of blacks and whites. In the first election under the plan on March 1, 1977, blacks won five of the nine seats.
34. See reference to the Voting Rights Act in *United Jewish Organizations of Williamsburgh* v. *Carey* 430 U.S. 144 (1977).
35. While education is not explicitly guaranteed in the federal Constitution, it is so guaranteed by many state constitutions. These provisions have provided the basis for relief against unfair property tax assessments and expenditures in several states.
36. See *Washington Post*, May 1, 1990; May 2, 1990; and May 23, 1990.

CHAPTER 6

COURTS, JUDGES, AND THE INTERACTION OF LAW AND POLITICS

Stare decisis is the preferred course because it promotes the evenhanded, predictable, and consistent development of legal principles, fosters reliance on judicial decisions, and contributes to the actual and perceived integrity of the judicial process . . . Adhering to precedent "is usually the wise policy, because in most matters it is more important that the applicable rule of law be settled than right." . . . Nevertheless, when governing decisions are unworkable or are badly reasoned, "this Court has never felt constrained to follow precedent." Smith v. Allwright, 1944. Stare decisis is not an inexorable command; rather it "is a principle of policy and not a mechanical formula of adherence to the latest decision." This is particularly true in constitutional cases, because in such cases "correction through legislative action in practically impossible." . . . Considerations in favor of stare decisis are at their acme is cases involving property and contract rights, where reliance interests are involved, . . . the opposite is true in cases such as the present one involving procedural and evidentiary rules.

Applying these general principles, the Court had during the past 20 terms overruled in whole or in part 33 of its previous constitutional decisions. Booth and Gathers were decided by the narrowest of margins, over spirited dissents challenging the basic underpinnings of those decisions. They have been questioned by members of the Court in later decisions, and have defied consistent application by the lower courts. . . . Reconsidering these decisions now, we conclude for the reasons heretofore stated, that they were wrongly decided and should be, and now are, overruled. We accordingly affirm the judgment of the Supreme Court of Tennessee.

Chief Justice William Rehnquist
from his majority opinion in
Payne v. *Tennessee* 111 S. Ct. 2597, (1991)

Power, not reason, is the new currency of this Court's decision making. Four Terms ago, a five-Justice majority of this Court held that "victim impact" evidence of the type at issue in this case could not constitutionally be introduced during the penalty phase of a capital trial. (Booth v. Maryland, 1987). By another 5-4 vote, a majority of this Court rebuffed an attack upon this ruling just two Terms ago. (South Carolina v. Gathers, 1989) Nevertheless, having expressly invited respondent to renew the attack, . . . today's majority overrules Booth and Gathers and credits the dissenting views expressed in those cases. Neither the law nor the facts supporting Booth and Gathers underwent any change in the last four years. Only the personnel of this Court did.

In dispatching Booth and Gathers to their own graves, today's majority ominously suggests that an even more extensive upheaval of this Court's precedents may be in store. . . . The majority sends a clear signal that scores of established constitutional liberties are now ripe for reconsideration, thereby inviting the very type of open defiance of our precedents that the majority rewards in this case. Because I believe that this Court owes more to its constitutional precedents in general and to Booth and Gathers in particular, I dissent.

Justice Thurgood Marshall
from his dissenting opinion in
Payne v. *Tennessee* 111 S. Ct. 2597 (1991)

INTRODUCTION

The resignation of Justice Thurgood Marshall and President Bush's subsequent nomination of Judge Clarence Thomas as his replacement illumined once again the interrelation and importance of courts and judges to American politics and public policy. And the fact that Justice Marshall, a black liberal, was being replaced by Judge Thomas, a black conservative, stirred the debate even more.

It would indeed be difficult to find any two persons whose views differ as widely as those of Justice Marshall and Judge Thomas along both policy and jurisprudential dimensions. And it clearly would prove more difficult, but not impossible, as Thomas's very appointment shows, to find two African

Americans whose views would prove as divergent on matters relating to problems of race and the role of government and courts in dealing with such problems. These and other matters were clearly and pointedly aired during the confirmation battle over Judge Thomas. A more detailed discussion of the nature and implications of the Thomas confirmation battle is reserved for Chapter 11. It may also, of course, be read profitably at this point.

But as difficult as the battle over Judge Thomas proved, the bitter and divisive controversy that erupted over President Reagan's nomination of Judge Robert Bork to the Supreme Court remains one of the most divisive and engulfing confirmation battles in court history. In recent times and in a real sense, the Bork controversy provides a sort of watershed context in which future Court nomination battles might be fought. The Bork battle reveals starkly the important relationship of courts and judges to politics and public policy and as with court nominations generally, illumines vividly the high stakes that various interest groups have, or at least believe they have, in who gets appointed to our courts, especially the U.S. Supreme Court. Indeed, judicial nominations, particularly highly controversial ones such as that of Judge Bork, reinforce the increasingly strongly held view that *who* is on the court determines largely *what* comes out of the court.

Thus, this chapter focuses mainly on a detailed case study of the Bork nomination. It illumines clearly the intimate and continuing interaction between law and politics and especially points up the crucial role of the Supreme Court in the formulation of public policy.

The chapter concludes with an analysis of the nature and importance of the judiciary to African Americans, and in doing so points up vividly the actual and potential role and functions of the judiciary in American politics and public policy.

THE BORK NOMINATION AND BLACK AMERICA: A CASE STUDY[1]

Kevin L. Lyles*

I. Parameters of the Controversy

The swirling controversy surrounding the nomination of Judge Robert Heron Bork to the United States Supreme Court has emanations throughout the landscape of American politics. While the controversy suggests a number of avenues for analysis and inquiry, it would seem especially useful to focus on the crucial role that blacks and civil rights interests generally played in the protracted confirmation battle that led

* Kevin L. Lyles is an assistant professor of political science at the University of Illinois–Chicago.

to the eventual rejection of Judge Bork by the United States Senate. Thus,i in this case study we focus on the nature and participatory role of blacks and civil rights interests in the fight over the Bork confirmation.

The Bork controversy indicates clearly that the nomination and confirmation process is sensitive to both institutional and societal pressures, for example, from the Senate, the president, organized interests and public opinion. The nomination commanded attention and engendered controversy and not without reason. Because retiring Supreme Court Justice Lewis Powell had been a "swing vote," especially in abortion, privacy, church-state and affirmative action decisions, the incoming justice stood to tip the balance of a closely divided Court and play a major role in shaping the general direction of that Court for years to come.

It was this potential for redirection that spurred the concerns and apprehensions of blacks and numerous civil rights groups. They feared that the "conservative" Judge Bork would move the Court in the directions that would be harmful to their interests. And their concern was well founded given Judge Bork's overall record, including his prolific scholarly writings as well as his decisional stances as a member of the federal appellate bench. The concerns of blacks and civil rights interests, however, went much deeper. These groups remain acutely aware of the pivotal role that the Supreme Court can and has played—through the landmark *Brown* v. *Board of Education* and other decisions—in the fight to overcome racial segregation and discrimination. Newspaper columnist Carl Rowan stated succinctly why many blacks were opposed to the Bork nomination: "The overriding reality is that when this nation was caught up in racial conflict a quarter of a century ago, whenever the constitution chips were on the line, Robert Bork came down on the wrong side."[2] Thus for blacks and their allies, President Reagan's nomination of Judge Bork was no less than a call to arms, a call that in the end rallied sufficient forces to keep Judge Bork off the Supreme Court.

II. Seeds of Conflict

On June 26, 1987, Justice Lewis Powell announced the end to his 16-year tenure on the United States Supreme Court. Associate Justice Powell was a centrist; he had been the swing vote in several cases of special significance to African Americans. Five days after Justice Powell's resignation, on July 1, President Reagan nominated Court of Appeals Judge Robert H. Bork.

At first glance, giving deference to objective criteria, 60-year old Judge Bork appeared more than well qualified. Receiving his J.D. from the University of Chicago in 1953, Bork had two successful private practices, Chicago, 1955-1962 and Washington D.C., 1981-82; had served as a professor at Yale Law School, 1962-1975 and 1979-1981; as solicitor general for the U.S. Department of Justice, 1973-1977[3]; as acting U.S. attorney general, 1973-1974; and was, at the time of his nomination, a U.S. Court of Appeals judge for the District of Columbia.

But President Reagan had chosen Judge Bork for reasons beyond objective qualifications. Even a cursory review reveals starkly the similarities in ideology between Judge Bork and President Reagan. The Reagan agenda included a constitutional amendment to ban abortion; restoration of voluntary prayer in public school; an end to the use of mandatory busing for racial balancing in schools; abandonment of quotas and ratios as a remedy for racial injustice; the relaxation of certain judicial rules that strengthen the rights of the accused; and, the overall rechanneling of power from the federal government to state and local governments[4].

Similarly, Judge Bork had been assessed as committed to a "strict construction" of the Constitution, arguing that "the Constitution can be law only if it is applied as intended . . . only a philosophy of original intention is legitimate for judges."[5] Judge Bork was known to generally favor school prayer, the death penalty, and to assume a most permissive position on antitrust and mergers. Moreover, Judge Bork had argued against decisions restricting racial covenants on real estate and had suggested that the Court cannot give substantive meaning to an idea as broad as liberty and that the Court should not enforce that concept in the Fourteenth Amendment.[6] For example, in testimony before a Senate Judiciary subcommittee in 1981, Judge Bork criticized the Supreme Court's 1973 *Roe* v. *Wade* abortion decision as "an unconstitutional decision, a serious and wholly unjustifiable usurpation of state legislative authority."[7] In another example, in 1963—the same year as Martin Luther King's "I Have a Dream" speech—Bork wrote an article opposing passage of provisions of the 1964 Civil Rights Act that prohibited discrimination in public accommodations.[8] And writing in 1971, Judge Bork severely chastised the Warren Court for what he termed "judicial activism." Bork wrote:

> We have also damaged the law, and created disrespect for it, through our failure to observe the distinction, essential to democracy, between judges and legislators. The era of the Warren Court was, in my opinion, deeply harmful to the prestige of law . . . If that court did inspire the young, it taught them to confuse the desirability of ends with the legitimacy of means, perhaps to confuse the idea of law with the fact of power.[9]

On balance, the strong confluence in ideological positions between President Reagan and nominee Judge Bork served to enhance—if not promote—his initial selection by the president. But it was also these ideologies that served to ignite and kindle bitter opposition as well as staunch support for the nominee.

III. The Call to Arms

Immediately following President Reagan's announcement, several civil rights leaders condemned the nomination. For example, within an hour of the announcement, Ralph Neas, executive director of the Leadership Conference on Civil Rights (LCCR), and Benjamin L. Hooks, executive director of the NAACP and chairman of the LCCR, said that Bork was "an ultraconservative" who would "dramatically alter the balance of the Supreme Court, jeopardizing the civil rights achievements of the past 30 years. Well-established law could overnight be substantially eroded or overturned."[10]

But overall it was Senator Edward Kennedy (D-Massachusetts) who led the charge against Judge Bork. Kennedy's opposition to Judge Bork on the Senate floor, less than an hour after the nomination, was immediate and unequivocal. The Senator said: "Bork stands for an extremist view of the Constitution and a role of the Supreme Court that would have placed him outside the mainstream of American constitutional jurisprudence in the 1980s, let alone the 1990s."[11] And making his position even more direct, Senator Kennedy bluntly charged that, "Robert Bork's America is a land in which women would be forced into back-alley abortions, blacks would sit at segregated lunch counters, rogue police could break down citizens' doors in midnight raids, school children could not be taught about evolution . . . and the doors of the federal courts would be shut on the fingers of millions."[12]

Senate Judiciary Committee Chairman Joseph Biden Jr. (D-Delaware) also responded on the evening of the nomination: "I continue to have grave doubts about the nomination and expect it to cause a difficult and potentially contentious struggle in the Senate."[13]

In contrast to the sharp criticisms of President Reagan's announcement, Judge Bork's supporters hailed the nomination saying that it signaled a move away from recent laws based on judicial overreaching and on the improper stretching of the Constitution to accommodate "modern times and liberal interests."[14] For example, Representative Henry Hyde (R-Illinois)—an outspoken opponent of abortion—viewed the nomination as a "chance to change the direction of the court."[15] Republican Senator Paul Trible of Virginia called Bork "an extraordinary choice" and Senator Orrin Hatch (R-Utah) said Bork was "one of the brightest legal minds . . . one of the quintessential judges in this country."[16] Senator Hatch further warned that if the Democrats tried to "play politics" with the Bork nomination, their strategy would be unsuccessful both in the Senate and with the public.[17]

IV. Preparing for Battle—The Interim Days

Seven days after the nomination (July 8), Democrats on the Senate Judiciary Committee caucused and agreed on September 15 as a starting date for the committee hearings on Judge Bork. This delay in the start-up date did not sit well with Republicans. Indeed, Senate Minority Leader Robert Dole (R-Kansas) suggested that Republicans were "willing to work through the August recess to help expedite the confirmation process."[18] Nonetheless and despite Republican opposition, Committee Chairman Joseph Biden strategically scheduled the hearings to begin 11 weeks after the initial nomination and refused to set a closing date. After the caucus, Chairman Biden told reporters, "Quite frankly, it goes well beyond Judge Bork. It's a question of whether the Reagan-Meese agenda is going to be accomplished through the Court and whether Judge Bork has been picked to be the vehicle to accomplish that."[19]

The refusal of Senator Biden and other Democrats to expedite the hearings signaled the role and influence of party, committee rules, and committee chairmanship in the nomination process by affording the Democrats time to mobilize interests, raise needed lobbying finances, and strategically order the testimony of witnesses. And as was subsequently reported in the *New York Times*: "The strategic advantage that Democratic control of committee procedures gave to opponents was augmented by sometimes counterproductive efforts of Republican Senators to discredit witnesses . . . For example, Orrin Hatch . . ., Gordon Humphrey . . . and others kept prominent and articulate anti-Bork witnesses on the stand for hours with sometimes fumbling cross-examinations."[20]

During the weeks before the Judiciary Committee hearings were to begin, the tone was intensified by frequent and scathing speeches on the floor of the Senate and numerous press releases by both sides. For example, Senator Biden made an hour-long speech in the Senate vowing to defeat the nomination on the ground that Judge Bork would shift the Court in too conservative a direction. In response, Senator Alan Simpson (R-Wyoming) called Biden's speech a "vapid rationalization," stating: "If we are going to oppose the Bork nomination simply because Judge Bork has been nominated by a conservative Republican president, why don't we just come out and say so."[21]

Additionally, one of the nomination subplots, adding fuel to the growing controversy and contentious atmosphere, was the fact that several senators were also running for the presidency. These included Judiciary Committee Chairman Joseph Biden who stridently opposed the nomination and Senator Robert Dole who was "making his support of Judge Bork a centerpiece of his Presidential bid."[22] Also running for the presidency was Judiciary Committee member Paul Simon (D-Illinois). Thus, the confirmation hearings stood to shape not only the image of Judge Bork but also the images of the senators involved—senators whose performances could potentially reflect on their presidential campaigns.[23]

V. Choosing Sides: Senators, Interest Groups, and the Public

Chairman Biden's refusal to expedite the Judiciary Committee hearings set the stage for one of the most controversial and contentious confirmation battles in modern history—and the sides were drawn quickly. At one point, Senate Minority Leader Robert Dole accused Committee Chairman Biden of "stalling the nomination." Biden countered, charging that "Dole was being his typical, partisan cheap-shot self."[24] Anticipating the conflict ahead, several members of the Senate began to express concern that the Senate had become too polarized too fast: "The sides have been drawn very quickly," said John Breaux (D-Louisiana), "they didn't wait for the hearings."[25] This was the scenario presented to the pool of undecided in the Senate. As still undecided Senator Max Baucus (D-Montana) commented, "What it comes down to is whether Bork turns out to be too much of an extremist."[26]

However, well before the 14-member Senate Judiciary Committee hearings began, all but 3 Committee members had expressed their stance either formally or informally. Democrats predicted most likely to oppose Judge Bork included Joseph Biden, Edward Kennedy, Howard Metzenbaum (D-Ohio), Patrick Leahy (D-Vermont), Paul Simon, and Robert Byrd (D-West Virginia). Republicans believed most likely to support Judge Bork included Strom Thurmond, Orrin Hatch, Charles Grassley (R-Iowa), and Gordon Humphrey (R-New Hampshire).[27] Consequently, the balance of power in the Judiciary Committee would be determined by the undecided "fence sitters": conservative Democrats Dennis DeConcini (D-Arizona) and Howell Heflin (D-Alabama), and moderate Republican Arlen Specter (R-Pennsylvania).[28] When questioned on the nomination, Senator Heflin told reporters a week prior to the start of the Committee hearings, "I'm basically a conservative with conservative propensities, but I don't want a right-wing activist that would end up reversing the progress that has been made in many areas by the courts."[29] Another of the swing votes, Senator Specter, was a liberal Republican who had in the past voted against several of Reagan's judicial nominees. As reported by *Congressional Quarterly* in 1986, Senator Specter had the lowest presidential support score of any Republican, 31 percent.[30]

In addition to the few "undecided" on the committee, others throughout the Senate were not quite ready to take sides. They wanted to see how the hearings would develop and wanted more information before taking a position. Critical among these "undecided" were the southern Democrats and the moderate Republicans. For example, on the day of the nomination (July 1) Arkansas Democrat Dale Bumpers refused to take sides but commented, "Let's put it this way. He certainly wouldn't have been my first choice."[31] Repeatedly, the special dilemma for moderate Republicans and southern Democrats was a topic of debate and analysis throughout the entire Bork controversy. As analyzed by one observer:

> Conservatives are threatening to "primary" wavering Republicans: Either you vote to confirm Bork, or we will run a conservative against you in the Republican primary. . . . Southern Democrats face the same problem in reverse. If they vote to confirm Bork, they get in trouble with the party . . . Black voters can create problems for southern Democrats in the primaries. Even worse, northern Democrats can charge them with disloyalty to the party and take away cherished leadership positions in the Senate. On the other hand, if southern Democrats vote against Bork, they get in trouble in the general elections.[32]

However, more than senators were choosing sides. Indeed, one of the most striking aspects throughout the whole of the Bork conflict was the plethora of organized interests that were mobilized to participate in the confirmation battle. Only days after Reagan's nomination, the Senate was under intense pressure from a "multimillion-dollar" lobbying effort from those who supported as well as those who opposed the nomination.[33] As direct-mail consultant Roger Graves put it: "This is equivalent of Jim Watt wanting to flood the Grand Canyon."[34] For example, the People for the American Way launched a $2 million media campaign against Judge Bork while the National Conservative Political Action Committee spent well over $1 million in his defense.

Judge Bork's supporters, led by President Reagan and the White House staff, assembled an impressive number of conservative and/or New Right organizations including the Moral Majority, American Conservative Union, American Life League, Concerned Women for America, the Free Congress Foundation, and Phyllis Schlafly's Eagle Forum, which were augmented by the assistance of such conservative legal analysts as Bruce Fein, a former Justice Department official and Tom Korologos, a veteran Washington lobbyist hired by the White House to aid Judge Bork during the confirmation hearings.[35]

But opposing the nomination were an abundance of civil rights and civil liberties groups including the NAACP, the National Organization of Women, United Mine Workers, Common Cause, the Leadership Conference on Civil Rights, numerous local Bar Associations, and others.[36] The American Civil Liberties Union called Judge Bork "unfit" to serve on the high bench and the AFL-CIO promised a "no-holds-barred battle."[37] In fact, many of the opposition groups found their causes in direct contravention to Judge Bork's views. For example, Planned Parenthood Inc. sharply disagreed with Bork's views on the right to privacy and a right to abortion.

In another example, Common Cause, one of the nation's largest "nonpartisan" citizens' lobbies—noted for a tradition of not taking a position on presidential appointees for ideological reasons—publicly opposed Judge Bork the same day President Reagan announced the nomination, maintaining that its longstanding position on civil rights ran counter to Bork's record."[38] And on August 31, the American Civil Liberties Union (ACLU) abandoned its 51-year-old policy against involvement in Supreme Court confirmation battles to oppose Judge Bork's nomination. ACLU President Norman Dorsen told a news conference that Judge Bork was "not a conservative" but a "radical" espousing so limited a vision of the Court's role in protecting individual rights that the Court would "atrophy" if his views prevailed.[39]

Additionally, both sides had initiated grass-roots campaigns. For example, undecided Senator Terry Sanford (D-North Carolina) had received 1,080 letters on Bork before the Senate Judiciary Committee had begun—600 for and 480 opposed.[40]

However, irrespective of senators, organized interests, and grass-roots lobbying, a majority public opinion had not yet formed against Judge Bork. As revealed in a New York Times/CBS poll, Judge Bork was still unknown to nearly two-thirds of the public; another 15 percent were undecided about Judge Bork, and for those with an opinion, support was equal to opposition. But this opinion was measured prior to the formal committee hearings.[41]

VI. The Formal Hearings—The Judiciary Committee Testimony

Beginning on September 15, the Senate Judiciary Committee kept Judge Bork for an unprecedented five days and over 30 hours of testimony—no previous Supreme Court nominee had ever spent more than four days before the Committee. And it did not take long to see how the battle lines would develop. Opening statements from individual senators illuminated at the very outset the overall combative nature of the hearings. For the most part, initial debate consisted of Judge Bork's supporters and opponents clearly stating their positions. The opening statements were sharp and direct. Chairman Biden set the tone and justification for weighing Judge Bork's philosophy. Said Biden:

> A vote to confirm you requires, in my view, an endorsement of your basic philosophic views as they relate to the Constitution. And thus the Senate, in exercising its constitutional role of advice and consent, has not only the right, in my opinion, but the duty to weigh the philosophy of the nominee as it reaches its own independent decision.[42]

Following Chairman Biden's opening remarks was Senator Thurmond's warning that "Judge Bork's opponents will try to raise questions about his character and integrity. Failing this," said Senator Thurmond, "they will assert that he is disqualified by virtue of his philosophy, by labeling him an extremist or 'outside the mainstream' . . . Do we really want to enshrine, for all time, every decision the Court makes? . . . I believe the Court should be allowed to correct errors it has made."[43]

Senator Kennedy's opening statement countered, challenging that "Robert Bork falls short of what Americans demand of a man or woman as a Justice on the Supreme Court. Time and again, in his public record over more than a quarter of a century, Robert Bork has shown that he is hostile to the rule of law and the role of the courts in protecting individual liberty." Senator Kennedy charged, "It is easy to conclude from . . . Mr. Bork's published views that he believes women and blacks are second-class citizens under the Constitution. He believes that, in the relation to the executive, Members of Congress are second-class citizens, yet he is asking the Senate to confirm him."44 "In Bork's America," said Kennedy, "there is no room in the inn for Blacks and no place in the Constitution for women, and in our America, there should be no seat on the Supreme Court for Robert Bork."45 It was this latter comment that set the overall tone of the "case" against Bork and that in time came to serve as a constant refrain and rallying point for those who opposed the nomination.

Following the initial statements by each member of the committee, Judge Bork began his opening testimony by thanking President Reagan for placing his name in nomination. He then presented his concept on the role of a judge.

> My philosophy is neither liberal nor conservative, when a judge . . . reads entirely new values into the Constitution, values the framers and the ratifiers did not put there, he deprives the people of their liberty. That liberty, which the Constitution clearly envisions, is the liberty of the people to set their own social agenda through the processes of democracy.[46]

Overall, these opening statements set the stage for what soon developed into long and often bitter charges and counter-charges, spirited defenses, and sharp cross-examinations. Indeed, for five days, the committee questioned Judge Bork about a variety of critical issues including Judge Bork's respect for legal precedent; the privacy issue, sterilization and women's rights; poll taxes, literacy tests and the "one man, one vote" reapportionment formula; restrictive racial covenants; free speech and pornography; separation of church and state; the Equal Protection Clause, and so forth. As demonstrated by the excerpts below, the debate and testimony regarding voting rights and the privacy issue as well as Judge Bork's respect for precedent were among those especially charged on both sides.

On Abortion/Privacy. Even before the hearings began, Judge Bork had stridently criticized such cases as *Griswold v. Connecticut*, striking down a Connecticut law banning the use of contraceptives, and the *Roe v. Wade* abortion decision. For example, Judge Bork had stated that the desire of a "husband and wife to have sexual relations without unwanted children" was indistinguishable, for constitutional purposes, from the desire of an electric company to "void a smoke pollution ordinance." "The cases," said Judge Bork, "are identical."[47] Thus, the related issues of privacy and abortion generated controversial testimony throughout the hearings.

In one heated exchange during the hearings, Judge Bork said that there was no right of privacy in the Constitution and that judges cannot place a higher value on marital rights than on economic rights.[48] For example, Senator Biden asked Judge Bork directly: "Does a state legislative body, or any legislative body, have the right to pass a law telling a married couple . . . behind their bedroom door . . . they cannot use birth control? Does the majority have the right to tell a couple that they cannot use birth control?" Judge Bork responded, "I do not know what rationale the state would offer or what challenge the married couple would make . . . All I have done was to point out that the right of privacy, as defined or undefined by Justice Douglas, was a free-floating right that was not derived in a principled fashion from constitutional materials."[49]

Later, following additional questioning by Chairman Biden and more by Bork-defender Senator Alan Simpson, Judge Bork said he believed that there were "several crucial protections of privacy in the Bill of Rights." However, later when Senator Howell Heflin addressed the same theme, Judge Bork said "I do not have available a constitutional theory which would support a general defined right [of privacy] . . . and I can only say that if someone has a constitutional theory, I will listen attentively."[50]

On Reapportionment: One Man, One Vote. Judge Bork was also sharply questioned throughout the hearings about the Supreme Court's decisions in voting rights and reapportionment cases. These concerns were seemingly well based given Judge Bork's widely publicized criticisms of *Baker* v. *Carr*, *Reynolds* v. *Sims*, and other voting rights cases. For example, in 1972, Judge Bork wrote that in *Katzenbach* v. *Morgan*[51] the Supreme Court was wrong in upholding provisions of the 1965 Voting Rights Act that banned literacy tests under certain circumstances.[52] In 1981, Judge Bork called the decisions in *Katzenbach* and *Oregon* v. *Mitchell*,[53] which upheld a national ban on literacy tests, "very bad, indeed pernicious, constitutional law."[54] Indeed, in an interview just weeks before his nomination to the Supreme Court, on June 10, 1987, Judge Bork stated:

> I think [the] Court stepped beyond its allowable boundaries when it imposed one man, one vote under the Equal Protection Clause. That is not consistent with American political history, American political theory, with anything in the history or the structure or the language of the Constitution.[55]

Senator Kennedy repeatedly challenged Judge Bork to clarify his position regarding these cases. Note the following:

> Kennedy: Well, I must say that you have indicated that position that you have expressed here on many different occasions. You said in 1973 before the Congress one man, one vote was too much of a straitjacket and that you, quote, "did not think that there is a theoretical basis for it." And then you indicated on June 10th of this year, you said in an interview, "Well, I think this Court stepped beyond its allowable boundaries when it imposed one man, one vote under the equal protection clause."
>
> Bork: Well, Senator, if the people of this country accept one man, one vote, that is fine. They can enact it any time they want to. I have no desire to go running around trying to overturn that decision. But as an original matter, it does not come out of anything in the Constitution and if the people of the country want it, they can adopt that apportionment any time they want to.

On Judicial Precedent. Throughout the hearings, senators questioned Judge Bork on his believed willingness to overturn past Supreme Court rulings. Near the end of the fourth day of testimony, in a rather dramatic effort, Senator Kennedy played a tape recording of a remark made two years earlier (1985) by Judge Bork. Bork stated in part: "I don't think that in the field of constitutional law, precedent is all that important . . . If you become convinced that a prior court has misread the Constitution, I think it's your duty to go back and correct it."[56] After playing the tape, Kennedy challenged the nominee: "In light of what we have just heard, how can anyone have confidence that you will respect the decisions of the Supreme Court . . ."[57] Judge Bork countered calling the recording an "off-the-cuff remark" and "not the kind of thing that ought to be weighed against my more considered statements."[58] But Senator Kennedy was not convinced and summed up his position by referring to Judge Bork as a "walking constitutional amendment [who] should not be confirmed by the Senate."[59]

In yet another sharp exchange, Democratic Senator Howard Metzenbaum told Judge Bork: "You are not a frightening man, but you are a man with frightening views . . . The basic problem, as I see it, is that to you, the Constitution is not a living document; it is not a charter of liberty . . . And if you cannot find protection for the individual in the fine print, then the people of this country are out of luck." Senator Metzenbaum then concluded, "You have stated views time and time again that would reverse progress for blacks, that would slam the door on women, that would allow government in the bedroom, that would adversely affect the rights of consumers, that would limit free speech, that would undercut the principles of equality under the law."[60] Clearly irritated, Judge Bork responded in part, "I think there is no basis for the concern you describe among women and blacks, and I regret to say I think there is no basis for the charges you have leveled at me."[61]

The final session of Judge Bork's testimony before the Judiciary Committee was highlighted by more than an hour-long dialogue between Judge Bork and the still undecided Republican Senator Arlen Specter. Senator Specter questioned Judge Bork on a number of issues, for example, sexual morality, privacy, speech, pornography, and religion, in an attempt to clarify what the senator viewed as inconsistencies and/or recantations. Note the following:

> Senator Specter: Judge Bork, I have not made up my mind on the confirmation process as of this moment. At the outset, I was very concerned about what I considered to be a sharp variance in your writings as opposed to the tradition of U.S. constitutional jurisprudence. You have made significant shifts in accordance with this testimony which I think, candidly, has to be evaluated. We don't expect a man to be in concrete on his thinking, and I understand that what you had written in the past was speculative and tentative and I respect that.
>
> Judge Bork: Senator, may I say just one word? I agree with you a great deal of what you say, I just want to talk about—you talk about significant shifts. I really haven't shifted that much. I have told you where I have changed my mind, explicitly political speech, and so forth.[62]

Judge Bork concluded his long days as a witness by reiterating a comment made at the outset of his testimony. "I will adhere to my judicial philosophy . . . I am a jurist who believes his role is to interpret the law and not make the law."[63] But this reiteration did little to clarify the situation. Indeed, after five days of testimony, the principal questions that now evolved concerned which of Bork's views—those he had expressed over many years and evidenced in his legal writings, or his more moderate statements during the hearings—were representative of his judicial philosophy.[64] In one exchange, for example, undecided Senator Heflin stated: "I wish I was a psychiatrist rather than a lawyer and member of this committee to try and figure out what you would do if you get on the Supreme Court." Senator Heflin maintained, "Well, now there are those that raise the issue that your changing your position and sort of renouncing of your positions on certain positions came only at a time when a carrot was in effect, being dangled before your eyes; and, . . . that you changed your mind on certain writings when you knew that you would have to come up and face questioning before a Senate panel on confirmation . . ." Replied Judge Bork: "I can assure you that is not the way I operate, never have."[65]

It was at this critical period—near the end of Judge Bork's testimony—that public opinion polls suggested Judge Bork was losing ground with the public. A *New York Times/CBS* poll conducted September 21 to 22 (during Bork's testimony) revealed 26 percent of those questioned had an unfavorable view of Judge Bork while only 16 percent had a favorable view. When the same question was asked earlier on September 9 to 10—before Judge Bork's televised testimony began—only 12 percent said they had an unfavorable opinion of Bork, and 11 percent had a favorable opinion.[66] Following Judge Bork's testimony, on September 26, a *Wall Street Journal/NBC* poll found 42 percent opposed to Bork and only 34 percent in favor, and a *Washington Post/ABC* poll showed 48 percent opposing Judge Bork and 44 percent supporting him.[67]

In yet another example, a Harris Survey released on September 28 revealed that the "American People" opposed the Bork nomination 57 percent to 29 percent. Significantly, among those who said they saw the hearings on TV or who followed them closely in the newspapers, a higher 61 percent to 32 percent majority opposed Judge Bork's confirmation.[68] Given the nature of electoral politics and the importance of "going public" in American politics generally, it seems clear that these polls undoubtedly had some impact on the eventual outcome of the Bork confirmation controversy.

The situation in the South was particularly affected by such polls. For example, a Roper Organization poll of 12 southern states published in the *Atlanta Constitution* showed 51 percent of respondents against Judge Bork and only 31 percent for him. Even southerners who described themselves as "conservative" opposed Judge Bork 44 percent to 39 percent.[69] Undecided Democrat John B. Breaux of Louisiana, in response to a growing opposition to Judge Bork among his constituency, told the *Washington Post* that if he voted to confirm Judge Bork, "I better have a hell of a good reason."[70] In another example, Senator Wendell Ford of Kentucky stated that "I think the whole block of southern Democrats is moving against him a little . . . just like the public seems to be moving against him."[71] Clearly, senators' attention to public opinion polls signaled concern about possible political fallout from the Bork vote. This fallout could be especially costly in the South, particularly in those states where the black vote can prove determinative in state-wide elections. But as we shall see, more than opinion polls were exerting influence on undecided senators; a host of witnesses attempted to affect the Senate as well.

VII. A Parade of Witnesses

After an unprecedented five days of testimony and questioning of Judge Bork, the committee was ready to begin the second stage of its formal hearings—testimony from a parade of some 120 witnesses either supporting or opposing Judge Bork's confirmation.

Those testifying in support of Judge Bork included Edward H. Levi, attorney general under President Ford, and William French Smith, attorney general under President Reagan. Former Attorney General Levi, for example, characterized Judge Bork as having an "inquiring and powerful mind." Similarly, William Smith described Judge Bork as "an able person of honor, kindness, fairness" and as one who "cares about our society and cares about people . . . a highly distinguished, fair-minded jurist and scholar of the highest professional integrity," with "all the earmarks of a great Supreme Court Justice"[72]

Support for Judge Bork also included testimony by former Chief Justice Warren E. Burger and Lloyd Cutler, a leading Washington lawyer. Burger called Judge Bork as "well qualified as any Supreme Court nominee in the past half-century" and condemned what he viewed as "a campaign of disinformation" by Bork opponents. "If Judge Bork isn't in the mainstream," said Burger, "neither am I."[73] Similarly, former White House Counsel Cutler referred to Judge Bork as "a highly qualified conservative jurist who is closer to the moderate center than to the extreme right."[74] Said Cutler:

> On the whole, I think he [Bork] would come much closer as a sitting Justice, if he is confirmed, to a Justice like Justice Powell and Justice Stevens—and I remind you that is precisely what Justice Stevens himself said, that "you will find in Judge Bork's opinions and philosophy similar to that you will see in the opinions of Justice Stewart, Justice Powell, and some of the things that I . . . have written."[75]

Also, Judge Griffin Bell, attorney general during the Carter administration, was among a number of prominent Democrats testifying in support of Judge Bork. Bell said, "I like to see a man go to the Court who is going to be his own judge, be his own man, and I think that is the way it is going to turn out."[76]

In an obvious attempt to rebut particular criticisms, Carla Hills, secretary of housing and urban development under the Ford administration and head of the civil division in the Department of Justice when Judge Bork was solicitor general, testified that she was "startled and saddened" by the "vociferous opposition" and stated there was not a "a scintilla of evidence" that Judge Bork was opposed to the equality of women.[77] In response, Senator Orrin Hatch was quick to extol Mrs. Hills's testimony and suggested that "Women ought to pay attention to you instead of the extreme misrepresentations put out by special interest groups."[78]

Though most black leaders opposed Judge Bork, a few did come to his support. For example, Thomas Sowell, a noted conservative economist and senior fellow at the Hoover Institute, testified that he had publicly urged that Judge Bork be nominated to replace retiring Justice Potter Stewart and again as a replacement for retiring Chief Justice Warren Burger. Sowell continued: "So I'm, of course, heartened to see him nominated now, though I'm disheartened to see the confused, hysterical, and even dishonest terms in which that nomination is too often discussed in the media and elsewhere."[79] Additionally, the final day of testimony, September 30, included a visceral defense of Judge Bork by Roy Innis, chairman of the Congress on Racial Equality (CORE). Innis praised the nominee, suggesting that "Judge Bork's presence on the Supreme Court can contribute mightily to the efforts to confront and mitigate one of the most pressing problems facing Black America today—urban crime. . . . Judge Bork's firm approach to criminal law is a matter that should be of interest to the civil rights community, for crime preys most savagely on the poor of our major urban centers."[80] Innis was also critical of those opposing the nomination. Consider the following excerpts from Innis' prepared statement:

> Judge Robert H. Bork has been roundly attacked by my colleagues . . . The tragedy of this misguided view is that this desire for an activist judiciary clearly shows how out of touch much of the civil rights movement is with the problems facing black Americans in the 1980s . . . Reliance on the Supreme Court to solve these problems is both foolish and sad.
>
> I believe black Americans . . . will be best served by courts staffed by judges who will apply the laws with honesty, impartiality, and fairness . . . for this reason . . . I strongly support . . . Judge Bork.[81]

But opposition to the Bork nomination was strong and seemingly well planned. Among those testifying against Judge Bork were Nicholas Katzenbach, who served as attorney general under President Johnson; Burke Marshall, professor of law at Yale University who had headed the Justice Department's civil rights division under President Kennedy; and Harvard law professor Laurence Tribe. Their testimony was especially critical of Judge Bork. For example, Marshall stated, "It appears to me that at every turning point in the past quarter-century on which there was still room for disagreement, Judge Bork favored positions that did harm to minorities." Similarly, Professor Tribe suggested that Judge Bork's approach to discrimination cases amounted to little more than "a dream and a prayer and a blank check."[82]

Judge Bork's nomination was also vigorously opposed by a host of black leaders and the civil rights community in general. Among those black leaders testifying in opposition to Judge Bork were William Coleman, transportation secretary under President Ford; Barbara Jordan, former Democratic representative from Texas (1973-1979); and Mayor Andrew Young, former U.S. ambassador and currently mayor of Atlanta, Georgia. On the whole, their testimony charged that Judge Bork's personal views and "restrictive approach to constitutional rights" posed a risk to racial justice and the rights of women and minorities.[83] But it was the testimony of William Coleman, not only a former cabinet member but also a highly respected jurist, that captured the attention and interest of the committee. Said Coleman:

> "I have tried very hard to avoid this controversy. The Supreme Court has played such an important role in ending so many of the horribly racially discriminatory practices that existed when I came to the Bar. As one who has benefitted so greatly from this country's difficult but steady march toward a free, fair, and open society, the handwriting on the wall—"mene mene tekel upharsin"—would condemn my failure to testify against Judge Bork.[84]
>
> I urge this committee not to send this nomination to the floor of the Senate with its approval; if it does go to the floor, I urge the Senate not to give its consent."[85]

And though Coleman's—as well as Andrew Young's testimony—are certainly worthy of more extensive review, it was Barbara Jordan's comments that strikingly illustrate the high stakes for African Americans in the Bork confirmation controversy. As Jordan stated:

> My opposition to this nomination is really a result of living 51 years as a Black American born in the South and determined to be heard by the majority community . . . When you experience the frustration of being in a minority position and watching the foreclosure of your last appeal and then suddenly you are rescued by the Supreme Court of the United States, Mr. Chairman, that is tantamount to be being born again . . . In 1962 . . . I filed for the election to the Texas House of Representatives . . . I lost . . . [I]n 1964, I ran again for membership in the House of Representatives . . . I lost . . . The Texas legislature was so malapportioned that just a handful of people were electing a majority of the legislature . . . I was dispirited. But something happened. A decision was handed down: *Baker* v. *Carr* . . . In 1966, I won . . . Do you know what Judge Bork says about those cases on reapportionment? He has disagreed with the principle of one person one vote many times.[86]

Other black leaders also testified against Judge Bork. Duke University Professor Emeritus Dr. John Hope Franklin, for example, recounted for the committee his "degradation and humiliation" as a seven-year-old child in the South when a train conductor "stopped the train and put us out in the woods" because his mother had "refused to go to the Negro coach." Said Franklin, "Nothing in Judge Bork's record suggests to me that, had he been on the Supreme Court at an earlier date, he would have had the vision and the courage to strike down a statute requiring the eviction of a black family from a train for sitting in the so-called white coach; or the rejection of a black student at a so-called white state university; or the refusal of a white restaurant owner to serve a black patron."[87]

On the final day of the hearings, Judge Bork's opponents released the names of 1,925 law school professors (representing 40 percent of the

Against Bork. The case study indicates that though most black leaders opposed the Bork nomination, it was the testimony of former Texas Congresswoman Barbara Jordan that most strikingly captured the reasons for that opposition. *(AP/Wide World Photos)*

full-time law faculty of the American Bar Association-accredited law schools in the United States), urging the Senate to defeat the nomination.[88] Still not all the fireworks were confined to Capitol Hill. Indeed many battles were played out at the White House and across the nation.

VIII. Away from Capitol Hill

At the White House. Throughout the battle, President Reagan continued to press for the confirmation of Judge Bork. From the outset, the White House strategy had been to depict Judge Bork as a moderate, as a mainstream conservative nominee, and to distance the whole effort from right-wing support. By the eleventh day of the Judiciary Committee hearings, however, the president launched a counterattack to the perceived increasing opposition to Judge Bork. Speaking to a meeting of the Concerned Women for America, President Reagan stated: "It's clear now that the charges that Robert Bork is too ideological are themselves ideologically inspired, and that the criticism of him as outside the mainstream can only be held by those who are themselves so far outside the mainstream that they've long ago lost sight of the moderate center."[89] Reagan's statements, coupled with several White House press releases, signaled the administration's growing concern of the increasingly mobilized opposition to Judge Bork. "Right now, we're losing the public relations battle," said one White House strategist. "All the little groupies are out there . . . this has turned into a political campaign."[90] Thus, the White House began to pull out all the stops. As one senior White House official stated, "We tried to present the issues in a dignified way, and it just didn't work. So now it's time to fight fire with fire."[91]

Consider the following paid telephone communication which was sent out across the nation:

> Senator Humphrey: Hello, this is Senator Gordon Humphrey. In my role as Honorary Chairman of the National Conservative Political Action Committee, I decided to speak to you by tele-computer because of the urgent need for citizens to rally behind the President. President Reagan needs your support in his effort to have Judge Robert Bork confirmed to the United States Supreme Court.
>
> Please hold for an important message from President Reagan.
>
> President Reagan: Judge Bork deserves a careful highly civil examination of his record, but he has been subjected to a constant litany of character assassination and intentional misrepresentation. Tell your Senators to resist the politicization of our court system. Tell them you support the appointment of Judge Bork . . .
>
> Announcer: And, if at all possible please consider making a contribution to help with this important battle . . . tell me your name . . . telephone number . . . so that one of our volunteers can contact you.[92]

Across the Nation. Although the committee hearings and Senate debates were televised in their entirety over the Cable News Network, public television, or C-SPAN, most Americans received their information from 30-second spots televised on the major networks' evening news programs. Mass media campaigns including television and newspaper advertisements as well as direct mail and other tactics of modern day interest-group politics were employed effectively against the Bork nomination in unprecedented fashion. One of the most noted examples was a television advertisement narrated by Gregory Peck which told viewers that

> Robert Bork wants to be a Supreme Court Justice. But the record shows he has a strange idea of what justice is. He defended poll taxes and literacy tests which keep many Americans from voting. He opposed the civil rights law that ended "white only" signs at lunch counters. He doesn't believe the Constitution protects your right to privacy. And he thinks that freedom of speech does not apply to literature and art and music.[93]

As such, the protracted confirmation battle had moved from the crucible of the Senate to the television and radio airwaves requiring additional and unprecedented strategies and resources.

IX. The Decision: The Judiciary Committee Rejects Judge Bork

As the hearings concluded, lawmakers on both sides continued to prepare for the final vote. President Reagan called the Bork nomination his "top domestic priority" and held private "arm-twisting" sessions with undecided senators and again urged the public to "[T]ell your Senators to resist the politicization of the court system."[94] At the same time opponents continued making phone calls keeping pressure on wavering senators.

Overall, it was clear that the Bork confirmation was continuing to lose ground. This was vividly reflected in a speech made by President Reagan in the Rose Garden at a ceremony marking German-American Day (October 2). President Reagan asserted that Judge Bork had "an outstanding record on civil rights," and added: "Those who have been distorting his record have said . . . he's going to turn back the clock on civil rights. It's amazing they can find a room big enough for them to get in front of the cameras, their noses must be so long by now." The president also attacked the "special interests" that had opposed Bork. Reagan added that "special interests are determined to pack the Supreme Court." "Their aim," said the president, "is to get through the courts what they can't get at the ballot box."[95] Interestingly, however, those who opposed Judge Bork claimed that it was Reagan's very nomination of Judge Bork that was in fact the attempt of a lame duck president to get through the courts what he could not get through the legislature. Nonetheless the president held fast to his position. On October 3, for example, President Reagan charged that "liberal interest groups seek to politicize the court system, [and] to exercise a chilling effect on judges to intimidate them into making decisions not on the basis of the law or the merits of the case but on the basis of a litmus test or a response to political pressure."96

Despite such intensive public and private lobbying efforts by President Reagan, just three days later (on October 6) the Judiciary Committee voted 9-5 to send Judge Bork's name to the full Senate with a recommendation that the nomination be rejected. Significantly, the crucial Judiciary Committee votes to reject Judge Bork were cast by the previously "undecided" senators; that is, Democratic Senators DeConcini and Heflin and Republican Senator Specter. Additionally, just days before the Committee vote, southern Democrats had begun to abandon the president's nomination. Speaking on the Senate floor on October 1, for example, Terry Sanford (D-North Carolina) was the first of the freshman southern Democrats to declare his opposition, followed by others like John Breaux and Bennett Johnson (Louisiana), Richard Shelby (Alabama), Bob Graham (Florida), Wyche Fowler (Georgia), John D. Rockefeller IV (West Virginia), and Lloyd Bentsen (Texas). Overall, the arguments cited by these southern senators focused on Judge Bork's views on civil rights and privacy and a desire not to "reopen old wounds and reconsider decisions that had been accepted in practice." Senator Sanford further commented, "In the course of his public life Robert Bork had been a socialist, a libertarian, a conservative, and now, most recently, a moderate. There is no way to predict what he will be as a member of the Supreme Court."[97]

The nine-member committee majority report summarized their position by stating that Judge Bork would threaten the important role of the Supreme Court in serving as "the ultimate bulwark of protection when the majority has attempted to impose its preference upon the fundamental principles of the Constitution—when it has attempted, in other words, to channel the force of government to override the rights of the individual."[98] The majority report stated:

> [Bork's] jurisprudence fails to incorporate the ennobling concepts of the Constitution. It is thus fundamentally at odds with the express understanding of the Framers and with the history of the Supreme Court in building our tradition of constitutionalism.[99]

But the five-member minority—all Republicans—were just as strong in their support of Judge Bork and their opposition to the committee report. The minority report insisted that "despite sloganeering and misrepresentations to the contrary," Judge Bork's testimony before the Judiciary Committee "place[d] him well within the conservative mainstream of American jurisprudence" and that "the major criticisms leveled at Judge Bork are the result of misunderstandings by his critics."[100] The minority report concluded:

> The failure of the Senate to confirm him [Bork] will be a failure larger than simply denying one qualified nominee a place on the Court. It will be a disservice to the process by rewarding those who have turned the nominating process into a negative campaign of distortions; it will be a disservice to the judiciary of this country who should not be forced to endure such a politicized process; and most importantly, it will be a disservice to the American people, who not only will be denied the service of this intellect on the Court, but will also see the judiciary have its independence threatened by activist special interest groups.[101]

Moreover, both minority members and Judge Bork were bitterly critical of the overall atmosphere in which the nomination battle was being fought, leading Senator Orrin Hatch to charge that those opposed to Judge Bork had converted the confirmation battle into "a freak sideshow."[102]

X. Judge Bork and the President Respond

Only a few days after being rejected by the Judiciary Committee, on October 9, Judge Bork openly declared that he would not ask the president to withdraw his nomination and said he was determined to have a "full debate and a final Senate decision." Though admitting that he held "no illusions" concerning his chances in the Senate, Judge Bork asserted that "a crucial principle was at stake" because opponents had "transformed the process into a political campaign that endangered the judicial system." "Federal judges are not appointed to decide cases according to the latest opinion polls," and when judicial nominees "are treated like political candidates . . . the effect will be to erode public confidence and endanger the independence of the judiciary," said Judge Bork.[103] Further, Judge Bork stated that if he withdrew, the "public campaign of distortions" against him "would be seen as a success, and would be mounted against future nominees."[104] But the judge's comments, however, seemed only to exacerbate the situation and increase the mounting tally of undecided senators opposed to his nomination. "Talk about arrogance," said Senator Dale Bumpers (D-Arkansas) of Judge Bork's remarks, "[W]hen you win around here, it's a great victory for the American people; when you lose, it's a lynch-mob mentality."[105]

Like Judge Bork, however, President Reagan also indicated his determination to fight to the very end. Indeed, soon after the committee vote, President Reagan made a stinging speech from the Oval Office, which the commercial networks chose not to broadcast, in an attempt to revitalize support for Judge Bork. President Reagan berated the tactics of opponents and angrily proclaimed that his next nominee (should Judge Bork not be confirmed) would "upset the Democrats just as much." The President charged that Bork's opponents had made the confirmation process an "ugly spectacle marred by distortions and innuendos and casting aside the normal rules of decency and honesty."[106]

But similar to Judge Bork, the President's comments also served to intensify the controversy. For example, Senator Terry Sanford (D-North Carolina) delivered the Democratic response to Reagan's speech and said that "[T]o suggest that [senators] have been swayed by anything but conscientious intellect is slanderous." Sanford further charged that it had been the president, not the Senate, who had politicized the confirmation process. "We are tired of having our integrity impugned . . . we are tired of having our sincerity questioned. We are tired of having our intelligence insulted. . . . The Senators who are voting for Judge Bork have no monopoly on honesty."[107] Others were equally harsh in their criticisms of the president's comments, including swing vote Senator DeConcini who called Reagan's speech "shameful, [and] an embarrassment for the president." Senator DeConcini further warned that Judge Bork's insistence on a Senate vote was a "big mistake." "[T]he President has really opened himself in the worst light."[108]

XI. The Full Senate Acts: Debate and Decision

On October 21, the Bork nomination went to the full Senate. But well before the final debates it seemed clear that the confirmation was doomed to defeat. Said Senator Byrd at the start of the session, "I do not think we ought to spend a lot of time on the Bork nomination. I think it is beating a dead horse. It is not going anywhere."[109] But Judge Bork's supporters were not ready to give up. Despite the bleak outlook, they at best hoped to portray his opponents as "abusers of the confirmation process," thus perhaps making it easier for the next nominee. As suggested by Bork supporter Phil Gramm (R-Texas), a tough floor debate would "put the facts before the American people and spare another good person some of the pain of the treatment Bork received."[110] Thus, what was termed a "debate" was actually a succession of speeches for over 23 hours by senators from each camp. In the main, Judge Bork's supporters focused on events outside the Senate while opponents focused more closely on the 12 days of Judiciary Committee hearings. Critical of Judge Bork's opponents' tactics, William Armstrong (R-Colorado) asserted that concentration on occurrences outside the Senate were appropriate because of a "deliberate, calculated strategy to move the focus of the debate out of this chamber, out of the Senate, into the public arena"; however, "what is not proper is the vicious personal nature of that attack [on Bork] and the untruthfulness of it."[111]

One of the most bitter attacks against Judge Bork's opponents was delivered by Senator Orrin Hatch. Hatch asserted that the nomination had been conducted like a "major political campaign," characterized by "distorted newspaper ads, erroneous radio commercials, 30 second TV smear campaigns, misleading appeals . . . dishonest polls . . . and deceptive direct mail solicitation. . . ." Further, Hatch dramatically held up enlarged mounted copies of several full-page newspaper ads insisting that the ads "were a campaign of ridicule" that "mischaracterize, misconstrue and mislead." "The Bork nomination has become a bruising political wrestling match, ultimately decided by political muscle in the form of lobbying strength, media attacks, fundraising, and majority party solidarity," said Senator Hatch.[112] At one point Senator Hatch even lambasted the Senate Judiciary Committee Report as "a very, very poor job," "grossly slanted," filled with "flaws and inaccuracies." And Senator Hatch responded to an objection by Senator Biden by saying that he would be "more than happy to debate any one of these points anytime, anyplace, anywhere."[113] Other Bork supporters similarly ridiculed the opposition. Senator Charles Grassley (R-Iowa) claimed Judge Bork's opponents spent "millions to smear an American citizen"; Senator Steve Symms (R-Idaho) accused "liberal propagandists" of engaging in "character assassination"; and Senator Gordon Humphrey (R-New Hampshire) called Judge Bork's opponents "a dozen clamoring special interest groups with selfish agendas screaming for Judge Bork's scalp."[114]

Some senators were even more directly critical of their fellow colleagues. Senator Malcolm Wallop (R-Wyoming), for example, charged that "the [Judiciary] committee started with a conclusion and came to a justification." And in an hour-long speech staunchly defending the nomination, Senator John Danforth (R-Missouri) charged that Judge Bork had been "trashed in our house . . . [and] some of us helped to generate the trash. Some of us yielded to it. But all of us have been accomplices to it."[115] Senate Judiciary Committee Chairman Biden responded sharply to Danforth's charges calling them "one heck of an indictment of your colleagues" in the Senate.[116]

However, Chairman Biden and others opposing the confirmation had tallied the preliminary votes and sensed victory. Thus for Judge Bork's opponents the debates were in the main pro forma. Even so, those who did speak continued to beat away at what they considered an "ideologically unfit" nominee. Senator Edward Kennedy, for example, reiterated once more his position that "Bork's constitution contains no real right to privacy for individuals against Government intrusion, no real protection for women against sex discrimination, no real support for civil rights, and no real limit on presidential power."[117] Kennedy's comments were sharp and direct:

> From the purchase of a home, to the ballot box, to the job site, to the indignity of "whites only" signs in public places, to the schools of the Nation's Capital, Robert Bork has made a career of opposing simple justice, and he does not deserve a new career on the Supreme Court of the United States."[118]

Senator Hatch immediately responded to Kennedy's remarks by calling them "wholly imaginary—an absurd bad dream."[119]

Additionally, "swing vote" Senator Arlen Specter defended the quality of the Judiciary Committee's hearings, saying that the "hearings established a proper and meaningful evaluation of a nominee's views . . ." Decidedly, Senator Specter maintained that he would vote against confirmation because of "substantial doubt" that Judge Bork would "apply fundamental principles of constitutional law." Said Senator Specter:

> I am troubled by his [Bork's] writings that unless there is adherence to original intent, there is no judicial legitimacy; and without such legitimacy, there can be no judicial review. This approach could jeopardize the most fundamental principle of U.S. constitutional law—the supremacy of judicial review.[120]

Although others continued to offer comments and reactions throughout the three days of floor debate, there is no evidence to suggest that any votes were changed or even decided during this time. And so, on October 23, 115 days after the nomination, Judge Bork was rejected by the full Senate by an unprecedented margin of 16 votes, 42 in favor and 58 against confirmation. The negative tally against Judge Bork was larger than either the Haynsworth (1969) or Carswell (1970) rejections. In the words of the chamber's presiding officer, "The nomination is not confirmed . . . the President is to be notified of the Senate's action." Six Republicans-Chafee (Rhode Island); Packwood (Oregon); Specter (Pennsylvania); Stafford (Vermont); Warner (West Virginia); and Weicker (Connecticut)-joined with the 52 Democrats (including all but one Southern Democrat) in voting against Judge Bork. Two Democrats, Hollings (South Carolina) and Boren (Oklahoma) joined the 40 Republicans who voted in his favor. Overall, Judge Bork lost both a crucial group of moderate northern Republicans and southern Democrats, making him the twenty-seventh U.S. Supreme Court nominee to fail but only the fourth to be voted down by the full Senate this century.

XII. The Battle in Perspective: Lessons and Observations

Several lessons or observations with respect to black politics may be drawn from the Bork nomination controversy.

1. Blacks used their recently increased voting strength not only to elect political candidates but also to influence and pressure elected officials to promote and support policy goals and preferences.

In broad strokes, the Bork nomination pitted President Reagan and judicial conservatives, who believed that Judge Bork would help turn the court away from "inappropriate judicial activism," against an assortment of liberal and civil rights groups—including many African Americans—suspicious that Judge Bork would work to undo significant precedents of the last three decades.

Perhaps more than any other single component, the defeat of Robert Bork can be attributed to the dawning and increasing political power of blacks—particularly in the South.[121] Since 1954, African Americans in particular have looked to the courts to intercede when states have attacked their freedoms, to shield them from unfavorable public opinions and majorities, from legislatures unwilling to act and presidents less than dedicated to upholding the constitutional rights of blacks and other minorities.

When reviewed in perspective, the "new black voter" played a crucial role in influencing the votes of senators, especially southern senators, on the Bork nomination. In the 1966 congressional election, fewer than 4.5 million blacks voted nationally; by 1986, that figure was more than 8.2 million with a vast percentage of the increase in the

South.[122] It is less than coincidence that a good portion of this increase can be attributed to the 1965 Voting Rights Act—several parts of which Judge Bork had harshly criticized.

The black vote played a key and determinative role in the 1986 elections that converted a 53-47 Republican majority in the Senate into a 54-46 Democratic one. Democrats retained a seat in Louisiana left open by Russell Long's retirement and gained seats in Alabama, Florida, Georgia, and North Carolina that Republicans had won in Reagan's first election in 1980. Without question, the balance of power in each of these Senate races was exercised by black voters. For example, Senator John Breaux of Louisiana got only 40 percent of the white vote in 1986 but won some 90 percent of the black vote. And Breaux was quite mindful of the influence of black voters. "Those who helped us get elected—the black voters . . . are united in their opposition to Bork, and don't think for a moment that we are going to ignore that."[123]

Yet, the votes by southern senators evidence more than the significance of increased black voting power in their home states. They also reflect uniquely that Supreme Court rulings such as those in *Baker* v. *Carr*[124], *South Carolina* v. *Katzenbach*[125] and other voting rights decisions which sought to protect the franchise for blacks and other groups have also empowered these very groups to shape the complexion of the Court itself by forging a Senate majority capable of rejecting a nominee perceived hostile to such judicial decisions.

Overall, the influence blacks exercised over southern senators serves as a good example of the interdependence of law, politics, and the Court. Combined with other political actors, blacks helped to shape the direction and nature of constitutional law, as well as the institution of the Supreme Court itself.

2. Blacks joined with other groups to form a meaningful coalition which maximized their influence in the American political system in order to promote or retard policy and/or institutional changes.

Overall, the importance of blacks joining with other groups to achieve political objectives cannot be overemphasized. Group unity and collective action are both fundamental and necessary in pluralistic democratic societies. The defeat of Robert Bork was in large measure the result of the collective efforts of blacks, women, Jews, civil libertarians, and others. The lesson to be learned is this: Although organizations are expected to further the interests of their members, they may also further the interests of broad categories of nonmembers in the process.[126] The potential for black political progress in the future could well depend on maintaining and developing these emerging, though unstable, coalitions.

But this situation is tenuous at best. Indeed, for some time, studies have suggested that blacks are the most distinctively liberal group in American politics and society. For example, virtually all blacks agree that they would vote for a well-qualified black presidential candidate. Yet some 35 percent of whites surveyed by the Gallup organization reported that a white candidate was more likely to be "intelligent" or to have "good judgment in a crisis"; and roughly 20 percent reported they would not vote for a black presidential candidate regardless of "qualification."[127] Additionally, most blacks think they should have a right to live anywhere they can afford and believe black and white children should go to the same schools. And while for many of these broad principles whites have reached a similar level of support, whites continue to demonstrate considerably less support for the implementation of these principles than blacks. For example, an average of about 85 percent of blacks favor federal intervention to ensure fair treatment in jobs while figures for whites are in the 36 percent to 39 percent range.[128] This suggests that on issues of voting, political candidate selection, and policy implementation, blacks and other groups may find it difficult to join into meaningful working coalitions. Under such circumstances, blacks may need to resort to more immediate and dramatic strategies and tactics than other groups may be willing to support.

3. Because party affiliation remains an important index to voting behavior, the Bork confirmation battle demonstrates clearly that blacks gained from their overwhelming support of and allegiance to the Democratic party.

It is difficult to ignore that after 115 days, countless hours of debate, special meetings, testimony by more than 120 witnesses, a barrage of media coverage, and an unprecedented mobilization of interest groups, in the final analysis it is clear that partisan polarization was the most obvious cleavage within the Senate vote. Put more directly, 96 percent of the Democrats rejected Judge Bork, while 91 percent of the Republicans voted to confirm him. Thus, the Bork nomination serves to illustrate the continuing importance and influence of party in Senate voting on Court appointments and suggests a confluence between partisan affiliation and voting behavior generally.

Plainly, recent national and state elections demonstrate that the black vote can prove crucial, even determinative, in election outcomes. Black support for the Democratic party has risen from 64 percent nationally in 1956 to nearly 100 percent by 1964, continued overwhelmingly through the late 1960s and 1970s, and in the 1990s is solidly aligned with the Democratic party at around 90 percent. However, it seems as if the Democratic party is continuing to profit primarily from the symbols and achievements of the Kennedy and Johnson years and not from continuing efforts and initiatives which address the enduring problems that still plague black America. Viewed in this context, nearly unanimous Democratic opposition to Judge Bork might be seen as party recognition of the increasing influence of the black vote. But blacks need to develop strategies to enhance party support for more of their major objectives.

Indeed, Jesse Jackson's campaigns for the Democratic presidential nomination in 1984 and 1988 starkly reveal the lack of tangible observable advances engineered by the Democratic party since 1968 that are in line with black and other minority policy interests. For example, on most measures of income and employment, wide economic disparities between blacks and whites have not lessened since 1960. The unemployment rate for blacks since 1960 has been uniformly twice that of whites and the median family income of blacks seldom exceeds 60 percent of that of whites. These continuing disparities reflect in part the inability—or unwillingness—of the Democratic party to substantively address such problems and make good on the symbols and promises that continue to attract black voters.

Thus it is prudent to argue that blacks may need to take steps to diminish the penchant of the Democratic party to take the black vote for granted. Indeed, a 1987 survey by the Gallup organization for the Joint Center for Political Studies found that younger blacks—those who had not gone through the civil rights struggles—are much less loyal to the Democratic party than older blacks.[129] In fact, in recent elections some Republicans have benefitted from the emerging black vote. For example, Republican Governor Kean of New Jersey won a majority of the black vote in his 1985 reelection and agreed "there is a message in the victories of governors" like himself but admitted nonetheless that "Republican efforts among blacks had been wholly inadequate."130 Put more directly by Eddie Williams, president of the Joint Center for Political and Economic Studies, "They [Republicans] want to woo black votes, but they want to do it in the dark."131 Thus, while blacks need to take steps to diminish the penchant of the Democratic party to take their vote for granted, blacks must at the same time hold to and encourage the potential benefits of party affiliation as the basis for building majority coalitions to promote their objectives—such as defeating Supreme Court nominees viewed as adverse to the interests of blacks and other minorities.

XIII. The Bork Controversy in Perspective

The Bork confirmation battle demonstrates vividly the role and dimensions of politics and policies endemic in the nature and institutional structure of the U.S. Supreme Court. At bottom, the battle was yet another round over the nature and extent of the Court's policy-making role in the political system, a role that since the 1950s has often been a major—and in some instances the only effective—source of redress for African Americans.

At still another level the Bork nomination was also of major symbolic importance. For many, Judge Bork came to symbolize the Reagan administration's continued attacks on rights won by blacks during the turbulent years of the civil rights movement. Judge Bork came to represent a retreat from certain legal doctrines such as those prohibiting segregated schools and restrictive covenants in the real estate market and policies protecting the right of privacy. One might also interpret the defeat of the Bork nomination as indicative of America's refusal to turn away from—and indeed as representing an added confirmation of—fundamental policies and precedents established by the Warren Court in the 1950s and 1960s.

The Bork nomination controversy may well be summarized as a bicentennial seminar on "America's commitment to the rule of law, to the principle of equal justice for all Americans and to the fundamental role of the Supreme Court in protecting the basic rights of every citizen."[132] Yet clearly it is also both instructive and warranted to view Judge Bork's defeat as a case where African Americans were able to cultivate and exploit expanding political power and collective influences in an effort to protect and defend these "basic" rights.

CONCLUSION COURTS, JUDGES, AND THE INTERACTION OF LAW AND POLITICS

Our discussion in this and the preceding chapter suggests clearly that changes in Court personnel have certainly brought with them changes in the judicial stance toward the rights of African Americans and other minorities. In short, it seems apparent that the legal fate of problems confronting African Americans was much more uncertain under the Burger Court than it was during the Warren Court, and the Rehnquist Court has moved in an even more openly negative direction.

What we have observed indicates the development and continuation of three somewhat interrelated trends in Supreme Court decision making during the Burger-Rehnquist Courts: (1) less inclination by the Court to expand Warren Court policies supporting racial justice; (2) less support for blacks and others who wish to use litigation to achieve objectives they cannot attain in political forums; and (3) less judicial support for individual or group claims against governmental authority.

These trends, if continued, hold important implications for blacks and for the political system generally. In general they could pose formidable barriers to one of the most vital points of access that blacks have come to have in the political system. Indeed, one of the chief functions assumed by the

Warren Court was to express and to respond to certain grievances of those who were unpopular, unrepresented, or underrepresented in the political system. The characteristics of the American judiciary, as opposed to Congress and the presidency, seem unique to this function. Particularly, the built-in insulation of the federal judiciary from conforming to various majoritarian pressures places judges in a very unique position to support the rights of "insulated and isolated" minorities.[133]

The problems that affect blacks and press the governmental system for solution are not trivial. They are the great issues of our time, which, as de Tocqueville observed long ago, sooner or later are resolved into judicial issues. The American political system, as it has developed, tends to translate economic and social conflicts into legal conflicts. This, it seems, accounts for the unique significance of the Supreme Court. Consider the kinds of major issues that occupied the Warren Court:

1. How to overcome problems of racial injustice
2. How to strengthen and extend political democracy—for example, fair and effective systems of representation
3. How to ensure fairness to all persons in administering criminal justice
4. How to safeguard the rights of the poor in distributing legal, political, and economic benefits
5. How to give maximum protection to individual freedoms

With all these problems, it was quite obvious dominant interests during the Reagan-Bush era were unlikely to be in the vanguard of change. Those who are the victims of these problems—the politically disadvantaged—would quite naturally turn to the judicial system. Numbers, social status, wealth, and influence presumably have less bearing on the decision. In short, one of the important contributions of the Warren Court is that it was in a position to place items important to such groups on its constitutional agenda. It also could deal with them. Among the results of these actions the symbol of constitutionalism and law was placed on the side of particular issues of concern to such interests.

As a result, blacks were able initially to overcome many of the defects of coalition building and isolationism that so often characterize minority group politics. Coalition politics, for example, would appear to be necessary for a minority group to achieve favorable policies in the majority-rule electoral system. But to gain coalition support, a minority more often than not must soften its original objectives, since failure to do so lessens the possibilities of success in coalition building. Or, a minority may hold to its original objectives but find itself isolated without the support necessary to achieve success. Then again the minority group may subscribe to general, vague, though favorable policies. These policies either postpone the specific goals or shift their realization to another area. This is the more plausible course for a minority group to follow in elective-political arenas. But such policies are more likely to involve matters that affect the very self-esteem and dignity of individuals and the group itself. Hence, it would be most difficult for the group to soften its original objectives. But it could be equally difficult for the group to hold its original objectives in isolation without any viable chance of even limited success.

The judicial process can offer a minority group a way to overcome certain limitations that are part of the elective political process. In the judicial process a minority group may push its original objectives to obtain fully specific constitutional-legal guarantees. Moreover, the entire judicial drama, though not separate from politics, is carried on in a strictly "nonpolitical" manner; the language used addresses outcomes in terms of what the Constitution—and justice and fairness—"commands." "Reasoned argument" and "legal principles" replace advice and majority rule as the "critical" determinants. The "myth" and structure of the judicial forum, unlike the practice and structure of elective political forums, such as Congress, strengthen a minority group's chances of success. In addition, since courts also serve important functions for political elites and the political system generally—for example, resolution of conflict in terms of "law and order"—a victory for a minority group in the judicial system takes on added significance. Specifically, favorable court action may increase and constitutionalize (legitimize) pressures on and in elective political institutions to deal with the issues involved. Indeed, the minority group may now, as a result of victory in the courts, seek to give effect to legal constitutional rights, not mere interest group objectives. This, in large measure, is what happened during the Warren Court.

However, the situation began to change during the Burger Court. The Supreme Court's leadership and strong support for civil rights and civil liberties became much more uncertain. Nonetheless, the Burger Court did seem to follow the basic thrust of the Warren Court with respect to school desegregation and even extended increased constitutional protection to women. In general, however, decisions of the Warren Court included a creative use and application of the law to stimulate basic policy changes, whereas the Burger Court showed no such inclination. An off-the-bench comment by Chief Justice Burger illustrates this point. "Those [young people] who decide to go into law primarily on the theory that they can change the world by litigation in the courts," cautioned the Chief Justice, "may be in for some disappointment." Litigation, he said, is not "the route by which basic changes in a country like ours should be made. That is a very limited role for courts in this respect."[134] This seems to have characterized rather well the posture of the Burger Court, and now the Rehnquist Court. And given the nature and number of Reagan and Bush appointments to the Supreme Court, and lower federal courts as well, this posture is likely to manifest a strong presence in judicial policy making for some time to come. Hence, the problem for African Americans will not be how to forge new changes through litigation.[135] Instead, it will be how to prevent continuous "chipping away" of legal supports already gained.

With the 1992 election of Democratic President Clinton, however, and his pledge to appoint judges who have "deep convictions about the Constitution," this "chipping away" might be slowed and in time even alleviated or turned around. But, as suggested throughout this chapter, such change in judicial policy depends in large measure on *who* is appointed to the Court.

Importance of Judicial Support In the current political climate, and without strong judicial support, blacks and other minorities might find it even more difficult to achieve their objectives—quality education, decent jobs, and adequate housing. Notwithstanding the election of a more sympathetic president (Clinton), given the nature of the political system, it seems unlikely that persistently strong leadership on civil rights and related problems can be expected from elective-political institutions including the presidency.[136] In other words, elective-political institutions, in large measure, respond to constituencies that have the resources necessary to win elections. These resources include votes, financial wealth, support from influential groups, and so on. The only resource that blacks have historically had in adequate supply is votes. However, even if blacks should achieve maximum voting strength (they are a numerical minority), this would not be enough to balance the scale, much less assure favorable action from elective-political institutions.

A higher degree of political participation among blacks, including voting and holding public office, might appear a desirable option. Yet it is unwise to build expectations regarding such activity beyond what we might reasonably expect. Reliance on political participation by "insulated and isolated" minorities to correct basic sociopolitical and legal problems must be tempered by an understanding of the limitations of American electoral politics. This latter point, as well as the overall inefficiency of elective-political institutions in dealing with racial problems, is illustrated in a study on black officeholders in the South by one of the coauthors of this volume (Mack Jones).[137] "While voting and holding office are necessary conditions," writes Jones, "they are not sufficient ones for realization of the democratic creed." This suggests, for example, that more than emergent black political majorities and elected officials in the nation's central cities may be needed for blacks to receive the full benefits of American society.[138] As the system presently operates, the authority and resources which cities need to deal effectively with urban problems make them greatly dependent upon institutions beyond their control, such as state and federal legislatures. This situation has led one scholar to conclude that future control of central cities appears to offer blacks "very limited" opportunities for gains and may well prove a "hollow prize."[139] But this need not be the case. The dynamic character of American politics suggests that in certain situations these "prizes" might not be that "hollow."

However, it could very well be that, given the nature and operation of the American political system, strong judicial support—similar to and even more than that given by the Warren Court—is one of the minimum conditions necessary for the full realization of the "democratic creed" by minority groups. The Court has had a long history of blocking and slowing down the constitutional rights of blacks, even when faced with strong congressional opposition. (An example is the civil rights cases of 1883). Even in relatively recent times, decisions of the Court offered only slight support for black interests. As long as the Court impeded black interests or supported them only slightly, nothing much was done to improve blacks' status. But once the Court began making decisions that strongly supported and expanded the constitutional rights of blacks, the situation began to change. Impetus was given to the civil rights movement. Support for its objectives was broadened. Congress and the president began to take action to deal with the problems of racial injustice. Initiatives taken by the Warren Court stand out as crucial in stimulating and developing policies designed to overcome these problems.

However, the Burger Court did not appear so disposed and the Rehnquist Court seemed even more inimical to concerns of blacks and minority groups. This is clearly suggested by another one of its 1989 Court decisions *Patterson* v. *McLean* (109 S. Ct. 2363) where the Court reconsidered its 1976 decision in *Runyon* v. *McCrary*. In the *Runyon* case the Court construed the Civil Rights Act of 1866 as prohibiting not only racial discrimination resulting from public action but from *private* actions as well. And though the Court agreed not to overturn *Runyon*, the manner in which it construed the reach of the 1866 Civil Rights Act represented a serious setback to civil rights advocates. Justice Kennedy, speaking for a 5-4 majority, held that section 1981 of the 1866 Act protects against race discrimination in the "formation of a contract, but not to problems that may arise later from the conditions of continuing employment." The Court reasoned that once the contract had been entered, Brenda Patterson's allegations of racial harassment, including promotion discrimination claims, were not protected under the 1866 law. Rather, the court suggested that such post-contract racial harassment could more properly be brought under Title VII of the Civil Rights Act of 1964. Justice Brennan, who spoke for Justices Marshall, Blackmun, and Stevens, disagreed sharply with the majority on this narrow construction of the 1866 statue. So apparently did a majority of Congress which through the Civil Rights Act of 1991 seeks to overcome the adverse effects of the 1989 *Patterson* decision as well as certain other decisions of the Court. As suggested in the last chapter, however, it remains to be seen how effective this legislation will prove.

Impact on Lower Courts and the Many "Others" If the Supreme Court—both the Burger and now the Rehnquist Court—continues to make uncertain, to narrow, or to negate the policies and posture of the Warren Court, we might expect such actions to have an important impact on lower federal and state courts. These courts, after all, perform crucial functions. They exercise a "gatekeeping" function to determine what issues enter the judicial arena. They determine, in large measure, how the few major issues that do finally reach the Supreme Court are phrased for decision by that body. Lower courts also implement Supreme Court mandates.[140] Moreover, decisions of lower courts are final in most cases. How lower courts exercise these functions may be determined largely by what they perceive to be, and what is, the actual posture of the Supreme Court. The same applies to the influence of the Supreme Court on the behavior of other institutions and officials in both the public and private sectors, including potential litigants and their lawyers.

Of course, the reverse is also true. Lower courts, for example, affect the substance and impact of Supreme Court decisions. These courts in large part sift and winnow the issues and arguments which constitute the record upon which the Supreme Court reaches its decision. Additionally, it is also lower courts who interpret and apply principles laid down in Supreme Court decisions to the bulk of cases and controversies that enter the judicial system.

These more generalized observations of the relative role and interaction of the Supreme Court and lower courts must be put in a more practical context. Indeed, as pointed out in Chapter 5, lower federal courts no less than the Supreme Court have come under the control and influence of Reagan-Bush judges. Though this could make for a high level of policy congruence between the Supreme Court and lower federal courts, that congruence could be disturbed, even turned around, in response to when and how President Clinton deals with the appointment opportunities that may come his way to shape and influence the federal judiciary.

Not by Judges Alone: The Court in Political Perspective Our discussion highlights the role of courts, primarily the Supreme Court, in the formation of racial policies. Indeed, the strong and persistent support given such policies by the Warren Court, in contrast to the uncertain posture of the Burger Court and now the Rehnquist Court, indicates that the position taken by the Court can prove crucial (even determinative) in gaining policy objectives. But court action in itself may not be enough to achieve the very goals and objectives expressed in court decision. Court pronouncements may be viewed as authoritative (and final) as to the law and the Constitution. Yet they are not necessarily authoritative and final as to ultimate policy and practice. This is especially true when dealing with the kind of tough political and social issues as those relating to race tend to be. Action from significant "others" is invariably needed to achieve benefits envisioned by court decisions. Specific and generalized support that the Court receives from other institutions, public officials, and various publics can prove crucial to the viability of particular decisions. This relates to specific support for a given court decision that might come from key officials such as the president, governors, mayors, and so on. It also relates very definitely to action taken by other political institutions—president, Congress, state legislatures—that might support and implement, or otherwise circumvent and impede, judicial policies.

There are, of course, other considerations that influence the importance of particular court decisions. But what we have suggested here is sufficient to illuminate the intimate interrelation of law, courts, and politics. This, however, is not meant to minimize the important, even crucial, role the courts play in the formulation of public policy and in the management of social conflict generally. Indeed, it may be suggested that the gross underrepresentation of blacks (and other minorities) in the legal profession accounts for their very limited influence not only in shaping judicial policies but also in shaping policies in other governmental institutions, such as in Congress, state legislatures, and administrative agencies.

At least the actions and policies of the Reagan administration, including appointments to the federal bench, indicate vividly how decisions in the judicial arena might be greatly influenced by decisions made by elective-political actors such as the president. This latter point, as well as many other observations made in this chapter, were illustrated quite vividly in the case study on President Reagan's celebrated and unsuccessful attempt in 1987 to appoint Judge Robert Bork to the U.S. Supreme Court and of course by the more successful effort of President Bush in appointing and winning confirmation of Justice Clarence Thomas.

Topics for Discussion

1. Consider the relative nature and dynamics of the appointment and confirmation of Justice Thurgood Marshall, Justice Sandra Day O'Connor and Justice Clarence Thomas to the Supreme Court. Point out the similarities and differences involved, especially as related to the interaction of law and politics.

2. As the case study has shown, Judge Bork was an outspoken conservative with a long paper trail and a precisely defined, controversial theory of constitutional interpretation. But Justice Scalia could also be similarly described. In the end, however, Bork was defeated, while Scalia was confirmed with little opposition. What factors might explain the differing outcomes?

Note: As to both questions, you might wish to consult the popular press as well as relevant government documents (e.g., Senate Judiciary Committee hearings).

Suggested Readings

Abraham, Henry J. *Justices and Presidents: A Political History of Appointments to the Supreme Court*. New York: Oxford University Press, 1974.

Abraham, Henry J. *The Judiciary: The Supreme Court in the Government Process*. Boston: Allyn & Bacon, Inc., 1980.

Barker, Lucius J. "The Supreme Court from Warren to Burger: Implications for Black Americans and the Political System." *Washington University Law Quarterly*, Vol. 1973 (Fall), No. 4.

Barker, Lucius J. "Third Parties in Litigation: A Systemic View of the Judicial Function." 29 *Journal of Politics* 41 (1967).

Barker, T. W. and Michael Combs. "Civil Rights and Liberties in the First Term of the Rehnquist Court: The Quest for Doctrines and Votes." 1 *National Political Science Review* 31-57 (1989).

Baum, Lawrence. *The Supreme Court*. 4th ed. Washington, DC: CQ Press, 1992.

Bell, Derrick, Jr. *Race, Racism and Law*. 3rd ed. Boston: Little, Brown, 1992.

Bork, Robert H. *The Tempting of America*. New York: Free Press, 1990.

Caldeira, Gregory A. and John R. Wright. "*Amici Curiae* Before the Supreme Court: Who Participates, When, and How Much?" 52 *Journal of Politics* 803 (1990).

Caldeira, Gregory A. and John R. Wright. "Organized Interests and Agenda Setting in the U.S. Supreme Court." 82 *American Political Science Review* 1109 (1988).

Caplan, Lincoln. *The Tenth Justice: The Solicitor General and the Rule of Law*. New York: Knopf, 1987.

Cardozo, Benjamin. *The Nature of the Judicial Process*. New Haven: Yale University Press, 1921.

Casper, Jonathan D. *Lawyers Before the Warren Court: Civil Liberties and Civil Rights*. Urbana, IL: University of Illinois Press, 1972.

Chayes, Abram. "Public Law Litigation and the Burger Court." 96 *Harvard Law Review* 4 (1984).

Chayes, Abram. "The Role of the Judge in Public Law Litigation." 89 *Harvard Law Review* 1281 (1976).

Choper, Jesse. *Judicial Review and the National Political Process*. Chicago: University of Chicago Press, 1980.

Dahl, Robert. "Decision Making in a Democracy: The Supreme Court as a National Policy Maker." 70 *American Political Science Reviews* 3 (March 1976).

Ely, John Hart. *Democracy and Distrust: A Theory of Judicial Review*. Cambridge, MA: Harvard University Press, 1980.

Epstein, Lee. *Conservatives in Court*. Knoxville, TN: University of Tennessee Press, 1985.

Fried, Charles. *Order and Law*. New York: Simon & Schuster, 1991.

Goldman, Sheldon and Austin Sarat eds. *American Court Systems: Readings in Judicial Process and Behavior*. 2nd ed. White Plains, NY: Longman Inc., 1989.

Horowitz, Donald L. *The Courts and Social Policy*. Washington, DC: Brookings Institution, 1977.

Kluger, Richard. *Simple Justice: The History of* Brown v. Board of Education *and Black America's Struggle for Equality*. New York: Knopf, 1976.

McCann, Michael W. and Gerald L. Houseman. *Judging the Constitution: Critical Essays on Judicial Lawmaking*. Glenview, IL: Scott, Foresman, 1989.

Murphy, Walter and C. Herman Pritchett. *Courts, Judges and Politics*. 3rd ed. New York: Random House, 1979.

O'Brien, David M. *Judicial Roulette: Report of the Twentieth Century Fund Task Force on Judicial Selection*. New York: Priority Press Publications, 1988.

Peltason, Jack W. *Federal Courts in the Political Process*. New York: Random House, 1955.

Perry, H. W. *Deciding to Decide: Agenda Setting in the U.S. Supreme Court*. Cambridge, MA: Harvard University Press, 1991.

Rabkin, Jeremy A. *Judicial Compulsions: How Public Law Distorts Public Policy*. New York: Basic Books, 1989.

Rehnquist, William H. *The Supreme Court*. New York: Morrow, 1989.

Rosenberg, Gerald N. *The Hollow Hope: Can Courts Bring About Social Change?* Chicago: University of Chicago Press, 1991.

Shapiro, Martin. *Freedom of Speech: The Supreme Court and Judicial Review*. Englewood Cliffs, NJ: Prentice Hall, 1966.

Simon, James. *In His Own Image: The Supreme Court in Richard Nixon's America.* New York: D. McKay, 1973.

Tribe, Laurence H. *God Save This Honorable Court: How the Choice of Supreme Court Justices Shapes Our History.* New York: Random House, 1985.

Warren, Elizabeth. *The Legacy of Judicial Policy-Making:* Gautreaux v. Chicago Housing Authority: *The Decision and Its Impacts.* Lanham, MD: University Press of America, 1988.

Wasby, Stephen L. *The Supreme Court in the Federal Judicial System.* New York: Holt, Rinehart and Winston, 1978.

Notes

1. This study was written specifically for this book.
2. *Chicago Sun-Times*, September 22, 1987, p. 176.
3. Indeed it was as solicitor general that Robert Bork carried out President Nixon's order—after Attorney General Elliott Richardson and Deputy Attorney General William Ruckelshaus had refused and resigned—to fire special "Watergate" prosecutor Archibald Cox. This incident, considered by many as legally and ethically questionable, came to be known as the "Saturday Night Massacre" on October 20, 1973, and prompted impeachment resolutions against President Nixon.
4. See Elder Witt, *A Different Justice: Reagan and the Supreme Court* (Washington DC: Congressional Quarterly, Inc., 1986), p. 100.
5. "Bork's Views: Interpreting the Constitution," *Congressional Quarterly Weekly Report* 45 (September 12, 1987), p. 2166.
6. See Anthony Lewis, "Bork on Liberty," *New York Times*, September 6, 1987, p. E15.
7. Nadine Cohodas, "Much at Stake as Senate Gets Ready for Bork," *Congressional Quarterly Weekly Report* 45, no. 27 (July 4, 1987), p. 1430.
8. See "Civil Rights: A Challenge," *New Republic*, August 31, 1963.
9. Cohodas, "Much at Stake," *Congressional Quarterly Weekly Report* 45, no. 27 (July 4, 1987), p. 1430.
10. Ibid., p. 1429.
11. Ibid.
12. *U.S. News and World Report*, July 13, 1987, p. 28; *Time*, July 13, 1987, p. 10.
13. Cohodas, "Much at Stake," p. 1429.
14. Ibid., p. 1430.
15. Ibid.
16. Ibid.
17. Ibid.
18. Tom Watson, "Polarized Senate Prepares for September Hearings on Bork," *Congressional Quarterly Weekly Report* 45, no. 27, (July 11, 1987), p. 1495.
19. Ibid.
20. Linda Greenhouse, "G.O.P. Challenges Bork's Opponents," *The New York Times*, September 28, 1987, p. 10.
21. Stuart Taylor, Jr., "Politics in the Bork Battle," *The New York Times*, July 24, 1987, p. 10.

22. See Linda Greenhouse, "Stakes of the Bork Fight," *The New York Times*, September 14, 1987, p. 1.
23. See Nadine Cohodas, "For Robert Bork, the Real Test Begins Now," *Congressional Quarterly Weekly Report* 45 (September 12, 1987), pp. 2160-2161.
24. *Congressional Quarterly Weekly Report* 45 (August 1, 1987), p. 1735.
25. Cohodas, "Polarized Senate," *Congressional Quarterly Weekly Report*, July 11, 1987, p. 1495.
26. Cohodas, "For Robert Bork," *Congressional Quarterly Weekly Report*, September 12, 1987, p. 2163.
27. See Nadine Cohodas and Tom Watson, "Undecided Feel Screws Tighten as Bork Vote Nears," *Congressional Quarterly Weekly Report* 45 (September 26, 1987), p. 2301.
28. See Nadine Cohodas, "DeConcini, Heflin Hold Key to Judiciary Committee Vote on Bork," *Congressional Quarterly Weekly Report* 45 (July 11, 1987), pp. 1496-1497. See also Linda Greenhouse, "The Alignments in the Bork Battle: How Each Member Is Likely to Vote," *The New York Times*, September 15, 1987, p. 12.
29. "The Judiciary Committee: Balance of Power Rests with Three Undecided Senators," *Congressional Quarterly Weekly Report* 45 (September 12, 1987), p. 2173.
30. Ibid.
31. Cohodas, "Much at Stake,"
32. See William Schneider, "Bork's Confirmation Would Shake Both Parties," *National Journal* (August 29, 1987), p. 2166.
33. Cohodas, "Polarized Senate,"
34. L. Greenhouse, "Bork as a Bonanza," *The New York Times*, Sept. 11, 1987, p A1.
35. Tom Watson, "Veteran Lobbyist Steps into Another Nomination Fray," *Congressional Quarterly Weekly Report* 45 (September 12, 1987), p. 2174.
36. A. Kornhauser, "Liberal Groups Take Early Jump in Bork Battle," *Legal Times*, July 20, 1987, p. 6.
37. E. Walsh, "ACLU Urges Senate to Reject Bork's Nomination to the Court," *Washington Post*, September 1, 1987.
38. See "Why Common Cause Opposed the Bork Nomination," in *PS* 20, no. 4 (Fall 1987).
39. See Linda Greenhouse, "ACLU Revising Policy, Joins the Opposition to Bork," *The New York Times*, September 1, 1987, p. 7.
40. Cohodas, "For Robert Bork," 45, no. 37 (September 12, 1987) p. 2161.
41. *CBS News/New York Times* poll released, September 14, 1987, 6:30 PM EDT. This poll was conducted by telephone September 9-10, 1987.
42. See Senator Biden's opening statement in Senate Committee on the Judiciary, *Hearings on the Nomination of Robert H. Bork to Be Associate Justice of the Supreme Court of the United States*, 100th Cong., 1st sess., September 15, 1987, pt. 1 of 5, pp. 95-96 (Washington DC: Government Printing Office, 1989). Hereafter cited as *Hearings*.
43. *Hearings*, September 15, 1987, pt. 1 of 5, pp. 30-32.
44. Ibid., p. 33.
45. Ibid., p. 34.
46. See "Bork Statement: 'Philosophy of Role of Judge,'" *The New York Times*, September 16, 1987, p. 16. See also Robert Bork, *The Tempting of America* (Riverside, NJ: Macmillan, 1989).

47. *Hearings*, October 13, 1987, pt. 5 of 5, p. 6216.
48. *St. Louis Post Dispatch*, October 4, 1987, p. C2.
49. *Hearings*, September 19, 1987, pt. 1 of 5, p. 116.
50. *Hearings*, September 16, 1987, pt. 1 of 5, pp. 288-296.
51. 348 U.S. 641 (1966).
52. *Constitutionality of the President's Busing Proposals* 1 (Washington, DC: America Enterprise Institute, 1972), pp. 9-10.
53. 400 U.S. 112 (1970).
54. Senate Committee on the Judiciary, *Hearings on the Human Life Bill before the Subcommittee on the Separation of Powers*, 97th Cong., 1st sess., 1982.
55. *Hearings*, October 13, 1987, pt. 5 of 5, p. 6226.
56. *Hearings*, September 18, 1987, pt. 1 of 5, p. 663.
57. Ibid., p. 664.
58. Ibid., pp. 666-667.
59. Ibid., p. 668
60. Ibid., p. 469
61. Ibid., pp. 469-470.
62. *Hearings*, September 19, 1984, pt. 1 of 5, pp. 840-842.
63. Ibid., p. 855.
64. See "Bork v. Bork," *The New York Times*, September 22, 1987, p. 26.
65. *Hearings*, September 16, 1987, pt. 1 of 5, p. 296.
66. *The New York Times*, September 12, 1987, p. 12.
67. See Cohodas and Watson, "Undecided Feel Screws Tighten as Bork Vote Nears," p. 2301.
68. *Hearings*, September 30, 1987, pt. 3 of 5, p. 3547.
69. Jacob V. Lamar, Jr., "Gone with the Wind," *Time*, October 12, 1987, p. 19.
70. Cohodas and Watson, "Undecideds Feel Screws Tighten," p. 2303.
71. *The New York Times*, September 27, 1987, p. 12.
72. Ibid.
73. See *Hearings*, September 23, 1987, pt. 2 of 5, pp. 2096-2116.
74. *The New York Times*, September 24, 1987, p. 1.
75. *Hearings*, October 13, 1987, pt. 5 of 5, p. 6314.
76. Ibid., p. 6313
77. Linda Greenhouse, "Foe Warns Bork Views Pose a Serious Risk to Freedoms," *The New York Times*, September 23, 1987, p. 15.
78. Ibid.
79. *Hearings*, September 25, 1987, pt. 2 of 5, p. 2310.
80. Ibid., pp. 3801-3803.
81. Ibid.
82. See Linda Greenhouse, "Foe Warns Bork Views Pose a Serious Risk to Freedom," *The New York Times*, September 23, 1987, p. 15.
83. See "At Hearing on Bork, Words of Warning and of Praise," *The New York Times*, September 22, 1987, p. 13.
84. *Hearings*, September 21, 1987, pt. 1 of 5, p. 867.
85. Ibid.

86. Ibid., pp. 1104-1005.
87. *Hearings*, September 23, 1987, pt. 2 of 5, pp. 2118-2121.
88. *Hearings*, September 30, 1987, pt. 3 of 5, pp. 3349-3412.
89. *The New York Times*, September 26, 1987, p. 1.
90. Ibid.
91. *The New York Times*, October 1, 1987, p. 1.
92. *Congressional Record*, 100th Cong., 1st sess., 1987, vol. 133, no. 164, S14571.
93. *The New York Times*, October 13, 1987, p. 26.
94. *The New York Times*, October 4, 1987, p. 1.
95. *The New York Times*, October 3, 1987, p. 7.
96. *The New York Times*, October 4, 1987, p. 15.
97. *The New York Times*, October 2, 1987, p. 14.
98. *The New York Times*, October 16, 1987, p. 8. For the complete report, see *Hearings*, October 13, 1987, pt. 5 of 5, pp. 6180-6307.
99. Ibid., p. 6185.
100. Ibid., p. 6308.
101. Ibid., p. 6403.
102. *The New York Times*, October 1, 1987, p. 15.
103. Nadine Cohodas and Mark Willen, "Angry, Defiant Bork Insists on Senate Debate," *Congressional Quarterly Weekly Report* 45 (October 10, 1987), p. 2435.
104. *The New York Times*, October 10, 1987, p. 12.
105. Nadine Cohodas, "Senate Warms Up for 'Divisive' Bork Debate," *Congressional Quarterly Weekly Report* 45 (October 17, 1987), p. 2511.
106. Ibid.
107. See text of Sanford speech in the *Congressional Quarterly Weekly Report* 45 (October 17, 1987), p. 2546.
108. Cohodas, "Senate Warms Up," p. 2511.
109. *Congressional Record*, 100th Cong., 1st sess., 1987, vol. 133, no. 164, S14549.
110. Cohodas, "Senate Warms Up," p. 2512.
111. *Congressional Quarterly Weekly Report*, October 24, 1987, p. 2600-2601.
112. *Congressional Record*, 100th Cong., 1st sess., 1987, vol. 133, no. 165, S14686.
113. *Congressional Record*, 100th Cong., 1st sess., 1987, vol. 133, no. 165, S14687.
114. Nadine Cohodas, "Senate Debates, Then Dispatches Bork, 42-58," *Congressional Quarterly Weekly Report* 45 (October 24, 1987), p. 2601.
115. *Congressional Record*, 100th Cong., 1st sess., 1987, vol. 133, no. 176, S14945.
116. *Congressional Record*, 100th Cong., 1st sess., 1987, vol. 133, no. 167, S14946.
117. *Congressional Record*, 100th Cong., 1st sess., 1987, vol. 133, no. 167, S14992.
118. *Congressional Record*, 100th Cong., 1st sess., 1987, vol. 133, no. 165, S14699.
119. *Congressional Record*, 100th Cong., 1st sess., 1987, vol. 133, no. 165, S14705.
120. *Congressional Record*, 100th Cong., 1st sess., 1987, vol. 133, no. 165, S14670. See also Senator Specter's additional comments in the majority committee report, *Hearings*, October 13, 1987, pt. 5 of 5, p. 6306.
121. See for example, Tom Wicker, "Bork and Blacks," *The New York Times* October 5, 1987, p. 23; "Saying No to Bork, Southern Democrats Echo Black Voters," *The New York Times* October 8, 1987, p. 1; David Lauter, "South Had Key Role in Bork

Rejection: White House Misjudged Black Voting Power," *Los Angeles Times*, October 24, 1987, sec. 1, p. 30.

122. Ibid.
123. *The New York Times*, September 27, 1987, p. 12.
124. 369 U.S. 186 (1962).
125. 383 U.S. 301 (1966).
126. See Mancur Olson, *The Logic of Collective Action* (Cambridge, MA: Harvard University Press, 1971).
127. Linda Williams, "White/Black Perceptions of the Electability of Black Political Candidates," *National Political Science Review* 2 (1990).
128. Howard Schuman with Charlotte Steeth and Lawrence Bobo, *Racial Attitudes in America* (Cambridge, MA: Harvard University Press, 1985).
129. See "G.O.P. Ponders an Appeal to Minorities," *The New York Times*, August 2, 1987, p. E4.
130. Ibid.
131. Ibid.
132. Senator Kennedy's closing remarks before the Senate, *Congressional Record*, 100th Cong., 1st sess., vol. 133, no. 167.
133. Jack W. Peltason, *Federal Courts in the Political Process* (New York: Random House, 1955).
134. *The New York Times*, July 4, 1971, p. 24.
135. Yet state supreme courts may offer alternative judicial forums in which blacks may be able to continue to forge new changes through litigation. Justice Brennan, writing in 1977, saw signs of the development as perhaps an indication of increasing dissatisfaction with the Burger Court's construction of the federal Bill of Rights and the due process and equal protection clauses of the Fourteenth Amendment. See William J. Brennan, Jr., "State Constitution and the Protection of Individual Rights," *Harvard Law Rev.* 90, no. 489 (1977), esp. pp. 495-500.
136. For commentary on the inability of the political system to deal with these problems, see James M. Burns, *Uncommon Sense* (New York: Harper & Row, Pub., 1972); Theodore J. Lowi, *The End of Liberalism* (New York: W. W. Norton & Co., Inc., 1969). See also Walter D. Burham, *Critical Elections and the Mainspring of American Politics* (New York: W.W. Norton & Co. Inc., 1970), pp. 91-193.
137. M. Jones, "Black Officeholders in Local Governments of the South: An Overview." Paper prepared for delivery at the Annual Meeting of the American Political Science Association, 1970.
138. For searing commentary on the problems which face a black mayor (and in many ways, problems common to elected executives generally), see Carl Stokes, *Promises of Power. A Political Autobiography* (New York: Simon & Schuster, 1972), pp. 118-20.
139. H. Paul Friesena, "Black Control of Central Cities: The Hollow Prize," *Journal of the American Institute of Planners* 35 (March 1969), pp. 75-79.
140. For a detailed and interesting account of lower court implementation of the school desegregation case, see Jack W. Peltason, *Fifty-Eight Lonely Men: Southern Federal Judges and School Desegregation* (Chicago: University of Illinois Press, 1961). A more recent study of lower court implementation of federal law is found in Charles Hamilton, *The Bench and the Ballot: Southern Federal Judges and Black Voters* (New York: Oxford University Press, 1973).

CHAPTER 7

CHANGE THROUGH POLITICS: INTEREST GROUPS

The new black politics demands a reevaluation of this age-old concept. Those who embrace the new black politics must couch their thinking in the fundamental concept that "what is good for minorities is good for the nation." This position out of necessity requires the development of a new philosophy that must be practical and selfish—the same as all others that presently exist in this country. Black politics must start on the premise that we have no permanent friends, no permanent enemies, just permanent interests. In matters strictly of a political nature, we must be determined to "take what we can, give up what we must." Those in politics who disagree with this approach should first analyze the composition of their own philosophy and if it does not parallel ours—they are qualified to disagree.

The second qualification for the new black politics is a relative degree of political independence. Those black politicians who are subservient to white controlled political machines cannot possibly stand the kinds of pressures which will come when the new black politics launches the campaign for total black equality in all areas of American life. This is not to say that blacks in politics cannot have a reasonable, legitimate coalition with white politics. To think otherwise would be absolute folly. But the kinds of techniques necessary to employ at this stage in black politics must be abrasive, retaliatory, obstructionist—all of which may be offensive to whites, even white liberals. The question is—can the white liberal follow the lead of blacks who have followed them for so many years?

Congressman William Clay (D-Missouri)*

INTRODUCTION

The above comments of Rep. Clay, though made in 1971, remain and appear increasingly relevant in 1993.

The transition from the Warren Court to the Burger Court and now the Rehnquist Court vividly illustrates that policies emanating from the judiciary are heavily dependent on the kind of support and policies that come from the "political" arena.

Even so, one can understand why blacks and other minorities have chosen to resort to "judicial" politics as opposed to "political" politics to pursue their goals. Indeed, success in the judicial arena, as shown by the civil rights movement, has had enormous impact on the political arena. Judicial policies have broadened the protection of those who have to resort to both traditional and nontraditional means to communicate and act on their views. The scope of the First Amendment guarantees has been interpreted so as to protect protest demonstrations and other forms of political expression. These latter forms include limiting the law of libel as applied to public officials and public figures; permitting those with common objectives to join in association with others without fear of recrimination; permitting interest groups to use litigation and to promote and advocate objectives which they perhaps could not otherwise achieve in other arenas.

Court actions have also eliminated the white primary and other similarly restrictive devices. In addition, formidable Court decisions in combination with the civil rights movement spurred the enactment of the most important civil rights legislation in almost a century—the Civil Rights Act of 1964 and the Voting Rights Act of 1965. Subsequently, the Court upheld the constitutionality of both laws. Moreover, in the reapportionment cases, the Court determined that representation was to be based on the "one person—one vote" formula so as to take account of massive shifts in population—mainly from rural to urban areas.

Such decisions have had variable effects on black participation and influence in the political arena. Mainly, however, their overall impact has had a healthy effect by stimulating blacks and others to use "politics" as a way to gain their objectives. Of course, it could very well be that both the judiciary and black groups recognized, and not without glaring evidence, that except for strong support in and from political institutions, judicial policies would not go very far. In any event, favorable judicial decisions have broadened participation and stimulated the use of political forums by blacks and others to deal with their concerns. And without doubt, many blacks have attempted to take advantage of the "new" openings in the political process, and they have met with a measure of success.

In this chapter we focus on (1) the nature of groups and factors that determine the relative success of interest groups in the political process; (2) the history, development, and present operations of black civil rights groups; and (3) some overall observations with respect to how blacks fare in interest group politics and in American pluralism generally. In the next chapter we discuss blacks and political parties.

INTEREST GROUPS AND THE POLITICAL PROCESS

FACTORS DETERMINING SUCCESS IN GROUP CONFLICT

In general, the relative effectiveness of interest groups in the political process may be explained by a number of factors. Perhaps the most important factor is the *nature of the membership* of the particular group. This includes the basis of group membership; that is, why people belong to certain groups; the commitment and attitude of group members toward group goals; and the position and standing of the group and its members in the socioeconomic structure. Clearly, the nature of leadership is an important factor (and resource) in determining group effectiveness. In large measure, the quality of the leadership determines the quality of the organization. Leaders have to be constantly on top of things: managing the day-to-day operations of the organization; carrying out its policies and programs; promoting consciousness and self-awareness among its members; and constantly devising ways to deal with and overcome persistent "free-rider" problems that may well affect the group's ability to recruit and maintain its membership. The "free-rider" problem is particularly vexing—leaders have to convince members and potential members that in addition to "collective benefits," there are indeed certain "selective benefits" that one gains from formal membership.

The *resources* that groups can bring to bear in achieving their goals is another factor to consider in assessing their influence in the political process. These resources relate to such elements as leadership, money, size of group membership, and how the group is organized (structured) to carry on its business. Of course, in this respect *strategy* and *tactics*, that is, how and in what manner groups actually use their resources, are directly and crucially related to group effectiveness. Groups utilize a number of ways to achieve objectives. They try to stimulate a favorable *public opinion*, for example, through the use of "propaganda" or "educational campaigns." Through *electioneering* groups seek to influence election outcomes by supporting candidates who are favorable (or at least not opposed) to their goals. Group participation in elections may take several forms. It may range from outright endorsement and support of particular candidates to outright opposition in other situations. This, of course, leaves other options in between.

In this connection political action committees (PACs) have come to take on increasing importance as a way for interests to promote their objectives. Organized labor has long had its political action committees which offer support to "friendly" political candidates, mostly Democratic. In 1974 legislation was passed to make PACs altogether legal for corporations, professional groups, or any other groups who wished to solicit money and give it to candidates who support their interests. As a result, the number of PACs has skyrocketed from about 600 in 1974 to more than 3,500 in 1984. The growth has occurred primarily among corporate, business and trade association PACs, although a number of ideological PACs—such as the National Conservative Political Action Committee (NCPAC)—have also burst on the scene. While there are limits on the amounts PACs may donate directly to federal candidates in a given year, PACs may spend any amount they wish on behalf of particular candidates so long as they do not contribute directly to candidates or coordinate their spending with the candidate's campaign.

Groups also *lobby* to influence public policy. Much of this activity focuses on Congress where groups spend large amounts of money each year to protect and promote their interests.[1] But a number of factors, including the inability or unwillingness of Congress to deal with particular problems, the centralization and bureaucratization of power in Washington, and the federal structure of our governmental system has led to a renewed interest in the role and authority of state and local governments. As a result, interest groups and lobbyists are increasingly looking to these governmental units as additional avenues through which to achieve their objectives.

Groups also use the judicial process to influence public policy. The two principal ways by which groups do this are by sponsoring (initiating, financing, and conducting) *litigation*, and by filing *amicus curiae* (friend of the court) *briefs*. For example, the NAACP has been quite vigorous in using litigation to achieve its goals. And the United States Supreme Court has held that such vigorous advocacy is constitutionally grounded in the First Amendment. As Justice Brennan put it:

> In the context of NAACP objectives, litigation is not a technique of resolving private differences; it is a means for achieving the lawful objectives of equality of treatment by all government, federal, state and local for the members of the Negro community in this country. It is thus a form of political expression. Groups which find themselves unable to achieve their objectives through the ballot frequently turn to the courts. Just as it was true of the opponents of the New Deal legislation during the 1930s, no less is it true of the Negro minority today. And

> under the conditions of modern government, litigation may well be the sole practicable avenue open to a minority to petition for redress of grievances.[2]

In general, the success of the NAACP and other such groups in this respect has been well documented elsewhere.[3] We will not repeat it here except to reemphasize that litigation remains a chief avenue by which groups seek to accomplish their objectives.

Direct action (marches, demonstrations, sit-ins, and violence) has long been used by groups to promote their causes. This is particularly true of groups that lack the traditional resources (money, skill, votes) needed to influence public policy. The more recent and widespread use of direct action and violence occurred during the civil rights movement of the 1950s and 1960s. But even though these methods have long been part of the American political scene, they have never really been accepted as consistent with American beliefs and traditions of resolving conflict through peaceful (even nonobstructive) means. But accepted or not, the potential use of such methods may yet be determined by whether politically disadvantaged groups gain a greater share of the *traditional* and *accepted* resources (for instance, money, political offices) they need to protect and promote effectively their interests in the American political system.

BLACKS IN GROUP POLITICS: PROBLEMS OLD AND NEW

The major black interest groups have been and are now concerned with those problems that affect black people and other minorities. These problems have been called civil rights problems; groups that focus on these problems have been labeled civil rights groups. Obviously, the nature and scope of civil rights problems and civil rights groups have changed over time. Until late in the 1960s these groups were mostly concerned with the formal recognition and definition of constitutional and legal rights. A major concern today, however, is with the practical implementation of these legal rights; but it has become increasingly and painfully clear to all that without corresponding economic rights and economic justice, legal rights are somewhat hollow and on their own do little to improve the quality of everyday living for African Americans. While black interest groups remain concerned about civil rights, the time has come to emphasize economic justice and improving the socioeconomic standing of blacks. Even so, it is no secret that black groups have differed and continue to differ in how best to achieve these objectives.

The difference between and among groups, as we discussed above, turns on a number of factors such as the nature of group membership, the nature of group resources, and the strategy and tactics groups use to achieve their objectives. The following section illustrates these factors as they relate to black interest groups. It describes the problems and successes of major black groups in forming a coalition that would give unity and direction to the civil rights movement in the 1960s.

COALITIONS IN THE CIVIL RIGHTS MOVEMENT**

On July 2, 1964, President Lyndon Johnson signed into law the Civil Rights Act of 1964. This enactment was important in two respects. First, it was one of the most significant pieces of civil rights legislation to get through Congress. Second, and most important for our purposes, the 1964 legislation displayed the strength and unity of the civil rights coalition. The 1964 legislation (along with the 1965 Voting Rights Act) marked the high point of the civil rights movement. More than 40 major interest groups united their efforts in order to pass it.[4] Anthony Lewis states that the passage of the 1964 legislation "emphasized the breadth of national commitment"[5] to civil rights.

The years following the "high point" of 1964, however, stand in sharp contrast to the unity and success enjoyed by civil rights groups during that year. The coalition which rallied around the 1964 legislation is all but dead today. Those organizations which formed the hard center of that coalition—the National Association for the Advancement of Colored People (NAACP), Urban League, and the Southern Christian Leadership Conference (SCLC)—no longer lay claim to the political influence that was their greatest strength. The two other components of the civil rights coalition which commanded considerable attention in the 1960s—the Student Nonviolent Coordination Committee (SNCC) and the Congress on Racial Equality (CORE)—are barely visible today. CORE no longer exerts the same influence over mainstream American politics it once did, and SNCC has ceased to exist.

To anyone familiar with the tenuous civil rights coalition during the 1960s, the dissolution came as no surprise. As the decade progressed past 1964, the signs became clear. The once effective civil rights coalition was rent by truculent diatribe. Debate over means (e.g., whether to use established legal and political channels to change a condition, or to protest by a massive march or sit-in, or to respond with violence) was replaced by debate over ends. The sympathetic white liberal, a basic component of the 1964 coalition, began to retreat and watch with anxiety.[6] The Reverend Martin Luther King, Jr., once the rallying point of the coalition, was by the time of his assassination in 1968 barely able to maintain a viable leadership position. And the NAACP, the major force behind the Supreme Court's *Brown* decision in 1954, struggled to retain some vestige of its moderate civil rights leadership.[7] The whole concept of racial integration was being rejected by some black leaders,[8] and nonviolence was being challenged by Black Power advocates.[9] In short, by the mid 1960s disunity rather than unity characterized the entire civil rights movement.

Among other things, this state of affairs focuses attention on the political problem of maintaining a coalition among civil rights groups. In an attempt to understand this problem and its implications for the American political structure at large, we begin by examining general profiles of each of the five organizations considered here: the Urban League, NAACP, SCLC, SNCC, and CORE. In addition, we will consider a sixth group, the Black Muslims, or Nation of Islam. While the Muslims were never a part of the civil rights coalition in any formal sense, they did offer a viable alternative to African Americans who found the message of racial integration weak or unresponsive to their needs.

This section on the civil rights movement is divided into three parts: a general profile of group characteristics and attitudes; a brief history of the rise of the coalition among civil rights groups; and an account of factors leading to disunity among the groups.

THE MAJOR CIVIL RIGHTS GROUPS

Civil rights groups are hardly cut out of the same cloth. They exhibit a variety of characteristics which tend to associate with, and perhaps produce, differing political outlooks. First of all, these groups can be visualized in terms of a continuum of high-low integration into the existing political system, as in Table 7-1.[10] Clearly, some civil rights groups seek to achieve their goals by using normal institutional approaches and channels, such as lobbying and electioneering. On the other hand, other groups consider these techniques ineffective in terms of institutional response and accordingly resort to "direct action" and "militant" methods to achieve their goals. Though generally within the legal limits of the political system, these direct-action approaches nevertheless defy traditional norms and political styles and in the process evoke strong negative reactions from many people including those in the policy-making positions.

At one end of the continuum we find two groups. Both of these, the Urban League and the National Association for the Advancement of Colored People, were, and still very much are, well integrated into the political and social structure of American life.

TABLE 7-1 Percentage of institutionally directed incidents as indicative of relative system integration, 1966-1967

ORGANIZATION	TOTAL REPORTED ACTIONS	ALIENATED ACTIONS	INTEGRATED ACTIONS	PERCENT INTEGRATED
Urban League	47	1	46	98
NAACP	133	23	110	83
SCLC	140	38	82	59
CORE	98	72	26	27
SNCC	101	85	16	16

The National Urban League[11] was founded in 1910 for the purpose of aiding southern blacks in their adjustment to the urban North. Over time, it has evolved into a large-scale social agency operating on a national level. Generally, the Urban League is a highly structured, biracial organization, run from the top with the help of a relatively large and well-trained professional staff. The league attempts to achieve its objectives through research, consultation, and persuasion. Since its beginnings, it has sought to integrate blacks into American society through the establishment of equal opportunities. The Urban League hastens to add that with new opportunities come new responsibilities for blacks. In this light, then, the Urban League divides its time between the white and black communities.

In attempting to push its social welfare approach to race relations, the Urban League has gone to the white community for much of its financial support. The main sources of money are foundation grants donated through fund drives such as the United Way. Consequently, even though the league devotes its major efforts to the unemployed and the poor, it tends to do so within the framework of "established" or "mainstream" America. It could be said that the League uses middle-class methods to achieve middle-class goals for lower-class people. The league has usually avoided participation in direct-action campaigns. Rather, it has emphasized welfare lobbying within the limits of existing institutions and practices, and, of the organizations discussed in this section, it is probably the most integrated into the American political system.

The National Association for the Advancement of Colored People (NAACP)[12] and the Urban League have much in common. Founded in 1909, the NAACP has attempted to work for change within the established political structure. While the Urban League has emphasized change through massive social welfare programs, the NAACP has dedicated much of its effort to conventional political arenas in an effort to make and change laws that would improve the legal status of African Americans. This legalistic approach can be observed in the NAACP's active role in legislative, administrative, and judicial decision making.

The NAACP, as well, has historically avoided direct-action approaches. The executive board prefers to use political and legal channels rather than direct action. The NAACP does, however, support the right of protest and has, under the leadership of Benjamin Hooks, increasingly participated in direct-action programs and the more action-oriented tenor of the civil rights movement. In terms of management, power in the NAACP is concentrated in the hands of the national executive board, and organization policy is largely determined at the top.

Membership is fundamentally middle-class and middle age. There are two outside bases of support, namely, white liberals and the religious community. Like the Urban League, the NAACP has been and still is relatively well-financed, "elitist," and highly integrated into the traditional or mainstream structure of American politics.

At the other end of the continuum, we find a cluster of three organizations: the Black Muslims (or Nation of Islam), SNCC, and CORE. Unlike the NAACP and the Urban League, these organizations were not, or are not, considered "politics as usual." On the contrary, these groups tend (or tended, as in the case of SNCC) to emphasize direct-action techniques.

During the 1960s, the Muslims were one of the most separatist and feared groups in American society.[13] A religious organization dedicated to the complete cultural and spatial separation of the races, the Muslims were strongly anti-Christian and anti-white, regarding all white people as "devils." Its membership was (and to a large degree still is) concentrated in the black urban areas of the northern and western United States, and its membership mostly consists of black students, workers, and poor people. Unlike many of the other groups discussed here, the Nation of Islam continues to enjoy increasing visibility and subscription. Much of this is due to one of the Nation's most vocal, charismatic, and controversial leaders, Minister Louis Farrakhan, and to the group's unwavering commitment to black separatism and black economic self-determination.

Founded in 1960, the Student Nonviolent Coordinating Committee (SNCC) grew out of heavy student involvement in the early civil rights movement.[14] Whereas students originally constituted the bulk of SNCC's membership, the composition of the organization changed considerably during the 1960s to the point where membership consisted primarily of young, non-student, working-class blacks.

SNCC, financed by contributions, began with some ties to the white community. As the decade progressed, however, those ties became weaker, reflecting the growing impatience SNCC's changing leadership had with the slow progress of non-violent protest. Accordingly, the organization became less influenced by the interests and pressures of the political establishment than the more integrated groups. SNCC differed from the NAACP and the Urban League in another way: It was truly a grass-roots organization. SNCC's national body, the coordinating committee, represented a variety of local protest groups. This system of representation promoted a close relationship between the national governing body and SNCC's local units.

Like its membership, SNCC's message changed dramatically after 1966, from "Freedom Now" to the more assertive "Black Power." However, "Black Power," even as defined by SNCC leaders, was a changing concept subject to varying interpretations. Stokely Carmichael, former SNCC chairman and originator of the phrase "Black Power," originally viewed SNCC as the political, economic, and social mobilization of an oppressed people, an effort to empower individuals through direct action (pickets, marches, and boycotts) and electioneering. As the 1960s wore on, however, Carmichael and other SNCC leaders defined "Black Power" and the goals of SNCC in more militant terms. "Black Power," Carmichael has said, embodies "the unification of the Negro population to fight for their liberation . . . to take up arms."[15] This new militant stance contrasted sharply with the "nonviolent direct action" message which characterized the founding of SNCC.

Much like SNCC, the Congress of Racial Equality (CORE)[16] has grown up with a history of protest. Founded in 1942, CORE has generally tried to abolish racial discrimination through the application of Gandhian philosophy and techniques of nonviolent direct action. Under the leadership of Floyd McKissick, however, CORE also adopted the rhetoric of Black Power. As was the case with SNCC, this more militant Black Power stance affected the organization in a number of ways. First, its biracial character gave way to uniracial emphasis. While a number of liberal whites left the group, many urban blacks were attracted to it. Second, losing the financial support of liberal whites hampered certain CORE programs, such as its "target city" program. The "target city" program combined a mild welfare approach with a strong dose of protest.

Like SNCC, CORE had few connections with the political establishment. Because of its philosophy and its orientation to lower-class African Americans, CORE rarely entered conventional political arenas. It relied primarily on direct-action methods. Consequently, CORE, just like SNCC, became increasingly alienated from the political system and from the more established moderate civil rights organizations such as the NAACP and the Urban League.

The Southern Christian Leadership Conference (SCLC)[17] falls in the middle of the continuum shown in Table 7-1. It holds this position probably because of its mixed characteristics. On the one hand, SCLC's organization, support, and connections with liberal whites have tended to integrate it into the political system. On the other hand, however, its techniques resemble those of low-integration groups. This mixture of characteristics probably accounts for SCLC's central position in the 1964 coalition. SCLC was organized in 1957 and has been one of the most effective groups in civil rights. It is based on a philosophy of racial reform through creative nonviolence. Martin Luther King, Jr. was, until his assassination in the spring of 1968, the president of SCLC. In fact, the organization was considered the personal embodiment of King. SCLC under King's leadership was very highly centralized. Despite elections, the organization was a synonym for the name Martin Luther King. It depended not only on his leadership and philosophical guidance but also his ability to raise money. King's speaking tours helped SCLC become one of the best financed civil rights groups. Given King's charisma, the organization was able to enlist the support of more than 100 church-affiliated groups. This religious support, in combination with the support of white liberals, provided King with many points of access.

In the 1960s, however, SCLC's power position became highly unstable. Some white liberals shied away from King in the mid- to late-1960s because of his increased use of direct-action techniques. (Yet King was able to garner additional white liberal support for his stand on the Vietnam War.) By contrast, some blacks were disappointed by his refusal to become more militant in his direct-action activities. At the time of his death, Martin Luther King seemed caught in the center. The year 1968 found SCLC in a central position, but that central position may have no longer been the rallying point for civil rights. Wherever that "rallying point" was, however, it appeared likely that (had he lived) King would have tried to find it.

THE POLITICS OF COALITION BUILDING

Between 1963 and 1965, the civil rights coalition proved to be a potent force in the American political scene. The question of how this coalition came about leads us to the politics of coalition building.

World War II brought the country into a new phase of civil rights.[18] This new era was an outgrowth of several factors. First, World War II was fought in the name of human freedom. This attuned the population, both black and white, to the importance of equality. Second, the war marked the end of the Great Depression. The depression reoriented the thinking of many Americans. The market had failed the United States in 1929. Because of this failure, the American people were willing to place other values above the rights of private property. As a result of this rethinking, Americans now placed a greater emphasis on political, economic, and social equality. Finally, World War II directly affected African Americans' lives by making them mobile. Able to compare two styles of life (thanks to military service or a wartime job in some northern factory), African Americans could see the southern caste system was not inevitable. Taken together, these factors set the stage for a new revolution in America.

The 1940s produced a flurry of civil rights activities. It was in this era that groups like CORE gained attention.[19] Frustrated by the gradualism of established civil rights groups, the younger groups dedicated themselves to more militant approaches. But during the tensions of the 1940s, groups tended to be concerned with their own immediate problems. For the most part, civil rights were still considered in terms of local interests. A civil rights movement per se did not yet exist.

Only in the 1950s can we observe the development of a coalition. Through a series of Supreme Court cases, one could note a gradual convergence of interested parties. There was now evidence that a civil rights coalition could be effective. This new realization sparked the desire to destroy finally the "separate but equal doctrine" of *Plessy* v. *Ferguson*. In *Brown* v. *Board of Education* (1954), several groups under the leadership of the NAACP pooled their resources[20] and won a monumental victory when on May 17, 1954, the Supreme Court declared racial segregation in public schools unconstitutional.

The 1954 decision fostered new hope in the civil rights movement. It also aroused in blacks a sense of impatience with racial conditions generally. In 1955, for example, nearly all blacks in Montgomery, Alabama, boycotted segregated transportation facilities. Indeed, "the once dormant and quiescent Negro community," as Martin Luther King expressed it, "was now fully awake."[21] The success of the 1955 bus boycott paved the way for subsequent nonviolent techniques, including sit-ins and freedom rides of the early 1960s. (It also skyrocketed Martin Luther King into national prominence.) These direct-action efforts were engineered primarily by the more recently established, more action-oriented groups, that is, CORE, SCLC, and SNCC. In the early 1960s these newer civil rights groups and the older groups were not united, yet there were many who felt that unity was necessary to combat racial discrimination.

The 1963 March on Washington represented, among other things, an attempt to promote and demonstrate unity among the various groups. A. Philip Randolph, veteran civil rights leader and president of the Brotherhood of Sleeping Car Porters, AFL-CIO, issued the call for the march at a time when there was considerable division and personal rancor among civil rights groups and their leaders.[22] Randolph originally conceived the march as a demonstration for jobs, but Martin Luther King thought the goals should be broadened to include all African American rights, not just economic rights. Randolph accepted King's "broadening proposal" and the march began to take shape. To actually plan the march, Randolph secured the services of Bayard Rustin. Rustin had a rich and varied background of experiences in civil rights activities and other human rights causes and at one time had served as secretary to Dr. King. Close attention had to be paid not only to promoting unity among the largely black civil rights groups but also to building a coalition that included white organizations such as labor.

Achieving unity and cooperation among the civil rights groups was not easy. One might have expected the June 13, 1963 murder of Medgar Evers, field director of the Mississippi NAACP, to serve as a rallying point for the various organizations. But such was not the case. Groups suspected each other of trying to "use" the emotional situation to promote their own particular causes. Frictions inevitably developed. Roy Wilkins attacked the "irritating incidents" caused by "local eager beavers," and openly criticized CORE, SNCC, and the SCLC for taking "the publicity while the NAACP provides the manpower and pays the bill."[23] "The only organization that can handle a long sustained fight," said Wilkins, "is the NAACP. We are not here today, gone tomorrow." A few days later, however, Wilkins called for cooperation among the various groups, noting that such collaboration was especially important at the "present time" because of civil rights legislation pending in Congress. "Intelligent work in the Capitol lobbies," said Wilkins, "could be more important than mass marches on Washington or sit-downs in the halls of Congress."

Responding to Wilkins' plea (and also, perhaps, to his earlier criticisms), Martin Luther King remarked:

> We all acknowledge that the NAACP is the oldest, the best established, it has done a marvelous job for many years and has worked rigorously. But we feel we also have a role to play in supplementing what the NAACP has done. Unity is necessary. Uniformity is not. The highway that leads to the city of freedom is not a one-time highway. New organizations such as SCLC are not substitutes for the NAACP, but they can be wonderful supplements.[24]

King's remarks sounded a note upon which there could be unity and cooperation among the various groups. The commonality of their goal overcame, for the time being at least, group differences in strategy and tactics and led to cooperative ventures. For example, in July 1963, SNCC, CORE, SCLC, NAACP, the Urban League, and two other groups formed an Ad Hoc Council on Civil Rights Leadership to coordinate planning and activities for "racial integration and equal opportunity."[25] A major goal of the Ad Hoc Council was to raise emergency funds for aiding organizations to meet rising and unexpected costs resulting from the "tremendous increase in civil rights activities . . . since their 1963 budgets were adopted."[26] Evidence that this cooperative fund-raising effort met with some success can be found in the more than one-half million dollars distributed among the various participating groups in July 1963.[27]

The cooperative mood of the times was further enhanced by pronouncements and resolutions emanating from the 1963 national conventions of the various organizations. CORE national delegates, for example, were warned against "rivalry" among organizations and were told of the necessity of cooperation.[28] But perhaps the most dramatic example of the growing cooperation and understanding among civil rights groups was pointed to by a resolution passed by the 1963 National Convention of the Urban League. While continuing to pursue its goals through negotiations and professional social work, the league nevertheless resolved to support legal picketing and sit-ins by other groups. The league even acknowledged that certain "stubborn problem situations have not responded to Urban League methods."[29]

The August 1963 March on Washington was the high point of coalition activity among civil rights groups and their allies up to that time. [The "Big Six" civil rights organizations, (SNCC, CORE, the NAACP, SCLC, the Urban League, and Randolph's Negro American Labor Council (NALC)) even agreed to accept as equal partners Walter Reuther, vice president of AFL-CIO, and one white officer apiece from Protestant, Catholic, and Jewish organizations.] For a moment, group priorities were set aside, with each group yielding something for the coalition. For their part, the Urban League and the NAACP agreed to participate actively in the form of direct action. On the other hand, the more militant participants such as CORE and SNCC agreed to seek and be content (for a while at least) with action through relatively conventional channels. Moreover, CORE and SNCC were dissuaded from other actions that

March on Washington. This August 1963 March on Washington was the highlight of coalition activity among civil rights groups and their allies. *(UPI/Bettmann Newsphotos)*

tended to offend white liberal sympathizers. For example, when Archbishop Patrick O'Boyle of the Washington, D.C., archdiocese threatened not to give the invocation at the March program unless John Lewis, then president of SNCC, changed his prepared speech, Lewis (after some negotiation) obliged. Lewis's original speech read:

> The non-violent revolution is saying we will not wait for the others to act for we have been waiting for hundreds of years. We will not wait for the President, the Justice Department nor Congress, but we will take matters into our own hands and create a source of power outside of any national structure that could and would assure us victory.[30]

O'Boyle discussed this part of Lewis's speech with Randolph and Reuther, both of whom agreed that the speech was not consistent with the tenor "of the rest of the program." Upon the urgings of Randolph and Reuther, Lewis revised this part of his speech. The revision read:

> To those who are saying, "Be patient and wait," we will say that we cannot be patient. We do not want our freedom gradually, but we want to be free now.[31]

Great care was taken to nurture march unity. For example, representatives of each of the ten sponsoring groups were given a place on the program. In this way no group could feel slighted. However, as on other occasions, it was the charisma and powerful oratory of Martin Luther King that highlighted the program and cemented a coalition unity that paved the way for future coordination and cooperation among civil rights groups and their allies.

The fruits of the cooperation and the spirit of unity exemplified in the 1963 March on Washington were reaped in 1964 and 1965 when Congress passed the most far-reaching civil rights legislation since the Reconstruction era. These acts contained provisions legally guaranteeing blacks the right to vote, access to most public accommodations, desegregated schools, and equal employment opportunities. Not only was the scope of these acts far broader than the earlier Civil Rights Acts of 1957 and 1960, but the provisions for enforcement by the federal government also gave hope that the provisions would be obeyed. Of course, passage of these two acts was not due solely to intensive lobbying; the northern Democratic-Republican coalition and vigorous assistance from the White House were crucial elements of the victory. Nevertheless, behind the near-consensus among the pro-civil rights coalition of politicians was a national mood; in the creation of that national mood the coalition of civil rights groups was perhaps the primary moving force. In Senate Republican leader Everett Dirksen's words,"the time has come."[32].

But there were signs, even in 1964-1965, that the coalition was in jeopardy. First, the less integrationist members of the coalition, such as SNCC, CORE, and SCLC, had always made their support contingent upon success in the society at large and not merely in Congress. As it gradually became clear that even the historic acts of 1964-1965 would not change the living conditions of African Americans rapidly, these groups began to search for means other than legislation to promote that change. Second, despite provisions for enforcement, considerable discrimination remained even in the areas covered by these two acts. For example, in 1967 the Civil Rights Commission reported that in the area of public education, the field in which federal government intervention had been tried the longest (since 1954), "racial isolation in the public schools was intense and growing worse."[33] Finally, there was the failure of the coalition to obtain legislative enactment of desegregation in certain crucial areas, such as housing. "Open housing" was not included in the 1964-1965 acts, and when it was included in the 1966 Civil Rights Bill the Senate killed the bill. Such legislation was finally passed in 1968.

THE POLITICS OF DISINTEGRATION

In July 1964, the leaders of the NAACP, SCLC, the Urban League, and the Negro American Labor Council (NALC) signed a statement urging major civil rights groups to curtail or postpone mass demonstrations until after the 1964 presidential elections.[34] SNCC (Lewis) and CORE (Farmer) did not sign the statement. "Our own estimate of the present situation," said the four leaders, "is that it presents a serious threat to the implementation of the Civil Rights Act of 1964."[35] The "present situation" was described as including the passage of the Civil Rights Act, the nomination of Barry Goldwater, and recent big city riots. "Therefore," the four leaders continued, "we propose a temporary change of emphasis and tactics because we sincerely believe that the major energy of the civil rights forces should be used to encourage Negro people, North and South, to register and to vote. The greatest need in this period is for political action."[36] Although Roy Wilkins said that SNCC and CORE leaders agreed with the statement "personally" and were withholding their signatures pending the meeting of their steering committees, there is no evidence that Lewis and Farmer ever agreed to the statement. In a second statement issued by the group, all but SNCC joined. This statement condemned rioting and looting and drew a sharp distinction between such activity and legitimate protest.

The year 1965 was the turning point for coalition activity within the civil rights movement. The year began on a cooperative note. A. Philip Randolph (NALC), who led the 1963 March on Washington, was once again in the forefront. He convened a two-day closed meeting of civil rights leaders to outline aims for 1965. Some 29 organizations attended, including representatives from all major civil rights groups, including SNCC, SCLC, CORE, the NAACP, and the Urban League.[37] In a carefully and broadly worded statement, the organizations agreed that "the thrust of the civil rights movement this year . . . would be toward guaranteeing the right to vote through increased registration, legislation, and peaceful demonstrations."[38] Randolph called the conference evidence of the "continued dialogue and shared experience" among civil rights groups.[39]

But support for the Voting Rights Act of 1965 was perhaps the final manifestation of a viable coalition among civil rights groups and their allies. Indeed, the "continued dialogue" was already finished. Disaffection, frustration, and friction began to develop and, ironically, the passage of the Civil Rights Act of 1964 and the Voting Rights Act of 1965 gave further impetus to these developments. Blacks by and large were frustrated because, though sweeping legislation had been passed, their social and economic situation remained the same; nothing had changed. It was this latter factor perhaps more than anything else which led to friction among civil rights groups. Some groups, such as SNCC and CORE, wanted immediate results, while the NAACP was willing to pursue enforcement through regular legal channels. Actually, this "division of labor,"[40] that is, the testing of laws through demonstrations by the more militant groups and legal challenges by the NAACP, seemed tailor-made for the situation. But, although their goals may have been the same, the difference in temperament and approach between the less moderate and more established organizations posed too great an obstacle to overcome for a sustained period. In addition, the insistence of

SNCC and CORE to link the "peace movement" (Vietnam) with the civil rights struggle also created friction among the groups.[41] For example, in August 1965, SNCC and CORE members openly joined the Assembly of Unrepresented People and staged a march on Washington, D.C. On the other hand, the NAACP's Roy Wilkins warned his members not to participate since the focus of the march was on Vietnam, not civil rights.[42] Wilkins undoubtedly was concerned that linking civil rights with the anti-war movement might cost the coalition some powerful friends, especially President Johnson.

The smoldering frictions of the coalition exploded into the open in 1966. This was the year that saw Stokely Carmichael and Floyd McKissick take over the reins of SNCC and CORE. Undoubtedly these changes in leadership in SNCC and CORE did much to bring the battle into the open. In May 1966, for example, Carmichael attacked integration as a goal of the civil rights movement and called it "irrelevant."[43] "Political and economic power is what black people have to have."[44] This kindling of black nationalism flew in the face of everything civil rights leaders had previously sought to accomplish. However, the man in the "middle" of the civil rights movement, Martin Luther King, remained in the middle in his criticism of Carmichael. "While I can't agree with the move toward a kind of black nationalism developing in SNCC," said King, "it is an indication of deep discontent, frustration, disappointment, and even despair in many segments of the Negro community."[45]

The June 1966 White House Conference on Civil Rights also pointed up the developing split among civil rights groups. SNCC refused to participate since it did not believe the Johnson administration was sincere in helping blacks and because of United States involvement in Vietnam. And though CORE participated, it did so, as its new national chairman Floyd McKissick put it, so that militants could "bring forth ideas that otherwise would not be brought forth."[46] This "militant" view included a CORE-sponsored resolution calling for American withdrawal from Vietnam. Though soundly defeated, the resolution nevertheless evidenced the growing schism between militants such as CORE and SNCC and the more established groups such as the NAACP. Martin Luther King attended the White House conference but apparently, and perhaps discreetly, remained "behind the scenes."

Other incidents also demonstrated the growing rift among the various groups. In June 1966, for example, James Meredith was wounded while walking through Mississippi on his "pilgrimage against fear." Major civil rights organizations came to his rescue and agreed to continue the march. For the moment, at least, it seemed as if the groups had patched up their differences. But this appearance was short-lived. The groups did not agree on what they hoped to accomplish by continuing the "pilgrimage." Three leaders—King, Carmichael, and McKissick—issued a joint statement declaring the march to be a "massive public indictment and protest of the failure of American society, the government of the United States, and the State of Mississippi to 'fulfill these rights,'"[47] "Most important of all," the statement continued, "the President of the United States must enforce those laws justly and impartially for all men."[48] However, Roy Wilkins of the NAACP and Whitney Young of the Urban League refused to sign the statement. Subsequently, Wilkins openly denounced CORE and SNCC and shed light on the apparent disagreement among the groups at the time of the Meredith march. Wilkins said:

> The refusal of the . . . organization to join in a strong nation-wide effort to pass the Civil Rights Bill (1966) was a civil rights tragedy. The Meredith shooting should have been and could have been a rallying cry for scores of organizations and groups in a concerted push for the Bill . . . The whole business showed the NAACP again how difficult it is to have genuine cooperation on an equal responsibility basis with groups that do not have the same commitments and which may well be pursuing certain goals that have nothing to do with civil rights at all.[49]

Wilkins decried the fact that his organization had to bear the major burdens in order to get cooperation with other groups. He recalled instances in which his group had helped SNCC, CORE, and SCLC. He talked of the $5,000 the NAACP sent to King during the Selma-to-Montgomery march in 1965 and said it was some six months later before his organization even got an acknowledgment, and then for only $3,000 (this was apparently the first hint of strained relations between Wilkins and King). Wilkins also denounced the Black Power aspirations of SNCC and CORE. This latter denunciation brought a sharp rebuttal from CORE's Floyd McKissick: "I think it is regrettable that Mr. Wilkins, a man whom I respect . . . has reached the point where he does not understand the community, possibly because of lack of contact."[50] Undoubtedly, the Mississippi "pilgrimage against fear" widened the split among civil rights groups and "Black Power"[51] became the symbol of that split. It was on this march that Carmichael popularized Black Power, and angry crowds repeated it time and again.

Black Power now became the divisive force among civil rights groups. Carmichael (SNCC) and McKissick (CORE) championed the new concept and expounded its meaning, including black mobilization, black leadership for black organizations, the promotion of self-pride, and the right of self-defense.[52] But the more established civil rights groups and leaders denounced the new concept. They viewed Black Power as damaging to the civil rights movement and alien to its principles. Accordingly, seven civil rights leaders, including Wilkins (the NAACP), Young (the Urban League), and Randolph and Rustin (leaders of the 1963 March on Washington) issued a joint statement reaffirming these principles lest Black Power advocates "be interpreted as representing the civil rights movement."[53] In this restatement of principles, the leaders reaffirmed their commitment to achieving racial justice through democratic institutions such as courts and legislatures, their commitment to integration and to "the common responsibility of all Americans, white and black, for bringing integration to pass." The leaders strongly denounced the violent "implications" of Black Power.

Once again, Martin Luther King took a "middle" position.[54] He endorsed the principles set forth by the moderate civil rights leaders but refused to sign the statement.[55] He called Black Power "confusing" but did not denounce those who espoused it. He said it was a false assumption that the slogan had brought about the so-called white backlash when actually it had been "exploited by the decision-makers to justify resistance to change."[56] In an oblique criticism of those who signed the statement, King said:

> Some consider certain civil rights groups inclusively and irrevocably committed to error and wish them barred from the movement. I cannot agree with this approach because it involves an acceptance of the interpretation of enemies of civil rights and bases policy on their distortion. Actually, much thinking, particularly by young Negroes is in a state of flux . . . the intensified resistance to civil rights goals has outraged and dismayed very sincere Negroes and . . . in frustration and despair, they are groping for new approaches. Negro unity and Negro-white unity, both of which are decisive, can only be harmed by a precipitated effort to excommunicate any group, even if silencing or isolating some groups is unintended.[57]

Basically, this general division among civil rights groups and leaders—with SNCC and CORE on the one side, the NAACP and the Urban League on the other, and Martin Luther King and his organization somewhere in between—was the pattern that emerged in early 1968.

Conclusion

The civil rights groups' policies differed throughout most of the 1960s because of substantial differences in the nature and structure of the groups. Moreover, these organizational differences tended to be cumulative: As these factors reinforced one another, coalition disintegration accelerated. In sum, it appears that the breakdown of the civil rights coalition originated from the organizational goals and characteristics of its member groups. Thus, we might conceptualize civil rights coalition behavior in terms of Figure 7-1. In the view presented here, the highly effective civil rights coalition of 1963-1964 was able to function in spite of a large number of factors tending toward disunity because of the moderating force of the SCLC and Dr. Martin Luther King, Jr. However, events after 1964-1965 exacerbated the frictions among the various civil rights groups and, of course, in the spring of 1968, assassination removed Dr. King from his central leadership position.

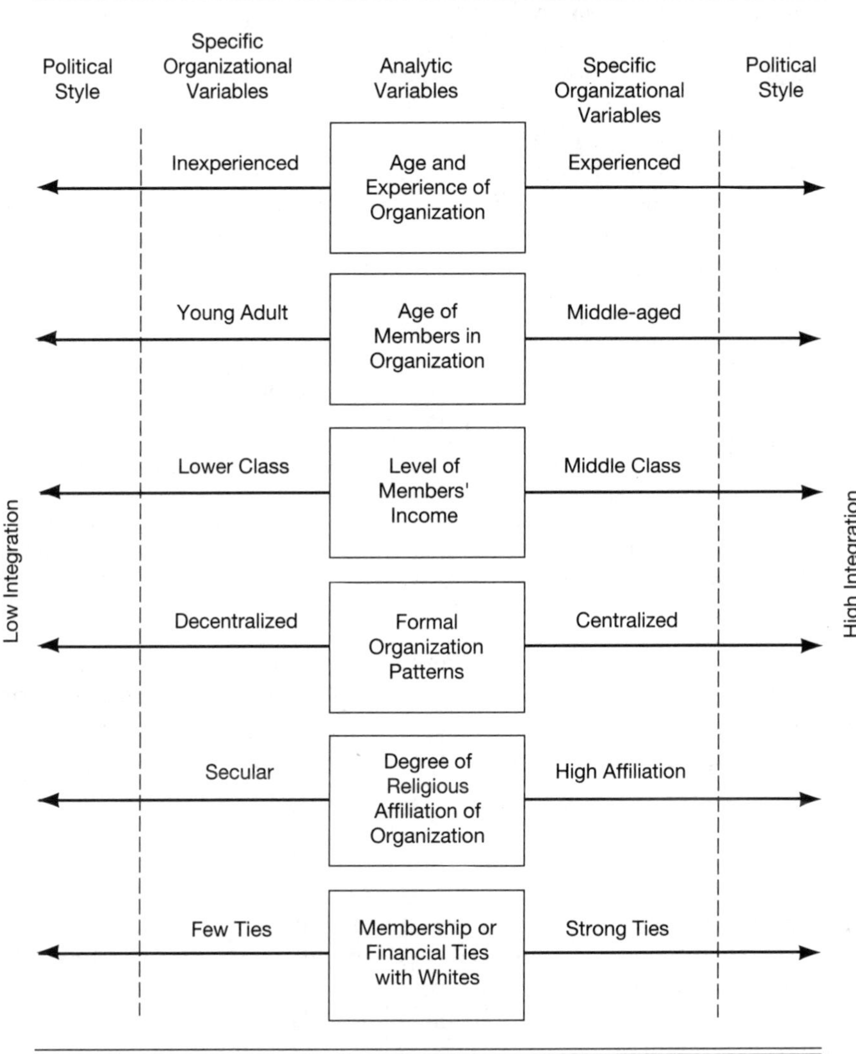

FIGURE 7-1
Factors contributing to the "Integration" of civil rights groups in the existing political system

CIVIL RIGHTS ORGANIZATIONS: QUEST FOR SURVIVAL AND ROLE

The 1960s were the high point of the civil rights movement. Unfortunately, the unity and direction that characterized that movement no longer exist; the focus of civil rights activity has changed. In the 1960s the push for formal recognition of legal rights provided a broad base around which civil rights groups and their white allies could rally. But in the 1970s, 1980s, and early 1990s the push for the actual implementation of those rights has commanded far less appeal and support. This situation has been caused by a number of factors. Perhaps the most significant factor is the belief that with the passage of major civil rights legislation in the 1960s, America's racial problems have been solved and civil rights need no longer be a priority on the nation's agenda.[58] To be sure, some very real, notable, and visible progress has been made by blacks and other minorities. This can be noted in both broad socioeconomic terms (e.g., income and education differentials) and also in the number of blacks elected or appointed to government positions. Such progress, however, has not had much effect on the circumstances of most blacks, and the progress that has been made, and especially the publicity which has accompanied such progress, serves, ironically, to lessen interest in civil rights.

Clearly, such visible signs of progress bolster the view that our civil rights problems are behind us and that ours is a society free from racism. This is the viewpoint that was nurtured and perpetuated by the Reagan administration, resulting in civil rights occupying low priority during Reagan's eight years. This should come as no surprise, however, given the comparative constituency support for civil rights between the two major parties. A similar situation prevailed during the Bush administration.

The small amount of attention paid to civil rights and racial problems in national politics is commensurate with the attitudes of the American electorate. In October 1965, for example, 27 percent of all Americans considered civil rights the most important problem facing the country. In September 1972, that figure had dropped to only 5 percent. And by 1978, race had all but vanished from the national conscience as one of our "most important problems."

During the last decade that trend has continued. Other issues such as the state of the economy (unemployment, inflation, energy, and most recently, taxes), crime, and international crises (such as the Iranian hostage crisis in 1979, the Soviet invasion of Afghanistan in 1980, the Iran-Contra scandal of 1987, the end of the Cold War in 1989 and the Persian Gulf crisis of 1990) have eclipsed the importance of civil rights in the minds of many Americans. In addition, public disinterest in civil rights was only reinforced by the Nixon, Reagan, and Bush administrations. Each of these Republican presidents relegated civil rights concerns to the back burner, exhibiting attitudes which were at best insensitive and at worst deliberately hostile to the interests of African Americans.

But it is clear that concerns of civil rights organizations today go beyond race-specific issues and embrace the whole range of economic concerns consistent with the significant problems that continue to disproportionately and negatively influence the overall quality of life of blacks and minorities. These problems include persistently high levels of unemployment; the dire need for more jobs, better educational systems, and job training; the continuing high incidence of poverty; inadequate health care and delivery; and the lack of decent housing. The mounting challenge for traditional civil rights groups in the future is how effectively they can garner the resources needed to deal with these socioeconomic problems. Their relative success and survival depend on how well they can meet this challenge.

Another very important factor complicating the life of civil rights organizations has been the general posture of the president, Congress, the Supreme Court, and other governmental institutions toward civil rights and racial problems. The general posture of these institutions and officials, of course, is closely related and responsive to changing events and changing moods of public opinion. Indeed, what is perceived as the "most important problem" will undoubtedly affect the agendas of these various institutions of government. The posture of the president is a good example. As intimated earlier, the Nixon administration, for the most part, projected a hostile attitude toward the problems of blacks, the poor, and minorities. Neither Nixon's campaigns for the presidency nor his administration were disposed to encourage or seek support from civil rights interests. And quite obviously, that support was not forthcoming. In addition, the Ford presidency did little to change the overall posture of the Nixon era toward blacks. It is true, of course, that Gerald Ford as president was somewhat preoccupied with the spillover effects of Watergate. And though not viewed as hostile to civil rights as Nixon, the Ford administration could well be characterized as a "benign" continuation of the Nixon years.

The 1976 campaign and election of Jimmy Carter as president undoubtedly rekindled the hopes and aspirations of blacks and civil rights interests. But this renewed hope was rather short-lived. Indeed, many believe that the low-keyed performance of Carter simply did not live up to his glowing rhetoric and visible symbols, that is, his appointment of blacks to administrative positions. This view was openly and straightforwardly articulated by Vernon Jordan, executive director of the National Urban League and one of the major black civil rights leaders.[59] In his opening address to the 1977 annual meeting of the Urban League, Jordan stated flatly that the Carter administration had "fallen short of blacks' expectations in terms of 'policies, program, and people.'"[60]

But two days later, in response to an earlier invitation by Jordan to address the convention, President Carter had his opportunity to react to Jordan's criticism and the president reacted sharply. The president said he had "no apologies" for his administration's record with respect to blacks and poor people. In fact, Carter said that Jordan's criticism itself damaged "the hopes and aspirations of those poor people."[61] However, despite the president's stirring defense of his record, there is little doubt that Jordan's criticism became an increasingly widely shared view among blacks. This was reflected by the immediate support for his position that Jordan received from other major civil rights leaders.[62] But by 1980 the Iran and Afghanistan situations directed attention away from domestic concerns, and President Carter gave his priority to foreign policy matters.

Black dissatisfaction with the Carter administration was mild when compared to their open dissatisfaction and anguish that ensued following Ronald Reagan's victory over Carter in the 1980 elections. Time and again, through word and deed, the Reagan administration demonstrated its lack of concern and generally negative posture toward matters that greatly affected blacks and minorities. Likewise, Reagan's overwhelming reelection victory over Mondale in 1984 sent ominous signals with regard to the future of black progress.

The posture and actions of the Reagan administration were clearly and concretely inimical to the continued progress of blacks and minorities (e.g., budget cutbacks in social welfare programs, lack of sensitive and systematic efforts to deal with severe and disproportionate unemployment and poverty among these groups, and hostile interpretations and enforcement of civil rights laws). Moreover, Reagan's appointments, including those to the federal judiciary, reflected clearly the president's negative posture toward blacks, minorities, and civil rights interests generally.

Overall, the attitudes and actions of the Reagan administration illustrate vividly how the work and effectiveness of interest groups, in this instance civil rights organizations, can be affected greatly by the posture and policies of governmental officials and institutions. Black elected officials, as well as black interest group leaders, were quite unified and vocal in complaining about lack of access and influence with the Reagan administration.

The Bush administration, despite attaining the highest sustained approval rating among blacks for a Republican president, continued its opposition to certain civil rights issues, most notably affirmative action. In 1989, the Supreme Court issued six decisions that further eroded affirmative action.[63] The Supreme Court rulings included restricting application of statutory provisions prohibiting discrimination in the formation and enforcement of contracts to hiring agreements and not to later conduct by the employer. They also included placing the burden of proving discriminatory intent on the individual claiming employment discrimination, and eroding the effect of consent decrees by allowing persons not involved in the discrimination lawsuit to subsequently challenge the consent decree.

In response to these Supreme Court decisions, Congress passed a bill to amend the Civil Rights Act to reverse the effect of these court decisions. Shortly after the bill's introduction, Attorney General Dick Thornburgh wrote the

Senate Labor and Human Resources Committee that he would recommend that President Bush veto the bill. Bush stated that he wanted to sign a civil rights bill and met with black leaders to reach a compromise on the bill. However, the Bush administration continued to oppose the civil rights bill, and in the end, the president vetoed the measure, alleging that the bill was an attempt to impose racial hiring quotas. Attempts to resurrect the legislation in 1991 by moderate Republican Senator John Danforth (Missouri) continued to encounter rebuff and resistance from the White House.[64] In the end, however, Danforth's strong commitment paid off and the Civil Rights Act of 1991 was approved.

In addition, a number of other forces seem to indicate that civil rights groups and their objectives are in for hard times. Mention has already been made of the mixed posture of the Burger Court toward civil rights, and this posture has become increasingly negative in the Rehnquist Court. Indeed, although the increasing influence of blacks and minorities in politics clearly found expression in the Senate's rejection in 1987 of President Reagan's nomination of conservative Judge Robert Bork to the Supreme Court, in the end the president succeeded in bolstering the conservative position on the Court through the appointment of Justice Anthony Kennedy. Similarly, President Bush's judicial appointments, highlighted by his nomination of black Judge Clarence Thomas to the Supreme Court, also portend to strengthen conservative trends in the federal judiciary. After twelve years of Republican administrations under Presidents Reagan and Bush, civil rights groups and many others greeted the election of President Clinton in 1992 with much relief and enthusiasm. But as we suggest later in this book (see Chapter 11), the hope and expectations generated by Clinton's election, especially on the part of African Americans, must be tempered by the nature and realities of the policy process and American politics in general. After the first few months of his administration, for example, it seemed increasingly problematical whether Clinton's apparent strong attachment to "centrist-mainstream" politics and policies would bode well for African Americans and other historically disadvantaged minorities.

Mention should also be made of another factor that seems to be influencing the general political-social climate as well as public policy. This is the increasing volume of published views—in books, pamphlets, the press, and other media—that foster an "outlook forged in reaction to sixties turbulence, . . . fierce in its attachment to political and cultural moderation, committed to stability as the prerequisite for justice rather than the other way around, pessimistic about the possibilities for long-range, or even short-range, change in America, and imbued with a foreboding sense of our civilization's decline."[65] And though dressed in sophisticated garb, much of this "outlook" has been informed by views that have been generally critical of governmental intervention and policies designed to overcome problems faced by blacks and other minorities. A great deal of this effort has been made by scholars—referred to by Peter Steinfels as "neoconservatives"—whose credentials and reputations lend considerable prestige to their views and positions.[66] "The neoconservatives," says Steinfels, "are a *powerful* [emphasis his] party of intellectuals."[67] "Their reputations are solid; they speak from the elite universities—Harvard, Berkeley, MIT, Chicago, Stanford."[68] But although a "party of intellectuals," Steinfels warns that it would be risky and unwarranted to dismiss their significance as many are wont to do because they are intellectuals. Writes Steinfels:

> Intellectuals serve as advisers to officeholders and political candidates, write speeches, propose programs, draft legislation, serve on special commissions. The mass media amplify their ideas to a wider public, though not without considerable distortion. In all this the intellectuals have two functions. As experts in particular fields relevant to public policy they work out the details of political measures. But as traffickers in society's symbols and values, as keepers of memories, as orchestrators of its spectacles and images, and, in Tocqueville's words, as political theorists and shapers of general ideas, intellectuals are legitimators. What will be the agenda of public concerns? Where will one set the outer limits of the "responsible" opinion to which busy decision-makers should attend? Will credibility of this or that set of policies, or of the schools of thought behind them, be eroded or maintained—or will they be eliminated from serious consideration altogether? The dueling in intellectual journals, the rallying of like-minded thinkers at conferences or in new organizations, the shifts of power within the disciplines are all elements in this process of legitimation. So, one might add, is the quality of scholarship and the cogency and eloquence of argument."[69]

But not all current activity comes from the pens of white scholars; a few black scholars may also be viewed as deemphasizing the importance of race as a barrier to enjoying the benefits and opportunities of the American political-social system. In general, that such scholars, especially those whom Steinfels calls the "neoconservatives," can influence public opinion and public policy is evidenced not only by their access to communications media but also by "their direct access to officeholders and the political elite generally." It is clear, for example, that repeated Republican control of the White House (from 1968 through 1992, with the exception of the Carter years, 1976-1980) has considerably strengthened the visibility and influence of black conservatives. This strengthening occurred mainly through the appointment of black conservatives to certain highly visible positions, such as General Colin Powell as chairman of the Joint Chiefs of Staff, and Judge Clarence Thomas to the Supreme Court.

More generally, the overall "conservative" and "neoconservative" trends in the 1980s and the early 1990s seem to be increasingly supported by attitudes and actions of not only Republicans but Democrats as well. To become more competitive in presidential elections, for example, a broad array of Democratic party leaders (conservatives, moderates and "neo-liberals") now apparently want to make once "liberal" party principles more palatable to "mainstream" politics and the current popular mood. And both the Democratic Leadership Council, which provided the "platform" for Clinton's successful presidential campaign, as well as particular actions taken during the early months of his administration, appear obvious efforts to channel and institutionalize "centrist-mainstream" politics into molding a "New" Democratic party.

Overall, then, when one considers the various changes in the political-social climate, it becomes somewhat more understandable why civil rights organizations, whose major purpose is to promote the interest of blacks and minorities, have come upon hard times. These hard times have also had their impact on the internal politics and operations of civil rights groups. To these matters we now turn.

CIVIL RIGHTS GROUPS: PROBLEMS AND PROSPECTS

Civil rights groups continue to face a number of problems. These problems include (1) the nature of the groups' organizations and leadership and the problem of leadership succession; (2) the need to define continuously the group's role, objective, and tactics consistent with changing circumstances; (3) the ability to attract and maintain unity and support of group membership; and (4) the ability to attract financial support. In one way or another, these are the types of problems that can threaten not only civil rights organizations but also other organizations and interest groups in general. It seems clear that SNCC and CORE have not been able to weather these problems and that the SCLC faces an uphill battle for survival. Even the more established groups, such as the NAACP and the Urban League, have also felt the crunch of hard times. Let us consider this matter in more detail.

FROM EARLY SUCCESS TO LATER PROBLEMS

At the time of their founding, civil rights groups had little difficulty in defining their role and objectives and in recruiting and maintaining flourishing memberships. The primary purpose of such organizations was clear: to overcome the problems and pains of racial segregation and discrimination. The symbols and practices of racism were pervasive and were supported by a rigid system of laws, customs, and traditions. White racism was crudely blatant and openly visible; for example, public accommodations and educational opportunities that were separate and inferior if indeed they existed at all, and restrictions and pressures (physical if need be) against blacks voting and holding public office. But civil rights groups and their allies were able to meet these blatant practices head-on and their success in these efforts is evidenced by Court decisions (e.g., *Brown*) and civil rights legislation (e.g., the Civil Rights Act of 1964 and the Voting Rights Act of 1965). Simultaneously, a number of programs and policies supported and advanced black progress in a number of areas, for example, the War on Poverty. Hence, in terms of their original objectives, civil rights organizations had indeed met with a great deal of success.

But it is this very success that has led to some of the problems now faced by civil rights organizations. Indeed, while the more blatant and visible forms of racism have been overcome—at least legally—there remains a great deal of racism which is much more subtle, more complex, and much less visible. In addition, a number of the socioeconomic problems that impact disproportionately on blacks and minorities remain, for example, dilapidated and overcrowded housing and rising unemployment. Under such circumstances, it is clear that civil rights groups must redefine their role and objectives. Simultaneously, their strategy and tactics must be tailored to meet this more subtle discrimination and to attack these more complex problems. Some civil rights organizations, such as CORE and SCLC, have obviously encountered severe problems with respect to redefining their role and objectives in the light of changing circumstances. By contrast, the extent to which the NAACP and Urban League retain a measure of viability is related directly to their programs and objectives which meet these new and more complex problems.

Of course, the ability of particular groups to adapt to changing circumstances depends greatly on the nature of the group's organization and leadership. It seems clear, for example, that the fortunes of the SCLC were closely tied to Martin Luther King. He founded the organization, articulated its purposes and programs, and provided the leadership. Charismatic personality, stirring oratory, and undaunted commitment to a noble cause held the organization together and attracted many followers. King was the very embodiment of the SCLC. He dominated the organization and shaped its character, and his leadership was as unquestioned as it was cherished. However, just about the time of King's tragic assassination, the overall civil rights movement was meeting a crucial turning point. Indeed, most of the major civil rights legislation, except for the Fair Housing Act of 1968, was on the books.

More importantly, by 1968 we began to see a few tangible effects of the 1964 Civil Rights Act, for example, the opening up of places of public accommodation and the impact of the cutoff threat of federal funds with respect to increasing desegregation of public schools. Moreover, mainly as a direct consequence of the 1965 Voting Rights Act, blacks began to register and vote in increasing numbers, and they began to run and be elected to public offices.

However, between 1965 and 1968 we were also experiencing massive urban rebellion and unrest that dramatically illuminated the wide gaps that remained between the lofty promises of laws on the books and the painful and cold realities that the overall effects of the civil rights movement—including these laws—had brought about little if any change in the everyday life of African Americans.

CHANGES IN CLIMATE AND PRIORITIES: STRUGGLE FOR SURVIVAL

By 1968, we began to experience a shift in the political climate and in the nation's priorities. Ending the war in Vietnam and wiping out crime (restoring "law and order") replaced race and poverty as the most pressing problems facing the country. This shift in priorities brought about drastic changes in the political climate. President Lyndon Johnson, for example, who had strongly championed civil rights and socioeconomic programs, found himself in a quagmire that proved to be his political downfall. Johnson's undaunted courage and support for civil rights was not enough to satisfy liberals. They say his dogged prosecution of the Vietnam War was not only detrimental to finding a peaceful solution but also detrimental to harnessing the resources (money) necessary to deal with serious domestic problems, including civil rights and the socioeconomic programs which the president supported. Even so natural a supporter of the president as Martin Luther King found it necessary to speak out against the Vietnam War. Thus, with his natural support eroding (e.g., liberals), Johnson shocked the nation by announcing that he would not be a candidate for reelection. The ensuing politics saw Hubert Humphrey win the presidential nomination in a party which, though united on civil rights, was badly divided by the Vietnam conflict. And Humphrey himself was viewed by many as being too avid a supporter of Johnson's Vietnam policies.

The Republican party undoubtedly stood to greatly benefit from these strong divisions among the Democrats. By nominating Richard Nixon for president the Republicans obviously were determined to take full advantage of both the antiwar and "law and order" (get tough on blacks) moods of the country. But the Nixon campaign and his successful election illuminated that the pro-civil rights mood of the country had indeed changed.

Given these markedly changed conditions in the nation's overall political-social climate, we began to see more clearly the extreme difficulties and problems that faced civil rights organizations. These organizations now had to survive in a hostile climate. They felt pressures from within the black community ("deliver on your promises") as well as pressure from the outside (e.g., an unsympathetic president and a strong current of public opinion that believed enough had been done for blacks). How could civil rights organizations bring about effective implementation of civil rights legislation in this sort of environment? How could they maintain the unity and spirit of their memberships? How could they attract necessary funds for survival? In short, how would or could civil rights organizations adapt their roles, objectives, and tactics to meet these changed conditions? These were not easy questions and they posed difficult problems even for organizations that enjoyed a stable leadership. But for an organization like the SCLC—whose founder and personal leader was swept away without warning—these problems have undoubtedly proved disillusioning and divisive. A loosely structured group such as SCLC particularly would seem to depend upon a charismatic leader in order to nourish those factors which make for an effective organization, for example, viable goals and objectives, a unified membership, and sufficient financial resources. Of course, we can only speculate as to whether Dr. King would have been able to surmount these problems had he lived. But it is unquestionable that if any one person could have done so, King would have been that person. And it is even more speculative whether SCLC—without King—can overcome such problems. Nonetheless, the SCLC leadership continues to give it a try and make the organization more responsive to the changing opportunities and realities of the political-social climate.

THE NAACP: RETROSPECT AND PROSPECT

Similarly, we find that the more established organizations such as the NAACP and the Urban League have not been immune from such problems. The changed political-social circumstances have also affected the operations of these groups. Take the NAACP for example. This organization has had a long tradition of decentralized leadership and control with power being wielded by a well-entrenched middle-class national board of directors and by a strong executive director. Local chapters of the organization (some 2,200 in 1991) operate under guidelines and charters of the national organization. In general, this organizational structure has apparently worked rather well in defining and achieving the goals and objectives of the group. But the group's viability also depends upon mutual understandings of the relative role expectations and authority of the various officials and structures within the organization. For example, for the effective operation of an NAACP-type organizational structure, it is important to reach certain kinds of understandings with respect to the role expectations that exist (1) between and among the national board of directors, the national executive director, and the permanent professional and administrative staff and (2) between the centralized national structures (e.g., board of directors, executive director) and the local units or chapters.

The sheer survival and vitality of the NAACP serve to confirm that the organization's structure has worked rather well. Much of this, of course, has undoubtedly been due to the fact that the NAACP has traditionally had a national board of directors and executive directors who have enjoyed rather long tenures. This has not only promoted stability but also institutionalized working relationships. The long tenures of Walter White and Roy Wilkins (when combined with their leadership skills and visibility) especially served to quiet and overcome internal differences. But some internal differences did begin to surface. For the most part, they became more evident near the end of Wilkins's tenure and involved a combination of elements that generally concerned the relationship and authority of various structures at the national level. These elements included a leadership vacuum mainly created by Wilkins's impending retirement (which was somewhat filled by the board of directors, especially in defining the agenda and articulating the position of the organization on various issues); the politics involved in the selection of a new executive director to replace Wilkins; and the accommodations and relations that had to be worked out between the new executive director and the national board of directors. In terms of NAACP leadership patterns, one could say that most of these tension points or elements should have become quieted and synchronized once a new executive director was chosen. But the problems appear more deep-rooted. The selection of Benjamin Hooks as executive director did not quiet the internal problems. At the time of his selection, Hooks' experience and background as a lawyer, judge, Federal Communications Commission commissioner, and a Baptist minister would seem to combine the talents necessary for the position. But some two years later, apparent problems remained in the national leadership structure. Some suggested, for example, that though Hooks had done a good job, he "made the mistake of underestimating the power of the national board of directors." In this regard, one writer described the 1979 NAACP annual convention as follows:

> While Mr. Hooks' popularity with the members is unquestioned, scores of interviews indicate that he has made less of an impact on the long-entrenched board of directors and that he has been quietly discouraged about the slow-to-change bureaucracy he inherited. "I don't want to give the impression that the organization does not function," one staff official said. "It does, but it could function so much, much better with fewer personal agendas at the top and a broadening of leadership base, as well as better communications within and without the organization—and more money, of course."

The above quote, among other things, points up several other problems that have plagued the NAACP. There has long been concern that the power of the organization was so centralized in the national organization and its board of directors that initiatives, programs, and activities of local branches have been thwarted. Thus, during the 1960s the national "establishment" (and even local establishments) had to deal with frustrations and petitions from NAACP youth groups who wanted to be more "militant." Since that time, friction between the national office and local chapters became evident when local chapters (e.g., Atlanta) sought to work out school desegregation problems that did not meet the approval of the national office. In general, however, the general membership seems to approve this centralization of power and authority. Indeed, a resolution in the 1979 annual meeting to restrict the power and influence of the national board of directors by limiting the terms of its members to 12 years was defeated. The resolution was primarily backed by young persons who reasoned that they were being shut off from positions of leadership. Some persons, who are believed to be influential, have been on the national board for more than 12 years. But the defeat of the resolution, as one writer put it, "is yet another indication of the board's strength and of the general membership's distrust of sudden change."

Lack of adequate financial resources is another problem confronting the NAACP. Just like other civil rights groups, the NAACP faces the situation of trying to cope with increasingly complex problems with decreasing financial resources and doing so in a political-social climate that ranges from indifference to hostility.

Overall, however, and despite its problems, the NAACP remains the most viable black civil rights organization. It has a relatively large mass membership, about 450,000 in 1989. It has an organizational structure that allows for centralized authority to be exercised by state and strong national leadership. It maintains an array of programs and activities that show an attempt to keep its agenda continuously consistent with the changing nature of problems and of the political-social climate. And it is clear that the organization is also taking steps to see that its operations and procedures are congruent with modern practice and technology. This is exemplified concretely by the infusion of younger, more aggressive and well-trained staff personnel into the organization.[70]

To be sure, these actions may be viewed as responses to critics who charge that both the NAACP agenda and operations are out of step with current needs and requirements. In a 1991 interview, for example, NAACP Board Chairman Dr. William Gibson "acknowledged that the organization had been complacent in recent years but said it was becoming more active in areas like legislative redistricting, with an aim of increasing minority political representation and influence." This and similar efforts are being spurred by the younger personnel (exemplified by the organization's 40-year-old general counsel—Dennis Hayes) and the modern technology (e.g., computers) that now occupy the NAACP's national headquarters in Baltimore.

Both Dr. Gibson and Hazel Dukes, the NAACP president, saw these moves as reflecting both organizational goals and strategy. "We plan to be more firm and aggressive with corporate America over economic empowerment," said Gibson. "If negotiations fail, we will be prepared to use economic clout through boycotts. We're restructuring ourselves," he continued, "to lobby at the local, state and federal levels, using new technology and communications, whatever it takes." And this "restructuring" was reflected in comments by Dukes, who said that "we're bringing in new people who, while they know how the NAACP operates, they're not from our tradition. They believe in the NAACP values, but are able to see beyond traditional approaches."

But at the time, it took the organization's executive director, Benjamin Hooks, to respond more directly to critics who suggest that the NAACP's agenda and priorities are out of step with current reality. In a 1991 interview, for example, Hooks joined the issue in sharp perspective:

> There are so many things we try to do with meager resources because the problems are so deep. . . . But one thing we won't do is to abandon the fight against racism. If we do, who's left?

> I don't know if our critics understand; our charter is to fight discrimination. If they're telling me there's no longer a problem with police brutality, no more job and housing discrimination and most people are not worried about it, they're wrong. We're not struggling to find a mandate; we've got one.

Overall, and despite its struggles and its critics, the oldest civil rights organization, the NAACP, has developed an image and strong allegiance and tradition among blacks and Americans generally as a moderate organization that is stable yet flexible, and sensitive yet rational, in its approaches to problems. These traits were exemplified vividly by the deliberate and studied manner in which the organization reached its decision to oppose the nomination of black federal Judge Clarence Thomas to the U.S. Supreme Court. In the dynamic and fast pace of the confirmation battle, however, some might suggest that this kind of deliberate studied strategy served to slow the opposition buildup mounting against Thomas and, ironically, might have helped rather than hurt his cause. Despite this and other criticisms, however, the NAACP remains the key civil rights organization. The extent to which it might be able to maintain this role in the future clearly will depend in great measure on what type of leader the organization would select as its executive director to succeed Benjamin Hooks, who stated his intention in 1992 to retire as soon as a replacement could be found. And in April 1992, that replacement was found when the NAACP announced that Dr. Benjamin Chavis, a 45-year-old black minister and long-time civil rights activist, would replace Hooks as executive director.[71] But the dynamics leading to Chavis' selection were anything but tranquil; in many ways they reflected the overall tensions that had for some time been affecting the organization. For example, some on the 64-member national Board of Directors, the body that actually selects the executive director, thought that the organization needed a more active, visible, and aggressive leader; in particular they apparently wanted Jesse Jackson.

Jackson's candidacy perforce commanded attention. Indeed, despite being the focal point of repeated criticism and controversy, Jackson remains one of the most widely known and popular leaders in the black community, having waged two highly publicized and in many ways largely successful campaigns for the Democratic presidential nomination in 1984 and 1988.

Even so, controversy continued to swirl about Jackson—this time in his candidacy for the position of executive director. To be sure, Jackson on occasion has openly suggested that the organization should become more aggressively involved in issues such as those reflected by the 1992 Rodney King incident and the subsequent Los Angeles riots. In this way, Jackson and others reasoned that the NAACP could thus attract the interest and support needed to cope with today's problems.

But others on the Board of Directors were opposed to, or at least a bit wary of, Jackson. They were apprehensive, for example, that Jackson might be more disposed to follow his own "agenda" rather than that of the national

Board or organization generally. More directly, some "expressed grave concern over the administrative ability and temperamental compatibility" of Jackson with the NAACP. As the selection process evolved, however, any impending battle over such concerns was averted when in the end Jackson decided to withdraw his name from consideration.

However, Jackson's comments on his withdrawal continued to fuel the controversy. In explaining his withdrawal, for example, Jackson charged that the national Board was "considering reducing the powers of the executive director," thus making the job less attractive and less doable. Other Board members, however, were quick to counter Jackson. They indicated that Jackson never was the "frontrunner" on the short list of four finalists, as he was wont to believe. In fact, the charge was made that Jackson withdrew "because he almost certainly would have lost if he had stayed in the race."

Whatever the situation regarding Jackson's candidacy and withdrawal, several things can be said. First, as we have discussed earlier in this chapter, on occasion the NAACP has been confronted in the past with tensions and disputes over the relative role and authority between the national Board of Directors and its executive director. And secondly, Jackson's withdrawal apparently smoothed the way for the selection of Chavis over the other two candidates that remained on the short list.

For his part, and as indicated earlier, Chavis, as a long time member of the NAACP and veteran of the civil rights movement, was not unaware of the problems surrounding both the organization and his own selection. In his acceptance speech as executive director, for example, Chavis took note of criticisms that had been levelled by Jackson and others against the organization. Indeed, Chavis acknowledged that he wanted to "sharpen the focus of the organization" consistent with the changing nature of the issues and the times. Moreover, Chavis in stating that he was no "stranger in the 'hood,'" similarly acknowledged that "I know we need to reach out and embrace our young people."

On the other hand, Chavis summarily dismissed criticisms that the NAACP has become "irrelevant" or "ossified." Indeed, said Chavis, "I think we need the civil rights movement more in '93 than [we did] in '63. And the great thing about the NAACP is its structure. It's in place." Overall, and when viewed in the total context of its goals, traditions, and continuing vibrancy, the NAACP is an organization that one expects to be around for some time.

THE URBAN LEAGUE: A CHANGING CIVIL RIGHTS POSTURE

The National Urban League has long been concerned with problems (e.g., housing, job opportunities) that strike at the very heart of the real everyday problems that affect blacks and other minorities. But given its nature—"an interracial, non-profit community service organization" with its main sources of financial support from corporate donations and federal grants—one would perhaps expect the Urban League to be among the more moderate civil rights groups; it is and has been. This is exemplified vividly by the League's decision to remain neutral on the controversial nomination of Clarence Thomas to the Supreme Court. Nonetheless, during the height of the civil rights movement, and also today, the League has somehow been able to project a relatively strong civil rights posture without alienating the necessary kinds of support it needs from the private and public sectors.

Undoubtedly, this has been due in large measure to the leadership skills and resourcefulness that the League has enjoyed in its executive directors, including the late Whitney M. Young, Jr., Vernon Jordan, and most recently, John Jacob. During the civil rights movement, for example, Young found a way for the Urban League to be a cooperative partner in direct-action activities, for example, the 1963 march on Washington. And in 1979, Jordan became the first leader of a major black civil rights organization to openly criticize the Carter administration for its record and lack of achievements with respect to blacks. It is true, of course, that during the 1960s the League was not in the forefront of the battle; but neither were other organizations. They generally followed the leadership of Martin Luther King.

Today, however, the situation is somewhat different. Jordan initiated, in terms of national visibility, the criticism of the Carter administration and other civil rights leaders rallied to his support. And under John Jacob, the Urban League through its annual state of the union reports has continued to systematize and crystallize this overall assessment of the progress or lack of progress that has been made to overcome the problems facing blacks. While these increased Urban League initiatives may be attributed to a number of factors, there is little doubt that they provide commentary on a changing leadership structure and perhaps on an apparent leadership vacuum or void that seems to have existed among civil rights groups and leaders since Martin Luther King. The Urban League, not unlike others, has acted to fill this void.

THE CHANGING STRUCTURE OF AFRICAN AMERICAN LEADERSHIP

The changing leadership structure among civil rights groups, and African Americans generally, may be attributed to a number of factors. For one thing, a number of other groups and organizations are now on the scene and are also seeking ways to deal with problems that affect blacks and minorities. Until the late 1980s, one of the most visible of these groups was Operation PUSH (People United to Save Humanity). Operation PUSH was founded by the Reverend Jesse Jackson, a former close associate of Martin Luther King and former national director of SCLC's Operation Breadbasket. But apparent differences between Jackson and the Reverend Ralph Abernathy, King's immediate successor as president of SCLC, led Jackson to launch a new organization initially devoted mainly to the economic development of blacks and other minority groups. PUSH subsequently expanded its programs and activities to reach into a number of areas, especially voter registration and education.

Undoubtedly, PUSH profited greatly from the charismatic personality and the fiery oratory of Jesse Jackson. In many ways, Jackson was the life of PUSH just as Martin Luther King was the life of SCLC. Through the organization's programs and his own charisma, Jesse Jackson was able to command a role and presence in the civil rights leadership structure that did not seem possible for him within the existing structure of the SCLC. And clearly that role was enhanced by Jackson's forays in Democratic presidential politics in 1984 and 1988. Inevitably, however, Jackson's presidential campaigns increasingly limited his role in PUSH—in 1990 forcing him to turn over the active running of the organization to others. Subsequently Jackson moved from Chicago to Washington, where he ran for and was elected as the "shadow" senator from the District of Columbia. This effectively removed Jackson from the Chicago national headquarters of PUSH, and since that time PUSH, like many other traditional civil rights organizations, has been struggling to survive. Without Jackson PUSH has not been the same.

Since 1965 there has been an increase in the number of organizations that retain offices in Washington and that deal with issues of primary interest to blacks and minorities. In general, these organizations, such as the Children's Defense Fund, focus on program implementation as a way of influencing public policy. Individually, these groups tend to be rather specialized, but collectively they cover a variety of policy areas of interest to blacks and minorities, such as housing, community development, day care and child development, food stamps and social services, business, and labor. The emergence of such groups symbolizes both the growth and increasing complexity of the problems facing blacks and other minorities. They also bring about a change in the overall leadership structure and influence affecting blacks and minorities.

The success of blacks in the political arena is another factor that has affected both the role of established groups—such as the NAACP—as well as influenced the general leadership structure among blacks and the civil rights community generally. Local voters leagues and other civil rights groups have been spurred and energized by the growing number of local black candidates and elected officials who view these groups as a way to solidify and expand their careers and influence in the black community and in politics generally. Undoubtedly, these local groups and organizations tend to vie for attention and serve as a viable substitute for some who might otherwise support—or at least support more fully—national civil rights groups and organizations such as the NAACP and Urban League.

By 1991 there were some 7,500 black elected officials—mainly at the state and local levels—and by virtue of their office, each of these officials has a leadership opportunity. Those in more visible positions, such as blacks in the

Congress, Governor Douglas Wilder of Virginia (1989-present), and those who serve as big city mayors, are obviously in positions to have more influence. Those at the state and local levels are especially important to the leadership structure since they have greater chances for day-to-day face-to-face contacts with more persons in the black community.

Of course, those in appointive positions also exercise and have political influence. Certainly blacks and minorities now widely recognize the importance of those in administrative roles as well as those who hold legal-judicial positions. Although the requirements and expectations of office vary and impose constraints somewhat different from those in elective office, it is undoubtedly the case that persons who hold appointive positions, be they high administrative officials or federal judges, are perceived as leaders by and in the black community. They are also obviously leaders in the general American community by virtue of their office and authority. In any event, when one combines the increasing leadership base in the public-political arena with the established and developing leadership structures (church, business), it is abundantly clear that the leadership base among African Americans has been considerably broadened with various persons "leading" from various vantage points. This broadening of the leadership base, to be sure, is indicative of the concrete advances that have been made. And it is this very success that makes it more difficult for blacks to have one leader or to speak with one voice (which in fact has never been the case) when there are so many different leaders and voices.

Several comments may be made about what seem to be the consequences of blacks gaining success in various leadership arenas. First, how they keep pressure on the system: From a practical standpoint, as blacks become more integrated into the "system" and the "establishment," they will tend to use more traditional and systematic means to achieve their objectives. The effectiveness of these efforts, however, will continue to depend upon the resources (i.e., leadership, money) that black organizations and their allies can develop and muster. Such resources should increase as system integration increases. However, a breakdown or failure in the development and harnessing of these resources could, of course, lead to a breakdown or failure in system integration and in the use of more traditional and systematic means to achieve objectives. Second, the inability of the black community to have one leader or speak with one voice: From a practical standpoint, it stands to reason that as the number of blacks in leadership positions increases, it will become much more difficult to harness the black community under any one leader. Or to put it another way, it will become increasingly difficult to have any one black leader who can speak for the black community. But it could very well be that in the future there could be events, circumstances, and common sense that will force the new "collective" black leadership to act with extraordinary unity on issues that tend to affect the self-esteem and life chances of blacks as a group.

INTEREST GROUPS: SOME CONCLUDING OBSERVATIONS

This discussion of interest groups permits us to make several conclusions and observations about these forums, especially as they relate to black politics.

1. American politics may well be described as a process that attempts to manage and accommodate the demands of conflicting and competing interests. Two dominant theories—pluralism and elitism—are most often advanced by political scientists to explain how that process works—for what ends and for whose benefit. Pluralist theory suggests that the number and diversity of interest groups and the competition among them place government in the role of a broker whose major function is to balance competing demands through compromise policies and actions. Under this theory no one group or coalition dominates; rather, in due course competing interests will realize some but not all of their objectives.

On the other hand, those who hold to the elite theory of American politics also recognize the presence of interest groups, but they suggest that such groups are in the main controlled by an elite corps of leaders. Elite theorists posit that these leaders share similar goals, values, and directions and as a result reach compromises among themselves with little or no influence or input from the masses. While these two theories offer conflicting interpretations, clearly elements of both are reflected in the political process. Thus plural elitism may prove a more apt and perhaps more accurate description of American politics.

But whether pluralism, elitism, or some such combination, those who are on the lower rung of the socioeconomic ladder—as most African Americans are—tend to be disadvantaged by the nature and operation of the American political process. Socioeconomic inequities in such resources as money, wealth, education, and expertise, which have come mainly as a result of racism and discrimination, continue to seriously impede effective black political participation. And these are the very resources groups must have in order to maintain the kind of sustained presence needed to meaningfully participate, compete, and achieve their objectives in the political process.

2. Staff and money, as we have seen, are important resources that groups need in order to promote their objectives in the political process. However, with the possible exceptions of the NAACP and the Urban League, black interest groups have such resources in only small measure, if at all. The lack of such resources is vividly portrayed by Harold Wolman and Norman Thomas in their study of black influence in the federal policy process as related to two policy areas that are of crucial importance to blacks, housing and education.[72] Wolman and Thomas found that "the civil rights movement did not result in extensive involvement by black groups in the federal policy process" in these two areas. Indeed, black groups suffer from problems such as small staffs, lack of technical expertise, and the resulting inability to influ-

ence policy at crucial stages of its formulation. When such groups do attempt to influence policy, say Wolman and Thomas, they do so in largely "formal and visible" ways such as testifying before congressional committees. More than this, these attempts occur "fairly late in the policy process, particularly at the stages of legislative consideration and implementation." "At those stages," the authors conclude, "certain actions can be prevented and marginal changes in policy outputs affected, but the major thrust of policies cannot substantially be altered, for they have been shaped in the earlier innovative and formulative stages when the basic agenda is set." In general, however, the lack of staff and money have forced black groups to concentrate what meager resources they have in ways and areas which they believe to be most useful. This might call for activities that are open and visible rather than those of the behind-the-scenes, low-profile variety, which ordinarily might indeed be the most effective. However, that temperament necessary for good lobbying ("compromise, accommodation, patience"[73]) is not at all surprising given the long history of factors that have retarded for so long the social, economic, and political development of African Americans.

3. "Social solidarity" and "expression of opinion" might best characterize black interest groups. Yet the stability and viability of these groups are related directly to the material benefits they can secure for the causes they represent. Hence the successes of the Urban League in employment have kept these organizations more viable than those where tangible successes are less continuously evident (for example, SCLC, CORE). Nonetheless, both the NAACP and the Urban League have had to modify or broaden the posture of their "nonmaterial" benefits (such as participation in direct action) to retain support and increase interaction with various segments of the black community.

4. Blacks can count on neither mass membership organizations (labor) nor high socioeconomic status groups (such as the American Bar Association or the American Medical Association) to support their goals. And, these are the groups that wield significant influence in American politics. Though less influential than in earlier times, the political arsenal of the AFL-CIO continues to remain quite formidable. That arsenal includes a large potential vote, a good amount of money, and lots of manpower to supplement and expand those things money can buy—for instance, time. To be sure, there are elements among labor that apparently still offer strong support to black interests. But racial friction and apprehension between labor's rank-and-file and blacks, for example, over such issues as school integration and job competition and job security (e.g., affirmative action), have tended to lessen labor's traditional support for blacks and other minorities. This phenomenon has many implications, including the problems it could cause for black candidates who now enjoy labor support in elections. No longer can it be assumed that the policy positions of blacks and organized labor are compatible or closely related. That they should be compatible or related is another matter.

The high socioeconomic status groups—for example, the American Bar Association, the American Medical Association—have money and standing as their major resources. While there is an increasing number of black lawyers and doctors, their numbers and success in terms of material wealth do not yet have a significant impact on these organizations and the policies they support. But the increasing growth and vitality of black professional organizations—National Bar Association and National Medical Association—could prove of potential value to black politics in terms of providing relevant resources.

5. Black interest groups, in many ways, are somewhat caught in a bind. This is so because a group's influence in politics may be related to how much its purposes and activities are congruent with American values and traditions. To be sure, to advocate freedom and equality for all is certainly in keeping with American values. But many perceive that it is not consistent with American values when groups seek to achieve such ends through means such as marches, protests and demonstrations. This view persists even though such means have long been used and continue to be used by whites to achieve their goals (e.g., farmers, organized labor, and more recently by various abortion action groups).

That this situation has not led to more violent outbreaks in the 1960s and now is due in large measure to the moderating influence of black leaders and organized groups such as the NAACP. By the same token, such moderating influences helped create the environment wherein some progress toward black goals has been made. Though that progress has come incrementally, it is nonetheless consistent with how change occurs in American politics. But it is also clear that even this incremental change might not have come about without direct-action pressures on the system. As mentioned earlier, this certainly has implications for the future leadership and strategy of civil rights groups.

Topics for Discussion

1. Do you agree with the view that civil rights groups, such as the NAACP, are no longer relevant or needed? What seems to be the basis of this view? What is your position—are such groups "relevant or needed"? Discuss thoroughly.

2. The text states that "the changing civil rights leadership structure may be attributed to a number of factors." What are these factors? Do you agree that these factors have brought about changes in the civil rights leadership structure? Discuss.

3. The authors state that changes in the political-social climate have brought about "hard times" for civil rights organizations. Discuss these changes and describe how and in what ways they have complicated the life of civil rights organizations.

Suggested Readings

Bentley, Arthur. *The Process of Government*. Chicago: University of Chicago Press, 1908.
A classic work on the whole body of literature on group analysis and interest group theory.

Blair, Thomas L. *Retreat to the Ghetto: The End of a Dream?* New York: Hill and Wang, 1977.
A critical analysis of how relevant the "Black Power" movement and the "Black Revolution" were to the crisis of survival faced by urban blacks.

Button, James W. *Blacks and Social Change: Impact of the Civil Rights Movement in Southern Communities*. Princeton: Princeton University Press, 1989.

Carmichael, Stokely, and Charles V. Hamilton. *Black Power: The Politics of Liberation in America*. New York: Vintage Books, 1967.
Pioneering work on the explanation and formulation of the meaning of the concept of black power.

Cigler, Allan J., and Burdett, A. Loomis, eds. *Interest Group Politics*, 2d ed. Washington, DC: Congressional Quarterly Press, 1986.

Epstein, Lee. *Public Interest Law*. New York: Garland Publishers, 1992.

Greenwald, Carol S. *Group Power: Lobbying and Public Policy*. New York: Praeger Publishers, 1977.
Describes the importance of interest groups in the development and application of general policies in the public policy process.

Harmon, Robert B. *Interest Groups and Lobbying in American Politics: A Bibliographic Checklist*. Monticello, IL: Council of Planning Librarians, 1978.
An extensive bibliography of sources dealing with the role of lobbying and interest *groups in the American political system.*

Hilliard, David. *This Side of Glory: The Autobiography of David Hilliard and the Story of the Black Panther Party*. Boston: Little, Brown, 1993.

Jennings, James. *The Politics of Black Empowerment*. Detroit: Wayne State University Press, 1992.

Key, V. O. *Parties, Politics and Interest Groups*. New York: Crowell, 1958.
An examination of American politics in light of the activities of parties and interest groups.

McCartney, John T. *Black Power Ideologies: An Essay in African-American Political Thought*. Philadelphia: Temple University Press, 1992.

Mundo, Philip A. *Interest Groups*. Chicago: Nelson-Hall Publishers, 1992.

Olson, Mancur, Jr. *The Logic of Collective Action: Public Goods and the Theory of Groups*. Cambridge, MA: Harvard University Press, 1965..
Explores the nature of interest groups, the behavior of members, the importance of size, and how these and other factors interact in realizing groups' objectives.

Salisbury, Robert. "Interest Groups." In Fred I. Greenstein and Nelson Polsby, *Handbook of Political Science*, Vol. 4. Reading, MA: Addison-Wesley Publishing Co., 1975.
Analysis of interest groups over a broad spectrum.

Schattschneider, E. E. *The Semi-Sovereign People*. New York: Holt, Rinehart and Winston, 1975.
A forceful commentary on the role of the people in the American political system.

Tate, Katherine. *From Protest to Politics: The New Black Voters in American Elections*. Cambridge, MA: Harvard University Press, 1993.

Walker, Jack L. *Mobilizing Interest Groups in America*. Ann Arbor: University of Michigan Press, 1991.

Notes

* *Congressional Record*, February 19, 1971, p. E936.

1. See, generally, *The New York Times*, October 19, 1979, p. 49; *Congressional Quarterly Almanac* (Washington, DC: Congressional Quarterly, Inc., 1978), p. 770; and John Felton "The Wealth of Congress," *Congressional Quarterly*, Report 35 (September 2, 1978), p. 2326.
2. *N.A.A.C.P.* v. *Button*, 371 U.S. 415 (1963), 429-430.
3. See Lucius J. Barker, "Third Parties in Litigation," *Journal of Politics* 29 (1967), pp. 41-69, and sources cited therein.

** From Lucius J. Barker and Donald Jansiewicz, "Coalitions in the Civil Rights Movement," in *The Study of Coalition Behavior: Theoretical Perspectives and Cases from Four Continents*, ed. Sven Groennings, E.W. Kelley, and Michael Leiserson. Copyright, 1970, by Holt, Rinehart and Winston, Publishers. Reprinted with permission of Holt, Rinehart and Winston, Publishers. (Footnotes congruent with chapter text.)

4. For a complete list of participating groups, see "Intensive Lobbying Marked House Civil Rights Debate," *Congressional Quarterly Weekly Report* 22 (week ending February 21, 1964), pp. 364-366.
5. Anthony Lewis, *Portrait of a Decade: The Second American Revolution* (New York: Bantam Books, 1965), p. 106.
6. See Murray Friedman, "The White Liberal's Retreat," in Alan F. Westin, ed., *Freedom Now: The Civil Rights Struggle in America* (New York: Basic Books, 1964), pp. 320-328.
7. See Louis Lomax, "The Crisis of Negro Leadership," in *The Negro Revolt* (New York: New American Library, 1963), pp. 160-176.
8. Lomax, "Crisis of Leadership," pp. 178-193. For more complete references, see Louis Lomax, *When the World Is Given* (Cleveland: World Publishing, 1963) and Elijah Muhammad, *Message to the Blackman in America* (Chicago: Muhammad Mosque of Islam No. 2, 1965).
9. See Stokely Carmichael and Charles V. Hamilton, *Black Power: The Politics of Liberation in America* (New York: Vintage Books, 1967).
10. This continuum is a reflection of group efforts to work within the institutional framework of American politics. It represents the percentage of actions or statements of a group that conforms to normal American institutional expectations.

    The data for the figures were drawn from nineteen and one-half months (January 1, 1966, through September 15, 1967) of *The New York Times Index*. Every time a group's representative went to formal government for redress of grievance, spoke positively about the viability of American institutions, or established and participated in complementary nongovernmental institutions, this group was given credit for one "integrated action."

    Every march, boycott, threat of picketing, or anti-institutional statement (or antisystem statement) is coded as an "alienated action." The assumption here is that picketing, boycotting, and threats of violence do not constitute institutionally oriented behavior patterns. Final calculations were then made in terms of a group's percentage of institutional incidents.

Three major methodological qualifications should be noted. The continuum does not weigh the intensity and forms of political behavior. Rather, it weights the direction. In this respect it does not distinguish between a peaceful march and the threat of violence. The forms of political behavior are merely classified as being institutional or alienated.

Secondly, the Muslims were left out of the analysis. Despite their consideration later in this article, the paucity of data prohibited useful analysis. In light of the organization's goals, the Muslims might be given a score of absolute zero, but in the absence of the necessary data they have been excluded from Table 7-1.

11. See Lomax, "Crisis of Leadership," pp. 112-132; Kenneth B. Clark, "The Civil Rights Movement: Momentum and Organization," in Talcott Parsons and Kenneth B. Clark, *The Negro American* (Boston: Houghton Mifflin, 1966), pp. 601-602; R. Joseph Monsen, Jr., and Mark W. Cannon, "Negroes," in *The Makers of Public Policy: American Power Groups and Their Ideologies* (New York: McGraw-Hill, 1965), pp. 143-144; Whitney Young, "The Urban League and Its Strategy," in Arnold M. Rose, ed., *Annals of the American Academy* 357 (January 1965), pp. 102-107; Norman Jackman and Jack Dodson, "Negro Youth and Direct Action," in *Phylon* 28 (Spring 1967), p. 13; James H. Lane, "The Changing Nature of Negro Protest," in Arnold M. Rose, *Annals of the American Academy* 357 (1965), pp. 120-125.
12. Lomax, "Crisis of Leadership," pp. 224-236; Clark, "Civil Rights Movement," pp. 598-601; Monsen and Cannnon, "Negroes," pp. 141-142; Morsell, "The NAACP and Its Strategy," in Arnold M. Rose, *Annals of the American Academy* 357 (January 1965), pp. 97-101; Jackman and Dodson, "Negro Youth"; Lane, "Changing Nature," pp. 120-122.
13. Lomax, "Crisis of Leadership," pp. 178-192; Monsen and Cannon, "Negroes," pp. 145-146; Lomax, *When the Word is Given.*
14. Lomax, "Crisis of Leadership," pp. 133-159; Parsons and Clark, *Negro American*, pp. 615-619; Monsen and Cannon, "Negroes," pp. 144-145; Lane, "Changing Nature," pp. 125-126; Jackman and Dodson, "Negro Youth," pp. 12-15; Howard Zinn, *SNCC: The New Abolitionists* (Boston: Beacon Press, 1964), pp. 1-40.
15. See generally, Don McKee, "SNCC Turns to Black Violence as Members' Support Dwindle," *Milwaukee Journal*, November 26, 1967, p. 24.
16. Lomax, "Crisis of Leadership," pp. 133-159; Clark, *Negro American*, pp. 608-610; Monsen and Cannon, "Negroes," pp. 144-145; Lane, "Changing Nature," pp. 125-126; Marvin Rich, "The Congress of Racial Equality and Its Strategy," in Arnold M. Rose, ed., *Annals of the American Academy* 357 (January 1965), pp. 113-118; Jackman and Dodson, "Negro Youth," pp. 12-15.
17. Parsons and Clark, *Negro American*, pp. 610-615; Monsen and Cannon, "Negroes," pp. 12-15; Lane, "Changing Nature," pp. 123-124.
18. Samuel Eliot Morison and Henry Steele Commager, *The Growth of the American Republic*, 7th ed. (New York: Oxford University Press, 1980), pp. 916-928.
19. Lomax, "Crisis of Leadership," p. 145.
20. For an account of the *Brown* litigation, see Barker and Barker, *Freedoms, Courts, Politics: Studies of Civil Liberties* (Englewood Cliffs, NJ: Prentice Hall, 1965), pp. 137-185. Also see Barker, "Third Parties in Litigation," p. 41ff.
21. Martin Luther King, Jr., *Stride Toward Freedom* (New York: Harper & Row, 1958), p. 40.

22. M. Kempton, "March on Washington," *New Republic* 149 (September 14, 1963), pp. 19-20.
23. "N.A.A.C.P. Leader Assails Other Civil Rights Groups," *The New York Times*, June 17, 1963, p. 12.
24. *The New York Times*, June 23, 1963, p. 56.
25. *The New York Times*, July 3, 1963, p. 10, and July 17, 1963, p. 15.
26. *The New York Times*, August 16, 1963, p. 9.
27. *The New York Times*, July 18, 1963, p. 10.
28. Ibid.
29. *The New York Times*, June 29, 1963, p. 10.
30. *The New York Times*, August 2, 1963, p. 11.
31. *The New York Times*, August 26, 1963, p. 20. Also see Paul Good, "Odyssey of Man and a Movement," *The New York Times Magazine*, June 25, 1967, p. 45.
32. Congressional Quarterly, Inc., *Revolution in Civil Rights*, 3rd ed. (Washington, DC: Congressional Quarterly Service, 1967), p. 68.
33. Ibid., p. 22.
34. See generally George D. Blackwood, "Civil Rights and Direct Action in the North," *Public Policy* (1965), p. 311.
35. *The New York Times*, July 30, 1964, pp. 1, 12.
36. Ibid.
37. *The New York Times*, February 1, 1965, p. 12.
38. Ibid.
39. Ibid.
40. Actually, this "division of labor" is suggested by Anthony Lewis in his *Portrait of a Decade*; that is, SNCC and CORE would protest while the NAACP would provide counsel and bail (pp. 118-120).
41. As leaders of a grass-roots movement comprised largely of young, working-class blacks, the directors of SNCC and CORE were keenly aware of what the Vietnam War meant in terms of African American lives. A disproportionate number of soldiers who fought—and died—in the jungles of Indochina were black working class. No fact more clearly illustrated the cruel irony: black soldiers defending the very civil liberties they were concurrently denied at home. To SNCC and CORE, civil rights and Vietnam were two sides of the same coin.
42. *The New York Times*, August 15, 1965, p. 73.
43. *The New York Times*, May 28, 1966, p. 1.
44. Ibid.
45. Ibid.
46. *The New York Times*, June 1, 1966, p. 33.
47. *The New York Times*, June 9, 1966, p. 1. For a general discussion of the Mississippi march and its consequences see Martin Luther King, *Where Do We Go From Here: Chaos or Community* (New York: Harper & Row, 1967), pp. 1-66.
48. *The New York Times*, June 9, 1966, p. 1.
49. *The New York Times*, July 8, 1966, p. 1.
50. Ibid.
51. See King, *Where Do We Go From Here.*
52. *The New York Times*, July 8, 1966, p. 16; see also *The New York Times*, July 3, 1966, p. 28; Carmichael and Hamilton, *Black Power.*

53. *The New York Times*, October 10, 1966, p. 35.
54. See, generally, Gene Roberts, "Dr. King on Middle Ground," *The New York Times*, July 17, 1966, Sec. 4, p. 5.
55. *The New York Times*, October 15, 1966, p. 14.
56. Ibid.
57. *The New York Times*, October 17, 1966, p. 42.
58. See *The Gallup Poll: Public Opinion* (Wilmington, DE: Scholarly Resources): 1982, p. 222; 1988, p. 166; 1990, p. 149; 1992, p. 160.
59. Ernest Holsendolph, "Jordan Urges Carter to Visit Looted Areas," *The New York Times*, July 26, 1977, p. 43.
60. Ibid., and Adam Clymer, "President Rejects Jordan's Criticism," *The New York Times*, July 26, 1977, p. B8..
61. Adam Clymer, "President Rejects Jordan's Criticism," *The New York Times*, July 26, 1977, p. 1
62. Ibid., p. B8.?
63. *Price Waterhouse* v. *Hopkins*, 490 U.S. 228 (1989). *Wards Cove Packing Co.* v. *Atonio*, 490 U.S. 642 (1989); *Martin* v. *Wilks*, 490 U.S. 755 (1989); *Lorance* v. *AT&T*, 490 U.S. 900 (1989); *Patterson* v. *McLean Credit Union*, 491 U.S. 164 (1989); *Independent Federation of Flight Attendants* v. *Zipes*, 491 U.S. 754 (1989).
64. For a background overview of the situation, see *The New York Times*, July 28, 1991, p. 10, cols. 1-4.
65. Peter Steinfels, *The Neoconservatives: The Men Who Are Changing America's Politics* (New York: Simon & Schuster, 1979), p. 1.
66. Ibid.
67. Ibid., p. 7.
68. Ibid.
69. Ibid., p. 6.
70. For an overview of these and related matters, see Paul Delaney, "Called Complacent, N.A.A.C.P. Looks to Future," *The New York Times*, June 10, 1991, p. C10. Materials and quotes in the next two paragraphs are drawn from the Delaney article.
71. Quotes and background materials for this section may be found in Neil A. Lewis, "Veteran of Rights Movement to Lead N.A.A.C.P.," *The New York Times*, April 10, 1993, p. 6, cols. 3-6. For an informative biographical profile on the new executive director, see Neil A. Lewis, "Deep Civil Rights Roots—Benjamin Franklin Chavis, Jr.," Ibid., April 11, 1993, p. 12, cols. 1-2.
72. Harold Z. Wolman and Norman C. Thomas, "Black Interests, Black Groups, and Black Influence in the Federal Policy Process: The Cases of Housing and Education," *Journal of Politics* 32 (1970), pp. 875-897.
73. Ibid., p. 893.

CHAPTER 8

CHANGE THROUGH POLITICS: POLITICAL PARTIES

To bring about change through politics in the American political system necessarily involves change in and through political parties. And undoubtedly the most striking feature of political parties in America is the two-party system. This refers to the dominant and overwhelming role of the Democratic and Republican parties in performing the major function of parties—the recruitment and election of public officials at all levels of government. The lifeblood of parties is to control government by electing its members to office. This is the central concern of parties, of their every move; every other function is geared toward this central concern.

THE TWO-PARTY SYSTEM

That two parties and only two parties dominate the American political scene has been explained by several factors. "At the root of the explanation," as Sorauf puts it, "lies the basic, long-run American consensus on fundamental beliefs. Traditionally, no deep rifts over the kind of economy, society or government we want have marked our politics."[1] But the more practical explanation by which this "consensus" is fostered lies perhaps in the symbiotic relationship that has developed between parties and the constitutional-legal system. In attempts to win control, parties have actually given life to our constitutional-legal structures and have in turn been influenced by these very structures.

Consider such features as federalism, the electoral college, separation of powers, regular and frequent elections, and the single-member district. Federalism, for example, means that a party must be organized to contest national and state elections. Federalism has also come to mean, of course, that frictions which inevitably erupt between national and state interests also erupt along these lines within the party organization. Overcoming such frictions could hold enormous consequences for party success. Consider the election of the president, by far the single most important government official.

To win the presidency, the party must win a majority of the electoral votes. And electoral votes of each state are awarded on a winner-take-all basis. This calls for viable party organizations in all states—organizations that can work together under a central umbrella. And given the varied politics of the states, that central umbrella must be large enough to cover and hold many divergent interests. Obviously, the resources needed by the party to win the presidency (such as nature of organization, type of candidate, the platform, and money) can differ from the resources needed by the party to capture other government offices (for example, state governors, U.S. senators, and representatives). Yet somehow the major problem for the central party organization is that these very resources must be made to work together if the party is to succeed and win the presidency and other offices. In any event, the party must be able to adjust to the many structures such as federalism that exist in the political system.

One way in which a party tries to adjust to and overcome these structures in presidential elections is through the national party convention. Meeting every four years to coincide with presidential elections, the main business of the convention is to nominate candidates for president and vice-president. But it must conduct that business so as to maximize party chances in the subsequent election. What this means is that at every turn party leaders must be alert to the tenuous foundations upon which party organizations are built and upon which they depend. Indeed, party organization generally corresponds with governmental organizations; that is, there is a national party organization, a state party organization, and local (county, city, ward, precinct) party organizations. And some of the same problems that plague operations at the various government levels also plague the party organization.

Essentially, then, one may well describe the two major parties as "grand coalitions." More often than not one can find this coalition flavor reflected both in the party platform (statement of policies) as well as in the presidential ticket. By and large, however, both the platform and party nominees represent the same interests. That is, the dominant interests that coalesce to mold the party platform also prevail in fashioning the presidential ticket and vice versa. What all this means is that it is highly unlikely (although not unknown) that any one group or interest in a given party will have its way. Put another way, party conventions as forums of decision making, similar to other national forums, are not likely to come up with sharp, clear, concise actions that might jeopardize their mass broad support base. Consequently, compromise and moderation rather than conflict and clarity usually characterize the operation of parties at the national level. As such, the character of the national party tends to support those interests who favor the status quo or those who believe in gradual change.

It becomes obvious then why black participation in national party politics has for the most part been frustrating. Let us take a brief look at black experience with the two major parties.

BLACKS AND THE REPUBLICANS: FROM FRIENDSHIP TO ALIENATION TO A "CAUTIOUS COURTSHIP"

Lincoln's Emancipation Proclamation and the policies of the Republican Reconstruction Congress stand out as historic benchmarks in African Americans' struggle for freedom. The circumstances surrounding these actions have led some to ascribe various motivations for them. But the fact remains that these actions were taken by Republicans. Lincoln's Proclamation did free the slaves. Moreover, the support of the Republican Congress for black interests was symbolized not only through legislation, such as the Civil Rights Act of 1866, but also through the eventual enactment of the Civil War Amendments, the Thirteenth, Fourteenth, and Fifteenth Amendments. Quite naturally these historic policies benefitted the Republican party by attracting black voters.

But this strong support given blacks by Republicans during Reconstruction was short-lived (an ironic fact, given that one of the main principles on which the Republican Party was founded was the abolition of slavery). As we have seen earlier, in the disputed election of 1876 Republican candidate Rutherford B. Hayes, in exchange for southern electoral votes, agreed to withdraw federal troops from the South and in effect adopted a "hands-off" policy toward the newly freed blacks. This agreement, called the Compromise of 1877, led to a widespread feeling among blacks that they had been abandoned by the Republican party and once again offered up to the whims of their former slaveholders. Consequently, black Republicans who had prospered during Reconstruction were brushed aside both by the reemergence of the Democratic party as well as by southern white Republican leaders who wanted to rid the party of its black image. This led to warfare between two factions of the party: the white faction, known as the Lily White Republicans, and the black faction, the Black and Tan Republicans. And although national Republican leaders sought to overcome this factionalism and effect a viable party organization in the South, they were unable to do so.

Southern whites took full advantage of the situation. They solidified their control of state governments through the Democratic party. They also instituted various devices that disfranchised black voters and relegated blacks in general to a subordinate status. In 1928, President Hoover squashed any hope that the Republican party would once again come to the rescue of blacks. Indeed Hoover, sensing an increasing wave of race prejudice throughout the country, sided with the Lily White Republicans and through his economic policies dealt a severe blow to the Black and Tan faction in the South. This move by Hoover, coupled with the attractive economic policies of President Roosevelt's New Deal, had by 1938 brought most blacks to the Democratic party. But though Democrats controlled national politics until 1952, they did little to unravel the web of subordination that enveloped the life of blacks in the South.

However, the national Republicans did even less to alleviate the plight of blacks and poor people. The GOP was pictured as the party of the rich and well-born WASP. The Republicans with General Eisenhower recaptured the White House from 1952 through 1960, and these were crucial years in the civil rights movement. It was during this time the Supreme Court handed down its decisions on public school desegregation, the Montgomery bus boycott, and the Little Rock school integration crisis. These were all situations that provided opportunities for the Republicans to regain some credence with African Americans. But, as is well known, President Eisenhower refused to endorse the Court decision. He remained aloof and uninvolved in the expanding civil rights controversy, limiting his role to one of enforcement. To be sure, the president did use federal troops to enforce federal court orders during the Little Rock crisis but only as a last resort.

The Republicans did not regain the White House until 1968, when Richard Nixon was elected president. Between 1960 and 1968, however, the Democrats through Kennedy and Johnson strengthened their hold on black voters. This black support for the Democrats was, of course, enhanced by the strong anti-civil rights posture and conservatism of the 1964 Goldwater campaign. In 1968, however, the Republicans won the presidency with a campaign that appealed to white America. The "law and order," "anti-busing," and "southern strategy" themes that characterized the 1968 and 1972 Nixon campaigns, as well as his administrations, were definitely not calculated as an appeal to black voters. Nixon had written off the black vote. But President Nixon and leading figures of his administration, including his chief law enforcement officer, Attorney General John Mitchell, became trapped in their own "law and order" rhetoric, in work and in (mis)deed. This, of course, included Vice-President Spiro Agnew, who, along with Mitchell, symbolized the antipathy of the Republican administration toward blacks, minorities, and the poor. The ensuing Watergate scandal led not only to the conviction of the leading officials of Nixon's administration but also to the resignation of the president himself.

Predictably, the elevation of Gerald Ford to the presidency did little to improve the civil rights image of the Republican party. And this well may have proved Ford's undoing. In his 1976 presidential campaign Ford did little if anything to win the black vote. In fact, a key strategist in Reagan's unsuccessful attempt to win the GOP nomination said that "Ford made so little effort (among blacks) it was an insult." And an Urban League official put the matter even more vividly, saying that "if Ford had gone to black churches in Ohio, he might still be president." But Ford did not do so. And as matters turned out, it was the overwhelming black vote (over 90 percent) that provided Carter's margin of victory in the 1976 election. In addition, the black vote also proved crucial in other races. For example, former Senator William Brock (R-Tennessee) inferred that it was the "awesome" black vote that perhaps led to his own defeat. Brock was defeated by some 77,000 votes while his Democratic opponent, the eventual winner, received some 130,000 or 93 percent of the black vote.

In any event, Brock and other Republican party leaders did not soon forget the importance of the black vote in 1976. Thus, in 1977 when Brock emerged as chairman of the GOP national committee, he was in a position to do something about this situation. In outlining the Republican strategy to attract blacks, Brock indicated that he wanted to provide blacks with alternatives to the Democratic party. Said Brock:

> I'm not sure it is realistic to establish goals with any degree of reason. . . . Fundamentally, I want this party to earn the support of the black community, to provide it with an honest and realistic alternative. How fast they seize the opportunity depends on how effective our efforts are.

The Republican alternative focused on three areas: "symbolic action, involvement of blacks in the party as policy makers and candidates, and legislation." Although "symbolic action" involves mainly rhetoric, some blacks believe that it is nevertheless "a step in the right direction." But as Brock himself put it, "It is going to take tangible results; we're going to have to prove the rhetoric." He thought Republicans must give close attention to problems that especially impact blacks and minorities, for example, unemployment, taxation, housing, and small business.

And the Republicans took several concrete and highly visible steps in their attempt to attract blacks. For example, the party retained a black consulting firm, Wright-McNeil Associates of Columbus, Georgia. The firm gave much of its attention to "advising candidates, mostly white, but it also worked in the recruitment of black candidates." This effort showed some modest but encouraging signs. Of course, the recruitment of black candidates at the state and local level is a very tangible and realistic way to attract black attention and black votes.[2]

In addition, the Republicans sought the views and reactions of various black leaders to their efforts to attract blacks to the GOP. For example, in 1977 the party invited the Reverend Jesse Jackson to address a meeting of the GOP National Committee. In his speech, Jackson took the opportunity to expose the political interests and attitudes of blacks toward the GOP efforts and party politics in general. Said Jackson:

> The only protection people have politically is to remain necessary. We must pursue a strategy that prohibits one party from taking us for granted and another party from writing us off. The only protection we have against political genocide is to remain necessary.

Notwithstanding the candor of his remarks, the inevitable question put to Jackson was whether the GOP was "trying to use blacks for their own ends." And to this Jackson replied: "Of course, they're trying to use us, in a broad political sense, and we're trying to use them in the same way."

Overall, given the apparent determinative role of the black vote in the 1976 election, especially for the presidency, it was quite understandable why the Republicans would attempt to attract blacks to their party and away from the Democrats. But such efforts seem to have been short-lived during the 1980s. The election and reelection of Ronald Reagan in 1980 and 1984 and the hostile attitudes and actions of his administration all but obliterated most efforts by the party to attract black support. Clearly, Ronald Reagan made it much more difficult to bring about any raproachment between blacks and the Republican Party.

Despite the antagonism of the Reagan administration to black interests, the Republican party once again attempted to reach out to blacks under the leadership of President Bush and Republican National Committee Chairman Lee Atwater. Shortly after George Bush's victory in 1988, Atwater announced that "we are now presented with a unique chance" to gain support among blacks.[3] Republicans believed that blacks were likely to look for an alternative to the Democratic party since the Democrats seemed to take black support for granted. Apparently, one key aspect of the Republican strategy was to seek greater support from blacks by appointing blacks to highly visible positions in government and in the party organization.[4] To be sure, Bush's appointment of Judge Clarence Thomas to the Supreme Court struck a responsive chord among many blacks. At the time at least this move won black support for the nominee's eventual confirmation despite the fact that Thomas's views were clearly inimical to major policies relevant to black interests and concerns. Overall, however, the racism implicit in the "Willie Horton" strategy of the 1988 Bush campaign apparently did much to temper whatever benefits might have accrued to the President from actions such as the Thomas appointment.[5] Moreover, as the 1992 election campaign unfurled, it became clear that President Bush and the Republican party generally made little effort to attract black voters. As a result, African Americans continued their strong support for the Democratic candidate (Governor Clinton), giving him 82 percent of the vote, with President Bush receiving only 11 percent.

BLACKS AND DEMOCRATIC PARTY POLITICS

Black ties to the Democratic party system can be traced in large part from the economic benefits which accrued during Franklin Roosevelt's New Deal era. These ties were strengthened during President Truman's Fair Deal administration. Truman not only continued Roosevelt's policies, but he also exhibited some concern for the civil rights of African Americans. This concern was symbolized by the report of a 1947 presidential commission on civil rights, "To Secure These Rights." Also of importance was the relatively strong support the Democratic party gave to civil rights in their 1948 convention—a posture that led to a conservative walkout and the formation of the Dixicratic party. In addition, black attachment to the Democratic party was undoubtedly strengthened by the sympathetic support given the civil rights movement from Democratic leaders (the Kennedys, Johnson, Humphrey) and Democratic-oriented groups (labor, Catholics, and Jews).

Moreover, the issue orientation of the Democratic party, in contrast to the Republicans has been more supportive of black concerns. Consider several examples of policy positions taken from platforms of the two parties since 1972. Indeed, the tone and substance of the 1972 Democratic platform in such key issue areas as civil rights, employment, housing, welfare, health insurance, education, law enforcement, and tax reform were undoubtedly more attuned to black interests than was the Republican position. Let us look at a few examples. The Democrats viewed busing as "another tool to accomplish desegregation," while the Republicans flatly said they were "irrevocably opposed to busing for racial balance." The GOP said that busing "fails in its stated objective—improved learning opportunities—while it achieves results no one wants—division within communities and hostilities between classes and races."

Take welfare. Both parties agreed that the present welfare system needs replacing. But agreement stopped there. The Democrats would replace welfare with "an income security program" that includes a guaranteed annual income "substantially more than the poverty level" to ensure standards of decency and health. In contrast, the Republicans flatly opposed "programs or policies which embrace the principle of a government-guaranteed income" and rejected as "unconscionable the idea that all citizens have the right to be supported by the government, regardless of their ability or desires to support themselves or their families." As to health insurance, the Democrats supported federally financed and federally administered national health insurance. The Republicans opposed "nationalized compulsory health insurance" and called for a plan "financed by employers, employees and the federal government." On law enforcement, the GOP platform praised President Nixon's anti-crime program and his strongly articulated "law and order" stance. The platform called for increased support for law enforcement. The Democrats were likewise against crime, but stated that

> We can protect all people without undermining fundamental liberties by ceasing to use "law and order" as justification for repression and political persecution, and by ceasing to use stop-gap measures and preventative detention, "no-knock" entry, surveillance, promiscuous and unauthorized use of wire taps, harassment, and secret dossiers. . . .

The Democratic platform concluded that "the problems of crime and drug abuse cannot be isolated from the social and economic conditions that give rise to them."

The positions taken by the two parties in their 1976 platforms continued to reflect a difference in the tone and substance on issues of obvious concern to blacks and minorities. In the area of education, for example, the 1976 GOP platform stated:

> We believe that segregated schools are morally wrong and unconstitutional. However, we oppose forced busing to achieve racial balance. . . . We believe that there are educational advantages for children in attending school in their own neighborhoods. . . . The racial composition of many schools results from decisions by people about where they choose to live. If Congress continues to fail to act, we would favor consideration of an amendment to the Constitution forbidding the assignment of children to schools on the basis of race. Our approach is to work to eradicate the root causes of segregated schools, such as housing discrimination and gerrymandered school districts. We must get on with the education of all our children.

By contrast, the Democratic party in its 1976 platform addressed the busing and school desegregation issues as follows:

> The essential purpose of school desegregation is to give all children the same educational opportunities. We will continue to support that goal. The Supreme Court decision of 1954. . . . was based on a recognition that separate educational facilities are inherently unequal. It is clearly our responsibility as a party and as citizens to support the principles of our Constitution. The Democratic Party pledges its concerted help through special consultation, matching funds, incentive grants and other mechanisms to communities which seek education, integrated both in terms of race and economic class, through equitable, reasonable and constitutional arrangements. Mandatory transportation of students beyond their neighborhoods for the purpose of desegregation remains a judicial tool of last resort for the purpose of achieving school desegregation. The Democratic Party will be an active ally of those communities which seek to enhance the quality as well as the integration of educational opportunities. We encourage a variety of other measures, including the redrawing of attendance lines, pairing of schools, use of the "magnet school" concept, strong fair housing enforcement, and other techniques for the achievement of racial and economic integration.

With respect to dealing with matters relating to employment and equal rights in job opportunities, the two parties also took divergent positions. The Republicans stated:

> There must be vigorous enforcement of laws to assure equal treatment in job recruitment, hiring, promotion, pay, credit, mortgage access and housing. The way to end discrimination, however, is not by resurrecting the much discredited quota system and attempting to cloak it in an aura of new respectability. Rather, we must provide alternative means of assisting the victims of past discrimination to realize their full worth as American citizens. Wiping out past discrimination requires continued emphasis on providing educational opportunities for minority citizens, increasing direct and guaranteed loans to minority business enterprises, and affording qualified minority persons equal opportunities for governmental positions at all levels.

Again in contrast, the Democratic position in the areas of employment and equal job opportunity was more supportive of black and minority interests. The 1976 Democratic platform stated:

> Minority unemployment has historically been at least double the aggregate unemployment rate, with incomes at two-thirds the national average. Special emphasis must be placed on closing this gap. Accordingly, we reaffirm this Party's commitment to full and vigorous enforcement of all equal opportunities laws and affirmative action. . . . (W)e pledge vigorous federal programs and policies of compensatory opportunity to remedy for many Americans the generations of injustice and deprivation, and full funding of programs to secure the implementation and enforcement of civil rights.

In general, while continuing to show more support for black interests than the Republican party did, the 1976 Democratic platform nonetheless reflected a softening tone in certain volatile issue areas such as "busing." Whereas in 1972 the Democrats viewed busing as "another tool to accomplish desegregation," in 1976 busing was viewed as a *"judicial remedy of last resort."* (Emphasis ours.) This obviously made the Democratic position more congruent not only with the changing mood of public opinion but also with the views of the party's eventual candidate, Jimmy Carter.

More recent party platforms reinforce these patterns. In 1980, largely as a result of the nomination challenge Senator Edward Kennedy (D-Massachusetts) mounted against President Carter, the platform sounded a more liberal tone than its 1976 predecessor. On jobs, the platform committed the Democrats to seeking a "12-billion-dollar antirecession jobs program, providing at least 800,000 additional jobs." On housing, the platform promised a restoration of the housing industry for lower-class Americans through the addition of 200,000 new units for low-and-moderate income families. On civil rights, the Democrats pledged to "[s]upport affirmative-action goals to overturn patterns of discrimination in education and employment," reiterating the Democrats' commitment to "appointing women and minorities to federal positions at all

Ron Brown, chair of the Democratic National Committee, 1992. *(AP/Wide World Photos)*

levels." And on busing, the party echoed the familiar phrase first enunciated in its 1976 platform: It was supported, but only as "a judicial tool of last resort."[6]

In addition to the old, there were new features about the Democrats' 1980 platform which appealed to blacks. The platform pledged to favor a federal scholarship program for "all the underprivileged who could benefit from a college education"; to increase federal dollars for "historically black colleges and universities"; to enhance minority businesses and to"[t]riple the 1980 level of federal procurement from minority-owned firms"; and to increase "pressure through legal diplomatic sanctions on the oppressive South African regime."[7]

By contrast, the Republicans' 1980 platform concerned itself primarily with tax reform and criticized such programs as "Meals on Wheels," arguing that they undermined voluntary programs.[8] Welfare programs, the Republicans contended, create a "welfare constituency," removing any incentive for individuals to take low-paying jobs.[9]

As for blacks specifically, the platform paid only cursory attention. While it promised to enforce the then-existing civil rights laws, the platform vigorously opposed affirmative action and school busing. Further, the platform contained no policy initiatives directed toward blacks specifically, instead saying "[o]ur fundamental answer to the economic problems of black Americans is the same answer we make to all Americans—full employment without inflation *through economic growth.*"[10] (Emphasis ours.)

The 1984 and 1988 Democratic and Republican platforms continued the familiar trend: Democrats addressing a far greater array of African American concerns than Republicans. In large measure, the Republicans did not feel any pressure to alter their rhetoric or policies with respect to blacks: They had been elected in 1980 and reelected in 1984 by the largest electoral vote landslides in American history.

What is interesting to note is the effect Jesse Jackson's 1984 and 1988 presidential candidacies had on the Democratic platforms, particularly in 1988. While the 1988 Democratic platform was one of the shortest in the Party's history—about 4,000 words—it bore the unmistakable stamp of Jackson's influence. The clearest example was in the platform's stand on South Africa's apartheid system:

> We believe that the time has come to end all vestiges of the failed policy of constructive engagement [the Reagan administration's South Africa policy], to declare South Africa a *terrorist state*, to impose comprehensive sanctions upon its economy, to lead the international community in participation in these actions, and to determine a date certain by which United States corporations *must leave South Africa*. (Emphasis ours.)

Predictably, the Republican platform opposed sanctions and reiterated its commitment to "constructive engagement."

Notably absent from the Democrats' 1988 platform was the familiar recitation of programs and commitments to various special interests. Instead, the platform committed the party to various principles, consistent with its past policies. The decision to omit such specific promises was a strategic one. Then Party Chairman Paul Kirk, along with others, felt the party had been painted (and successfully so) as the party of "Big Government" and higher taxes. A short, broad platform statement would allow Massachusetts Governor Michael Dukakis, the Party's 1988 nominee, flexibility in staking out his policy positions during the campaign.

In 1992, and consistent with democratic symbols and values, both parties gave their expected allegiance to the importance of civil and equal rights for all. The relative overall thrust and image of Clinton and the Democratic party, however, seemed to be far more attuned and sympathetic than Bush and the Republicans to the traditional interest and concerns of women, blacks, and minorities. In their platform, however, the Democrats couched the matter of race in the more general context of "the fight to ensure that no Americans suffer discrimination or deprivation of rights on the basis of race, gender, language, national origin, religion, age, disability, sexual orientation or other characteristics irrelevant to ability." Democrats also pledged to support "ratification of the Equal Rights Amendment, affirmative action, stronger protection of voting rights for racial and ethnic minorities; to reverse the Bush administration's assault on civil rights enforcement; . . . support comparable remedies for women; aggressively prosecute hate crimes; strengthen legal services for the poor; . . . provide civil rights protection for gay men and lesbians and an end to Defense Department discrimination; . . . and fully enforce the Americans with Disabilities Act." The Democrats charged that the Republicans,"by playing racial, ethnic and gender-based politics . . . have divided us against each other, created an atmosphere of blame, denial and fear, and undone the hard-fought battles for equality and fairness." The platform continued:

> America's special genius has been to forge a community of shared values from people of remarkable and diverse backgrounds. As the party of inclusion, we take special pride in our country's emergence as the world's largest and most successful multiethnic, multiracial republic. We condemn anti-semitism, racism, homophobia, bigotry and negative stereotyping of all kinds. We must help all Americans understand the diversity of our cultural heritage. But it is also essential that we preserve and pass on to our children the common elements that hold this mosaic together as we work to make our country a land of freedom and opportunity for all.

Similarly, although with somewhat different nuances, the Republican platform pledged that its "agenda for equality of opportunity runs throughout this platform and applies to all Americans." Said the Republican platform:

> There is no such thing as segregated success. We reject the Democrats' politics of division, envy and conflict. They believe that America is split into classes and can be healed only through the redistribution of wealth. We believe in the economics of multiplication: free markets expand opportunity and wealth for all.
>
> That is true liberation. It frees poor people not only from want but also from government control. That is why liberal Democrats have fought us every step of the way, refusing congressional action on enterprise zones until Los Angeles burned—and then mocking the expectations of the poor by gutting that critical proposal. They can kill bills, but they cannot kill hope. We are determined to pass that legislation for the sake of all who are waiting their chance for the American Dream.

In general, however, the parties seem to cancel out each other with respect to two other highly volatile issues: They both emphasized "law and order," pledging toughness on crime and criminals and advocated significant reforms with respect to the welfare system. These have been two issues which in past elections have been exploited to suggest racial overtones. But on two other issues that also carry racial implications the parties differed sharply, with the Democrats supporting statehood for Washington, D.C. and Republicans opposing statehood and the Republicans favoring a "school choice voucher" plan for low-income children that would include private-school "choice."

Overall, however, it must be remembered that what a party stands for in practice is viewed in large measure by what the respective presidential candidates and party leaders say during the campaign. It also depends on the overall image that prevails about the party. In this context,and insofar as women, blacks, and other minorities were concerned, there is little doubt that Clinton and the Democrats were viewed as much more favorable to their causes than Bush and the Republicans. Of course, much of this image was shaped by President Bush's strong opposition to and then reluctant approval of the Civil Rights Act of 1991, designed to overcome certain adverse Supreme Court affirmative action decisions. Moreover, the overall tenor projected during the Republican convention, especially by the vituperative and mean-spirited implications of the fiery speech made by Patrick Buchanan, also hurt the Republican cause with these groups and with others. Indeed, the tenor and tone of that speech and convention served to plague the image of the Republican party throughout the 1992 campaign.

In general, this sample of issue positions of the two parties clearly supports the disposition of blacks to favor the Democratic party. This should not be construed to suggest that blacks are satisfied with the position taken by Democrats on particular issues. It simply means that between the two major parties, blacks tend to favor the Democrats. Blacks, more than any other minority group including women and youth, have given strong and consistent support to the Democrats. That support continued to be apparent in the 1984, 1988, and 1992 presidential elections (see Table 8-1).

In terms of party identification, blacks have shown an overwhelming preference for the Democratic party, although in recent years that preference seems to be on the decline. Nonetheless, such support would certainly suggest that blacks would and should expect more tangible rewards and benefits from a government controlled by the Democratic party. But by 1977, black leaders were openly expressing dissatisfaction with how little President Carter and his Democratic administration were doing in return for the large black vote received by the Democratic party (especially for the presidency) in the 1976 elections. To be sure, President Carter made some visible attempts, as, for example, through political and judicial appointments, to reward and satisfy black interests. Even so, the image and reality of the Carter performance among blacks (and many others) continued to decline, so much so that it was fairly clear that the Democrats—at least Carter—could no longer take the black vote for granted. And in 1979 Carter apparently attempted to project a new image—by changing his own leadership style and reshuffling his cabinet to deal with pressing domestic problems—in order to overcome the "crisis of confidence," as he put it, that was continuing to envelop black Americans and many others. Whether due to Carter's actions, opposition to Ronald Reagan's

TABLE 8-1 Black and white voting patterns-1952–1992

YEAR	RACE	DEMOCRATIC	REPUBLICAN	OTHER
1952	Black	80%	20%	12.–%
	White	40	60	–
1956	Black	64	36	–
	White	39	61	–
1960	Black	71	29	–
	White	48	52	–
1964	Black	100*	0	–
	Whie	65	35	–
1968	Black	97	3	–
	White	36	52	12.0
1972	Black	87	13	–
	White	30	70	–
1976	Black	94	5	–
	White	50	48	–
1980	Black	85	11	3.0
	White	36	55	7.0
1984	Black	89	9	–
	White	35	64	–
1988	Black	86	12	–
	White	40	59	–
1992	Black	82	11	7.0 (Perot)
	White	39.2	40	20.7 (Perot)

*The 100 percent voting of blacks for the Democratic party probably results from the small size of sample. Certainly a few blacks voted for Goldwater as probably a very few voted for Wallace in 1968. Furthermore, the reported 100 percent Democratic support is consistent with a bias to report having supported the winner-a well known artifact in recall data.

candidacy, traditional voting patterns, or a combination of these and other factors, the 1980 elections demonstrated once again the loyalty of blacks toward the Democratic party. In 1980, blacks gave Carter more than 90 percent of their vote while giving Reagan only 7 percent.

Even so, all was not well with blacks and the Democratic party. This was exemplified most dramatically by the candidacy of Jesse Jackson in the 1984 Democratic nomination battle. Time and again Jackson talked in such terms as fashioning a "new covenant" between blacks and the Democratic party so party officials could or would no longer take the vote of blacks and minorities for granted. He warned the party that these groups should have voice and tangible benefits commensurate with the fierce loyalty and overwhelming vote they had long given Democratic candidates. In his campaign Jackson sought to give "teeth" to his warnings by developing strong voter and delegate support for his positions. And though he met with a great deal of success on both scores, in the end Jackson's candidacy seems to have come up short in terms of winning tangible benefits from the party for those he sought to represent. A combination of factors, including Walter Mondale's commanding delegate lead for the nomination and the apparent inability of Jackson and Mondale's black supporters to unite behind a common set of policy positions, clearly lessened the incentive and need for party leaders to reach meaningful accommodations with blacks.

In the subsequent 1984 presidential election, however, blacks continued their traditionally strong allegiance to the Democratic party and gave Mondale more than 90 percent of their vote even while other traditional sources of Democratic strength (white Southerners) lessened their support considerably for Mondale and increased their support measurably for President Reagan. On the surface, these voting patterns indicate that there is little need for party leaders to be concerned about the black vote: They have it. Indeed, activities of Democratic leaders since the 1984 elections, including the party's 1992 eventual nominee (Governor Clinton) suggest rather strongly that the party leaders had decided to focus their attention and policies on those groups they hoped to win back, particularly white Southerners and middle- and working-class whites. And though efforts to recapture this vote stood to alienate a number of blacks, the party seemed disposed to take that chance, and in combination with other factors, succeeded in winning the election. As a result, the success of this strategy gives increasing credence to those who describe the two-party system as one in which blacks are taken for granted by one party (the Democrats) and written off by the other (the Republicans). On the other hand, however, it clearly enhanced Democratic chances to recapture the White House, allowing President Clinton to promote socioeconomic policies that could improve the lot of poor Americans generally, of which blacks contribute a disproportionate share.

PARTY POLITICS IN PERSPECTIVE

Black participation in national party politics has for the most part been frustrating. To be sure, blacks have gravitated to the Democratic party and have generally tended to support its candidates. Attitudes and benefits that carry over from Roosevelt's New Deal and from the Truman, Kennedy, and Johnson administrations still claim a dominant allegiance from blacks. Moreover, when one views the membership characteristics of the two major parties (such as education, race, income, occupation), blacks and other minorities still continue to have more in common with Democrats than with Republicans.

It is true, of course, that recent studies have pointed to an increasing dissatisfaction with both Republicans and Democrats in general. Blacks undoubtedly perceive a growing insensitivity and inaction coming from both major parties with respect to the very serious problems, such as poverty, that they still face. One manifestation of this dissatisfaction came in early 1980 when a national Conference on a Black Agenda for the 1980s addressed problems facing African

Americans. And as a result of resolutions adopted at the Richmond, Virginia meeting, black leaders could more vigorously push their concerns before the two major parties and other forums as well. These concerns focused on politics, economics, social and cultural concerns, and international issues. And, of course, this dissatisfaction was also reflected by Jesse Jackson's candidacy for the Democratic presidential nomination in 1984 and 1988. Clearly, however, Clinton's election seems to have given renewed hope to many Americans, particularly women, blacks, and minorities. But, as we discuss in Chapter 11, that hope is likely to be tempered by various factors that reflect the stark realities of American politics and the political system.

POLITICAL PARTIES: SOME CONCLUDING OBSERVATIONS

1. The central concern of the two major parties is to win elections—all else must be conducive or subordinate to this end. At the national level this means that above all the party wants to win the presidential election. Consequently, drafting the party platform, nominating its candidates, and even conducting convention business are geared toward fashioning a winning majority. This calls for the presentation of policy positions (platforms) and candidates (president and vice-president) that have broad appeal. Special efforts are made to minimize controversy and to promote harmony. Given this situation, party policies or candidates are rarely strongly committed to the interests of African Americans. For in the context of American politics, those interests (goals) involve the type of controversy that party leaders more often than not wish to avoid. In a sense, Jesse Jackson's 1984 and 1988 campaigns forced the Democrats to deal with the concerns of blacks and others more than they might have wished or expected. By contrast, however, Clinton's 1992 campaign tended to adhere rather closely to "mainstream positions" and to avoid such controversy.

2. Winning presidential elections, however, might require support from black and minority voters. In fact, such support has been especially important to the eventual elections of recent Democratic presidents—Kennedy, Johnson, Carter, and Clinton. The structure of the electoral college and the concentration of black voters in key states offer certain advantages to blacks in a presidential election situation. In the main, blacks have given their support overwhelmingly to the Democratic party, and such strong black support can prove decisive in closely contested elections. In a three-way race in the 1992 presidential election, Clinton received approximately 44.9 million popular votes (43.3 percent); Bush 39.1 million (37.7 percent); and Perot 19.7 million (19 percent). But in terms of the "winner-take-all" of electoral votes, however, Clinton won 370 electoral votes, more than doubling the 168 received by Bush. Perot received no electoral votes.

Conventional wisdom says that party leaders must consider ways to attract votes while simultaneously attempting to keep a "mainstream" or "middle of the road" stance. In practice, this could mean recognition of black and minority concerns in the party platform but not in the candidates or vice versa. Ronald Reagan's landslide victory over Mondale in the 1984 election and George Bush's decisive triumph over Michael Dukakis in 1988 are evidence of a popular conservative trend, and as a result Republican attempts to attract black votes have lessened. While the black vote continues to overwhelmingly support Democratic candidates, party leaders cannot overlook the fact that increasing white support for Republican candidates has more than overcome the persistently overwhelming black vote for the Democratic party and resulted in Republican victories in four of the last five presidential elections. As a result, particularly since the 1984 election, Democratic party leaders through party pronouncements and informal groups, especially the Democratic Leadership Council (DLC), have made overt efforts to placate the middle class and the white vote, especially in the South. The strategy clearly risked alienating much of the black vote, especially if an attractive alternative candidate, such as Jesse Jackson, decided to actively campaign for the party's presidential nomination. Moreover, the Democratic strategy also assumed that the Republican party, even without Ronald Reagan and under George Bush, would continue to hold little appeal for blacks. Democratic candidate Clinton and party leaders came out right on both scores: Jackson did not run, and the Republican party continued to hold little attraction for blacks.

But as blacks gain in political influence, voting, and officeholding, they will undoubtedly expect and demand a greater role in the activities of the major parties, especially in the selection of nominees for president and vice-president. Given the present pattern of party participation, however, the matter is not as crucial for the Republicans as it is for the Democrats. Nonetheless, the sheer size and distribution of the potential black vote, plus the need to satisfy certain symbolic functions, make it almost necessary for both major parties to at least make some effort to attract black votes. But whether, how, and to what extent the Republican and Democratic parties attempt to meet the expectations and demands of blacks will tell us much about the nature of our two-party system, American politics, and the future course and direction of black politics.

Topics for Discussion

1. It has become obvious in some instances that both the Democratic and Republican parties have abandoned (or refused to give high priority to) the political aspirations of African Americans. Would you suggest that blacks organize a political party to represent their interests? Do you think that blacks could overcome such differences and problems as might exist among themselves to form a viable party organization? What would be the costs and benefits to blacks (and to the political system generally) if such a party were organized?

2. Suppose you were a consultant of the Democratic (or Republican) party whose job was to hold or attract more blacks to the party. What would you propose? Would your proposal gain support of "party professionals"? Would it hold or attract more blacks? Might such developments alienate other important segments of the party? of the voting public? Discuss thoroughly.

Suggested Readings

Baer, Denise L. and David A. Bositis. *Elite Cadres and Party Coalitions: Representing the Public in Party Politics*. Westport, CT: Greenwood Press, 1988.

Barker, Lucius. "Black Electoral Politics," *National Political Science Review*, Vol 2 (1990).

Black, Earl and Merle Black. *The Vital South: How Presidents Are Elected*. Cambridge, MA: Harvard University Press, 1992.

Burnham, Walter D. *Critical Elections and the Mainsprings of American Politics*. New York: W. W. Norton & Co., 1970.

An excellent analysis of aggregate electoral behavior in historical perspective.

Burns, James MacGregor. *Cobblestone Leadership: Majority Rule, Minority Power*. Norman, OK: University of Oklahoma Press, 1990.

Dawson, Richard. *Public Opinion and Contemporary Disarray*. New York: Harper & Row, 1973.

Describes and analyzes the distribution of opinions on current social and political issues.

Fiorina, Morris. *Divided Government*. New York: Macmillan, 1992.

Ginsberg, Benjamin. *Politics by Other Means*. New York: Basic Books, 1990.

Key, V. O. *Public Opinion and American Democracy*. New York: Alfred A. Knopf, 1961.

The formation of public opinion and its political implications.

Key, V. O. *Parties, Politics and Interest Groups*. New York: Crowell, 1958.

An examination of American politics in light of the activities of parties and interest groups.

Lake, Celinda C. *Public Opinion Polling*. Washington, DC: Greenwood Press, 1987.

Mayhew, David R. *Divided We Govern*. New Haven, CT: Yale University Press, 1991.

Petracca, Mark P. ed. *The Politics of Interests: Interest Groups Transformed*. Boulder, CO: Westview Press, 1992.

Reichley, James. *The Life of the Parties: A History of American Political Parties*. New York: Free Press, 1992.

Schattschneider, E. E. *The Semi-Sovereign People*. New York: Holt, Rinehart and Winston, 1975.

A forceful commentary on the role of the people in the American political system.

Schramm, Peter W. and Bradford P. Wilson ed. *American Political Parties and Constitutional Politics*. Lanham, MD: Rowman & Littlefield, 1993.

Sorauf, Frank J. and Paul Allen Beck. *Party Politics in America*. 6th ed. Boston: Little, Brown, 1988.

Considers the nature, role, and functions of political parties in the American political system.

Sullivan, Denis G., Jeffrey L. Pressman, Benjamin I. Page, and John J. Lyons. *The Politics of Representation*. New York: St. Martin's Press, 1974.

A case study of representation and decision making at the 1972 Democratic National Convention.

Sundquist, James L. *Dynamics of the Party System*. Washington, DC: Brookings Institution, 1983.

A study of the alignments and realignment of political parties.

Walton, Hanes. *Black Political Parties: An Historical and Political Analysis*. New York: Free Press, 1972.

Traces the historical development of black political parties.

Notes

1. Frank J. Sorauf and Paul Allen Beck, *Party Politics in America*, 6th ed. (Boston: Little, Brown, 1988), p. 47.
2. In fact, some believe that more GOP black candidates well financed by the party may well determine the success of the party's efforts. As Eddie N. Williams of the Joint Center for Political Studies put it:

   > The more black candidates they have the more black voters the Republicans will attract. . . . Right now ideology is too locked in and you need intermediaries. The intermediaries are (black) candidates.

   Charles W. Hucker, "Blacks and the GOP: A Cautious Courtship," *Congressional Quarterly Weekly Report* 36 (April 29, 1978), p. 1051. In any event, for recruiting black candidates and for other work in 1977, the Wright-McNeil firm received $257,300 from the Republican National Committee and in 1978 the firm received a $550,000 contract

   Note: Quoted remarks on pp. 221-222, except where otherwise noted, are taken from Hucker, "Blacks and the GOP: A Cautious Courtship," as cited above.
3. Rhodes Cook, "GOP Planning to Woo Blacks to Widen Its Local Base," *Congressional Quarterly Weekly Report* 47 (March 4, 1989), p. 474.
4. Ibid., p. 475.
5. There was a ray of hope, however. In November 1990, for example, Gary Franks of Connecticut succeeded in becoming the first black Republican elected to Congress since 1935. Franks, who ran in a Republican district against a liberal Democrat, won by five percent of the vote and carried seven of the eight mostly black, heavily Democratic precincts in his district. See "New Star for G.O.P. Is Conservative and Black," *The New York Times*, November 25, 1990, p. 1. The question of whether black support for a black Republican continues beyond the initial election was answered in part when Franks was reelected in 1992.
6. See "The Promises Democrats Made," *U.S. News & World Report*, August 25, 1980, p. 62.
7. Ibid.
8. "Reagan's Platform: One He Can Run On In Wooing Democrats and Independents," *National Journal* 12, no. 30 (July 26, 1980), p. 1220.
9. Ibid.
10. Ibid.

CHAPTER 9

AFRICAN AMERICANS AND THE CONGRESSIONAL ARENA

In the orderly process of government, success of an issue often depends on the skill of its advocates in understanding who holds the key to power on that issue, and how to approach that person in a friendly or persuasive manner . . .

. . . Congress evidently gave little thought to the fact that if the poor people had the means to do things the right way—to hire a full-time lobbyist to touch the vital pressure points, to provide position papers, inserts for the Congressional Record, steaks and wine for the congressmen—they wouldn't be poor.

Nick Kotz,
Let Them Eat Promises:
The Politics of Hunger in America[*]

Perhaps the gravest distortions in congressional representation come from the extraordinary difficulty of defeating incumbents, and the great dependence of congressional campaigns on large contributions from interests with very specific legislative objectives. The slow turnover of members causes Congress to be always dominated by members with a vested interest in the organizational status quo. Sometimes it also isolates the legislative branch from changes in public attitudes. The members' dependency on business, unions, and the more affluent professions greatly increases the difficulty of enacting legislation to reform these institutions.

Gary Orfield,
Congressional Power:
Congress and Social Change†

Congress is the chief law-making institution in our governmental system. The legitimacy of this law-making function is enhanced by the fact that all of its 535 members (100 senators and 435 representatives) are elected directly by the people. Consequently, they are the people's representatives in Washington. And if there is anything about the principles of democratic government that undergirds our overall constitutional system, it is that our government is based upon the concept of popular representation. That is, the people (the governed) have the right and obligation to select directly those who represent them in the government (the governors). Hence, our government may be referred to as a *representative government*. This contrasts with the "town-meeting," or "direct democracy" idea in which all citizens participate directly in the governing process. But in a country as large as ours, direct democracy is both unworkable and impossible. Hence, our Constitution provides for a representative government with fixed terms and periodic elections for elected officials. This allows us to hold to the principle of *popular sovereignty* without suffering the pains and problems of direct democracy. In short, representative government makes popular sovereignty a practical, operational concept.

However, the idea of representative government, while a noble concept, continues to pose some perennial and troubling questions. For example, what do we mean by "representative"? and "representative" of what? of whom? These were and are exactly the kinds of questions that keep the *reapportionment* controversy alive. And such problems, as we know, have received and continue to get the attention of the United States Supreme Court. The prevailing view of our constitutional system was expressed dramatically by the Court in its "one-man, one-vote" formula, when it held that "the fundamental principle of representative government in this country is one of equal representation for equal numbers of people. . . . "[1] Said the Court:

> Legislators represent people, not trees or acres. Legislators are elected by voters, not farms or cities or economic interests. As long as ours is a representative of people, the right to elect legislators in a free and unimpaired fashion is a bedrock of our political system.[2]

However, despite this emphasis on the concept of popular representation based on numbers, there remains a measure of deviation from the strict numerical formula, especially at the state and local levels.[3] Of course, representation in the United States Senate is based on equality of representation from each state and not on population. But this does not dilute the essential principle that representation should be based on population since, as the Supreme Court put it, representation in the United States Senate was a necessary arrangement (compromise) in order to bring about the basic structure (constitution) of the union, "the birth of the nation" (*Reynolds* v. *Sims*). In any event, the fundamental principle of representation based on population applies both to the House of Representatives and to most other elective-legislative bodies in American state and local government.

But, for many Americans, the concept of popular representation encompasses much more than an automatic formula that apportions legislative representation based on population. Indeed, there has been increasing attention focused on how representative Congress really is. This more general question seems to be reflective of the more deeply held concern that Congress overrepresents particular socioeconomic strata of the American population. Specifically, Congress is criticized as being a predominantly white male, middle-class institution whose members are better educated and come from professional occupations, especially the legal profession (See Table 9-1). The number of women in Congress has fluctuated from 8 in 1947 to 27 in 1989 to

TABLE 9-1 "Representativeness" of the 103rd Congress: Members' Occupations

	HOUSE			SENATE			CONGRESS
	D	R	Total	D	R	Total	Total
Acting/entertainment	0	1	1	0	0	0	1
Aeronautics	0	2	2	1	0	1	3
Agriculture	7	12	19	4	5	9	28
Business or banking	56	75	131	14	13	27	158
Clergy	1	1	2	0	1	1	3
Education	44	21	66[a]	7	5	12	78[a]
Engineering	2	3	5	0	0	0	5
Homemaking	0	1	1	0	0	0	1
Journalism	11	12	24[a]	6	2	8	32[a]
Labor officials	2	0	2	0	0	0	2
Law	122	59	181	33	25	58	239
Law enforcement	8	2	10	0	0		10
Medicine	4	2	6	0	0	0	6
Military	0	0	0	0	1	1	1
Professional sports	0	1	1	1	0	1	2
Public service	51	35	86	9	3	12	98
Real estate	9	18	27	1	3	4	31

Note: Because some members have more than one occupation, totals are higher than total membership.
[a]Includes Sanders, I-Vt.
SOURCE: *Congressional Quarterly Weekly Report* 49 (Jan. 16, 1993), p. 13.

TABLE 9-2 African American Members of Congress, 1947-1993 (by numbers)[a]

CONGRESS	SENATE	HOUSE
103rd 1st sess.	1	38
102nd	0	25
101st	0	23
100th	0	22
99th	0	19
98th	0	20
97th	0	17
96th	0	15
95th	1	15
94th	1	16
93rd	1	15
92nd	1	12
91st	1	9
90th	1	5
89th	0	6
88th	0	5
87th	0	4
85th	0	4
84th	0	3
83rd	0	2
82nd	0	2
81st	0	2
80th	0	2

[a]Listed by Congress are the numbers of African-American members of the Senate and House of Representatives since the 80th Congress. The figures do not include the nonvoting delegates from the District of Columbia and the Virgin Islands.

SOURCE: Adapted from *Congressional Quarterly Weekly Report* 49 (Jan. 2, 1993), p. 10: *Congressional Quarterly Weekly Report* 49 (Jan. 16, 1993), p. 12.

54 in 1993. Even so, Congress remains a predominantly white male institution. (For rich and informative data on Congress, including data on women, blacks, occupational information with respect to the "representativeness" of Congress, see Norman Ornstein, Thomas Mann, and Michael Malbin, *Vital Statistics on Congress, 1989-1990* (Washington, DC: Congressional Quarterly, 1990). With respect to black representation, in 1947 there were 2 blacks in Congress and a new high of 39 as a result of the 1992 elections (See Table 9-2). The impact of the Voting Rights Act of 1965 in the South has been obvious with the election in 1972 of the first black members of Congress from this region in the twentieth century—Barbara Jordan (D- Texas) and Andrew Young (D-Georgia).

Another reason congressional membership reflects a distorted image of American society has to do with the kinds of people who generally become representatives. Although their numbers have declined in recent years, almost half of the people who make our laws are lawyers (See Table 9-1). But, blacks and women have yet to achieve the kind of representational parity in the legal profession that their relative population numbers would suggest. Thus, while lawyers are well represented in the membership of the Congress, blacks, women, and other minorities—in terms of sheer numbers—are woefully underrepresented.

Obviously, the implicit and explicit view is that the interests of these groups would be better represented if more persons from such groups were in Congress. While this does not necessarily follow, it is nevertheless a widely and strongly held view. Consequently, one of the major concerns of this chapter is whether, and to what extent and in what ways, black members of Congress attempt to represent the interests of blacks. An equally important consideration is how the aspirations of black representatives may be limited or enhanced by the rules, requirements, and expectations of the overall congressional environment. But there remains the strong prior question, and undoubtedly the more basic one, of how and to what extent the structural and dynamic aspects of congressional elections affect the election opportunities of blacks and minorities to gain membership in Congress.

BLACKS IN CONGRESS

There are 39 blacks in Congress, all of whom except one are members of the House of Representatives. Only two blacks have served in the Senate since 1880, Republican Edward Brooke (Massachusetts), who was defeated in his reelection bid in 1978, and at present, Senator Carol Moseley-Braun (D-Illinois) elected in 1992 (See Table 9-3). This represents a net increase of 13 blacks over the previous 26 in the 101st Congress, with most new House members coming from largely black districts created through reapportionment. While fewer than half of the 26 blacks in Congress in 1992 had prior experience in elective office, all of the 17 elected in 1992, except for one (Mel Reynolds of Illinois who replaced Gus Savage) come with a rich background of experience in state government or local office.[4]

A brief review of the socioeconomic characteristics of blacks in the House indicates a variety of career background patterns with no one pattern predominating (See Table 9-4). Overall, however, the fact that blacks in Congress come from a variety of career patterns may reflect a general trend away from any particular career avenue to the Congress. If this is true, then Congress may become more "representative," at least in terms of broadening the range of occupational interests now represented in the Congress.

In addition, a look at the congressional districts represented by blacks reveals a striking homogeneity in the types of districts represented by blacks

TABLE 9-3 African American Members of Congress: 1870-1993 (by name)

Senate	
Hiram R. Revels (R-Miss.)	1870-71
Blanche K. Bruce (R-Miss.)	1875-81
Edward W. Brooke (R-Mass.)	1967-79
Carol Moseley-Braun (D-Ill.)	1993-present
House	
Joseph H. Rainey (R-S.C.)	1870-79
Jefferson F. Long (R-Ga.)	1870-71
Robert B. Elliott (R-S.C.)	1871-74
Robert C. De Large (R-S.C.)	1871-73
Benjamin S. Turner (R-Ala.)	1871-73
Josiah T. Walls (R-Fla.)	1871-76
Richard H. Cain (R-S.C.)	1873-75; 1877-79
John R. Lynch (R-Miss.)	1873-77; 1882-83
James T. Rapier (R-Ala.)	1873-75
Alonzo J. Ransier (R-S.C.)	1873-75
Jeremiah Haralson (R-Ala.)	1875-77
John A. Hyman (R-N.C.)	1875-77
Charles E. Nash (R-La.)	1875-77
Robert Smalls (R-S.C.)	1875-79; 1882-83; 1884-87
James E. O'Hara (R-N.C.)	1883-87
Henry P. Cheatham (R-N.C.)	1889-93
John M. Langston (R-Va.)	1890-91
Thomas E. Miller (R-S.C.)	1890-91
George W. Murray (R-S.C.)	1893-95; 1896-97
George H. White (R-N.C.)	1897-1901
Oscar De Priest (R-Ill.)	1929-35
Arthur W. Mitchell (D-Ill.)	1935-43
William L. Dawson (D-Ill.)	1943-70
Adam C. Powell Jr. (D-N.Y.)	1945-67; 1969-71
Charles C. Diggs Jr. (D-Mich.)	1955-80
Robert N. C. Nix (D-Pa.)	1958-79
Augustus F. Hawkins (D-Calif.)	1963-91
John Conyers Jr. (D-Mich.)	1965-present
Louis Stokes (D-Ohio)	1969-present
William L. Clay (D-Mo.)	1969-present
Shirley Chisholm (D-N.Y.)	1969-83
George W. Collins (D-Ill.)	1970-72
Ronald V. Dellums (D-Calif.)	1971-present
Ralph H. Metcalfe (D-Ill.)	1971-78
Parren J. Mitchell (D-Md.)	1971-87
Charles B. Rangel (D-N.Y.)	1979-present
Yvonne B. Burke (D-Calif.)	1973-79
Cardiss Collins (D-Ill.)	1973-present
Barbara C. Jordan (D-Texas)	1973-79
Andrew Young (D-Ga.)	1973-77
Harold E. Ford (D-Tenn.)	1975-present
Julian C. Dixon (D-Calif.)	1979-present
William H. Gray III (D-Pa.)	1979-91
George T. Leland (D-Texas)	1979-89
Bennett McVey Stewart (D-Ill.)	1979-81
George W. Crockett Jr. (D-Mich.)	1981-91
Mervyn M. Dymally (D-Calif.)	1981-93
Gus Savage (D-Ill.)	1981-93
Harold Washington (D-Ill.)	1981-83
Katie Hall (D-Ind.)	1983-85
Charles A. Hayes (D-Ill.)	1983-93
Major R. Owens (D-N.Y.)	1983-present
Edolphus Towns (D-N.Y.)	1983-present
Alan Wheat (D-Mo.)	1983-present
Alton R. Waldon Jr. (D-N.Y.)	1986-87
Mike Espy (D-Miss.)	1987-93
Floyd H. Flake (D-N.Y.)	1987-present
John Lewis (D-Ga.)	1987-present
Kweisi Mfume (D-Md.)	1987-present
Donald M. Payne (D-N.J.)	1989-present
Craig Washington (D-Texas)	1990-present
Maxine Waters (D-Calif.)	1991-present
Gary Franks (R-Conn.)	1991-present
William Jefferson (D-La.)	1991-present
Barbara-Rose Collins (D-Mich.)	1991-present
Lucien E. Blackwell (D-Pa.)	1991-present
Earl F. Hilliard (D-Ala.)	1993-present
Walter R. Tucker (D-Calif.)	1993-present
Corrine Brown (D-Fla.)	1993-present
Alcee L. Hastings (D-Fla.)	1993-present
Carrie Meek (D-Fla.)	1993-present
Sanford Bishop (D-Ga.)	1993-present
Cynthia McKinney (D-Ga.)	1993-present
Bobby L. Rush (D-Ill.)	1993-present
Mel Reynolds (D-Ill.)	1993-present
Cleo Fields (D-La.)	1993-present
Albert R. Wynn (D-Md.)	1993-present
Bennie Thompson (D-Miss.)	1993-present
Eva Clayton (D-N.C.)	1993-present
Melvin Watt (D-N.C.)	1993-present
James E. Clyburn (D-S.C.)	1993-present
Eddie Bernice Johnson (D-Tex.)	1993-present
Robert C. Scott (D-Va.)	1993-present

SOURCES: *Congressional Quarterly Weekly Report* 49 (Jan. 2, 1993), p. 10: *Congressional Quarterly Weekly Report* 49 (Jan. 16, 1993), p. 12. In addition to the members listed above, John W. Menard, R-La., won a disputed election in 1868 but was not permitted to take his seat in Congress. Walter E. Fauntroy, D (1979-1991) and Eleanor Holmes Norton, D (1991-present) have served as non-voting delegates from the District of Columbia.

TABLE 9-4 Blacks in Congress: Socioeconomic Characteristics

NAME	AGE	EDUCATION	RELIGION	CAREER
Sanford Bishop (D-Geo., 2)	46	B.A., 1968, Morehouse College; J.D., 1971, Emory University	Baptist	Attorney, state legislator
Lucien E. Blackwell (D-Penn., 2)	61	West Philadelphia High School	Baptist	Labor official, city councilman, state legislator
Corrine Brown (D-Fla., 3)	46	B.S., 1969, Florida A&M University; Ed.S., 1974, University of Florida	Baptist	College guidance counselor, state legislator
William L. Clay (D-Mo., 1)	62	B.S., 1953, St. Louis University	Catholic	Real estate, life insurance, union business representative
Eva Clayton (D-N.C., 1)	58	B.S., 1955, Johnson C. Smith University; M.S., 1962, North Carolina Central University; 1967, University of North Carolina Law School	Presbyterian	County commissioner
James E. Clyburn (D-S.C., 6)	52	B.S., 1962, South Carolina State College	African Methodist Episcopalian	State human affairs commissioner
Barbara-Rose Collins (D-Mich., 13)	54	Wayne State University	Pan-African Orthodox Christian	School board member, state legislator, city councilwoman
Cardiss Collins (D-Ill., 7)	61	Northwestern University	Baptist	Stenographer, accountant, revenue auditor
John Conyers, Jr. (D-Mich., 1)	64	B.A., 1957, LL.B., 1958, Wayne State University	Baptist	Legislative assistant, workman's compensation referee, attorney
Ronald V. Dellums (D-Cal., 9)	57	A.A., 1958, Oakland City College; B.A., 1960, San Francisco State College; M.S.W., 1962, University of California	Protestant	Social worker, city councilman
Julian Dixon (D-Cal., 32)	59	B.S., 1962, Los Angeles State College; J.D., 1969, Southwestern Law School	Episcopalian	Special legal counsel, legislative assistant, state legislator
Cleo Fields (D-La., 4)	30	B.A., 1984, J.D., 1987, Southern University	Baptist	State legislator

TABLE 9-4 Continued

NAME	AGE	EDUCATION	RELIGION	CAREER
Floyd H. Flake (D-N.Y., 6)	48	B.A., 1967, Wilberforce University; Payne Theological Seminary, Northeastern University	African Methodist Episcopalian	Marketing analyst, college administrator, minister
Harold E. Ford (D-Tenn., 9)	48	B.S., 1967, Tennessee State University; L.F.D., L.E.D., 1969, John Gupten College	Baptist	Mortician, state legislator
Gary A. Franks (R-Conn., 5)	40	B.A., 1975, Yale University	Baptist	Real estate, alderman
Alcee L. Hastings (D-Fla., 23)	56	B.A., 1958, Fisk University; 1958-60, Howard University; J.D., 1963, Florida A&M University	African Methodist Episcopalian	Federal judge
Earl F. Hilliard (D-Ala., 7)	51	B.A., 1964, Morehouse College; J.D., 1967, Howard University; M.B.A., 1970, Atlanta University	Baptist	Attorney, insurance, state legislator
William J. Jefferson (D-La., 2)	46	B.A., 1969, Southern University; J.D., Harvard University, 1972	Baptist	Legislative aide, attorney, state legislator
Eddie Bernice Johnson (D-Tex., 30)	57	B.S., 1967, Texas Christian University; M.P.A., 1976, Southern Methodist University	Baptist	Business consultant, state legislator, regional director of Department of Health, Education, and Welfare
John Lewis (D-Ga., 5)	53	B.A., 1961, American Baptist Theological Seminary; B.A., 1963, Fisk University	Baptist	Civil rights activist, city councilman
Cynthia McKinney (D-Ga., 11)	38	B.A., 1978, University of Southern California; 1981, Georgia State University; 1984, Wisconsin, Fletcher School of Law and Diplomacy, Ph.D. candidate	Catholic	Professor, state legislator
Carrie Meek (D-Fla., 17)	67	B.S., 1946, Florida A&M University; M.S., 1948, University of Michigan; 1979, Florida Atlantic University	Baptist	Education administrator, state legislator
Kweisi Mfume (D-Md., 7)	44	B.S., 1976, Morgan State University; M.A., 1984, John S. Hopkins University	Baptist	City councilman

Continued

TABLE 9-4 Continued

NAME	AGE	EDUCATION	RELIGION	CAREER
Carol Moseley-Braun (D-Ill.)	45	B.A., 1967, University of Illinois-Chicago; J.D., 1972, University of Chicago	Catholic	Attorney
Eleanor Holmes Norton (D-Wash., D.C.)*	56	B.A., 1960, Antioch College; M.A., 1963, LL.B., 1964, Yale University	Episcopalian	Assistant legal director of ACLU, head of EEOC, professor
Major R. Owens (D-N.Y., 12)	57	B.A., 1956, Morehouse College; M.S., 1957, Atlanta University	Baptist	Library administrator, community development official, state legislator
Donald M. Payne (D-N.J., 10)	58	B.A., 1957, Seton Hall University	Baptist	Teacher, businessman, city councilman
Charles B. Rangel (D-N.Y., 15)	63	B.S., 1957, New York University; LL.B., 1960, St. John's University	Catholic	Attorney, state legislator
Mel Reynolds (D-Ill., 2)	41	A.A., 1972, Chicago City College; B.A., 1974, University of Illinois; LL.B., 1979, M.A., 1981, Oxford University	Baptist	Professor
Bobby L. Rush (D-Ill., 1)	46	B.A., 1973, Roosevelt University; 1975-1977, University of Illinois-Chicago	Protestant	Civil rights activist, insurance, college administrator, alderman
Robert C. Scott (D-Va., 3)	46	A.B., 1969, Harvard University; J.D., 1973, Boston College	Episcopalian	Attorney, state legislator
Louis Stokes (D-Ohio)	68	1946-1948, Western Reserve University; J.D., 1953, Cleveland-Marshall Law School	Methodist	Attorney
Bennie Thompson (D-Miss., 2)	45	B.A., 1968, Tougaloo College; M.S., 1972, Jackson State University	Methodist	Teacher, alderman, mayor
Edolphus Towns (D-N.Y., 11)	59	B.S., 1959, North Carolina A&T University; M.S.W., 1973, Adelphi University	Presbyterian	Teacher, social worker, hospital administrator, deputy borough president

TABLE 9-4 Continued

NAME	AGE	EDUCATION	RELIGION	CAREER
Walter R. Tucker (D-Cal., 37)	36	1974-76, Princeton University; B.A., 1978, University of Southern California; J.D., Georgetown, 1981	Baptist	Attorney, mayor
Craig Washington (D-Tex., 18)	51	B.S., 1966, Prairie View A&M University; J.D., 1969, Texas Southern University	Episcopalian	State legislator
Maxine Waters (D-Cal., 29)	54	B.A., 1970, California State University	Christian	State legislator
Melvin Watt (D-N.C., 12)	47	B.S., 1967, University of North Carolina; J.D., 1970, Yale University	Presbyterian	Attorney, state legislator
Alan Wheat (D-Mo., 5)	41	B.A., 1972, Grinnell College	Church of Christ	Economist, legislative aide, state legislator
Albert R. Wynn (D-Md., 4)	41	B.S., 1973, University of Pittsburgh; 1973-1974, Howard University; J.D., 1977, Georgetown University	Baptist	Attorney, state legislator

*Non-voting member.
SOURCES: Michael Barone et al., *The Almanac of American Politics 1992* (New York: Dutton, 1992); *Congressional Quarterly Weekly Report* 49 (Jan. 2, 1993); *Congressional Quarterly Weekly Report* 49 (Jan. 16, 1993).

in terms of race, urbanization, and poverty. Included are representatives from districts in the three largest cities in the United States—New York, Los Angeles, and Chicago. And a number of districts have a greater percentage of families below $3,000 in yearly income than their respective state averages. Overall, then, the constituencies represented by black members of Congress tend to be mostly black, poor, and urban.

There is another dimension on which congressional districts represented by blacks are homogeneous. That is the degree to which black representatives come from what are called "safe" districts. In this context, "safe" refers to the probability that an incumbent will continue to be reelected. A "safe" seat is usually one in which a candidate receives a high proportion of the votes cast. Using the percentage of votes received as a yardstick, in the 1990 elections we see that all but one of the winning black candidates received at least 68 percent of the vote—Republican Gary Franks of Connecticut who received 52 percent of the vote in a mostly white district.

An alternative measure of the safeness of a district for black representatives is the extent to which blacks replace blacks (or contest black incumbents) in a specific seat. For example, in the 1992 elections, of the 16 newly elected blacks only 3 come from districts previously represented by blacks, the other 13 coming from mainly new black districts resulting from state reapportionment policies in 1990. This suggests that there is a fairly stable number of congressional districts that will continue to elect black representatives. The "safeness" of these districts, insofar as electing blacks, seems very much related to the size of the black population in the particular district. That is, the larger the black population, the greater chance a black has of being elected. Thus, the probability of black representation still seems directly related to the size of the black population.

In addition, it should be mentioned that particular court decisions on discriminatory voting procedures may also help aid the election of blacks to Congress and other offices.[5] It is true, of course, that the Supreme Court in *City of Mobile, Alabama* v. *Bolden* [446 U.S. 55 (1980)] rejected a case challenging Mobile's at-large election districts for city commissioners since it diluted the black vote. But in response to this decision, Congress passed an amendment to the Voting Rights Act of 1965 that prohibited any voting procedure that abridged the right to vote on account of race. And in *Thornburg* v. *Gingles* [478 U.S. 30 (1986)], the Supreme Court held that a district containing a majority of minorities should be created when, among other factors, effects of discrimination are evident and the area has a sufficiently large and geographically compact minority population, the minority is politically cohesive, and minority candidates have been previously defeated due to bloc voting by whites. It is expected that these cases may affect the manner in which districts are drawn in the future. Clearly these court decisions have and will have an impact on the manner in which state legislatures reapportion their districts in the future.

THE CONGRESSIONAL ARENA

"All legislative power herein granted," says the Constitution, "is vested in a Congress of the United States. . . ." But the Constitution says much more. It makes similar statements about the executive power being vested in the president and the judicial power being vested in the federal courts. However, as discussed in Chapter 3, the Constitution follows the separation of powers doctrine only so far. After seeming to delegate total power to each of the three branches, the Constitution goes on to give each branch just enough of the other's powers to make them *interdependent* with rather than independent of each other. Accordingly, it is not accurate, either in theory or in practice, to say that the whole of any of these powers resides in any one branch exclusively. But exclusiveness aside, however, the fact is that Congress is the chief repository of legislative power under our system of government. As such, Congress has been and remains a major forum in the formation of public policy.

For one thing, the composition of Congress enhances its role in the policy-making process. Congress, as we know, is a *bicameral* institution consisting of the House of Representatives and the Senate. The members of the House are closest to the people because they are from smaller districts. House members are elected for two-year terms from 435 single-member districts into which the various states are apportioned. This apportionment is figured on the basis of population[6] by the respective state legislatures. No state has less than one member in the House. While there are 435 members of the House, there are only 100 senators each elected for six-year terms with 2 senators from each state. The Senate elections are staggered so that one-third of the Senate members are elected every two years.

COMMITTEES

The basic organizational and working unit in both houses is the *standing committee*. The main work of Congress, both legislative formulation and legislative oversight, takes place in these committees. How they function in larger measure determines what Congress actually does.

Standing committees are generally organized along subject matter lines such as labor, finance, agriculture, budget, and foreign policy. There are 16 such committees in the Senate with from 11 to 29 members. In the House there are 22 standing committees with an average membership of about 37. In addition, there are a number of *joint committees* with membership from both houses. Finally, there are *select committees* which are created for special purposes and have limited tenure.

Committees differ with respect to the perceived status and prestige conferred on their members. This variation between types of standing committees is reflected in the rules of the House which separate committees into three groups: exclusive, semi-exclusive, and nonexclusive. A member of an exclusive committee cannot sit on any other committee. These are the really important and prestigious committees that have impact on the work of all other committees and the entire House. There are three such committees in the House: (1) Appropriations, (2) Rules, and (3) Ways and Means. Next in order of prestige are the semi-exclusive committees; there are eight such committees in the House, including Agriculture, Education and Labor, and the Judiciary.[7] Members can sit on only one semi-exclusive committee but can also serve on a nonexclusive committee. A bit lower in rank and prestige, but not in terms of their particular functions, are the nonexclusive committees. There are also eight nonexclusive committees in the House, including the District of Columbia, Government Operations, and Post Office and Civil Service.[8] A member may serve on two nonexclusive committees. These restrictions, however, apply only to standing committees and not to selective or joint committees.

Membership on the major working committees—the standing committees—is bipartisan. Each party is represented roughly in proportion to its strength in the particular house. Both parties provide formal rules and structures for assigning members to committees. In the Democratic party, for example, it is the Steering and Policy Committee which makes committee assignments. This committee is made up of House leaders, congressmen nominated by the Steering and Policy Committee, and members elected by the caucus on a regional basis.[9] However, in the end, it is the House leadership that usually has the most influential voice in allocating committee assignments.

The political jockeying for what are considered "plum" committee assignments is politically intense. This is because committees are the focal point of congressional work and because congressmen perceive that committee assignments can make or break their careers. Representatives fight for those committee assignments that can do the most to further their interests. Interests of congressmen can be distinguished as influence within the House, ensuring reelection through aiding constituents, and making good public policy.[10]

Different committees allow representatives to attain those goals in various ways. For example, Appropriations and Ways and Means are seen as committees that bestow influence and prestige on their members. The Interior and Post Office committees are the type that aid a member's reelection through constituency service. Members of committees such as Education and Labor and Foreign Affairs have as their goal the making of good public policy.[11] Thus, one factor which can explain committee assignments is the motivation of individual members.

However, even if the desires of a representative are known and that representative gets the committee assignment, it is sometimes difficult to establish a direct causal relationship between the two. Take, for example, the case of the black representative from Texas, the late Mickey Leland.[12] Leland wanted to be on the Interstate and Foreign Commerce Committee to work on health issues which were in his main area of interest while serving in the Texas state legislature. He was, however, only one of a number of new representatives who wanted to fill one of the few vacancies on that committee. In fact, both Leland and another newly elected Texas representative (now Senator, Phil Gramm) sought membership on the Commerce Committee. This was possible since two of the seats open on the Commerce Committee had been vacated by Texans. Most important, however, is that the Commerce Committee has jurisdiction over oil and gas matters, a subject very dear to the hearts of Texans. Consequently, Texas representatives thought that their delegation and interests should be well represented on the committee. In any event both Leland and Gramm lobbied for support among members of the Texas delegation to fill the two seats vacated by departing members of the delegation. (It should be pointed out that both Leland and Gramm had earlier received the endorsement of the Texas freshman representatives, who numbered seven in all.) However, some members of the delegation felt that Leland was soft on energy issues, but Gramm was not so viewed. While consumer groups were concerned with Gramm's stand on issues such as his strong opposition to government regulation, the oil industry was pleased by his prospective membership on the Commerce Committee. Eventually, both Leland and Gramm received the support of the full Texas delegation, including Jim Wright, the House Majority Leader. Leland, in addition, also had the support of the Congressional Black Caucus (CBC) and Ralph Nader's Congress Watch Organization. The CBC supported Leland by expressing that he should be given the seat on the committee left vacant by the death of Ralph Metcalfe, a black representative from Illinois. In the end, both Leland and Gramm won seats on the committee. And though they did not lobby or campaign as a team, Leland thought that "Gramm's candidacy assisted him because . . . many welcomed them as representatives of diverse viewpoints."[13] Thus, Leland received the committee assignment he wanted, but primarily for reasons not included in his original desire to seek the appointment.

This example serves to show, to some extent, the political maneuvering necessary to get a valued committee assignment. Although it is difficult to state with certainty the factors responsible for gaining a particular assignment, a large part of Leland's success was due to his own lobbying efforts. He thus gained the support from his own state congressional delegation, which included Jim Wright, who was House Majority Leader at the time. This support undoubtedly provided the key to Leland's winning a seat on the committee he preferred.

By way of summary, we have suggested that the major working units of the Congress are its standing committees. The committees are classified as exclusive, semi-exclusive, and nonexclusive, describing the limits to the number of committees on which an individual representative may serve. These categories reflect the general perceptions of the prestige and importance of given committees, but there remain difficulties in attempting to attach importance and prestige to any particular committee except as it relates to the needs and desires of individual congressmen. In short, how and why members gain particular committee assignments is apparently a very dynamic process subject to the push and pull of a number of factors. Despite the complexities involved, however, it is possible to make several observations on committee assignments of black representatives. Particular committee assignments for each member of Congress can be found in the *Congressional Directory* published biennially for each Congress by the U.S. Government Printing Service. To begin with, a number of black representatives serve on the exclusive committees that are perceived as the most influential and prestigious assignments. Moreover, black membership on semi-exclusive and nonexclusive committees seems to be related to black policy interests. Indeed, as indicated above, the importance of any given committee depends, in large measure, upon the relationship of committee jurisdiction to constituency interests.

COMMITTEE CHAIRPERSON

What comes out of the committee, as well as how the committee conducts its work, dependslargely upon the committee chair. The power of an individual chairperson, of course, depends upon many factors—his or her personal prestige and standing among colleagues, the tradition and norms of the particular committee, and so on. Nonetheless, the committee chair occupies a central position in the work of the committee. He or she controls the committee staff, schedules or postpones committee meetings, determines the agenda, and generally sets the pace of the committee. Though recent rules changes have somewhat diminished their powers, chairpersons retain a great deal of influence over the committee's operations.

Historically, the only way in which a member could become a committee chair was through *seniority*. This tended to favor southerners from safe districts. However, because of the changes in Democratic party rules, seniority, though still an important factor, is not the only way to become a committee chair.[14] While a number of factors operated in concert to break the seniority system, a primary reason was the number of new representatives elected to Congress in the 1970s. The turnover rate in Congress reached the point that in 1978 more than half of the House members had been elected since 1974.[15] The result was a steady and large influx of new members who did not owe anything to the House senior establishment. But the seniority system rebounded in the 1980s with a dramatic reduction in the turnover rate. For example, the return rate for the current Congress—those who were members of the previous Congress—was 92 percent. In fact, 97.5 percent of those who sought reelection in 1988 won. In 1990, the rate for the House was 96 percent.[16] Black incumbents have been particularly successful in winning reelection, so much so that although blacks make up only 5 percent of the 435 voting members of the House, they chaired 25 percent of the standing and select committees in the 100th (previous) Congress.[17] These gains have come largely as a result of the seniority of black members.

For example, four blacks chair key congressional committees, including John Conyers, Jr. (D-Michigan), chair of the Government Operations Committee, and Ronald Dellums (D-California), who chairs the important House Armed Services Committee. This is quite a departure from the very recent past when in 1978, Dellums was the only black serving as chair of a committee—the District of Columbia Committee. He had replaced another black, Charles Diggs (D-Michigan), who became chair in 1972. Diggs was forced to resign the chairmanship following his conviction in October 1978 on felony charges relating to the diversion of his congressional employees' salaries to personal use.[18]

The two men who became committee chairmen prior to Diggs are names familiar to many of us: Representatives William L. Dawson (D-Illinois) and Representative Adam Clayton Powell (D-New York). Dawson was elected to

Currently the chair of important House Armed Services Committee, Rep. Ron Dellums (D., CA) is shown here in December, 1990 talking to reporters outside U.S. District Court in Washington, regarding the lawsuit of Democratic lawmakers challenging the constitutional authority of the president to wage war in the Persian Gulf without congressional approval. *(AP/Wide World Photos)*

Congress in 1942 and served as chairman of the House Committee on Government Operations from 1955 until his retirement in 1970. Powell was elected to Congress in 1944 and became chairman of the very important House Committee on Education and Labor in 1961. Powell remained as chairman of the committee until 1967 when he was ousted from that position and eventually from Congress. Let us take a more detailed look at the politics and chairmanships of Dawson and Powell.

Since the depression there has always been at least one black member in the House. But until Dawson and Powell came on the scene, blacks did not hold positions of significant influence in congressional policy making. Dawson's situation is especially important, we believe, since he seemed so enmeshed in the Chicago *political machine* that it was difficult, if not impossible, for him to attend to black interests. However, it should be stated that Dawson's committee did not at the time handle matters of salient interest to blacks. The jurisdiction of the committee has been described as:

> [b]udget and accounting measures other than appropriations, reorganization in executive and legislative branches of government, studying intergovernmental relations between U.S. and the states and municipalities, general legislative oversight of executive branch.[19]

Possessing institutional power in this instance did not lead to generalized political gains for blacks. In this regard, Hanes Walton has stated:

> Dawson used his institution and personal power to enhance his political position and influence in Congress and did not serve blacks in general.[20]

By the time Dawson became chairman he had reached an advanced age and his health was deteriorating. Effective use of power requires a degree of vigor and energy which he did not possess. And, finally, the amount of bargaining with colleagues for the interest of a black constituency was limited since Dawson's position furnished fewer resources with which to negotiate.

Unlike his colleague from Chicago, Adam Clayton Powell, Jr. was a maverick. The minister of the largest black Protestant congregation in New York City, Congressman Powell exploited this resource in fighting the Tammany machine of New York. Powell emerged at an opportune time. The influence of political machines was declining, but of equal importance was a growing political consciousness among northern urban blacks. This consciousness partly resulted from long-standing frustration over unresponsive government institutions. African Americans were becoming increasingly resentful of the continued discrimination and other forms of social injustice to which they were subjected.

Because of his flamboyant style and the explicit emphasis which Powell placed on race, he has generally been criticized by political commentators and scholarly analysts. James Q. Wilson, for example, characterized Powell as a political leader who substituted "personal charisma and bellicose militancy" for organization.[21] We agree that Powell had charismatic appeal and that he was (for his time) militant. But personalizing leadership is a characteristic of black ministerial style, especially in the Baptist denominations. And in the absence of more tangible rewards, charisma is a functional substitute for holding a constituency together. It should also be kept in mind that a religious congregation is similar to a political machine; it provides welfare services to members. This function is, of course, more limited in scope in a church.

As a political base, Powell's congregation was both durable and large enough to return him to office repeatedly. In consequence, he became chair of the House Committee on Education and Labor when Graham Barden resigned from Congress in protest against packing the committee with new members who favored more liberal legislation. Powell's tenure as chair was important since it spanned the period during the development of legislation needed to wage the War on Poverty. His committee was a focal point for many of the crucial legislative debates in this effort. Powell's committee leadership has not been evaluated favorably. Unlike some of the other chairpersons, Powell was not considered an "expert" in his assigned responsibilities. Much of the work of Education and Labor, as with other House committees, was done by subcommittee chairs. The flamboyant style that characterized Powell's leadership also militated against his effectiveness as committee chair. In addition, he could not be attentive to the business of the committee because of his high rate of absenteeism from Congress.

Perhaps Powell's fall from power was an inevitable consequence of his behavior. He was never a popular figure in Congress. His troubles grew in New York and Washington as well. Powell had gone against congressional norms, including what a special House committee found to be a misuse of federal funds. As a result, the House fined Powell and stripped him of seniority and his chairmanship. The racial themes which he espoused offended the white majority at the same time that they gained him widespread admiration among blacks. But in the end, it was Powell's Harlem constituents who did what his House colleagues wanted to do but could not: deprive him of a seat in Congress.[22] Powell was defeated in the 1970 primary and died soon thereafter.

Subcommittees: Their Increasing Influence While standing committees retain their role as the chief working units of both houses, subcommittees are increasingly being looked upon as the chief working units of the standing committees themselves. Indeed, the committee structure of the Congress provides members with the opportunity to gain expertise and visibility in discrete areas of public policy. This is important both for a member's efforts at reelection through constituency service and for the development of innovative and important policy initiatives. Almost all work done in Congress begins in a subcommittee. This is also the place where much of the investigation pursuant to legislative oversight occurs. Thus, because of their rather small size and discrete areas of jurisdiction, it is possible for one or a few members of Congress to exert significant influence in both the larger standing committees and in the legislative process generally.

Subcommittees exist under the jurisdiction of committees. In the House of Representatives, for example, there are approximately 150 subcommittees. As with committees, subcommittees vary with size, jurisdiction, and prestige. Historically, subcommittees existed as the personal fiefdoms of powerful committee chairmen. But no more. Along with changes to lessen the power of committees and committee chairs have come changes which have increased the role and authority of subcommittees and their chairs.

The major changes occurred in 1973 and have come to be known collectively as the "*subcommittee bill of rights*."[23] These reforms, for example, now allow committee caucuses, rather than committee chairs, to select chairs of the subcommittees, establish their jurisdictions, provide for adequate subcommittee budgets, and ensure all members of a major subcommittee assignment.

They also require committee chairs to refer legislation to appropriate subcommittees within two weeks. This, of course, prevents committee chairs from killing bills by not scheduling them for action. Furthermore, the changes allow subcommittee chairmen and their ranking minority members to hire one staff person each to work for them on the subcommittee. Such staff assistance allows subcommittees more independence of and from committee chairmen. Thus, subcommittees are becoming an increasingly important stage in the legislative process.

How do blacks fare in subcommittee assignments? Do they serve on subcommittees which can have a significant impact on the social welfare policies affecting African Americans? As with full committee assignments, answers to such questions can prove difficult, but we can suggest that black representatives, not unlike others, tend to serve on at least one subcommittee that addresses the interests of their constituents, for example, health, education, social welfare policy.

Subcommittee Chairpersons The reforms of the Democratic party and House rules which changed the committee and subcommittee structures also affected the power of subcommittee chairs. Decreasing the power of committee chairs over subcommittees provided subcommittee chairs with more autonomy. Again, as with committee chairs, seniority has ceased to be the only factor in selecting chairpersons. Thus, there has been an element of unpredictability added to who will become subcommittee chairs. The Democratic Caucus of each committee, established in 1973, typically decides who the subcommittee chair will be. However, one qualification to this general rule occurs with the Appropriations Committee in which all subcommittee chairs are approved by the Democratic Caucus of the House.

How successful have black representatives been in becoming subcommittee chairs? Just as in other areas, as black representation grows in numbers and seniority, so do their role and influence in chairing subcommittees. For example, probably the most influential subcommittee chaired by a black member is the Select Revenue Measures Subcommittee of the Ways and Means Committee chaired by Charles Rangel (D-New York).

Other Congressional Leaders In addition to committee and subcommittee chairs, there are other key positions in Congress. In the House there is the Speaker of the House, the majority *floor leader*, and the minority floor leader. Though each of these officials is selected by his party *caucus*, only the Speaker (the presiding officer) is officially elected by the entire House. The Speaker is by far the single most important official in the House. He wields great influence in his party, the House, and the Congress generally. Together, the Speaker and the majority and minority floor leaders significantly influence the outcome of business in the House. Similarly, the majority and minority leaders in the Senate set the pace of business in that house.

In general, the party leadership and various party committees decide standing committee assignments and committee chairs and control the operations and flow of business in each house. For these reasons, to be active in the party is extremely important to a congressional career.

Thus, another role for members of Congress has been identified. In addition to proposing legislation, engaging in oversight activities, providing services to constituents, and serving as members of committees and subcommittees, legislators must also attend to important party business which influences the inner workings of the House. If congressional careers can be made or broken by the type of committee assignment a member receives, a source of considerable power must be the bodies that decide committee assignments. Thus, it is in the interest of black members in furthering their careers and dealing with the problems of their constituents to gain leadership roles and membership in various congressional party structures.

Currently, several black members hold party committee assignments. Prior to his resignation from Congress in 1991, Representative William Gray III (D-Pennsylvania) held two positions. He served as Democratic Party Whip and, very importantly, was a member of the Steering and Policy Committee along with Harold Ford (D-Tennessee). The whip's function is to enforce party discipline in roll-call votes. The whip gets members to the floor and tries to get them to vote as the party leadership wants. The Steering and Policy Committee assigns members to committees and, thus, wields a great deal of power within the Democratic membership of Congress.

The Legislative Bureaucracy: Congressional Staffs The executive bureaucracy and administrative agencies bear the brunt of studies, investigations, and humor about what all those "faceless" federal bureaucrats do and how they operate. And, since this bureaucracy operates primarily under the direction of the president and his cabinet, it plays an important role not only in the implementation of public policies but also in the development of those policies. Thus, attention is properly focused on what and how these officials operate. However, similar attention has not been given to another group of staff persons who work for the federal government—the *legislative bureaucracy*.[24] This bureaucracy includes (1) professional staff persons who work for congressional committees and (2) those persons who serve as staff for individual members of Congress. These persons assist the Congress in carrying out day-to-day operations. Their work runs the gamut from research and data collection needed for hearings, investigations, and bill drafting to the kind of things needed to nurse a constituency, such as responding to letters from the people back home.

In short, the work of Congress is greatly dependent upon the work of various staffs. As such, legislative bureaucrats—just like bureaucrats in the executive branch—play a crucial and influential role in the legislative process. They provide ideas, information, and insight that help to shape legislation and congressional decision making. As such, the work effectiveness, standing, and influence of individual members of Congress and of congressional committees depend in large measure upon the work and resourcefulness of the various staffs.

This apparent and increasing role of legislative bureaucrats in the work of the Congress is (or at least should be) of obvious interest to blacks and minorities. And just as attention is focused on the "representativeness" of Congress and the executive bureaucracy in terms of minority representation, so must we devote similar attention to the "representativeness" of the legislative bureaucracy. And, in this regard, it remains the situation that blacks and minorities remain woefully underrepresented and unrepresented both on congressional committee staffs and on staffs of individual members of Congress. The situation is little different, if anything worse, than it was some 20 years ago. A 1979 *National Journal* study of congressional committee staffs, for example, found that committee staffs were "dominated by white males."[25] Indeed, as to committee staffs, the study indicated that blacks and other minorities constitute only about 5 percent of the staffs (85 out of 1,669). Moreover, the study pointed up that the few blacks who are on committee staffs are "often" selected by black members who serve on these committees.[26] Consider, for example, the following excerpt from the *National Journal* study:

> Of the 50 committee staff directors, not one is a woman. The only black holding the job is the staff director of the House District of Columbia Committee, which is chaired by a black member. No women or blacks are to be found heading any of the major administrative support offices and (at the time of the 1979 study) the only woman filling an important post in the legislative bureaucracy is Alice Rivlin, director of the Congressional Budget Office.[27]

Staffs of individual members, of course, are selected by and work for the various members of the Congress. Here again, however, the 1979 *National Journal* study indicated that just as on committee staffs, blacks constituted only about 5 percent of the staff personnel in members' offices. Moreover, a breakdown by staff position shows that just as is true in other contexts, blacks are clustered in the lower prestige and salaried jobs. Almost one-half (49 percent) of all blacks in members' offices are in "clerical" positions, with 75 percent clustered in the bottom three categories. By contrast, whereas only 25 percent of the blacks employed in staff positions are in the top four categories, more than 50 percent of the whites in staff positions (54 percent) hold jobs in these top categories.

Overall, however, and despite the fact that staffs have more than tripled since 1979, little has changed in terms of the continued paucity of black and minority representation in legislative staffs and the congressional bureaucracy. Indeed a 1991 survey by black staff groups in both houses indicates that blacks hold "only about 300, or 3.7 percent of the 8,200 power jobs [in Congress] that influence legislation and political decisions." Other minority groups are also seriously underrepresented with Hispanics holding about 150 of these jobs while another 45 are held by Asian Americans. And almost half of these minority staffers work for congresspersons who come from these minority groups. With the increase in number of members of Congress from these groups we would also expect the number of staff persons from the group to increase accordingly.

"Power jobs" are defined as including administrative assistants, legislative assistants, press secretaries, and senior committee staff. The 1991 report indicates, for example, that in the Senate blacks hold some 68, or 2.5 percent of the 2,700 persons who fill these most important positions. The situation is only a little better in the House where blacks hold about 240, or 4.4 percent of the 5,500 most important staff jobs. Mention is made, however, that more than half of these black staffers at the time worked for the 26 black members of the House.

Various explanations, of course, are offered for the paucity of blacks in the legislative bureaucracy. One may be that Congress (and the judicial branch) was not covered by the anti-discrimination provisions of earlier civil rights legislation such as the Civil Rights Act of 1964, even though both subsequently adopted policies against such discrimination.[29] It is true, of course, that the 1991 Civil Rights Act offers congressional (and White House) employees protection against job discrimination, but neither house is required to follow affirmative action guidelines. In short, there is a lack of any effective enforcement mechanism to insure greater representation of blacks and minorities among congressional staffs, and litigation as a way of enforcing rights remains a long and tortuous process. Thus, on balance, the lack of more blacks and other minorities in congressional staff positions might very well be due to the lack of any effective anti-discrimination as well as affirmative action policies. It is indeed ironic that the Congress which passed so much civil rights legislation should itself be found wanting in giving full effect to the kinds of policies that it has imposed on others.

On a more practical level, the lack of blacks in staff positions is explained by the fact that it is hard to find blacks who have the qualifications and experience needed for such positions. This, of course, is a timeworn excuse that is used in many contexts. Qualifications are ofttimes so nebulous that they can easily be tailored to permit or prevent certain persons from gaining particular positions. And while it is true that experience can be an important asset for given jobs, this explanation becomes somewhat circular and self-fulfilling since blacks, by not being employed initially, have not had the opportunity to gain such experience.

Overall, then, blacks are grossly underrepresented both in the membership of Congress and in the various congressional staffs. Accordingly, very few blacks participate in the fashioning of laws by which they, and all other Americans, are governed. And this could prove of major consequence since such staff positions "tend to become springboards to even more powerful positions."[30] Indeed, some current members of Congress, as well as persons in other branches such as Justice Clarence Thomas, a former aide to Senator John Danforth (R-Missouri), got their starts by working on congressional staffs.

Legislation and Legislative Oversight The main business of Congress is legislating or passing laws. Congress, however, is concerned with more than passing laws; it is also interested in how those laws once enacted are carried out. The enactment of laws and their implementation are obviously dynamic processes, involving as they do the interaction of the president, Congress, interest groups, administrators, and others. A discussion of these dynamics is reserved for the next chapter. Our purpose here is to give a brief overview of the process by which Congress passes laws and how Congress goes about finding out what happens once such laws are enacted.

Generally, the initiative in law making comes from the president, although a myriad of legislative proposals come from the Congress. Nonetheless, before any proposals (bills) can become law, they must run the legislative gamut in Congress, which includes (1) introduction and referral to committee; (2) committee consideration, including the full range of options open to the committee; for example, whether or not to hold public hearings, whether the bill should be amended, redrafted, or substituted altogether, whether or not the bill should be reported out; and (3) consideration, or debate, and vote by the entire house. If passed by one house, the bill is sent to the other house where basically the same procedures are followed. If both houses pass the bill in identical form, then the bill is sent directly to the president. However, if a similar but different version of the bill is passed by one house, a conference committee made up of members of both houses convenes to resolve the differences. If such differences are resolved, the identical measure worked out by the conference committee is presented to both houses. If passed in this identical form, the bill is then sent to the president for his approval or disapproval (veto). If the president approves and signs, the bill becomes law; if he disapproves (vetoes), the bill might still become law if two-thirds of both houses of Congress vote to override the president's veto. The overriding of a presidential veto, however, is seldom accomplished. Or, if the president does not take action on the bill within ten weekdays, the bill becomes law without his signature. However, if the Congress adjourns within this ten-day period, the president—by not taking any action—can kill the bill.

The activities of Congress do not stop once a bill becomes law. Indeed, there is an increasing interest in Congress to determine whether particular laws are being implemented by the executive branch in accord with congressional intent. This continuous review by Congress of the executive branch is generally known as *legislative oversight*.

Legislative oversight is on the increase. A major reason for this increase is perhaps due to a belief that certain implementation activities of government bureaucrats—such as the issuance of rules, regulations, and guidelines—violate legislative intent or otherwise abuse executive discretion. Moreover, many Americans believe that the government, especially the executive bureaucracy, has become too big and insensitive to their needs, and therefore, constant surveillance is required if adequate control on legislative implementation is to be maintained. Members of Congress, ever sensitive to voters in their quest for reelection, have increased their oversight of the bureaucracy to meet this perceived need.

The efforts of Congress to oversee the activities of executive agencies were dealt a blow when the United States Supreme Court held the legislative veto unconstitutional in *Immigration and Naturalization Service* v. *Chadha* [462 U.S. 919 (1983)]. The legislative veto, a mechanism whereby either house of Congress could overturn an executive agency's decision, was included in hundreds of laws to provide Congress with a weapon to combat bureaucratic decisions that it opposed. The Immigration and Nationality Act included a provision that allowed either the House of Representatives or the Senate to pass a resolution rejecting the decision of the attorney general and the Immigration and Naturalization Service to suspend a deportation proceeding. Through the use of a resolution, it was not necessary to present the action to either the other chamber or the president. In *Immigration and Naturalization Service* v. *Chadha*, the House of Representatives overturned the attorney general's decision to suspend the deportation of an East Indian, Jagdish Rai Chadha, and to allow him to remain in the United States. Chadha had a nonimmigrant student visa, but he remained in the United States after its expiration. The Supreme Court struck down the legislative veto because the resolution was not presented to the president for his approval. The result of this decision was to lessen Congress's ability to check the actions of executive agencies.

The brunt of the oversight function is carried on by various committees and subcommittees. A variety of methods are used by Congress in its oversight activities. The most prevalent of these methods are *hearings*,[31] wherein executive branch personnel appear before committees to give testimony on administrative implementation of legislative mandates.

Insofar as blacks and minorities are concerned, the increase in oversight activities by Congress can cut both ways. On the other hand, the time spent on oversight is time not spent on developing creative legislation and policy initiatives to deal with problems of blacks and other minorities. Of course, it may be argued that legislative oversight activities are necessary to protect and make more effective programs such as those embodied in the mass of legislation passed during the 1960s, for example, the Civil Rights Act of 1964. Indeed, such activities might point to the need for corrective or supplemental legislation to profit from new information.

However, the continuing inequities (e.g., in housing and employment) suffered by blacks and other minorities lend credence to the view that minorities do not appear to derive much benefit from the oversight activities of the Congress. Indeed, in the past few years Congress has done little, if anything, to fill in the "gaps" (in legislation) and come to grips with the persisting problems of racism. But, as we shall see, one of the major objectives of the Congressional Black Caucus is to push Congress to deal with these persistent problems.

DISTRICT REPRESENTATIVES WITH A NATIONAL CONSTITUENCY: THE CONGRESSIONAL BLACK CAUCUS[32]

"When we started the Caucus [in 1969]," said Representative Louis Stokes, "we had no idea that it would have the kind of impact on black America that it's had.[33]. . . All we were trying to demonstrate was that nine blacks, given the responsibility to be in the U.S. Congress, could come together to try to work on behalf of black people as best as we knew how."[34] Stokes's remarks capture well the notion that blacks in Congress represent more than just their district constituencies; in a very real sense, they also represent what Matthew Holden would call the "Black Nation."[35] This is indeed a tremendous burden, and it is one that is shouldered by (or that haunts) black leaders in various contexts. In short, whether individual blacks want to or not, those in visible leadership positions—such as black members of the Congress—are perceived by many Americans, not only blacks but whites as well, as representing the hopes and aspirations of all blacks. Apparently, in the main, blacks in the Congress have accepted this additional responsibility and have sought ways to carry it out. In this sense, the Congressional Black Caucus (CBC) symbolizes, in a very formal way, the commitment and concern that black members of Congress have toward their "national" constituency.

The formative years of the CBC, 1969-1971, saw the organization searching for its role and identity. At times, the organization served as an investigative body calling nationwide attention to everyday problems and perils faced by blacks. At other times, the CBC served as an information agency collecting and dispensing data on black concerns. But, according to one source,[36] the incident that gave the CBC national visibility and stature was its protracted battle with President Nixon. Essentially, the CBC was concerned and disturbed, as were many others, over Nixon's negative posture toward blacks. Hence, in February 1970, the organization requested a meeting with the president to discuss its concerns. But the President ignored the request. Apparently, this upset CBC members to the extent that they let it be known that they would boycott Nixon's 1971 State of the Union message, and they did. Obviously, the boycott created some concern and embarrassment to the president. In any event, some two months after this incident, on March 25, 1971, the president met with the CBC, and the group had done its homework. The organization "confronted" the president with 61 recommendations covering the range of problems facing blacks and other minorities, for example, health, welfare, poverty, civil rights. Not unexpectedly, the president's response was anything but encouraging. However, the "confrontation" meeting with the president was not without benefits. It served to bring the CBC to the fore as a major force in black politics. Perhaps, also, it served to crystallize the common dislike which blacks generally had for Nixon's policies. And this, in turn, undoubtedly helped to overcome or quiet stresses and divisions not only within the CBC but also between the CBC and other civil rights groups and leaders.

In 1971, the CBC sharpened its focus and direction and mushroomed as a force in national politics. This was symbolized by a number of things: a highly successful fund-raising dinner; the shaping of a permanent CBC staff; and more systematic attention to and study of black problems. Even so, however, the CBC had to define carefully its role and purpose to supplement, not duplicate, the work of other groups Eventually, the CBC decided that it would abandon some of its "national forum" functions—such as conferences and hearings—and would instead concentrate on matters consistent with the role and expertise of its members. Thus, the primary focus of the CBC would be on legislation and the legislative process.

This was indeed the new direction of the CBC and it was well reflected by the workshops, speeches, and other activities in connection with the group's third annual fund-raising dinner in 1973. As Caucus Chairman Stokes put it, the primary purpose of the CBC is to "utilize the legislative process to help bring about full equality of opportunity in American society." The CBC, continued Stokes, is now at the point where it hopes to put "the black perspective into all legislation."[37]

In February 1974, Representative Charles Rangel (D-New York) became the new chairman of CBC, replacing Stokes. Rangel cited the successful passage of "home rule" for the District of Columbia as evidence of the Caucus's acting with a new "sophistication." He reemphasized that the CBC must limit itself to legislative concerns. Said Rangel:

> I plan to present to the Caucus a legislative agenda that we can work on that will get us more realistic support rather than the spiritual support we have already. We have no permanent friends, no permanent enemies, just permanent interests of blacks and minority constituents.[38]

In looking to the future, Rangel indicated his intention to strengthen the CBC staff and to stimulate more participation from black elected officials in the national black convention movement.[39]

But perhaps the biggest challenge and opportunity that faced the Caucus involved its relations and access to the then-new president, Gerald Ford. As a U.S. representative from Middle America (Grand Rapids, Michigan), Ford's record was far from sympathetic to the needs and goals of blacks. But as president, Gerald Ford made the first move.[40] Within three days after assuming the presidency, Ford called Congressman Rangel directly, indicating his desire to meet with the CBC. Rangel admitted that different interpretations had and would be made of the president's initiative in calling the meeting. But, said Rangel,

> [w]hatever interpretation you choose, both sides undeniably reaped benefits. Clearly, the President's initiation of the meeting just three days after taking office means he saw it in his own self-interest. Our quick acceptance reflected the majority view that we could only gain by making this effort at establishing communication with the new national administration.

The meeting between the president and the CBC took place on August 21. Although disappointed that the president's very first speech to the Congress indicated little if any sympathy for black concerns, the Caucus nevertheless decided "to give him the benefit of the doubt and approach the meeting in good faith as an effort to communicate." Accordingly, the CBC agreed "to meet the President halfway" and to structure its presentation for the meeting around "double digit inflation," the "domestic enemy number one" that the president had identified in his speech to Congress. Such emphasis, said Rangel, "did no violence to our own priorities, for it is the poor and minority communities that have suffered most because of runaway inflation." In keeping with the inflation theme, the CBC "warned" the president that budget cuts in such areas as housing, health, and education would be counterproductive, saying that "those who can least afford to lose federal aid will be hurt the most."

The Caucus also asked the president to appoint blacks and other minorities who would be "sensitive" to the needs of poor and minority communities "at every level of his administration." As to this request, the president responded that he "fully intended" to make such appointments. Rangel called this the "most important commitment" to come out of the meeting. Indeed, said Rangel, "the best and most lasting way to achieve institutionalization of communication between the executive branch and the CBC is to have the type of executive agency appointees in this administration who will be sympathetic to the needs of the poor and minorities because of their ideological and philosophical commitment and, equally important, because of who they are." Overall, there appeared to be some optimism that the meeting would lead to improved relations between the CBC and "The Man" in the White House. But, as Rangel put it, "optimism cannot be sustained unless it is fed by concrete accomplishment, and although we stand ready to work with the President if he proves his good will, we stand equally ready to oppose him if he does not."

Subsequently, the president took some actions that undoubtedly caused the Caucus to be "less optimistic" about future relations with the president. For one thing, his "full and unconditional" pardon of former President Nixon did nothing to convince blacks and other minorities that all men are equal under the law. Moreover, in an October 1974 news conference the president served to provoke rather than quiet racial friction when he indicated sharp disagreement with "forced busing" (and a federal court order) at the very time that the Boston school situation was erupting in violence over the issue.[41] Consequently, given the situation, this attitude of the president toward "forced busing" greatly overshadowed his announced intention to enforce the law (the federal court decision). In any event, actions such as these were definitely not calculated to improve relations between the president and the CBC.

CARTER AND THE CBC

Jimmy Carter won the 1976 presidential election, and the CBC—from all apparent indications—now had a more friendly president in the White House. For one thing, Carter was a Democrat, as were all members of the CBC. Moreover, Carter received some of his strongest support during the election from particular members of the CBC, especially Representative Andrew Young (D-Georgia). And, perhaps most important of all, Carter won the presidency with overwhelming support from African Americans—more than 90 percent of blacks voted for Carter. Hence, along a number of dimensions, the CBC and African Americans had reason to be optimistic about the new president.

In general, however, relations between the CBC and Carter, just as with African Americans generally, were mixed and fluctuated greatly. To be certain, the president did appoint blacks to a number of positions throughout the federal government, including the appointment of two blacks to cabinet-level positions: Patricia Harris, Housing and Urban Development (HUD) and Andrew Young (U.N. Ambassador). In addition, the president consistently expressed sympathy and support for the hopes and aspirations of blacks and other minorities. On the other hand, however, many blacks—including some members of the CBC—did not think the president lived up to his campaign promises. As discussed in Chapter 2, many blacks saw little if any improvement in the everyday problems that affect blacks, for example, unemployment and poor housing. Consequently, though relations between the president and blacks remained friendly, they were also somewhat strained.

An example may serve to illustrate this rather friendly yet uncertain relationship. The CBC, pursuant to its new legislative focus, adopted the passage of the Humphrey-Hawkins bill as one of its major legislative objectives. The bill, co-sponsored by CBC member Augustus Hawkins (D-California) and the late Senator Hubert Humphrey (D-Minnesota), was aimed at reducing unemployment, an all-too-common status among blacks and other minorities. Simply put, the Humphrey-Hawkins bill sought to reduce unemployment by 4 percent by 1983. But there was a great deal of doubt about whether or not the bill should be passed. Apparently it took an incident, not unlike the CBC confrontation with President Nixon, to provide the impetus necessary to get the bill through Congress. In any event, the CBC met with President Carter to discuss the status of the measure. During the meeting, however, CBC member John Conyers, Jr., (D-Michigan) charged that the president was not doing enough to support passage of the bill. And when Vice-President Mondale objected to this assessment, Conyers walked out of the meeting. Obviously, it is difficult to ascribe motivation to any one particular incident, but apparently after this incident the president lobbied intensively in support of the bill.[42] Conservative opposition, however, loaded the measure with what many viewed as crippling amendments. Eventually, though, with the president's help the bill did pass but in a form which made its lofty goals difficult if not impossible to achieve. Nevertheless, both the president and many civil rights leaders hailed the new law as an important victory for blacks and for all the poor. And in many ways the passage of the bill was a victory, even if primarily along symbolic dimensions. One thing seems clear, however. The unity and feeling of the CBC in its meeting with the president did much to spur the bill's passage.

THE REAGAN YEARS

After winning the 1980 presidential election, Ronald Reagan met with the CBC during his first year in the White House. The relationship got off to a remarkably smooth start and continued that way through the first months of the Reagan presidency. The president even met personally with then-CBC chair Mickey Leland (D-Texas) in December 1982 to discuss famine relief in Africa. "He (Reagan) immediately upon our request diverted a ship that was going to India with food to Ethiopia," Leland said. "I was really happy—for the first time proud—that President Reagan was our President. He was far greater concerned than I had seen him on any issue dealing with human beings."[43] But Reagan's relationship with the CBC soon soured. The president rejected further meetings with the CBC, leading Leland to describe the relationship as "non-existent." Refusing to meet with the CBC "is past being just insensitive," Leland said. "It is an evil character who refuses to spend time with people who have a deep abiding concern about humanity when we are in severe jeopardy."[44]

It is the latter sentiments expressed by Leland that most characterized the president's relationship with the CBC during Reagan's two terms in office. Several issues polarized the White House and the CBC, including Reagan's handling of South Africa, his economic policies that reduced inflation at tremendous costs in terms of unemployment (especially among young blacks), and his opposition to civil rights legislation. Although the balance of power between the CBC and the White House obviously favors the president, the CBC won some significant victories over the Reagan administration. For example, the CBC led the fight in Congress to pass legislation calling for economic sanctions against South Africa. After Reagan vetoed the bill, Congress overrode the president and enacted the Anti-Apartheid Act of 1986, which was sponsored in the House by the CBC's Ronald Dellums (D-California).[45]

The CBC also built coalitions with like-minded groups in Congress—such as the Hispanic and Women's caucuses[46]—to oppose Reagan's widely perceived hostility to civil rights legislation. The technique paid off in passing the Civil Rights Restoration Act over Reagan's veto, with the CBC's Augustus Hawkins (D-California) playing a prominent role in the House override. The act was designed to overturn the effects of the 1984 Supreme Court *Grove City* v. *Bell* decision, which limited the reach of federal anti-discrimination laws in institutions that receive federal funds.[47]

However, beyond the battle over specific pieces of legislation, some CBC members considered the Reagan years as a big setback in general for blacks and other minorities. This sentiment was succinctly expressed during the 1984 presidential campaign by former U.S. Representative and CBC member Parren J. Mitchell (D-Maryland); "Even if Reagan gets kicked out, what you have in this country is a whole new mindset. There is an antiblack mood and an economic problem that we must address. The question for us is who will best cushion blacks."[48] Reagan did not get "kicked out" in 1984, and his vice-president, George Bush, won the 1988 presidential election after running what some observers considered a racially divisive campaign.[49]

CBC AND THE BUSH ADMINISTRATION

However, the Bush administration, in contrast to the Reagan administration, seemed more open to contacts with the Congressional Black Caucus. In May 1989, President Bush met with the CBC and agreed to a schedule of regular meetings and instructed administration officials to meet with CBC members.[50] In their meeting with Bush, the CBC members urged the president to tackle the problems underlying the drug crisis, such as the system for caring for the poor, and to shape military policy on the changing relations with the Soviet Union.

This willingness to consult with the CBC, however, did not mean an absence of conflict between members of the CBC and the Bush administration. An early conflict arose over the nomination of William Lucas to head the civil rights division of the Justice Department.51 Lucas, a former FBI agent, sheriff, and county executive, had little trial experience or knowledge of civil rights issues. Some members of the CBC, such as William H. Gray III (D-Pennsylvania), felt that his inexperience in civil rights issues disqualified him for the job. On the other hand, other members of the CBC, including John Conyers (D-Michigan) supported the nomination. In the end, the Lucas nomination was defeated. Similarly, in 1991 the CBC was the first black organization to openly oppose President Bush's nomination of Judge Clarence Thomas to the U.S. Supreme Court. To the CBC, the fact that Thomas was an African American was not as important as his policy positions, especially those taken in his role as director of the Equal Employment Opportunity Commission. Representative Gary Franks (R-Connecticut) was the only member of the CBC to vote against the Caucus position.

THE CBC AND THE CLINTON ADMINISTRATION

As a result of the 1992 elections, the Congressional Black Caucus seemed to be in its most promising political position since its formative years in 1969-1971. Most important of all, of course, is the election of a Democratic president who portends to stem the tide of confrontations and setbacks of the Reagan-Bush administrations. Indeed the election of President Clinton suggests an occupant of the White House who is clearly more sympathetic and supportive of policy interests of concern to blacks and minorities. Hence, this time the perennial loyal support blacks have given to Democratic presidential candidates over the years seems to have proven crucial in allowing Clinton and the Democrats to recapture the presidency after 12 years of Republican rule. And initially, given his policy initiatives (that is, health care, jobs), and his appointment of four African Americans to his cabinet, President Clinton seemed to be creating an environment that would portend to increase understanding and support from the Congressional Black Caucus.

Another important development, of course, which would portend to increase cooperative interactions with the White House, is the fact that as a result of the 1992 elections, the number of black members of the Congress has grown from 26 in 1991 to 40, a net increase of 13 new members in the House. It also reflects the election of Carol Moseley-Braun (D-Illinois) as the only black member of the Senate. And overall, this growth in members has also been accompanied by a growth in congressional seniority and influence. For example, the fact that Ron Dellums (D-California) is now chair of the House Armed Services Committee is not likely to escape the attention of President Clinton and other members of his administrative team, especially given the important role and relationship of the defense budget to the president's overall socio-economic initiatives (e. g., major increases in health care, education, and creation of more jobs.)

Despite these signs of friendship and cooperation, points of friction began to emerge between the CBC and President Clinton in the first few months of the new Democratic administration.[52] By May 1993, for example, the CBC openly expressed frustration and anger over certain revisions the president had made in his original budget proposals, especially those calling for additional cuts in both entitlement programs (e.g., Medicare) and domestic programs (e.g., creation of jobs to help alleviate massive unemployment particularly among black and minority youths.)

The CBC and other black leaders as well (e.g., Jesse Jackson) also expressed deep concern over the President's subsequent reversal of his campaign promise to admit Haitian refugees and do away with the more "inhumane" restrictive Haitian immigration policy of the Bush administration. As president, however, Clinton decided not only to essentially follow the more restrictive Bush immigration policy, but also acted to successfully defend that policy in the Supreme Court.[53]

But perhaps the most dramatic and visible friction between the CBC and President Clinton occurred when the president decided to withdraw his nomination of Lani Guinier as assistant attorney general for civil rights. Guinier, a black law professor at the University of Pennsylvania, was thought by many to have been superbly and uniquely qualified for the job. Black leaders, for example, were especially angered that the president, in withdrawing Professor Guinier's nomination, seemed to have succumbed to Republican and other critics who charged that Guinier had expressed views in her scholarly writings that were outside "mainstream" American political thinking, a charge that Democrats and others had levelled against Judge Robert Bork in his abortive attempt in 1987 to win Senate confirmation for a seat on the Supreme Court (see Chapter 6, *supra*). These critics, who subsequently were supported by President Clinton, particularly thought that Guinier's views with regard to more effective representation of minority interests in majority-rule legislative forums were beyond the pale of "centrist-mainstream" politics.

Whatever the case, the Guinier affair and other friction points came to a head in a three-hour meeting of the CBC on June 9, 1993, whose tone was described by one account as "decidedly angry." Indeed, comments made after the meeting by the CBC chair, Representative Kweisi Mfume (D-Maryland), in apparent reference to what was viewed as the president's retreat in his budget proposals, seemed to have captured well the overall strains created by these various friction points between the CBC and the White House. Mfume said that the CBC was not prepared "to accept additional cuts in entitlement programs . . . and is something that becomes a point of non-negotiation and imperils efforts to pass this legislation." Mfume said that all 37 black House Democrats, who had supported the president's earlier budget bill, were not ready to give the president "blind loyalty" and "be seen and not heard." "We want first-class partnership," said Mfume, who noted that support from the CBC for the final budget bill would surely be needed since the original bill passed the House the month before by only a narrow 219-213 vote.

Overall, however, it is much too early to suggest what effect these friction points will have on the continuing relations between the CBC and President Clinton, especially given the range of interests involved and the ever-changing dynamics of American politics and policy making. What can be said, however, is that these friction points clearly have done nothing to stabilize or strengthen the somewhat fragile relations and unity that prevailed generally between Clinton and African Americans during the 1992 campaign and election and at least in the first few months of the new administration.

THE CBC IN PERSPECTIVE[54]

Overall, the CBC now seems to have become an institutionalized part of the Washington and national scene. Its role and purpose are well recognized: to serve as "a more effective catalyst for the economical, educational and social concerns of Blacks and other underrepresented Americans" by working with other groups to develop and implement "legislative strategies and mandates for minorities."[55] Its annual fund-raising dinners have now blossomed into "Annual Legislative Activities Weekends," the proceeds from which support a full-time staff. And it is this permanent staff that provides "the legislative research, information coordination and technical support of Caucus activities."[56]

In many ways the CBC operates as an interest group. It certainly exhibits "*social solidarity*"—the need for people holding similar views "to enjoy the support, fellowship, and solidarity of one another." The Caucus also resembles the *expressive interest groups* which people join to symbolize and express more effectively their values and opinions with respect to certain causes. The CBC provides an excellent forum (including those provided during the Annual Legislative Weekends) for the expression of opinion. In short, the Caucus as an interest group acts in a sense as a "Washington Lobby" for blacks and the poor, and it has a staff and funds to support these ends.

Just as with other groups, there are factors that affect the cohesion of the CBC. Consider, for example, those factors that tend to plague group unity. For one thing, each member operates from an independent power base (his or her district) and has an independent staff; this promotes independence from the Caucus as a group. In such a situation, for example, the CBC staff becomes of less importance to individual Caucus members who have their own staffs. As a consequence, these independent sources of strength, which accrue from the nature of the office itself, can lead to independence in action that could impair a group unity. In addition, the once unanimous Democratic CBC has now been penetrated by its first Republican member—Representative Gary Franks of Connecticut. And as we have seen, Franks's vote against the CBC resolution to oppose the nomination of Judge Clarence Thomas to the Supreme Court suggests that black Republicans might well see the political world quite differently than black Democrats.

To be sure, there are strong factors that tend to promote group cohesion. Indeed, whether through a formal organization such as the CBC or not, the basic unity and cohesion of black members of Congress in legislative matters would seem to persist for some time. In this sense, the move of the CBC to concentrate (and restrict) its attention on legislative matters appears to be good strategy. To be sure, there is one overriding factor that promotes a large measure of unity among black legislators: The similarities in the needs of their constituents invariably lead to similarities in policy positions. This is reflected well in the socioeconomic characteristics that are common to most of the congressional districts from which Caucus members come.[57] Undoubtedly, these common characteristics will serve to promote a large measure of common policy positions among black congressional members.

In addition, we suggest that the *force of blackness* itself stimulates cohesion and identification among blacks in Congress. It remains as true today as it ever was that as long as blacks are disadvantaged as a group they must work as a group to remove those disadvantages. This might help to explain why the Congressional Black Caucus in 1975 refused to approve the application of a white member of Congress [Representative Fortney H. Stark, Jr. (D-California)] for membership in the Caucus. Indeed, in rejecting Stark's application, then-Caucus chair Charles Rangel (D-New York) stated that "the Caucus symbolizes black political development in this country. We feel that maintaining this symbolism," continued Rangel, "is critical at this juncture in our development."[58] Rangel and the CBC reasoned that just as separate caucuses of Democrats and Republicans "have unique interests to protect and project and would not include non-party members in their respective groups, we too have the same needs and concerns." Rangel then drove the point home. "The Black Caucus," he said, "is composed of seventeen House Members who share the common social, cultural and political experience of being black in America."[59] This latter point, it seems to us, vividly illuminates that the force of blackness remains a powerful (though not always articulated) influence enhancing black unity.

We may view the Congressional Black Caucus from yet another perspective. The change from "protests to politics" reflects a concern to increase black influence (power) in political institutions such as the Congress. The formation and continuing activities of the CBC symbolize this concern. A more tangible measure of increasing black political influence, however, relates to the number of blacks gaining seats in the Congress. In part, such an increase will depend upon whether or not those congressional districts that have significant black populations[60] will stimulate and put forth strong candidates and strong campaigns.

But black influence in Congress depends upon more than how many blacks happen to be members at any given time. As the dynamics of power in Congress now operate, it is not enough to gain membership in that body; members must be able to remain there for a long time. They need to gain seniority. By doing so, a member can normally become a committee chairman, and such positions provide crucial influence in the congressional power system. Obviously, members wish to gain seniority on the right committee, that is, a committee that is important to the interests of the member's constituents. Of course, if a member does not gain such an assignment initially, there is always the possibility of getting a preferable assignment later. But, as we have also seen, in changing from one committee to another, the member loses whatever seniority he or she had accumulated on the first committee.

The important question that arises here is how to get the right committee assignment in the first place, or how to gain such an assignment later. To a great extent, this depends upon the standing of the particular legislator with congressional leaders and with his or her colleagues. Moreover, such standing enhances or retards a member's ability to build coalitions and to gain sufficient support to enact legislation that is important to the legislator and to his/her constituents. To achieve standing, however, members must conform to congressional norms. In general, this means giving proper deference to established procedures and rules and recognizing the importance of bargaining, accommodation, and compromise in the conduct of business. All this, of course, helps members to maintain good personal relations with colleagues and vice versa. In short, "don't push too far too fast," and above all, "don't buck congressional leaders." The leaders, after all, achieved and maintain such positions because they followed the norms. And there are strong built-in temptations and pressures for others to do likewise.

Let us attempt to view this discussion of seniority and standing in terms of black influence in Congress and black politics generally. Consider the situation of black members of Congress. As mentioned earlier, for the most part these representatives come from *"safe" districts*—"safe" insofar as a black will more likely than not be elected to represent the district. As the district becomes more "safe" in this sense, however, we might find an increasing competition among blacks as to which black can best represent the district. In 1992, for example, Representative Gus Savage of Illinois was defeated in the Democratic primary by another black (and the eventual winner), Mel Reynolds. In general, however, black incumbents seem to follow the incumbency pattern of being highly successful in reelection bids. This continued electoral success, however, could run into trouble. For example, while black representatives may be attempting to meet the needs of their constituents and may indeed have introduced measures and taken other actions toward this end, the fact is that these needs more often than not have not been met and are not being met. Thus, the problems of the district remain. And the incumbent faces the not uncommon campaign charge of having done nothing about the situation. An important difference, of course, is that problems in heavily populated black districts, such as unemployment and poor housing, are highly visible and affect the everyday life of constituents. Under such circumstances, the black incumbent becomes increasingly susceptible to strong campaign challenges. This could pose a serious problem for black incumbents. As one of a few blacks in a collegial institution (House of Representatives) whose majority may not be especially sympathetic to his or her goals, it will be the rare occasion when a black incumbent can show a record of tangible accomplishments in meeting the immediate problems of his or her district.

To appreciate the context in which black officials operate in a collegial institution requires a measure of sophistication (and a prolonged acceptance of the status quo) on the part of black voters which is perhaps unparalleled in American political history. No other group in America has been required to hold to such understanding and with such patient endurance for such a long period of time! Indeed, the problems that blacks face are by definition "controversial" in the context of American politics. Nonetheless, these problems are perceived by many blacks in terms of "non-negotiable demands" that must be met now, not later. But the bargaining, accommodation, and compromise needed to gain widespread support might lead the black congresspersons to temper these demands to get some type of legislation and to show some record of accomplishment. But in doing so, the black legislator will more likely than not have to temper the rhetoric of his or her arguments that could provoke friction between the legislator and his or her white colleagues.

This could place severe strains on a black legislator. While perhaps understanding the necessity of compromise on substantive matters in terms of legislative strategy, the black legislator takes certain risks in compromising the rhetoric of his or her argument. Indeed, such rhetoric might prove necessary to satisfy the long-term demands and desires of his or her constituents while simultaneously making present-day substantive compromises more palatable to them. And more important, it might be necessary for political survival—that is, reelection, the one indispensable criterion for gaining influence in Congress. In any event, seniority and standing continue to pose serious and persistent problems not only for black congressmen but also for black politics generally. Of course it is true, as we discussed earlier in this chapter, that seniority can work to the advantage of blacks and civil rights interests. But as we have also seen, seniority is no longer an automatic guarantee to becoming committee chair. Under these circumstances, standing and good personal relations with colleagues take on added significance. It remains to be seen what the actual costs and benefits of such relations will be to the future of black politicians and black politics generally.

BLACK OFFICIALS WITH MOSTLY WHITE CONSTITUENCIES

Although blacks constitute 11 percent of the nation's voting-age population, less than two percent of all elected officials in the nation are black.[61] For blacks to reach proportionality in elected office and, specifically, for blacks to increase their membership in Congress, it seems clear that more whites will have to start voting for black candidates. But that is not likely, given the results of a recent public opinion poll of white voters' attitudes toward black candidates.[62] Analysis of the results indicates that whites generally consider blacks as less capable of achieving goals, less likely to possess important personal attributes, and less qualified for higher political offices. In addition, a majority of whites who were polled agreed that most whites vote on the basis of race rather than qualifications.[63] Nonetheless, some blacks have been elected to public office in constituencies that are mostly white. For example, U.S. Representative Alan Wheat (D-Missouri) comes from a constituency that is about 80 percent white,[64] and so do some black mayors in big or medium sized cities, for example, Los Angeles and Seattle. But blacks seem to face special difficulty in gaining statewide election office. Let us consider these matters in more detail.

Mayor Tom Bradley's gubernatorial campaigns in 1982 and 1986 are especially instructive. Bradley is a well-qualified, noncontroversial politician who had also been able to allay the fears and suspicions that white voters often have about black candidates.[65] However, after leading all of the pre-election polls against his Republican opponent in 1982, Bradley lost the California gubernatorial election to George Deukmejian. Bradley also lost heavily in a 1986 rematch. What went wrong? Analysis of electoral data indicates that racism played a significant role in Bradley's defeat—even taking into account other political factors, such as a high turnout of conservative voters in 1982 to defeat a controversial gun control measure and the Democratic candidacy for the U.S. Senate of the unpopular incumbent Governor Jerry Brown.[66] The influence of racism in the Bradley defeat is somewhat surprising, because Bradley did not associate himself primarily with black issues and did not even court the black vote in California during his gubernatorial campaigns.[67] Thus, the prospects seem bleak for black candidates in white constituencies, notwithstanding, for example, Douglas Wilder's victory in 1989 as the nation's first elected black governor.

Indeed, Wilder was elected governor of Virginia with 50.15 percent of the vote. In an election marred by negative campaigning, Wilder won approximately 40 percent of the white vote and 95 percent of the black vote. Wilder's opponent, J. Marshall Coleman, attempted to portray Wilder as a liberal. Coleman framed Wilder as soft on crime and untrustworthy. Wilder, who responded with attacks on Coleman, campaigned as a moderate on many issues, including support for the death penalty and right-to-work laws.[68]

Wilder had the most success in attracting white support in Northern Virginia and the Tidewater area, but failed to gain much support in the rest of the state.[69] The white support for Wilder was particularly important since the black population is 20 percent of Virginia's electorate. Wilder appealed to the white voters in suburban Northern Virginia by claiming that his opponent, who received $3 million in contributions from developers, was the pawn of real estate developers. In addition, Wilder gained support among the suburban voters in Northern Virginia for his pro-abortion position while his opponent took what was generally viewed as an anti-abortion stance. In the remainder of the state, Wilder did not fare as well as his white Democratic running mate for lieutenant governor, Donald S. Beyer, Jr., who won support in many parts of "Old Virginia," including Richmond and Southside. This suggests that the racial factor may have been more salient in these areas.

Additionally, and as mentioned earlier, blacks such as Alan Wheat (D-Missouri) have also shown it is possible to be elected and reelected to high public office in mostly white constituencies—even when the candidate is sensitive to and supportive of policies of primary importance to black constituents. In fact, some studies indicate that it is a political liability for black candidates to distance themselves from issues important to blacks and other minorities.[70]

Wheat was first elected to Congress from Missouri's Fifth Congressional District as a liberal Democrat in 1982. He is well known for the ability to strike a balance between his core constituency—blacks and white liberals in Kansas City—and other interests, such as the city's business community. He also placed whites along with blacks in key staff posts in his campaign and in Congress in a deliberate effort to not be regarded as solely a black congressman.[71] The strategy has worked well for Wheat, who has won every reelection bid since 1984.

However, the election of black candidates (such as Wheat) who must appeal to white constituents for support raises questions about the future of black politics. For example, how will the need to appeal to white constituents affect the issue positions and campaigns of black candidates? How might the new coalition politics affect a black official's support from black voters? With respect to the CBC, for example, will the need to articulate issues beyond the special concern of black members of Congress diminish the voice of the CBC as the advocate of black concerns in the legislative process?

Along with Wheat, the four newly elected black members to Congress in 1986 were described as a new generation of black legislators.[72] Four of the five took the seats of white members, and all appealed to white support in their campaigns [Mike Espy (D-Mississippi), Floyd Flake (D-New York), John Lewis (D-Georgia), and Kweisi Mfume (D-Maryland)].[73] It is interesting to note, however, that in 1992 all of the newly elected House members of the caucus came from congressional districts with large black populations (30 percent or more). Some of these districts were expressly created to enhance the possibilities of increased minority representation. As the number of congressional districts with sizable (20 percent or more) black populations continues to fluctuate, as black members appeal more and more for white support, and as more conservative blacks are elected, the nature and future of black politics in the legislative process are likely to become increasingly unclear.

Some Concluding Remarks

Let us make several concluding observations with respect to the structure and operations of the Congress as a law-making body and as a representative institution, especially as these relate to the problems and opportunities of blacks and other minorities.

1. The structure of elections and representation in the House of Representatives makes it more likely that blacks will have more representation in the House than in the Senate. The concentration of blacks in particular congressional districts makes it more possible for potential black candidates to gain their party's nomination and mount a viable election campaign. Financing a campaign in a single congressional district, for example, is much more within the reach of potential black candidates at this stage of black economic and financial development. On the other hand, governors and U.S. senators are elected on a statewide basis, and chances of blacks getting the necessary

resources to launch effective campaigns for their party's nomination for the subsequent general election are much more remote.

2. The structure and operation of the law-making process are such that those who propose new legislation have numerous procedural and political obstacles to overcome before they can achieve their ends. By the same token, those who oppose such new legislation are presented with many opportunities to impede and block its passage. Consider the necessity of gaining subcommittee and committee approval, the agreement of both houses, and the approval of the president (except that a two-thirds vote in both houses could override his veto). Consider, moreover, other factors such as the operation of seniority and the *filibuster*. It is, of course, true, as one writer points out, that certain perceived obstacles such as the filibuster and the seniority system can also work for liberal ends.[74] But mostly the filibuster has been used to block and impede passage of civil rights legislation. We should note, however, that recent changes in Senate rules now ostensibly make it easier to end filibusters and limit debate.

It is also true that the seniority system has made somewhat of a comeback in Congress and that black members are among the beneficiaries. Such changes may also mean that the CBC's agenda will be increasingly reflected in public policy. That will be determined by a number of other factors, including, as party loyalties stand at present, the stance of President Clinton and the Democratic majority in Congress and the degree to which CBC members must compromise their positions in order to pass legislation through the long and difficult legislative process.

3. Congress, as a body, is spending more time on legislative oversight functions than in the past. It is true, of course, that such activity might indeed reveal the need for new or corrective legislation. But an overemphasis on oversight activities might well blunt the time and efforts needed to develop creative and innovative legislative initiatives necessary to deal effectively with the myriad problems faced by blacks and other minorities. Moreover, rule changes which have limited the importance of seniority and decreased the power of committee chairpersons, when coupled with the breakdown of party discipline, would seem to make it increasingly difficult to enact major social welfare legislation of the type enacted in the mid-1960s. Historically, for example, if one could convince congressional and party leaders and committee chairmen of the need for a particular legislative measure, it was very likely that such legislation would be passed by the Congress.

But the situation is somewhat different today. Now there seems to be more fragmentation in the leadership in the Congress as well as growing independence among individual members of the Congress. This means that a larger group of leaders (e.g., subcommittee chairmen) as well as individual members have to be won over. Thus, getting legislation through Congress and monitoring its implementation are becoming increasingly difficult and complex tasks, and they require the continuous mobilization and utilization of the kind of resources (money, lobbying, votes) which are generally in short supply among blacks. What one can conclude from this is that due to both personnel and institutional changes, Congress is less likely to come to grips and deal effectively with the kind of major social-welfare problems (e.g., unemployment) that impose a disproportionate hardship on blacks and other minorities.

4. There are other effects that some of the changes mentioned in the previous observation can have on blacks. For example, we have focused on the general legislative role of Congress, but there are other particular types of work which occupy the time of members of Congress. These are *pork barrel* and *casework*.[75] Pork barrel is a term that applies to the efforts of senators and representatives to bring federal projects (dams, federal office buildings, urban redevelopment, etc.) to their states and districts. Casework refers to the help rendered by members of Congress to answer requests made to them by individuals or groups within their constituencies. Typically, these requests are for information or for enlisting the aid of a senator or representative in dealing with an executive agency. Both pork barrel and casework impart particular benefits. This means that the benefits typically accrue to certain individuals or groups within a given constituency.

Thus, recent changes in the House of Representatives which have expanded the powers of subcommittees and subcommittee chairpersons can have positive impacts for constituencies represented by blacks in Congress. For example, while black representatives have been only minimally successful in becoming committee chairs, they are beginning to meet with more success in chairing subcommittees. These subcommittee chairs can provide the opportunity for pork barrel and casework activities to deal with problems of at least some of the "people back home." And the fact that many of these activities (e.g., federal office building, urban redevelopment) occur in large urban areas gives black representatives—who primarily come from central city districts—added opportunities and influence to secure such benefits for their constituents. However, these mainly particularistic benefits are far from the sort of comprehensive congressional actions needed to alleviate the broad and multifaceted problems faced by blacks and other minorities.

5. In general, there seems to be a dire need for more black and minority representation in the Congress. As mentioned earlier, the number of blacks in Congress is almost invariably related to the size of the black population in a given district. In short, as the black population nears a majority, chances increase for a black representative to be elected. In 1988, for example, studies indicated that of 71 congressional districts having a sizable black population—20 percent or more,[76] only 23 of those districts were represented by blacks. Georgia's Fifth Congressional District provides an interesting study of the switch between black and white representation in a district with a sizable black population (60 percent). The district was once represented by a black, Andrew Young (former U.N. Ambassador under President Jimmy Carter and current mayor of Atlanta). Young was succeeded by Wyche Fowler, Jr., who won the

Democratic runoff primary over a black candidate, John Lewis, who had long been involved in black voter registration in the South. However, after Fowler stepped down in a successful Senate bid in 1986, Lewis won the Democratic primary, beating widely known civil rights leader Julian Bond. Undoubtedly, the story of this unusual switch[77] from black to white to black representation can tell us much about the dynamics of black politics and black-white relations in such congressional districts.

More than this, however, we need to know more about the behavior and responsiveness of elected white officials from districts where there are very large and discrete black and minority populations. Conversely, we need to know how black members of Congress deal with the matter of representing white populations in their districts. In general, this raises anew the perennial question of whether or not a particular group can have effective representation in government without actually having a member of (from) that group in government itself. Given the historical and present context of racial politics and race relations in this country, this could prove a most difficult problem for any given representative, black or white. But we suggest that it will be those representatives who are able to overcome such difficulties who will do much to improve both race relations and the overall quality of life in this country.

Topics for Discussion

1. "Due to both personnel and institutional changes, Congress is less likely to come to grips and deal effectively with the kind of major social-welfare problems (e.g., unemployment) that impose a disproportionate hardship on blacks and other minorities." What are these "personnel and institutional changes"? Do you agree with the view presented here?

2. Explain what is meant by the statement that "the structure of elections and representation in the House of Representatives makes it more likely that blacks would have more representatives in the House than in the Senate."

3. What are the advantages and disadvantages of the seniority rule for blacks and for the legislative process in general? Is the seniority system defensible? What alternatives are there to it? Discuss.

4. If a white person in Congress applies for membership in the Congressional Black Caucus (as has happened), should that person be admitted? Why or why not?

Suggested Readings

Arnold, R. Douglas. *Congress and the Bureaucracy: A Theory of Influence*. New Haven, CT: Yale University Press, 1979.
A study of how congressmen influence bureaucratic decisions concerning the geographic allocation of resources.

Berman, Daniel M. *A Bill Becomes a Law: Congress Enacts Civil Rights Legislation*, 2d ed. New York: Macmillan Company, 1966.
Discusses the role and impact of congressional procedures that led to passage of the Civil Rights Acts of 1960 and 1964.

Ceaser, James W. *Upside Down and Inside Out: The 1992 Elections and American Politics.* Lanham, MD: Rowman & Littlefield, 1993.

Cox, Gary W. and Mathew D. McCubbins. *Legislative Leviathan: Party Government in the House*. Berkeley: University of California Press, 1993.

Dymally, Mervin, ed. *The Black Politician: His Struggle for Power*. Belmont, CA and North Scituate, MA: Duxbury Press, 1971.
Readings on black politics and political and legislative strategies.

Fenno, Richard. *The Power of the Purse*. Boston: Little, Brown, 1966.
A detailed analysis of the operation of the House Appropriations Committee.

Fenno, Richard. *Home Style: House Members in Their Districts*. Boston: Little, Brown, 1978.
How members of Congress view their constituencies and the impact of such perceptions on their behavior.

Fiorina, Morris P. *Congress: Keystone of the Washington Establishment*, 2nd ed., New Haven, CT: Yale University Press, 1989.
A concise, readable analysis of how Congress works and what congressmen seek to accomplish.

Hinckley, Barbara. *The Seniority System in Congress*. Bloomington: Indiana University Press, 1971.
A study of the operation of congressional committees and the impact of the seniority rule.

Jacobson, Gary C. *The Politics of Congressional Elections*. 3rd ed. New York: Harper Collins, 1991.

Kiewiet, D. Roderick. *The Logic of Delegation: Congressional Parties and the Appropriations Process*. Chicago: University of Chicago Press, 1992.

Lindblom, Charles E. and Edward J. Woodhouse. *The Policy-Making Process*. 3rd ed. Englewood Cliffs, NJ: Prentice Hall, 1993.

Manley, John F. *The Politics of Finance*. Boston: Little, Brown, 1970.
A study of the House Committee on Ways and Means.

Mayhew, David. *Congress—The Electoral Connection*. New Haven, CT: Yale University Press, 1974.
Views congressional behavior and activity in the context of members of Congress as "single-minded seekers" of reelection.

McCubbins, Mathew D. and Terry Sullivan ed. *Congress: Structure and Policy*. New York: Cambridge University Press, 1987.

Orfield, Gary. *Congressional Power: Congress and Social Change*. New York: Harcourt Brace Jovanovich, 1975.
A study of the changing role of Congress in the development of public policy and social change.

Polsby, Nelson. *Congress and the Presidency*, 3rd ed. Englewood Cliffs, NJ: Prentice Hall, 1976.
An examination of the interaction between these two governmental branches.

Shepsle, Kenneth A. *The Giant Jigsaw Puzzle: Democratic Committee Assignment in the Modern House*. Chicago: University of Chicago Press, 1978.
Focuses on the dynamics of how one gains particular committee assignments in the House and its implications for the inner workings of Congress.

Notes

* 1969 by Nick Kotz. Published by Prentice Hall.

† 1975. Reprinted with permission of the publisher, Harcourt Brace Jovanovich, Inc.

1. *Reynolds* v. *Sims*, 377 U.S. 533 (1964).
2. *Ibid.*
3. See *Mahan* v. *Howell*, 410 U.S. 315 (1973); *Brown* v. *Thompson*, 462 U.S. 835 (1983); *Karcher* v. *Daggett*, 462 U.S. 725 (1983); and *Davis* v. *Bandemer*, 106 S. Ct. 2792 (1986).
4. For an informative overview of these and related factors see Ronald Smothers, "Black Caucus Gains a New Experience," *The New York Times* (November 10, 1992), p. A10, cols. 1-3.
5. James A. Barnes, "Minority Mapmaking," *National Journal* (April 7, 1990), p. 837.
6. *Wesberry* v. *Sanders*, 376 U.S. 1 (1964).
7. The other semi-exclusive committees are Armed Services; Banking, Finance and Urban Affairs; Foreign Affairs; Interstate and Foreign Commerce; and Public Works and Transportation.
8. The other nonexclusive committees are House Administration; Interior and Insular Affairs; Merchant Marine and Fisheries; Science and Technology; and Veterans Affairs. In addition, there are three standing committees whose status has not yet been defined; among these is the increasingly important House Budget Committee. The other two committees are Small Business and Standards of Official Conduct.
9. "Origins and Development of Congress," *Congressional Quarterly* (Washington, DC: Congressional Quarterly, Inc., 1976), p. 160.
10. Richard F. Fenno, Jr., Congressmen in Committees (Boston: Little, Brown, 1973), p. 1.
11. *Ibid.*, pp. 2-12.
12. The following account is taken from Richard Cohen,"How to Win—or Lose—Committee Seats," *National Journal* (February 3, 1979), pp. 183-188.
13. *Ibid.*
14. *Congressional Quarterly*, Origins and Development of Congress, pp. 160-161.
15. Christopher Buchanan, "House: Modest Gains for the Minority," *Congressional Quarterly Weekly Report* 36 (November 11, 1978), p. 3251.
16. *Time*, (November 19, 1990).
17. Julie Rovner, "Record Number of Women, Blacks in Congress," *Congressional Quarterly Weekly Report* 46 (November 12, 1988), pp. 3293-3295.
18. Diggs was sentenced to three years in prison, but the sentence was postponed pending appeal. His conviction was upheld in November 1979 by a three-judge panel of the U.S. Circuit Court of Appeals for the District of Columbia, and again in June 1980 by the Supreme Court. Despite being censured by the House in July 1979, Diggs remained in office until May 1980, when he announced his resignation. See the *1980 Congressional Quarterly Almanac* 36 (Washington, DC: Congressional Quarterly, Inc., 1981), p. 525.
19. Nelson Polsby, *Congress and the Presidency*, 3rd ed. (Englewood Cliffs, NJ: Prentice Hall, 1976) Table 3, p. 79.
20. Hanes Walton, Jr., *Black Politics: A Theoretical and Structural Analysis* (Philadelphia, Lippincott, 1972), p. 171.

21. Cf. James Q. Wilson, "The Negro in Politics," in *Daedalus* 94 (Fall 1965), p. 961. For more extended analysis of Powell, see Wilson's "Two Negro Politicians: An Interpretation," *Midwest Journal of Political Science* 4 (November 1960), pp. 360-69.
22. Actually, the House denied Powell his seat in 1967, but the Supreme Court later ruled that he had been unlawfully excluded. *Powell* v. *McCormack*, 395 U.S. 486 (1969).
23. See Robert Salisbury and Kenneth Shepsle. "Congressional Staff Turnover and the Ties-That-Bind," *American Political Science Review* 75 (1981), pp. 381-96.
24. But a major research project on "The Role and Impact of Congressional Staffs," has been undertaken by two political scientists, Robert Salisbury and Kenneth Shepsle, both of Washington University in St. Louis.
25. (June 2, 1979), p. 913.
26. See Daniel Rapoport, "The Imperial Congress—Living Above the Law," *National Journal* (June 2, 1979), pp. 911, 913.
27. *Ibid.*, p. 912.
28. Miles Benson, "Government Lax in Hiring Minorites," *San Francisco Examiner*, Dec. 1, 1991, p. B-10.
29. *Ibid.*
30. *Ibid.*
31. For a review of these methods, see Walter J. Oleszek, *Congressional Procedures and the Policy Process* (Washington, DC: Congressional Quarterly, Inc., 1978), pp. 202-208.
32. The number of congressional caucuses has mushroomed in recent years. These include the Blue Collar Caucus, Congresswomen's Caucus, the Irish Caucus, the Steel Caucus, and the Suburban Caucus. For an interesting account of this development, see Sarah E. Warren, "The New Look of the Congressional Caucuses," *National Journal* (April 29, 1978), pp. 677-679.
33. Alex Poinsett, "The Black Caucus: Five Years Later," *Ebony* (June 1973), pp. 64-73.
34. Ibid.
35. Matthew Holden, *Politics of the Black Nation* (New York: Chandler, 1973).
36. See Poinsett, "The Black Caucus."
37. See *The New York Times*, September 27, 1973, p. 13; September 30, 1973, p. 28; and October 1, 1973, pp. 1, 23.
38. Ibid.
39. Ibid.
40. The discussion is based on Representative Rangel's account of the meeting in "The President and the Black Caucus," *Focus* 2 (September 1974), pp. 4-5.
41. For an account of the Ford statement on the Boston situation and "forced busing" see *The New York Times*, October 13, 1974, Sec. 4, p. 2.
42. See *National Journal* (October 21, 1978), p. 1688.
43. Jacqueline Trescott, "Leland and the War on Hunger," *Washington Post*, September 7, 1983, p. B1.
44. *Ibid.*
45. "Congressional Black Caucus Rejoices in Growing Strength," *The New York Times*, October 6, 1986.
46. Nadine Cohodas, "Black House Members Striving for Influence," *Congressional Quarterly Weekly Report* 43 (April 13, 1985), pp. 675-681.

47. "A Salute to the CBC," *Focus* 16, no. 9 (September 2, 1988) Joint Center for Policy Studies.
48. "Pessimism Marks Gathering of Black Lawmakers," *The New York Times*, October 1, 1984.
49. "Bush's Chance With Blacks," *Focus* 16, nos. 11 and 12 (November-December 1988).
50. *Washington Post*, September 18, 1989.
51. *Washington Post*, May 14, 1989.
52. Quotes and overall context for discussion in this section are found in Adam Clymer, "Black Caucus Threatens Revolt on Clinton Budget," *The New York Times*, June 10, 1993, p. A10, cols. 5-6.
53. *Sale* v. *Haitian Centers Council*, No. 92-344 (1993).
54. For an interesting and perceptive account of the role, organization, and prospects of the CBC, see Marguerite Ross Barnett, "The Congressional Black Caucus and the Institutionalization of Black Politics," *Journal of Afro-American Issues* 5 (Summer 1977), pp. 202-27.
55. Included in Caucus mailing materials announcing the 1979 CBC Annual Legislative Weekend.
56. *Ibid.*
57. For a systematic and easily accessible profile on congressional districts, see Michael Barone et al., *The Almanac of American Politics* (New York: Dutton, 1992). This volume also includes similar data on U.S. senators.
58. Quotes on the refusal of the Caucus to admit Representative Stark are taken from Congressional Black Caucus press release dated June 19, 1975. Also see "Congress' Black Caucus Rejects White as Member," *Washington Star*, June 19, 1975, p. A13.
59. *Ibid.*
60. For a detailed look at these districts—those having 30 percent or more black population—see Joint Center for Political Studies, *Guide to Black Politics '72*, (The Republican National Convention, Washington, DC, August 1, 1972), pp. 48-53.
61. Linda Williams, "White-Black Perceptions of the Electability of Black Political Candidates," *National Political Science Review* 2 (1990), pp. 45-64.
62. *Ibid.*
63. *Ibid.*
64. "Wheat Faces Challenge from Palermo in 5th District Race," *St. Louis Post-Dispatch*, July 15, 1984.
65. Thomas F. Pettigrew and Denise A. Alston, *Tom Bradley's Campaigns for Governor: The Dilemma of Race and Political Strategies* (Washington, DC: Joint Center for Political Studies, 1988).
66. *Ibid.*
67. *Ibid.*
68. Rhodes Cook, "Wilder Win Marks Differences of Old Dominion and New," *Congressional Quarterly Weekly Report* 47 (November 11, 1989), p. 3101.
69. *Ibid.*, p. 3102.
70. *Ibid.*
71. *St. Louis Post-Dispatch*, July 15, 1984.
72. Richard E. Cohen, "A New Breed for Black Caucus," *National Journal* (September 26, 1987), pp. 2432-2433.

73. Representative Espy was appointed Secretary of Agriculture by President Clinton, and the special election for Espy's House seat was subsequently won by another African American and Democrat, Representative Bennie Thompson (D-Mississippi).
74. Gary Orfield, *Congressional Power: Congress and Social Change* (New York: Harcourt Brace Jovanovich, Inc., 1975), esp. pp. 38-44.
75. Morris P. Fiorina, *Congress: Keystone of the Washington Establishment* (New Haven, CT: Yale University Press, 1977), pp. 41-49.
76. *Congressional District Fact Book*, 3rd ed., Joint Center for Political Studies, 1988, pp. 23-24.
77. Except for the rather special circumstances which undoubtedly contributed to the defeat of former Republican Senator Edward Brooke (Mass.), this is the first switch from a black to a white representative since the turn of the century.

CHAPTER 10

THE PRESIDENCY AND THE POLICY PROCESS: THE "POVERTY" OF BLACK POLITICS

The essence of a President's persuasive task with Congressmen and everybody else, is to induce them to believe that what their own appraisal of their own responsibilities requires them to do is in their interest, not his. Because men may differ in their views on public policy, because differences in outlook stem from differences in duty—duty to one's office, one's constituents, oneself—that task is bound to be more like collective bargaining than like a reasoned argument among philosopher kings . . . This is the reason why: persuasion deals in the coin of self-interest with men who have some freedom to reject what they find counterfeit.

Richard E. Neustadt, *Presidential Power*[*]

The weakness of existing civil rights groups . . . was that they came to Washington once a year and talked to the Secretary of Labor or of HEW; the groups pushed for a big law once every three or four years, and forgot about the legislation once it was passed. No one remained to watch when agencies formulated guide-lines or were slow to enforce the laws. Someone was needed in Washington "to run a monitoring operation at the federal level . . ."

Robert Borosage, et al., "The New Public Interest Lawyers"[†]

THE PRESIDENCY AND THE POVERTY OF BLACK POLITICS

The presidency of the United States is perhaps the most powerful political office in the world. Without question, it is the most powerful and most sought after political office in America. It should come as no surprise that blacks have frequently looked to the incumbent in this office for support of their interests. Indeed, since the election of Franklin D. Roosevelt during the Depression African Americans have been a large part of the Democratic party's presidential coalition, that is, the diverse collection of ethnic groups and classes which come together every four years in an effort to elect their candidate to office.

Blacks believed, like others, that their support would produce gains for their causes as it appeared to produce gains for those of others. To some extent this did happen. But, for blacks it did not seem that what was received was commensurate with the effort. Desired corrections in the system of segregation and discrimination did not come quickly. In part, black political strategies failed to adequately consider the nature of the American political system. They did not take into account the fact that the system of politics is also a product of the larger society. It is important for blacks and others who put their hopes on strong presidential action to correct perceived social and political ills to remember that the president is one of a number of political officials who are involved in making and executing presidential decisions. To some, this may seem to be a rather small point; but many Americans fail to appreciate the difficulties involved in presidential decision making. It is for this reason that this case study was introduced by the excerpt from Neustadt's work.

There are many presidential roles. The president is indeed the chief executive and must take care that the laws be faithfully executed. This, in a sense, casts the president in the role of chief administrator. But the president is also chief legislator. He not only supervises the administration of the laws, but he is also expected to suggest laws that are needed. In addition, as the office has developed in terms of both the formal requirements of Article II of the Constitution and the practices and uses of power by particular occupants, the president performs many other roles. He is commander in chief of the armed forces, chief policy maker, chief of party, and chief of state. When combined, these roles make the president, as many others have suggested, both king and prime minister.[1] Because these roles tend to overlap and reinforce one another, of course, they add to the powerful position of the president in the political system.

Becoming President

As powerful as the president is, he is not all-powerful. Both the process by which he is selected and the way in which he is able to carry out his various roles limit his power. Take the process of selection. "To win the presidency," as one writer put it, "the aspirant must travel a long, hard, treacherous road abounding in bumps and quicksand and divisible into three distinct segments: the pre-convention buildup, the national nominating convention, and the post-convention electoral campaign."[2]

But before one can start this long journey with any viable chance of success, one must possess more than the formal requirements for the presidential office. It is not enough to be a native-born citizen, at least 35 years of age, and to have lived in the country for at least 14 years. Indeed, one must also meet (or have a reasonable chance of meeting) the informal requirements. One must have secured or be able to secure great financial backing. One must be well known, perhaps by having held high office or having rendered distinguished service to the country in some other way. Nor can one be too controversial; a candidate needs the support of a broad, often diverse, spectrum of people and interests. What is "controversial" could include those things over which a person has control, for example, his stand on major issues. Or it could involve matters over which he has little or no control—religion, race, color, sex. A potential candidate can and may alter his stand on issues as the campaign develops. But in terms of ethnic consideration, a candidate has to convince many others that such factors should not stand as barriers to his efforts to become president. For example, it was not until 1960 that John F. Kennedy, who had everything going for him (money, organization, charm) was able to overcome the traditional anti-Catholic barrier, and even then just barely. Consequently, one shudders to guess, despite an increasing number of blacks and women in public office, how long race, sex, and other factors will continue to make particular candidates too controversial.

Generally, the "pre-convention" phase provides a testing ground in which a presidential aspirant can assess his chances. Through presidential primaries, state party conventions, and other campaign forums one might indeed overcome or gain the necessary informal prerequisites to become a viable candidate for her party's nomination. She can gain publicity and become better known. One might also attract more financial backing, assuming enough money initially to gain additional funds.[3] One might also overcome or temper apprehensions or controversy with respect to one's position on issues, or regarding one's religion, race, or sex. Finally, and very important, one might gather the kind of popular support and delegate commitment needed to do battle at the convention stage.

To win the party's nomination at the convention, the candidate must be able to fashion a majority of the delegates. That is, he/she must be willing to form coalitions through negotiating and practicing the art of compromise. One might have to compromise in such areas as the party platform, a credentials fight, the vice-presidential nominee, the national party chairman, and his/her likely position on key issues and appointments if he/she should become president. Managing and overcoming conflict in any of these areas may determine not only who wins the nomination, but also how well the nominee can carry on in the third stage—the post-convention election campaign.

In the post-convention phase the nominee must try to hold on to the coalition that fashioned the nomination in the convention and must also try to add to it. The nominee needs more campaign workers. He/she needs to appeal to a broader spectrum of voters and will invariably need more money. But gaining new support involves risks of losing old support. A candidate must constantly assess costs and benefits, advantages and disadvantages. In the end, the candidate who receives a majority of the electoral vote (and almost always a plurality of the popular vote) becomes president. And after becoming president the kind of broad support that put the candidate into office will continue to be necessary to effectively carry out the various roles and responsibilities of office.

Once in Office

In addition to this broad popular support, the president also needs the support of those specifically charged to help fulfill the various roles. The president appoints many people in offices and agencies of the executive branch. The heads of the major departments—for example, State, Defense, Housing and Urban Development (HUD), Health and Human Services—are all appointed by the president. These officials (or secretaries) and several others form the cabinet. Formally, the cabinet members are the president's principal advisers on governmental policies. In making these and other appointments, the president has to remain alert to factors that affect the policies and programs of his administration. For example, will a particular appointment lessen support from an important party leader or an important member of Congress, or endanger the support of an important segment of those who voted for him in the presidential election? However, the overwhelming majority of the thousands of employees in the federal government are career civil servants. As such, they are not subject to presidential appointment and their career status also shields these permanent bureaucrats from attempts at blatant manipulation.

The president also relies heavily on the Executive Office for the president. This office, just like the larger departments, consists of presidential appointees and career civil servants. It is divided into various units such as the White House Office, National Security Council, Office of Management and Budget, and Council of Economic Advisers. While these various units are all directly responsible to the president in helping to carry out many functions, the White House Office is made up of the president's "own people." This allows the president to overcome certain political considerations (such as satisfying different factions of the party) that may dictate whom the president can appoint to administer the more formal governmental structures, such as the various cabinet departments. But in the White House Office the president can appoint aides and assistants of his/her own choosing. And their influence on the president in a given area might be greater than the cabinet member charged with that responsibility. However, the Watergate scandal, and subsequent revelations that some of President Nixon's closest "personal" assistants were involved, caused his successors to be more careful in making such appointments and in assigning responsibilities. In any event, to carry out his many roles the president needs the help of these administrators, both in the Executive Office and in the bureaucracies of the large departments, such as Health and Human Services or the Department of Defense. The quality of help received determines how well the president does his job.

Clearly, the person who occupies the office of the president has enormous influence in American politics. Through various messages to Congress and to the nation (for example, in the State of the Union address), the president sets the nation's agenda. He/she can thus propose legislation and through the veto power can dispose of legislation passed by the Congress. Further, the president sets the nation's priorities, and budgetary, legislative, and administrative powers give her/him great leverage to make those priorities stick. Also, the many ceremonial functions serve to strengthen the president in exercising formal powers.

The powers at the president's disposal are indeed impressive. Because they are, it is little wonder that blacks tend to focus on the person and the office in their struggle for social justice. In part, this concentration can be seen as an attempt to use the symbolism of the presidency to capture broad public attention and support. But to be successful blacks need the president to support their causes.

Whether or not a president supports the range of issues that are important to African Americans depends on the overall shape of American politics. Thus, just as the issues flow from political circumstances, so too do a president's political attitudes. But there is more to it than that. Presidential views and attitudes on all political issues are also products of the individual incumbent's conception of the presidency.[4] That is to say, a given president may see the office as an agent for change utilizing the various powers to vigorously move the country in new directions. That was the view that many observers held of the Kennedy presidency. And it was clearly the conception that Lyndon Johnson had of his proper role in the civil rights struggle of blacks. But not every president will see his responsibilities in such a light.

Presidents may, as was Eisenhower, be less venturesome. Eisenhower's view can be characterized as rather narrowly construing the provision that a president sees to the effective implementation and execution of the laws of the land.

Using the concept of office idea is merely another way of trying to understand what it is that a president believes should be done, fully recognizing that there are numerous constraints on what can be done. Of course, it is also true that "change-agent" presidents need not always do things of which particular groups approve. Black interests, for example, were not advanced by the Nixon administration. But, in general, blacks have fared better under presidents who had an activist and expansive view of their tenures. And because of this African Americans are probably more likely than others in the mass public to approve of a strong president.

The concept of office is not the exclusive creation of the individual. It results from the interaction between the incumbent president (or other officeholder) and the political environment. Messages and cues received are digested and converted into political actions and programs. But this process works both ways, for the president can also influence the views held by those within the political environment, thereby affecting the kinds of messages and cues he will get in return. Thus, Lyndon Johnson's rhetoric in describing a War on Poverty could elicit strong positive responses from the disadvantaged and their supporters that were used to overcome sources of opposition. Similarly, Richard Nixon could marshal broad public support, even among blacks, for a campaign of law and order in the nation's big cities. Obviously, public views are an important part of presidential decision making, but it would be foolhardy for any president to look to the mass public for specific policy guidance. Public opinion, at least as expressed in polling results, is too variable and contradictory. Thus, while Americans want a president to use the powers of office for the well-being of the nation, they also seek to reassure themselves that the use of these powers will not be unrestrained.[5]

From the perspective of black policy interests, public opinion has another flaw. It is simply that the specific concerns of blacks, or any other minority, are amalgamated into generalized policy positions. And as so often happens when there is a particular point that African Americans want to call to the president's attention, it is difficult to discern in the midst of "public" opinion. For a time after the election of President Jimmy Carter, African Americans believed that this problem had been corrected.

Perhaps more clearly than in any previous presidential election, black votes made a difference in the outcome of the 1976 contest between Carter and the incumbent president, Gerald Ford.[6] Initially, blacks were not enthusiastic about the Democratic race for it produced few candidates attractive to them. But the Republicans could derive little satisfaction from this fact for their man, like the party as a whole, lacked any significant black constituency.

Initially, the Carter candidacy was given little credence by blacks or virtually anyone else. As a one-term governor from Georgia, Jimmy Carter was almost unknown to the public. Moreover, from the point of view of many blacks, his Deep South background was a serious disadvantage. To make matters worse, two racial incidents during the campaign only heightened black distrust of the southerner.

The first incident involved Carter's response to a question about housing patterns in the urban North. The candidate responded with a reference to maintaining the "ethnic purity" of neighborhoods. For most blacks this was not a dramatically new statement of white views on residential integration. Nor at first was there much attention paid to the statement. Carter's difficulties came when he was asked to explain what he meant by the phrase. As is so often the case in politics, the candidate's attempts to clarify his position only made matters worse. It was an embarrassment that the media and the other candidates were quick to exploit.

However, Carter weathered the controversy. In this he was aided by a sizable contingent of southern black supporters. At the time, Representative Andrew Young of Atlanta, Georgia had been Carter's most prominent black supporter. But Young, a member of the Congressional Black Caucus, had no choice but to join with other members of the Caucus in denouncing the "ethnic purity" statement. However, this was more a pro forma gesture than a rejection of Carter.

According to Witcover, the people most troubled by Carter's statement were the white liberals for whom the Deep South candidate's "black support had become a kind of badge of Carter's acceptability (to) white liberal activists."[7] In other words, as long as blacks were not overly concerned with the statement and its subsequent explanations, it was safe for the liberals to support the Carter campaign. And when Carter received the "blessing" of Reverend Martin Luther King, Sr., the father of the slain civil rights hero, the incident was over.

Throughout this affair blacks showed a much more pragmatic attitude toward racial politics. It was also apparent that African Americans were more important to the Carter candidacy than their own numbers suggested. Black support, especially that of prominent individuals such as Representative Young and Reverend King, made it easier for him to garner northern white supporters. The Carter campaign was also shielded against some of the usual charges of being anti-black that one hears during presidential races. The explanation of this difference was not solely because of black support. Jimmy Carter helped himself by removing a principal source of racial antagonisms when he defeated his fellow southerner, former Governor George Wallace of Alabama. It was the combination of black support and the elimination of Wallace that contributed significantly to Carter's national acceptance.

The race between the one-term Georgia governor and President Ford was close. And, as we said earlier, the black vote was critical. Almost two-thirds of registered black voters went to the polls in November 1976. Of this number, over 90 percent cast their ballots for Carter. Without this massive black support the former governor would have lost. Indeed, Carter was the minority choice of all white voters, receiving approximately 48 percent of their votes to Ford's 52 percent.[8]

While we noted in an earlier chapter that the distribution of the black vote is not always a political advantage, it clearly was one for Carter in 1976. Their concentration in states with large blocks of electoral votes made it possible for Jimmy Carter to win while carrying only one state (Texas) west of the Mississippi River. An almost "solid South" and the industrialized Northeast gave Carter the necessary votes in the electoral college.

The nature of the Carter win helps shed some light on one of the little-noticed aspects of black politics. That is to say, while the black political agenda is often viewed as change-oriented, some reforms favored by white liberals, such as abolishing the electoral college, would work to the disadvantage of blacks. The electoral college system of deciding presidential races is a long-standing target of liberals who believe that it undermines the principle of "one person, one vote." African Americans, who in other instances would agree with this principle, also recognize that in contests like the 1976 campaign between Carter and Ford their votes had a larger impact than would be the case if the popular vote alone determined the winner. But this inconsistency does not weaken black efforts to gain a greater measure of political power. And in the glow of their contribution to the newly elected Jimmy Carter, blacks had high expectations of making significant strides toward that objective. Attention was directed to how the new president would repay his supporters. It was generally acknowledged that a cabinet appointment was in the offing. In the end, Carter surprised most observers by appointing two blacks to his cabinet. Patricia Roberts Harris, an attorney and a prominent actor in national Democratic party politics, became the secretary of Housing and Urban Development (HUD), and Representative Andrew Young, who had perhaps been Carter's staunchest black supporter, was named as Ambassador to the United Nations.[9]

In addition, President Carter appointed several blacks to prominent and politically significant subcabinet positions. Eleanor Holmes

Norton was appointed to head the Equal Employment Opportunity Commission, Drew S. Days, III, was named assistant attorney general for civil rights, and Clifford Alexander became the secretary of the army.

In some respects, one might have expected blacks to occupy several of these posts because of their importance in policy areas of concern to African Americans. While the "naturalness" of the positions spurs criticism in some quarters, it should be remembered that presidential appointments do take account of various constituency interests. Moreover, in the case of Carter's appointees, it can be argued that he chose blacks for these offices precisely because of the special sensitivities and insights they would bring to their jobs.

President Carter's appointments reflect the power of the black electorate in his 1976 victory and his effort to maintain the support of that part of his constituency should he choose to run for a second term—a choice he subsequently made. And though black voters remained fiercely loyal to the Democrats—giving Carter more than 80 percent of their votes—the president's bumbling image and increasingly conservative mood helped Ronald Reagan and the Republican party to win the White House. Under Reagan, blacks and minorities came in for very rough times.

Reagan entered the presidency with the stated intention of dismantling and cutting back many social welfare-type programs that in his view accorded the federal government too great a role in the lives of individual Americans and largely at the expense of the legitimate realms of state and local governments. And the president made good on his promise. He repeatedly ignored the traditional bargaining process with other governmental leaders and instead appealed directly to the American people for support.[10] His position was considerably strengthened by the fact that in the 1980 elections the Republicans won a majority in the Senate and gained 33 seats in the House of Representatives.[11] These Republican gains, in addition to a number of sympathetic conservative southern Democrats already in the Congress, provided the kind of legislative support the president needed for really key policy initiatives, reflected vividly in budget cuts and paring down of social programs that were mainly designed to help blacks, minorities, and the poor. This gave a more restrictive role to the federal government in American politics generally, and resulted in more leeway for state and local governments to fashion policy and practice in a number of policies especially crucial to blacks, including civil rights enforcement. Additionally, President Reagan made special efforts to see that insofar as possible, his overall ideological and policy positions were reflected in the large number of judicial appointments (almost half of all federal judges) he made to our federal courts. For many, Reagan seemed to summarize his administrations's attitude towards the interests of African Americans in early 1989 when he accused unnamed civil rights leaders of exaggerating American discrimination towards blacks in order to further their own political careers.

Ironically, it was at this very time that President-elect Bush was attempting to show a less strident opposition to the civil rights legacy. For many, Bush seemed to have at least some credentials as a proponent of the federal government's role in actively pushing for racial equality. At Yale, Bush headed the United Negro College Fund. Furthermore, as a congressman from Texas, Bush was one of the few southern legislators to vote for the 1968 landmark fair housing bill, despite protests from his conservative district in Houston. Yet many African Americans were horrified by what they considered Bush's racially divisive campaign tactics. Campaign manager Lee Atwater's attempt to tie Michael Dukakis to the image of Willie Horton—a black convict who raped a white Maryland woman and stabbed her husband while on furlough from a Massachusetts prison—seemed to prey upon white voters' most ugly fears.

But almost immediately after his landslide election in November 1988, President-elect Bush attempted to reassure blacks that his administration would be sensitive to their needs. Speaking to about 500 members of the American Bicentennial Presidential Inaugural Afro-American Committee, a predominantly black group of Bush supporters, Bush pledged that "bigotry and indifference to disadvantage will find no safe home on our shores, in our public life, in our neighborhoods, or in our home, and that Reverend [Martin Luther] King's dream for his children and for ours will be fulfilled. It will, I promise, be my mission as President of the United States."[12]

Yet Bush's leadership was much less forceful than his rhetoric. Indeed, the major difference between the Bush administration and the Reagan administration's agenda seemed to be one of style rather than substance. Bush seems to have quietly carried on the Reagan administration's agenda, only pausing to avoid the most stigmatizing embarrassments. For instance, in early 1990, the Department of Education announced new policy guidelines which would prevent any school receiving federal funds from earmarking scholarship money exclusively for certain minority groups. Within a week, however, Bush intervened to reverse this policy after the news media pointedly criticized his administration for chipping away at minority opportunities at home, while at the same time sending hundreds of thousands of African Americans to the Persian Gulf in defense of "the national interest." On the other hand, despite his eventual signing of the Civil Rights Act of 1991 (designed to overcome several adverse Supreme Court decisions), Bush's early and repeated opposition to that legislation clearly did not sit well with women, blacks and minorities. Moreover, and in the final analysis,

Bush did little if anything to improve his civil rights record by appointing to the Supreme Court Judge Clarence Thomas, a black arch-conservative, to replace Justice Thurgood Marshall, fondly and accurately referred to in the black community and American politics generally as "Mr. Civil Rights."

In any case, the 1992 election saw President Bush's bid for a second term rebuffed by Democratic candidate Governor William Clinton of Arkansas, whose victory was due in no small measure to the overwhelming support Clinton received from black voters.[13] Clinton's election excited the hopes and expectations of African Americans, and many others, in a manner quite reminiscent of those following the election of the late President John F. Kennedy in 1960. More extended commentary on the Clinton election as it relates to African Americans is given in Chapter 11. For our purposes here, however, it is sufficient to say that the general actions of Clinton in the early months of his administration suggested that blacks and minorities would both have access and become active participants running the new Democratic-controlled government and administration. This is evidenced in part in by Clinton's appointment of blacks to key posts in his transition team as well as in his cabinet, to which four blacks were appointed. Additionally, the president promised to have the kind of representation in the executive branch and in the federal judiciary that is reflective of the richness and diversity of the American population. But only time will tell how far the president is willing or able to push policies and programs designed to overcome the serious problems that continue to disproportionately plague and hamper the life chances and opportunities of blacks and minorities.

Overall, this suggests the changing nature and scope of issues facing the black community. Indeed, passing laws to secure or protect civil rights is no longer a priority. Blacks are now demanding presidential action on issues that are less susceptible to legislative initiatives. This does not mean that the issues themselves are new. Indeed, employment and housing are persistent problems for blacks. But neither of these areas offers a president much freedom to act. The difficulty with such issues is that most of the proposed solutions would require a redistribution of wealth and social advantage. Given present conditions, it is highly unlikely that the American political system would support these kinds of changes because to do so would imply some fundamental changes in the roles of government in the society. Presidents, no matter how ambitious or daring, do not usually win elections on pledges to make such changes.

But to overcome severe economic problems that disproportionately affect blacks and similar minorities, it is precisely these types of changes that may be needed—changes that could well modify current patterns of political influence and access. To achieve such changes,

Keeping in Touch. During the campaign, presidential candidates make efforts to keep in touch with their major constituencies. *(AP/Wide World Photos)*

however, would seem to call for blacks and others to take a much broader and more active role in politics than they have in the past or have ever taken before. Jesse Jackson's campaigns in 1984 and 1988 for the Democratic presidential nomination suggest that blacks can clearly do just this: Jackson's campaigns—and his relative success—reflect a clear, discernable growth in the sophistication and breadth of policy concerns among blacks. It also reflects the studied attempts on the part of Jackson and others to illuminate and show how the much broader common interests among blacks, poor whites, and others more than overshadow the perceived divisions that may exist among them.

Campaigns like Jackson's and those of others have clearly advanced the political knowledge and awareness of blacks and minorities. But only in marginal terms, at least thus far, has this won for these groups more leverage and clout in presidential politics. This can be seen clearly in the 1992 presidential elections where Clinton overwhelmingly won the black vote without—except in most general terms—promising much in return.

Nonetheless, black advances into the mainstream of presidential politics have given them new vantage points from which to view the workings of the presidency. This can be sobering because we can see that a president is not all-powerful. The president cannot govern by fiat because there are other powerful actors who have competing interests. Because the president is a part of a complicated political environment, the ability to initiate major change is limited. But in uncommon circumstances, in which the environment itself is more conducive to fundamental change, the posture of the president can be crucial, even determinative. Such was the case for Roosevelt during the New Deal years, Johnson during the "Civil Rights Revolution," Nixon during the period of "law and order," and Ronald Reagan during his first term when he capitalized on the conservative mood and made severe cutbacks in civil rights and social welfare programs.[14] It remains to be seen how crucial or determinate a role President Clinton is willing or able to play in this regard.

In any case, in American politics, broad scale and fundamental changes in national policies may require the kinds of unusual circumstances that aided presidents in the past, and certainly such fundamental changes are needed to deal with the problems faced by blacks. But most policy making takes place under normal, routine circumstances where the president need not be and is not always the most appropriate focal point for policy interests. And it is in this relatively routine area of policy making where African Americans will need to devote more careful attention and resources, for it is this routine, day-to-day policy making that can make a great deal of difference in the quality of life enjoyed (or endured) by most Americans, including blacks and minorities.

In the next section, you will see that we do not give the president as much prominence as he is generally thought to have in the making of public policy. Still, he remains the principal policy maker in the federal government. As we show later, presidential appointees loom much larger and play a much more crucial role than many are willing to acknowledge. The prominence of their roles may reflect individual presidential styles of policy making. For example, a factor illuminated during the 1987 Iran-Contra hearings was President Reagan's management style. Some presidents, such as Reagan, appear quite willing to allow department heads considerable discretion in policy development. Others, however, prefer to retain as much policy discretion as possible within the White House. The discussion that follows illustrates these points as well as the rich interactive nature of the policy process.

THE POLICY PROCESS—AN OVERVIEW

For our purposes here, the policy-making process is divided into four different phases:[15]

1. Agenda setting and initiation
2. Initial outcome: The legislative product
3. Secondary outcome: Administration and impact
4. Response, feedback, and future prospects

Within this framework one finds an interconnected series of actions and interactions involving private and public individuals, groups, and institutions. Also included are the president and his apparatus comprising the institutionalized presidency, members of Congress, the agencies, bureaus, and the political parties as well as the national news media.

We should emphasize that the process under discussion is not limited to a short period of time, say a single congressional term. It can take (and it has) a decade or more before an issue becomes a realistic part of the policy agenda. Sometimes it is even longer before specific policy results. Initiatives may fail but may not be forgotten. Such was the case, for example, with the lengthy struggle for black civil and political equality. This example, and there are others that stimulated less public concern, illustrates one of the most criticized features of the policy process: It is slow to respond to demands. Neither the strong feelings surrounding a group's claims nor their presumed justice weigh quite so heavily in political decision making as one might think. Despite the moral phrasing of the Constitution and the Bill of Rights, appeals to such ideas are of limited use in the political arena if the history of the civil rights struggle is any indication. Minority demands, such as those made by African Americans, mean a sharp break with practices which have matured during the course of American history. Adopting new programs or initiating new ways of dealing with continual problems may pose serious threats to existing social and political arrangements. Thus, policy making can, especially when dealing with questions that affect the scope of political influence, engender dramatic confrontations within and outside government.

Another reason why some things don't get done, or are sometimes done very slowly, stems from congressional "sampling."[16] Since members of Congress cannot attend to every demand made of them, they pick and choose among the issues brought to them for action and decision. Sampling, however, implies the existence of bias; by definition some things are ignored. Constitutionally, both Congress and the president are required to do certain things at fixed times. Congress convenes on a firm date every year (January 3) unless changed by law. And because some legislation expires after a set time, the legislature must act promptly if those laws are to be continued in force. An example of this is the use of the "continuing resolution." This device has financial importance for government agencies whose fiscal year begins on October 1. If Congress has not completed its work on an appropriations bill, the continuing resolution "allows agencies to spend at the rate set for that agency in the previous year . . . [O]r if only the House has passed the appropriations bill, at whichever rate is lower, or, if both Senate and House have passed the bill, at whichever of those two rates is lower."[17]

To be sure, Congress can move with more than "deliberate speed" when the circumstances demand swift action. An acute, or crisis, situation presents a must-act condition; other business has to be postponed while elected officials deal with the crisis. A chronic problem of the body politic—for example, structural unemployment for some of the labor force—can be put aside.

We should add that while the president and the "institutionalized presidency," that is, the White House and Executive Office staffs, have a preeminent role in policy making, members of Congress may also and do initiate legislation. Thus, the technique of sampling described above must also allow time for the many bills sponsored by the congressional membership. In addition, even though it is not explicitly included under sampling, the particular ideology (that is, the beliefs of committee chairpersons in a policy area) will also influence what and how proposals are considered. This means that a president will try to avoid giving policy proposals to a committee chair who is known to be hostile. However, this searching for a receptive committee chairperson may affect the content of the proposed legislation because the congressional policy system tends to be functionally specific in its organization.

Let us now examine the four policy phases. Although we believe these elements of the policy process are so closely connected that they can be combined, we see a number of patterned relationships.

AGENDA SETTING AND INITIATION

National policy initiation has increasingly become the province of the presidency. Once elected to office, a president stands a good chance to be reelected, though the record since 1960 has been rather rocky. In any event, presidents know that getting their programs through Congress takes time, and those elected to a second term stand a better chance of getting their policies through. A president's first term can be viewed then as a time to build a record on which to run for his second four years in office. Therefore, the first four years tend to be oriented toward accomplishing those things which can be done quickly. However, "quickly" is a relative term in the relations between president and Congress. The relationship between initiation and agenda setting focuses upon the expanded role of the executive branch as the initiator of legislation. Through communications such as State of the Union messages, budget messages, and specific program proposals, the president not only initiates policy but also makes an agenda for congressional consideration, debate, and action. What the president wants is made clear, not left to the congressional imagination.

Since the administration of Franklin D. Roosevelt, presidents have also had another means of getting their message to the legislative branch. They have increasingly used the media, especially when there is a potentially strong opposition in Congress. President Clinton seems especially to be taking advantage of major technological advances and different forums and contexts (e.g., electronic and in-person town meetings) in talking directly to the American people. In part, this is an educational technique to inform the public of proposed government actions. But it is also a device to create public support for the president's programs. For example, when former President Nixon wanted to halt court-ordered busing as a means to achieve school integration, he went to the public via television. He told the listening public that lower federal courts

> [h]ave gone too far; in some cases, beyond the requirements laid down by the Supreme Court in ordering massive busing to achieve racial balance. . . . There are many who believe that a constitutional amendment is the only way to deal with this problem . . . But as an answer to the immediate problem . . . of stopping more busing now, the constitutional amendment approach has a fatal flaw—it takes too long. . . . And there's only one effective way to deal with the problem now. That is for Congress to act. That is why I am sending a special message to the Congress tomorrow urging immediate consideration and action.[18]

Likewise, President Reagan was given high marks by the media and others as a great communicator and for taking his proposals—aid for the Nicaraguan Contras, for example—over the heads of Congress directly to the people. And similarly, in the early months of his administration President Clinton went to the public to try to bring the federal budget under control and showed every indication of continuing to do so for his other major policy initiatives.

AGENDA SETTING AND ELECTORAL POLITICS

It is, however, realistic to ask where the president's program originates. Certainly technical details are fleshed out by topical experts, both appointive and career officials. But the ideas for presidential programs may also originate in less formalized ways. While somewhat vague and symbolic, campaign promises of a presidential candidate and united parties in mid-term elections may suggest potential agenda items for future legislative and executive attention. Electoral campaigns may show what the candidate(s) think about different issues.

Part of the explanation for the absence of clear policy and issue discussion during the campaigns is that getting elected is different from actually doing the job. Quite naturally, a prospective president doesn't want to commit himself too strongly before taking office. In addition, if a candidate does take a firm position on a particular question, as Walter Mondale did on the need to raise taxes in his race against President Reagan in 1984, he or she may find himself giving the opposition an exploitable issue to use against him, which Reagan did. Similarly President Clinton in the early months of his administration gave Republicans and some Democrats an "exploitable issue" with respect to Clinton's strong pledge during the 1992 campaign to end discrimination against gays and lesbians in the military services.

Perhaps of greater importance, however, is that the campaigns are not designed for a discussion of the issues. Rather, they serve to attract, and make the candidate attractive to, the great middle of American politics. If the presidential hopeful gets too specific, he or she is likely to alienate the middle ground. This is the condition which Senator McGovern unwittingly created in his 1972 campaign with his proposal to pay $1,000 to welfare recipients. On issues like welfare, which have a high degree of ideological content, being specific entails risk. The extent that a campaign tells us anything at all about the kinds of policies we might expect from a candidate if he or she is successful is by way of inference. That is, assuming that the candidate is not a total unknown, his past political activity should give some evidence of what he will be like as president. Positions which he has previously taken on public issues can, if carefully studied, be reasonable indicators of future stances on similar or related issues.[19] This kind of presidential watching, however, requires an investment of time and energy which the general public does not make.

AGENDA SETTING AND INTEREST GROUPS

Certainly organized interest groups are involved in agenda setting through support of candidates likely to include their needs and wishes on an agenda for action. In American politics it is assumed that patience will at some future time be rewarded by positive government action in desired policy areas. While the denied group waits for these outcomes, it must also attempt to form coalitions with others. Such coalitions may require modification or even subordination of one group's goals in exchange for wider support. Sometimes the goals of the petitioning group can become the umbrella for the larger group. In either case, a broad base of support is often a necessary first step in getting the government to respond favorably to public demands.

Group formation and coalition building has been treated by many scholars as important means by which the interests of politically active publics are placed in the political marketplace.[20] More recently, there have been examples of small-sized interest groups placing their concerns on policy agendas without developing active wide-scale support. Small and less highly structured groups have been able to use the mass media to bring certain situations and viewpoints to public attention. Through use of the media such groups have activated third-party interests which may be "inconvenienced" by the publicity surrounding the issues in question. These third parties, then, may become concerned enough for their own self-interests to become active in seeking a political solution. The implication is clear that this tactic is more likely to be used by a relatively weak group. Third parties' resources are brought to bear on the agenda-setting process on behalf of a weak organization. Such political action tends to be issue-specific rather than broad and general. Moreover, its use seems to be limited so far to urban political systems rather than national. The restriction appears to result from the ad hoc character of these groups' formation. They are unable to sustain an active membership and effective leadership over time once the original demands are met.[21]

AGENDA SETTING AND DOMESTIC CRISES

Events such as a war and an energy shortage can bring issues to the policy agenda rather quickly. But the natural processes of American policy making, especially on domestic concerns, tend to be characterized by slowness. This was noted by President Nixon in his speech on busing. This incrementalism, as it is frequently called, is closely related to the problem of providing funds for government activities.[22] In addition, we should keep in mind that the two-party system seldom reflects sharp differences on matters of public policy. The basic agreement on political values between Democrats and Republicans reinforces the incremental character of policy making.

When a crisis situation develops it is difficult for the legislative and executive branches to respond. This is partly because their habitual patterns of response are oriented to regularities or the chronic problems of the political system. The solution to critical problems will generally require an abrupt change in the way the public's business is handled by its officials. However, the nature of that change depends upon political choices made among competing definitions of the problem(s) to be addressed by government action. The timing of crises also contributes to the ways in which they are handled. Most situations defined as crises in political terms are in fact not wholly novel phenomena. That is, one can usually find their antecedents in some one or another chronic problem that has gone unattended. A chronic problem becomes a crisis, in this view, when some part of the public is concerned enough about it to want to act. Moreover, those most directly concerned must also be able to get others to share their concern. The issue, in other words, must have a "ripple effect" among the public.

Naturally, the media has an important part to play in the evolution of a crisis, for they can enhance the "ripple effect." Direct political activity by individuals and groups in bringing the issues to the attention of legislators adds to the role of the media. Nontraditional forms of political behavior—for example, violence or mass protest demonstrations—help foster a sense of crisis, especially if the issue is relatively specific. This specificity implies that possible solutions will be narrow in scope and impact. The tendency then is to define a crisis situation in its narrowest terms consistent with its key issue(s).

If this is not possible, the attempt is to find a solution that is politically feasible and satisfactory to the petitioning group but that is, at the same time, not so broad that its scope and impact are likely to have effects within other policy arenas.

AGENDA SETTING AND THE IDEA WHOSE TIME HAS COME

Specific policy proposals may receive little support or interest when first introduced. With the sponsorship of skillful political actors in the legislative and/or executive branch such proposals gradually gain supporters. Many bills introduced by potential presidential candidates fit into this category; although such proposals may have little chance of current passage, they can help "build a record," induce interest group support, and perhaps garner media attention. There is a strong relationship between this "idea whose time has come" and the process described in the previous section. Evaluating the civil rights movement in this context clearly yields some rich perspectives on the nature and operation of American politics. For example, the stage for the Model Cities program was created by several articles that appeared in national magazines. These articles emphasized the terrible conditions of the urban poor in the central city. There were pictures of the Watts riots in Los Angeles and other disturbances that occurred in the nation's cities. Consequently, in 1965, a letter and later a conversation between Walter Reuther, president of the United Auto Workers, and President Johnson provided the catalyst to action. They proposed to concentrate federal programs in the center city and give the cities enough money to begin urban renewal programs. As mayor of Detroit, Jerome Cavanaugh, in several conversations with Reuther, had emphasized the need for a massive renewal program based on the existing Model Neighborhood in Detroit. President Johnson found the proposal to his liking. Consequently, the president formed a Task Force headed by then-Professor Robert G. Wood of the Massachusetts Institute of Technology, later under secretary of the Department of Housing and Urban Development.[23]

The Task Force was composed of academicians and federal officials who were unfamiliar with the problems confronting urban areas. Wood did possess some expertise in the field of urban renewal. Whether he understood the complicated "human" problems of the urban poor sufficiently to design an adequate program is another question. The Task Force included only one individual who could really represent the interests of the urban poor, of whom the majority were black. This was Whitney Young, president of the Urban League, an organization not known at the time for aggressively championing black interests. To some extent, it might be argued that these interests were generally represented by the U.S. Conference of Mayors, whose constituencies were increasingly made up of these groups. But, the president and Dr. Wood deliberately selected persons who had not been too strongly committed to or identified with any existing program such as those of the Office of Economic Opportunity (OEO).

What did the Task Force propose? Why? The Task Force was strongly encouraged to develop new and innovative programs. In fact, Dr. Wood was given great latitude in terms of the type of proposals that could be submitted. But President Johnson also had some preferences. He instructed Dr. Wood and the Task Force to construct programs with the following characteristics: (1) Mayors and city councils were to have a principal role; (2) social and physical planning should be coordinated; and (3) racial integration and citizen participation were "desirable goals but would have to be played down in order to facilitate congressional passage."[24]

Initially, the Task Force had planned to propose that the program be enacted in only six or eight cities. However, they were aware of the congressional process. That is, the members of the Task Force were aware that congressional approval depended upon whether or not the congressmen's districts would benefit. With these instructions and considerations in mind, the Task Force set to work.

In January 1966, the Task Force formally presented its proposal which contained a number of "innovations." These were clearly fashioned so that they would be accepted by Congress. The most drastic innovation was the concentration of resources in a defined neighborhood in a prescribed number of cities. The proposal also included a number of grant-in-aid programs that were to be coordinated by local officials and the neighborhood. The planning efforts were to be placed in a community development agency which would link the mayor's office to the affected neighborhood; the bulk of the funds would come from existing programs and agencies.[25] This arrangement would supposedly satisfy the demand for participation as well as congressional concerns for official control. Indeed, the Task Force was very concerned about the proposal's fate in Congress. The "reprogramming" of existing appropriations would also satisfy those members of Congress who did not want to increase federal spending. As we shall see later in this chapter, the Task Force got a good deal of what it, and the president, wanted in the legislation. And, of course, some congressional modifications were included.

INITIAL OUTCOME: THE LEGISLATIVE PRODUCT

A convenient way to view the legislative phase of the policy process is in terms of coalition building. The sponsor or sponsors of proposals must build coalitions in both houses of Congress as well as in the relative subcommittees.

Several factors are important to policy coalitions. First, there are the attitudes and actions of the president. Through White House staff and representatives of executive departments, the president lobbies for or against a bill at hearings, with individual legislators, and through the media. Tactics will largely depend on the partisan and ideological makeup of Congress. And naturally, if the bill is an administration bill, the president and his "helpers" will do all they can to help the measure along. Despite the absence of disciplined legislative parties, the president's policy position will usually be a major factor in defining the position of most members of both parties. It is also important to consider whether a president is working to pass or to defeat a bill on its merit, or whether he is trying to gain political advantage for electoral purposes. His tactics will vary accordingly. Compromises may be made in the former situation, but seldom in the latter. Thus, key members of Congress will try to find out the president's feelings on a particular measure before they commit themselves fully one way or the other.

Second, department and agency bureaucrats contribute to coalition construction. In many instances, these institutional representatives have a monopoly of information. How has a program worked? Its administrators have answers that are documented with mountains of supporting data. How will a new program work? Its technical authors can explain the prospects in exquisite detail. In other instances, bureaucrats use long-standing associations with individual legislators to rally support for proposals concerned with their agency. But there is little or no role for the public.

Coalition building in support of or in opposition to proposed legislation is also influenced by a third characteristic, the committee structure of Congress. Because the bulk of congressional work is performed in committee and subcommittee and not on the floor of the House or Senate, these smaller, functionally devised groups can significantly influence the final shape of the legislative product. For example, the policy areas of some committees are more conducive to "log-rolling" or "pork-barrel" tactics than others. That is, the issue being considered may have implications for some tangible interests of the members' constituencies. If the representatives are convinced that those interests will not be adversely affected by the "marked-up" bill, a strong committee coalition is likely when the bill is presented to the full House or Senate for debate and vote. The bill is likely to even attract the support of members whose constituents will not benefit from the bill, since these members count on the support of other coalition members when a bill benefiting their constituents is considered later. If such a committee coalition is bipartisan, strictly partisan voting on the floor is unlikely. This is especially true when the subject matter is not of great interest to many of the legislators.

On the other hand, a committee whose policy areas are subject to ideological conflict—the House Committee on Education and Labor is a good example—is less likely to arrive at a consensual coalition. Therefore, the House or Senate floor becomes the primary arena for coalition building on bills from such committees. Partisan and/or ideological differences are likely to be important factors. These differences will be revealed in the debate that precedes the final vote on the issue.

Similarly, it is important to note that the style of committee operation vis-à-vis House action will often determine whether much, little, or no bargaining and compromising go on at the committee level. When a powerful committee chairperson is determined to bring out a bill that will pass, committee activity is strongly oriented toward coalition formation—even though the subject matter itself may be controversial.

Fourth, legislative parties also affect congressional coalition building. There are several important variables: whether the White House and Congress are controlled by the same party, the relative strength of the majority and minority, the style and influence of party leadership, the amount of cohesiveness in each party, the role and influence of party subgroups such as the Democratic Study Group, and the anticipated closeness of the next election.

A fifth factor can be generally described as constituency influence. However, this does not mean only letters from home. Of course, constituents do include organized groups that serve as important referents—civil rights groups, labor unions, expressive associations, farmer organizations, associations of business and industry, and the like. Such organizations can influence legislators for several reasons. Their members or those they claim to represent may actually be an important segment of electoral constituencies and the organizations may be important to electoral success. Or the groups may simply share the legislator's own ideological leanings, a factor especially important for upwardly mobile representatives and senators. The coalition-building role of such groups typically centers around two tactics: (1) supporting tried-and-true friends and urging them to take more active roles in specific policy battles and (2) shoring up others who might waver in certain instances.

Another important constituency influence is the legislator's perceptions of how the "folks back home" feel about a policy area. It seems likely that what is calculated is not what most voters feel about a particular bill, but what they feel about a given issue area. How this is calculated varies, but certainly communications from major supporters, party leaders, and other key local individuals weigh heavily. Obviously, in many cases the legislator must realize that most of the home folks neither know nor care about the matter at hand!

In any given instance, one or more of these factors will be significant in developing congressional support for a policy proposal. In addition, several studies have indicated that certain policy decisions are more closely tied to presidential influence while others are related to party affiliation or constituency attitudes.[26]

This discussion has revealed the multiplicity of actors and some of their roles in making public policy. Although the general public's direct influence on this process is limited in most cases to letter writing, it is often remarked that their concerns are indirectly articulated through the "interest aggregation" function of the two major political parties. But if some part of the public is perceived or in fact is not influential in the party's decision, even indirect articulation loses much of its meaning. In general, this has been the case with national policy that is relevant to black interests. Thus the inability of African Americans to exercise significant influence in the policy process on matters that greatly affect them (unemployment, overcoming problems of poverty) reflects the relative weak position of blacks in the political system.

In some respects the lack of influence can be viewed as a byproduct of black urbanization. Many problems that affect blacks most severely are related to their urban concentration. Therefore, we could expect that the way in which urban policy is handled would strongly affect African Americans. In general, however, the American "love-hate" relationship with their large cities has been greatly affected by racial problems and conflicts more visible in urban areas. This condition is, of course, intensified by the fact that the potential for urbanization was not considered when Congress was initially organized. Cities, to the extent that they were considered at all by the founders, were the responsibilities of the states, not of the federal government.

Thus, despite the severe dislocations which urban populations suffered during the Great Depression and the obvious implications of the general urbanization of the nation since the 1920s, Congress and the president gave little specific attention to urban affairs. That is, unlike agricultural interests, there was no committee specializing in the affairs of urban communities.[27] Not until the Kennedy administration was an effort made to give urban policy questions an institutionalized status in the policy system. And, Kennedy's attempt to create a Department of Urban Affairs failed in part because some influential southerners in Congress viewed it as having racial/civil rights implications to which they were opposed. The Johnson administration met with greater success. However, that success came at a high price. The creation of the Department of Housing and Urban Development, with America's first black cabinet member as its head, came after several years of violent urban political activity by blacks and extensive damage to some of the nation's largest cities. The passage of the Demonstration Cities Act (hereafter referred to by the more common name of Model Cities) gives us an opportunity to see the policy system in action.

MODEL CITIES: THE POLICY PROCESS IN ACTION

The Model Cities program was introduced as three separate bills in the House of Representatives. The bills were referred to the House Committee on Banking and Currency chaired by Wright Patman (D-Texas). Patman was a staunch supporter of the legislation. And, it is useful to indicate that Patman was also a longtime friend of President Johnson. From the president's point of view it made good political sense to have potentially controversial legislation considered not only by a supporter but also by a friend. That legislation of this type should be handled by the Committee on Banking and Currency may at first appear strange. However, in addition to its jurisdiction over the general area of banking and currency, and the Federal Reserve system, Patman's committee also oversaw matters of housing and home finance and urban redevelopment. Although the president and his Task Force conceived of the Model Cities program as something new, in terms of committee perceptions it was a variation of the urban renewal legislation with which members were familiar. As such, it was likely that they would not think of the proposed legislation along the lines of novelty that its creators intended.[28]

The Model Cities legislation authorized participating cities the full array of available grants and aid in the fields of housing, urban renewal, transportation, welfare, economic opportunity, and related programs. In addition, the bill provided special grants amounting to 80 percent of the nonfederal cost of the programs included in the demonstration. It also included programs currently being financed under existing federal grant-in-aid programs and those proposed initially as part of the demonstration.

A second bill provided collateral programs for urban development. This was not a major concern in the legislation submitted by the president. The third and final bill authorized federal assistance to finance and equip facilities for group medical and dental practices. It too was a minor segment of the Model Cities program.[29]

The three bills attracted a variety of supporters and opponents. The testimony of the groups' spokesmen indicated their concerns; but it also furnished a basis for evaluating their roles and influence in the final legislative product.

The first individual to testify before the committee was Dr. Robert E. Weaver, later to become secretary of Housing and Urban Development and the first black to hold a cabinet post. He impressed upon the committee members the importance of the legislation in solving the physical, social, and economic problems confronting the nation's central cities. Weaver's comments went directly to the point of community involvement when he discussed the proposed eligibility criteria. Blight alone was insufficient. In addition to urban blight, the applicant would also be required to demonstrate that local officials and residents were able to work constructively together. Weaver stated:

> The areas (must be) willing and able to bring together the public and private bodies whose joint action is necessary to solve their problems—willing to commit fully their energies and resources—willing to undertake actions which will have widespread and profound effects on the physical and social structures of the city.[30]

Unlike the Community Action Programs (CAP) of OEO which emphasized a dominant role for the "grassroots," the Model Cities programs sought to create a less abrasive relationship between the lay public and elected officials.

Weaver also indicated that federal control would be limited; "this will be a local program."[31] He was attempting to gain the support of legislators and interest groups who had criticized the red tape in the administration of the poverty programs. Weaver continued, "All assistance under the program would be channelled into a demonstration agency established or designated by the local governing body to administer the program."[32] Despite the emphasis placed on local initiative, Weaver also indicated the likely nature of federal involvement. Undoubtedly, Weaver was aware of congressional doubts about urban officials' competence in handling large sums of money. He proposed that a federal coordinator be designated for each approved area; this federal coordinator's function would be to provide liaison and coordination services.

Weaver was followed by spokesmen from the U.S. Conference of Mayors. The support of this body is easy to understand. Cities were in financial trouble and physically deteriorating because the suburban areas were attracting the commercial enterprises, the financially stable families, and other taxable entities. Their livelihoods and the viability of their cities depended upon how well they were able to deal with the complex problems. H.J. Addonizio, mayor of Newark, endorsed the legislation on behalf of the U.S. Conference of Mayors.[33] The mayors strongly supported the idea of federal coordinators to provide liaison services in each approved project area. Surprisingly, however, they also urged that coordination be broadened by designating an assistant secretary or an assistant director for participating agencies. Mayor Addonizio was joined by several more colleagues before the committee in support of the proposed legislation. Among these were Mayors John Lindsay of New York City, Richard Daley of Chicago, and Jerome Cavanaugh of Detroit.[34]

Organized labor, of course, had supported the Model Cities proposal from its inception as a result of Reuther's active involvement. Labor also had a self-interest in the program because it would increase the number of jobs available. The legislation called for an enormous amount of construction. Boris Shiskin, secretary of the AFL-CIO housing subcommittee, termed the bills "an important and auspicious step in the right direction."[35] But, he reminded the committee that the anticipated funding level was insufficient to deal adequately with the urban blight and the associated social and economic problems confronting the urban poor.[36]

Additional interest group support came from several groups directly involved in the nation's urban areas. The organizations and their representatives included the executive director of the metropolitan Atlanta region of the National Association of Housing and Redevelopment Officials; the president of the National Association of Home Builders; the president of the National Housing Conference; and the president of the National Farmers Union.[37] Each of these representatives tried to impress upon the committee the importance of the legislation. They argued that the legislation would greatly decrease the misery of the urban areas and their people.

Technical experts also testified in support of the program. Harold Wise, chairman of the national legislative committee of the American Institute of Planners (AIP), strongly endorsed the Model Cities proposals but criticized their presentation as separate bills. He contended that the Demonstration Cities Act (H.R. 12341) and the Urban Development Act (H.R. 12939) could serve the needs of urban areas more adequately if they were consolidated under the same act. Wise felt that the administration was proposing two separate types of programs for two different constituencies—urban areas and growing suburban areas. Another to testify was Morris Ketchum, Jr., president of the American Institute of Architects (AIA), who endorsed the "New Towns Provision." He argued very strongly for specifying high standards for design technology, including cost reduction techniques.

Both the AIP and AIA saw potential gains for members of their respective professions. The architects naturally were interested in the jobs the program might provide. But they also saw Model Cities, as an opportunity to introduce new concepts in housing design and construction techniques. The planners meanwhile saw the requirement for comprehensive planning as a vehicle that would put into practice their belief in integrated social and physical planning. And, there was a less obvious dividend for the planners. They were a smaller and less prestigious group than the architects. The possibility of acquiring increased stature and influence through work in Model Cities programs was a consideration.

Although the administration had drawn the legislation in such a way as to gain support from several parts of the political spectrum, there was opposition. Indeed, some legislators believed that their constituents might sustain a loss if the legislation were to pass. For these critics of Model Cities it was essential for Congress to anticipate the "horrible" effects of the legislation. One of these groups was the National Association of Real Estate Boards (NAREB). This association has had a reputation for opposing the liberal viewpoint in housing and urban renewal matters. It had consistently opposed earlier housing acts and it opposed Model Cities.[38] The realtors argued that the proposal for another federal attempt would further reduce local initiative. In their view the proponents of the legislation should

> stop attempting to spoon feed the Congress and the [American] people in the area of federal assistance to whole communities. We should recognize that a gap in local initiative cannot be bridged by money alone.[39]

And, with reference to traditional conservative thinking, the NAREB contended that the legislation was an "unwarranted intrusion of Government in the control of the future use of land . . . [which] would lead ultimately to the federalization of the nation's communities."[40]

The NAREB opposition was not based entirely upon its fear of federal domination, the unwise use of land, and the cities' lack of initiative to do their jobs. Its position also reflected a belief that its members might lose economically because of the federally sponsored housing.

James F. Steiners, spokesman for the Chambers of Commerce of the United States, opposed the measures on similar grounds. He also argued that the proponents of the program were assuming without real proof that the cities did not have adequate resources to solve their own problems. He was harshly critical of the liaison function as well. He foresaw a possibility that the federal coordinator would become a "commissar or czar who would possess vaguely defined powers."[41]

That part of the legislation which provided for federal monies to finance and equip facilities for group medical and dental practice in blighted areas was strongly opposed by the American Medical Association and the American Dental Association. The doctors argued that the proposal was a weapon to put the individual practitioners out of business. Arguments which suggested that the urban poor received poor health and dental care were given only limited attention.

However, opposition to the Model Cities legislation was not that substantial. Nor were the arguments that the realtors and doctors presented persuasive to the committee members. And, in any case, the NAREB position was weakened by the enthusiastic participation of that industry in other federally assisted housing and urban renewal efforts. As for the medical profession, their almost traditional fears of socialized medicine as well as their expected opposing views carried little weight. The Committee on Banking and Currency was not studying medical legislation; it was considering problems of urban blight. It was an easy matter for the members of the committee to focus their attention on questions of urban renewal and to downplay the possible implications for socialized health and dental services.[42] The Model Cities bill was accepted by Congress on the president's terms with two exceptions: The federal coordinator was eliminated and the funding level was reduced.

It is useful, then, to ask one final question about policy making. Who benefits? But merely asking that question implies a larger number of related queries. One would like to know how a particular group or class of beneficiaries benefited from governmental actions. Answers to such questions are difficult to find, as we noted above. But there is usually some evidence available from which those who make such inquiries can develop reasonable inferences. The Model Cities program gives us an illustration of this point.

WHO BENEFITED?

Model Cities was expected to relieve the conditions of the urban poor, that is, blacks. It was purported to have been designed to enhance the quality of life within the central cities of metropolitan America. In fact, this was the first national program whose purpose was to deal with the social, economic, and health needs of the urban poor. It was the program that President Johnson viewed as giving meaning to the lives of the urban poor. But what has really been the impact of the Model Cities program on the lives of the urban poor? Has it enhanced the quality of life in the center cities? Or has it worked toward strengthening the local government—that is, the mayor's position as a decision maker?

The studies of the center city areas since the implementation of the Model Cities have produced discouraging findings. They revealed that the urban poor are still living under conditions that were prevalent before the enactment of Model Cities.[43] A study conducted by the National Urban Coalition discovered that the conditions reported in the Kerner Commission Report were still present in the urban areas. The study indicated that the quality of life had not been improved in the cities investigated. In fact, the study revealed that the quality of life had really changed for the worse: (1) Housing is still the national scandal it was then; (2) the rates of crime, unemployment, disease and heroin addiction are higher; (3) welfare rolls are larger; and (4) relations between minority communities and the police are just as hostile. One change for the better has been the more positive attitude blacks and the urban poor gained of themselves. This is not necessarily connected with Model Cities.[44] Some community activists and planners, however, criticized what they saw as the most detrimental aspects of the program: (1) breaking up ethnic neighborhoods—destroying a sense of community and (2) the forced relocation of the urban poor without adequate provisions for new housing.[45] Similar criticisms were also made of the urban renewal programs that had preceded Model Cities by more than a decade. There was no effective answer to these criticisms.

Some observers have taken the view that the federal government simply cannot correct some of the urban problems which plague American life.[46] And not all those who take this position can be dismissed as conservatives. The politically active among urban blacks have increasingly blamed the government for the failures (real and imagined) of programs like Model Cities. However, passage of a bill by Congress does not end the policy process. Indeed, as we shall see in the following section, the congressional action sets in motion a wide range of activities by other parts of government.

SECONDARY OUTCOME: ADMINISTRATION AND IMPACT

The impact of legislation approved by Congress can be viewed in terms of the following questions:

1. Does the act actually allocate or reallocate resources to certain groups or individuals?
2. If so, who gets what benefits and who pays what costs?
3. Does the act place regulations on individuals or groups?

4. If so, who is to enforce these regulations? With what sanctions?
5. Does the bill delegate authority to make allocations or regulations? If so, to whom?

Unless a policy is self-executing, or the guidelines as to "who gets how much of what" are unusually clear and explicit, there will be some administrative discretion in implementation. To discover the actual impact that a program has on a target population or problem area, several features of administration should be considered.

First, who is given administrative authority? An old-line agency, one that has been upgraded for the task, or a newly created structure? For both the War on Poverty and Model Cities programs, new agencies were developed: the Office of Economic Opportunity (OEO) for the former and a new department, Housing and Urban Development, for the latter.[47] The creation of new agencies may arouse jealousies in the older agencies which heretofore have had responsibility in the particular policy area. For OEO and Model Cities this problem was compounded by the emergence of interagency conflict around President Johnson's desire that federal efforts in the cities be coordinated. This meshing of sometimes competing energies and interests does not just happen; it has to be made to happen. And if the president or someone with his proxy isn't there to see it through, coordination is unlikely to become fact.

Second, if a new administration structure is created, will it be visible and thus vulnerable to political attacks?[48] If so, can such attacks affect the allocation or regulatory function? The staff of a new administration is also important: recruitment patterns, political ties, past experience in similar policy areas, and possible links to clientele groups must be considered in the selection process.

Third, changes in administrative practices and orientations over time greatly affect the impact of policy. The concept of life cycles of regulatory commissions is one important pattern to be considered. This phenomenon might well apply to structures created to deal with areas such as civil rights, environmental protection, and product safety. Agencies can be and are "captured" by clientele groups, even by those that they are supposed to regulate. In fact, administrator and client can become so closely tied that it is often difficult to distinguish precisely who is making administrative decisions.[49]

Fourth, just as it is possible for an agency to be "captured" by its clientele, so too can a similar "capture" be made by a legislator whose committee works in that particular functional area. The relationships developed between administrators and members of Congress can affect future funding and thus lead to expansion or reduction of program benefits and/or program scope.[50]

Fifth, if administrative structures have discretion in establishing program guidelines, setting standards of eligibility for program participation or approving funding of projects at the state and local levels, what criteria are used for making such decisions? It is quite possible that such discretion can lead to different results from those envisioned by sponsors and supporters of original legislation. Yet many such decisions go unchallenged. This may well be because many congressional coalitions can be built only for statements of general intent and would break down if specific allocations were involved.

Sixth, administrative functions may be diffused through various levels of bureaucratic structures. Until very recently, all the categorical assistance programs were administered in part at the federal level and in part at the local or county level. Such dispersion of administrative discretion created hundreds of welfare "systems." Under such circumstances, the impact of a "national" policy is difficult to discern or measure.

RESPONSE, FEEDBACK, AND FUTURE PROSPECTS

This phase of the policy process theoretically leads back to the beginning of the cycle, assuming first that adoption of a policy has some kind of impact and second that someone notices it. Responses ideally should come from those persons or groups affected by a specific program. However, if those targets are unorganized and without access to political actors or public attention, their pleasure or displeasure with program results may be unnoticed. While young men from low-income families were being drafted in greater proportions and receiving fewer deferments than youths of higher socioeconomic status, there was no available feedback route for complaints about this feature of the Selective Service System.[51] However, when large numbers of middle- and upper-class youths began attacking the draft as part of the Vietnam War protests, this response to an established policy was attended to by both political actors and the national media.

Since few national programs are systematically evaluated in terms of how much change is produced in target populations or whether specific governmental actions actually "solve problems," it seems that much of the content of response is quite subjective in nature. At best, praise or disappointment will often be registered by leaders, real or self-appointed, of target groups. Nevertheless, how leaders with ties to policy actors respond can affect the future of a given policy. Equally important can be the response of persons or groups affected by an unplanned consequence of a program. The reaction to community action registered by local elected officials was important in modifying OEO programs and activities, such as the Green Amendments of 1966 (former Representative Edith Green, (D-Oregon) which gave elected officials a stronger voice in the use of these federal funds. In turn, these modifications were made part of the Model Cities legislation, as we have seen.

Because many programs require the creation of extensive administrative networks, they may also create new constituent and clientele groups with an interest in program maintenance. While part of their feedback may entail suggestions for improvement, it is also safe to predict that their overall response will be positive. Thus policies that create a significant number of administrative units more or less create support groups for the future. We should also note the importance to future modifications, increments, or terminations of specific policies to the responses of original sponsors, supporters and opponents.

Of course, presidents, legislators, and even "experts," like other mortals, often see what they want to see. They too can be seduced by symbolic assurances. However, if association with a certain policy has aided one of these actors politically, it is likely that the actor will wish to continue this association if expansion or modification appears promising. If opponents feel that the program has not produced the dire consequence they predicted, or if their reference groups no longer care very much about the issue, they may accept incremental expansion.

One of the more troublesome situations in the policy process stems from the recognition by participants in the process that they have sponsored and carried through programs which are not fulfilling their promises. This seems to be the current dilemma of many critics concerning many of our current social programs. While negative responses and feedback are easy to find, new policy approaches to chronic problems are slow to emerge. And, we recognize that radical proposals are not likely to be accepted quickly, though they may be at some future time. Perhaps this is simply another indication that there are time lags at all points in the policy process. Or perhaps it substantiates the notion that there is "periodicity" to policy actions which expand the role of government.[52]

In the meantime, the higher levels of political participation among blacks do imply that the feedback mechanisms of the policy system will contain more politically relevant information from that section of the population. But the pervasive and persistent levels of low educational attainment in most black communities will continue to constrain the effectiveness of African Americans in the policy process, for black legislators, like their white colleagues, need technical and expert information on policy questions. The educational inequalities, which we discussed in an earlier chapter, compounded by the absence of viable alternative resources distributed among black citizens, impose limits upon the ability of black legislators to compete in forming the policy agenda. The inability of blacks to affect the policy process significantly is further evidence of their weakness in the nation's political life. Admittedly, corrective actions to overcome these deficiencies will take time, but the question is how much time.[53]

Topics for Discussion

1. Do you think that a black candidate can marshal the kinds of resources and support needed to become president? Discuss thoroughly, indicating a familiarity with the various considerations involved in the presidential nominating process and the presidential election.

2. Suppose you were asked by a black interest group to suggest concrete ways to increase black political influence in the policy-making process. What would you suggest? Why?

3. The text states that "black advances into the mainstream of presidential politics have given them new vantage points from which to view the workings of the presidency." Discuss the meaning and implications of this statement for black politics.

Suggested Readings

Allensworth, Donald. *Public Administration: The Execution of Public Policy*. Philadelphia: Lippincott, 1973.
A study of the problems of implementing congressional legislation.

Barnett, Marguerite R., and James Hefner. *Public Policy for the Black Community: Strategies and Perspectives*. Port Washington, NY: Alfred Publishing, 1976.
Analyzes various options through which the black community can attain its policy options in the political system.

Berger, Raoul. *Impeachment: The Constitutional Problems*. Cambridge, MA: Harvard University Press, 1973.
An historical and legal analysis of the constitutional provision relating to impeachment.

Brauer, Carl M. *John F. Kennedy and the Second Reconstruction*. New York: Columbia University Press, 1977.
Discusses Kennedy's role and attempts to overcome racial barriers in American life.

Braybrooke, David, and Charles Lindblom. *A Strategy of Decision*. New York: Free Press, 1970.
The classic formulation of the idea of incremental decision processes in government.

Blumenthal, Richard. "The Bureaucracy: Antipoverty and the Community Action Program." In Allen P. Sindler, ed., *American Political Institutions and Public Policy: Five Contemporary Studies*. Boston: Little, Brown, 1969.
A study of the infighting between agencies over administration of the resources of the Community Action Program.

Clausen, Aage. *How Congressmen Decide: A Policy Focus*. New York: St. Martin's Press, 1973.
A study of the forces and motives which influence the behavior of congressmen in the legislative role.

Cronin, Thomas E. *The State of the Presidency*, 2nd ed. Boston: Little, Brown, 1980.
Analyzes the role of the president in the modern era.

Crouse, Timothy. *The Boys on the Bus*. New York: Random House, 1973.
A description of the 1972 presidential campaign and election.

Goldman, Peter, and Tom Mathews. The Quest for the Presidency: The 1988 Campaign. New York: Simon & Schuster, 1989.
A detailed account of the dynamics of the 1988 presidential race.

Hargrove, Erwin C. *The Power of the Modern Presidency*. New York: Alfred A. Knopf, 1974.
A succinct discussion of the nature and powers of the presidential office.

Heclo, Hugh. *A Government of Strangers: Executive Politics in Washington*. Washington, DC: The Brookings Institution, 1977.
A penetrating study of the relations between political appointees (executives and high-level bureaucrats), and the implications of those relationships for change and continuity in government.

Kernell, Samuel. *Going Public*. Washington, DC: Congressional Quarterly Press, 1986.
A study of the presidential strategy of taking policies directly to the public.

Martin, Roscoe C. *Cities and the Federal System*. New York: Atherton, 1967.
An examination of the role of the federal government in the political and policy processes of local governments.

Moe, Ronald C., ed. *Congress and the President*. Pacific Palisades, CA: Goodyear Publishing Company, 1971.
A collection of readings that focus on various aspects of presidential-congressional relations.

Moynihan, Daniel P. *Maximum Feasible Misunderstanding*. New York: Free Press, 1969.
A description and analysis of the problems plaguing the implementation of public policy decisions during the Johnson years.

National Urban League, *The Urban League Review*. Washington,DC: National Urban League.
A semi-annual publication devoted to research and analysis of selected policy areas relevant to black Americans (e.g., housing, unemployment, energy).

Nelson, Michael, ed. *The Presidency and the Political System*, 2nd ed. Washington, DC: Congressional Quarterly Press, 1988.
A compilation of essays on the relationship between the presidency and the political system.

Neustadt, Richard. *Presidential Power*. New York: John Wiley & Sons, 1980.
An examination of the sources and limitations of the political power of the president.

Phillips, Kevin. *The Politics of Rich and Poor*. New York: Random House, 1990.
An analysis of the policies of Republican administrations benefiting the rich and harming the poor.

Pious, Richard M. *The American Presidency*. New York: Basic Books, 1979.
Describes the evolution of the American presidency and the various roles that the president must play in the American political system.

Polsby, Nelson and Aaron Wildavsky. *Presidential Elections*, 6th ed. New York: Charles Scribner's Sons, 1984.
A study of the strategies involved in presidential elections with an evaluation of possible reforms.

Pomper, Gerald M., et al. *The Election of 1992*. Chatham, NJ: Chatham House Publishers, 1993.
A collection of essays concerning various aspects of the 192 presidential and congressional elections.

Schneier, Edward V. and Bertram Gross. *Legislative Strategy Shaping Public Policy*. New York: St Martin's Press, 1993.
A penetrating empirical-theoretical analysis of congressional policy making.

Sindler, Allan, ed. *America in the Seventies: Cases in Politics and Public Policy*. Boston: Little, Brown, 1977.
Case studies of various policy problems in the 1970s.

Sundquist, James. *Politics and Policy*. Washington, DC: Brookings Institution, 1968.

A comparative study of the interplay between congressional and executive politics and policy formulation during the Eisenhower, Kennedy, and Johnson administrations.

Thomas, Norman C., ed. *The Presidency in Contemporary Context*. New York: Dodd, Mead and Co., 1975.
A collection of readings that view the presidency in various contexts.

Watson, Richard. *The Presidential Contest*, 3rd ed. Washington, DC: Congressional Quarterly Press, 1988.
A discussion of the development and dynamics of contests involving presidential nominations and presidential elections.

Wildavsky, Aaron B. *The New Politics of the Budgetary Process*. Glenview, IL: Scott, Foresman & Company, 1988.
An excellent analysis of budget making and its policy implications.

Notes

* Copyright 1990 by The Free Press. Reprinted by permission of The Free Press; p. 35.

† Reprinted by permission of the Yale Law Journal Company and Fred B. Rothman & Company from *The Yale Law Journal*, vol. 79, p. 1081.

1. James W. Davis, Jr., *An Introduction to Public Administration* (New York: Free Press, 1974), p. 21. Of course, literature on the presidency is voluminous. Among the most useful are Richard Neustadt, *Presidential Power* (New York: John Wiley, 1964); Clinton Rossiter, *The American Presidency* (New York: Harcourt Brace Jovanovich, Inc., 1964); Nelson Polsby and Aaron Wildavsky, *Presidential Elections*, 2nd ed. (New York: Scribner's, 1968); and Nelson Polsby, *Congress and the Presidency*, 2nd ed. (Englewood Cliffs, NJ: Prentice Hall, Inc., 1971).
2. Louis W. Koenig, *The Chief Executive*, 3rd ed. (New York: Harcourt Brace Jovanovich, Inc., 1975), p. 35.
3. Candidates, of course, might qualify for funds under the Federal Elections Campaign Act of 1974.
4. In recent years a growing number of political scientists have sought to use the tools of psychology and psychiatry in an effort to explain presidential behavior. While interesting and suggestive of substantial insights, this literature is a source of considerable controversy. For the students (and others) who are interested in this area, we recommend Alan C. Elms, *Personality in Politics* (New York: Harcourt Brace Jovanovich, Inc., 1976) as a useful starting place. The Elms' work also contains a lengthy bibliography for those who might wish to pursue the issues in greater depth.
5. Emmett John Hughes, *The Living Presidency* (New York: Penguin, 1974), pp. 69-74.
6. On the impact of black votes see *The Black Vote: Election '76* (Washington, DC: Joint Center for Political Studies, August 1977). More general discussions of the 1976 campaign can be found in Gerald Pomper, *The Election of 1976: Reports and Interpretations* (New York: David McKay, 1977) and Jules Witcover, *Marathon: The Pursuit of the Presidency 1972-1976 (New York: Viking, 1977). Witcover's book is especially useful for its treatment of the campaigns for election by the two major parties.*
7. Ibid., p. 306.
8. Pomper, *The Election of 1976*, pp. 60-61.

9. However, some critics noted that filling only two cabinet positions with blacks was hardly a sufficient return for their efforts on Carter's behalf. In 1979 Harris was transferred from HUD to HEW, and Ambassador Young resigned his position. For more on Young's resignation, see Chapter 9.
10. See generally Samuel Kernell, *Going Public* (Washington, DC: Congressional Quarterly Press, 1986) esp. pp. 115-117.
11. Congressional Quarterly, *CQ Guide to Current American Government* (Washington, DC: Congressional Quarterly Press, 1981), p. 14.
12. Maureen Dowd, "Bush Says the Dream of Dr. King Will Be a Vision for His Tenure," *The New York Times*, January 17, 1989, p.1.
13. For an overall detailed analysis of the 1992 presidential elections along with commentary on the congressional elections see Gerald Pomper et al., *The Election of 1992: Reports and Interpretations* (Chatham, NJ: The Chatham House Publishers, 1993).
14. There are a number of recent works available on the presidency. We suggest that an interested student should begin with Richard E. Neustadt, *Presidential Power*. Two readers providing a broad sampling of literature are Michael Nelson, ed., *The Presidency and the Political System* (Washington, DC: Congressional Quarterly Press, 1988), and George C. Edwards III, Steven A. Shull, and Norman C. Thomas, eds., *The Presidency and Public Policy Making* (Pittsburgh, PA: University of Pittsburgh Press, 1985).
15. These phases represent a combination of ten functional activities of policy making presented in Charles O. Jones, *An Introduction to the Study of Public Policy* (Belmont, CA: Duxbury Press, 1970).
16. Polsby, *Congress and the Presidency*, pp. 4-6.
17. Richard F. Fenno, *The Power of the Purse: Appropriations Politics in Congress* (Boston: Little, Brown, 1966), p. 421.
18. Quoted in George A. Davis and O. Fred Donaldson, *Blacks in the United States: A Geographic Perspective* (Boston: Houghton Mifflin, 1975), pp. 157-158.
19. See, for example, James David Barber, *The Presidential Character: Predicting Performance in the White House (Englewood Cliffs, NJ: Prentice Hall, Inc., 1985). A somewhat more accessible discussion of some of the points made here is contained in Nelson Polsby's "Our Quadrennial Drama," in his work Presidential Promises: Essays and Commentary on American Politics* (New York: Oxford University Press, 1974), pp. 165-171.
20. See, for example, David B. Truman, *The Governmental Process* (New York: Alfred A. Knopf, 1951); Robert H. Salisbury, *Interest Group Politics in America* (New York: Harper & Row, 1970); Earl B. Latham, *The Group Basis of Politics* (Ithaca, NY: Cornell University Press, 1952); and Robert A. Dahl, *A Preface to a Theory of Democracy* (Chicago: University of Chicago Press, 1956).
21. See Michael Lipsky, "Protest as a Political Resource," *APSR* 62, no.4 (December 1968), pp. 1144-1158.
22. Charles E. Lindblom discusses this feature of policy making in his essay, "The Science of Muddling Through," *Public Administration Review* 19 (Spring 1959), pp. 79-88. Additional details on incrementalism can be found in Aaron B. Wildavsky, *The New Politics of the Budgetary Process*, 3rd ed. (Glenview, IL: Scott, Foresman, & Company, 1988).
23. Judson L. James, "Federalism and the Model Cities Experiment," *Publius* (Spring 1972).
24. Ibid., p. 72.

25. Ibid., p. 73.
26. See Aage Clausen, *How Congressmen Decide: A Policy Focus* (New York: St. Martin's Press, 1978) and John Kingdon's *Congressmen's Voting Decisions*, 3rd ed. (New York: Harper & Row, 1989).
27. For a useful discussion of this failure, see Frederic N. Cleaveland, "Congress and Urban Problems," *Journal of Politics* 28, no.2 (May 1966), pp. 289-307; also see the insightful study by Roscoe C. Martin, *Cities and the Federal System* (New York: Atherton, 1967).
28. See Aaron Wildavsky, "The Analysis of Issue Contexts in the Study of Decision Making," *Journal of Politics* 24 (1962), pp. 717-732, for a perceptive discussion of the influence of issue contexts and settings on the formation of public policy.
29. U.S. Congress, House Committee on Banking and Currency, *Congressional Quarterly*, no. 9 (1966), p. 463.
30. Ibid., p. 493.
31. Ibid., p. 494.
32. Ibid., p. 495.
33. Addonizio was later defeated in his bid for reelection by Kenneth Gibson, the first black mayor to emerge in the wake of the mid-1960s urban violence. In 1987, Gibson was defeated by Sharpe James, a black candidate. For a useful discussion of lobbying by mayors and other government officials, see Donald H. Haider, *When Governments Come to Washington: Governors, Mayors, and Intergovernmental Lobbying* (New York: Free Press, 1974).
34. U.S. Congress, House Committee on Banking and Currency, *Congressional Quarterly*, no. 10 (1966), p. 563.
35. Ibid.
36. Ibid., p. 564.
37. Ibid.
38. Ibid.
39. Ibid., no. 11, p. 605.
40. Ibid.
41. Ibid.
42. It should be stated, however, that similar arguments by the medical profession were successfully used in opposing earlier efforts to develop a national health care plan. Data from Survey Research Center election surveys for 1956-1971 suggest that public support for such a plan was at a consistently high level over this 15-year period. Cf. Richard E. Dawson, *Public Opinion and Contemporary Disarray* (New York: Harper & Row, 1974). More recent evidence of the medical profession's effectiveness can be found in an examination of the defeat of President Carter's "hospital cost containment" proposals of 1979.
43. See National Survey of Housing Abandonment, conducted by Center for Community Change, National Urban League, April 1971; George J. Washnis, "An Overview of the Program's Progress," *Model Cities Service Center Bulletin* 2, no. 9 (June 1971); and National Urban Coalition, "State of the Cities," 1972.
44. "State of the Cities."
45. Ibid., p. 9.
46. See, for example, Edward Banfield, *The Unheavenly City* (Boston: Little, Brown, 1971). A different perspective on many of these issues can be found in the Advisory Commission on Intergovernmental Relations report, *City Financial*

Emergencies, The Intergovernmental Dimension (Washington, DC: Government Printing Office, 1973).

47. Actually, the Department of Housing and Urban Development was simply given this function. It had been created in the administration of former President John F. Kennedy. Model Cities was its first "new" activity.
48. Matthew Holden has suggested that political attacks may not all be of a partisan type. Interagency rivalries may also lead to conflicts which he calls "imperialism;" see his essay, "Imperialism in Bureaucracy," *APSR* 60 (December 1966), pp. 943-951.
49. See Francis E. Rourke, *Bureaucracy, Politics and Public Policy* (Boston: Little, Brown, 1969), pp. 11-24, and Grant McConnell, *Private Power and American Democracy* (New York: Albert A. Knopf, 1966). See also Philip Selznick, *TVA and the Grass Roots* (New York: Harper & Row, 1966). For those who think that pressure politics is engaged in only by big corporations, a look at the actions of professional social service organizations should prove instructive. See, for example, Gilbert Steiner, *The Children's Cause* (Washington, DC: The Brookings Institution, 1976).
50. For a discussion of this phenomenon, see Wildavsky, *The New Politics.*
51. See James W. Davis and Kenneth M. Dolbeare, *Little Groups of Neighbors: The Selective Service System* (Chicago: Markham Publishing Company, 1968).
52. See James Sundquist, *Politics and Policy* (Washington, DC: The Brookings Institution, 1968). For a detailed examination of the problems involved in presidential-agency relationships and program management techniques, see Richard Rose, *Managing Presidential Objectives* (New York: The Free Press, 1976).
53. One study specifically addresses these weaknesses of blacks; see Harold L. Wolman, Norman C. Thomas, "Black Interests, Black Groups and Black Influence in the Federal Policy Process: The Cases of Housing and Education," *Journal of Politics* 32 (1970), pp. 875-897.

CHAPTER 11

THE AUTHORS SPEAK OUT: SOME PERSPECTIVES AND INTERPRETATIONS

In the past ten chapters we have attempted to offer a systemic and structural analysis of how African Americans fare in the political system. This analysis especially points up the nature and scope of problems that confront blacks; provides commentary on particular strategies used to overcome these problems; and offers a systematic description of the nature, capacity, and limitations of the role of governing institutions—primarily at the national level—to deal with such matters.

In this concluding chapter, we have decided to depart from the traditional kind of summary and conclusions that might be drawn and that usually end such volumes. Rather, this chapter offers perspectives and interpretations concerning how we as scholars and as African Americans view and interpret particular issues and developments. In this way we hope to (1) illuminate continuing and current problems that are or have been both important and highly visible and (2) stimulate discussion and argument about matters that might well affect the future course of our overall politics and society.

To do this most effectively, each of the authors offers his own perspectives and interpretations on topics of his own choosing. Three of the contributions or essays concern problems of a more general and enduring nature, for example, problems of black leadership; while the other three discuss more topical and recent developments, pointing out both their immediate and long-range implications, for example, the Clarence Thomas confirmation battle.

There has been no attempt to sort out similarities, differences, or contradictions that might exist within or between and among the various essays or contributions. Nor has there been a focused and systematic attempt in these essays, in contrast to materials in earlier chapters, to convey in a rather orderly and organized manner basic facts and information about a range of fundamental problems and issues as they relate to how blacks fare in the American political system. Each contribution stands on its own and may be used by students and others as a way to utilize information and insights drawn from earlier chapters in assessing the views presented or in formulating alternative interpretations and perspectives of their own.

We are hopeful that the contributions will prove interesting and stimulate discussion and debate. The essay on "Deracialization, Routinization, and the Depreciation of Black Political Participation," for example, views deracialization as an argument to ignore issues of especial importance to African Americans and therefore conceptualizes deracialized politics as a politics for the continued domination of black people. "The Black Underclass" essay argues that the black underclass is not a new development and that there has always been a significant number of African Americans who, because of systemic conditions, have no realistic chances of upward mobility. The essay on "Black Leadership and the Continuing Struggle for Racial Justice" suggests that contemporary black leadership is increasingly irrelevant as it fails to address the economic problems of the black rank-and-file.

The other three essays focus on more discrete events and occurrences of high salience and visibility. One essay uses the highly charged controversy over the confirmation of Justice Clarence Thomas as a way to illuminate "The Continuing Paucity of Black Political Influence." Another essay views "Rodney King and Los Angeles" as yet "another defining opportunity" to deal with underlying causes of urban unrest and violence and points out that these "lessons" of history both inform and warn us about the nature and operation of the American political system. The last essay on "Black Americans and the 1992 Presidential Election" suggests that blacks and others should temper the excitement and euphoria that accompanied the election of President Clinton by "matching their hope with reality." The essay argues that the nature of Clinton's overall campaign and election, especially when viewed in terms of more enduring systemic factors and structures, serves to inhibit and impede the kind of fundamental change needed to deal with major problems that continue to hurt blacks disproportionately.

DERACIALIZATION, ROUTINIZATION, AND THE DEPRECIATION OF BLACK POLITICAL PARTICIPATION

If the American political system can be viewed as a game, it is safe to say that the objectives of the game and the rules through which they are to be realized have not served the interests of African Americans. Indeed, these rules grounded in the liberal philosophy and adulterated by the ideology of white supremacy were instrumental in creating a largely impoverished and powerless black community. As discussed throughout this text, black political participation was circumscribed by a variety of legal and quasi-legal devices and reinforced by economic intimidation and terror. However as the twenty-first century approaches, all of these impediments have been removed. Black political participation at every level, national, state and local and in every geographical region is now taken for granted. Blacks hold mayorships in a disproportionately large number of major cities, constitute a critical mass in the U.S. House of Representatives and in several state legislatures, and hold a small but growing number of statewide elective offices. Black political participation has become routinized, but it has become routinized in the ongoing game of American politics. The rules of the game and the fundamental priorities of the game have not changed significantly.

The routinization of black political participation, however, has come at a time when the country is becoming more conservative and less willing to support race-specific initiatives designed to correct historically driven inequities between the two races. Under these circumstances black political actors are faced with the daunting task of trying to consolidate their newly achieved positions in the system while at the same time trying to change the system itself. Deracialization and crossover appeals have been suggested as strategies for pursuing these dual objectives.

Deracialization refers to the practice of blacks articulating political demands in terms that are not racially specific so that they appeal to a broader group and presumably do not alienate those who are predisposed to oppose black efforts. Crossover appeal, on the other hand, refers to the ability of black officials to attract and cultivate white voter support with the hope of becoming politically prominent in majority white electoral districts.

The strategies have proven to be useful for integrating blacks into the system and consolidating their position as equal participants. The election of Douglas Wilder as governor of Virginia and Gary Franks as a congressman from a preponderantly white Connecticut congressional district and the appointment of Colin Powell as chairman of the Joint Chiefs of Staff and Ronald Brown as chair of the national democratic party are cases in point.

However, while deracialization and crossover appeal may be helpful in integrating black political actors in the political system, they may run counter to efforts to change the system. If that turns out to be the case, and we think that such an outcome is highly likely, routinization of black political participation driven by deracialization and crossover appeals may do little to change the unequal position of blacks in the United States. To the contrary it may serve to reinforce the legitimacy of the very structures and practices which give rise to the unequal socioeconomic conditions that characterize black life in America.

To defend our speculations and projections, brief comments about the nature of the game and the process through which black political participation has become routinized are in order.

As is widely known, if not so widely discussed, the United States began quite unapologetically as a class-based inegalitarian society. As conveyed by the *Federalist* essays, the founding fathers argued that unfettered majority rule would threaten the privileged position of the propertied classes and they established a political system with that in mind. The vote was limited for the most part to property-holding white men, and the selection of the principal officials, the president, U.S. senators, and members of the judiciary was insulated from mass influence. Inequality of wealth and income was rampant and the political system established in 1789 was carefully crafted to ensure that it remained so. Since that time the American people have struggled to bring about political democracy and a more egalitarian economic order. The struggle for black political participation has been a key element in the broader societal quest.

Passage of the Voting Rights Act of 1965 and subsequent extensions marked the culmination of the struggle for black political participation and for political democracy. Presently, there are more than 7,500 black elected officials who hold a wide variety of positions.

However, the struggle for black political participation was not merely a struggle for inclusion. Inclusion was not considered to be an end but rather a means toward an end. Inclusion was expected to be a means through which desired changes in the socioeconomic conditions of blacks could be stimulated. Black political participation was expected ultimately to have a salutary effect on the black-to-white ratio of factors such as unemployment, family income, labor force participation rates, and other indices of well-being. To the extent that discrepancies between blacks and whites on such indices were systemic outcomes, black participation was seen as a means through which the system could be changed for the better. As noted in chapter 4, this has not happened. Black political participation has become routinized in more of a *system supporting* than a *system challenging* fashion.

To be sure many of the black officials elected in the past two decades were viewed as outsiders challenging the existing order, but the challenges they posed were more to the irrational remnants of the era of state-sanctioned racial discrimination than to the fundamental political, social, and economic practices which create and maintain black subordination in a formally integrated social order.

For example, black officials successfully challenged discriminatory electoral systems and apportionment schemes, secured black appointments to critical administrative and regulator positions, garnered more equitable access to government contracts, reduced the volume of repressive police practices, and promoted a fairer distribution of government services. But all of this accrued within the constraints of the existing regime.

We do not mean to depreciate the significance of these achievements because they were and continue to be important milestones in the struggle for racial justice. Nevertheless, they did not require fundamental changes in the system. Nor did they challenge the material interests of major economic actors or social groups. They were the least threatening changes. The more difficult and threatening problems remain. They will be the foci of black political activity in the future.

In our view, problems such as constant double-digit unemployment, declining labor force participation rates, rampant poverty, inadequate schools, blighted crime-ridden neighborhoods, and related socioeconomic ills are systemic. That is to say that they arise when the various legitimate political and economic actors and institutions perform their roles in societally expected and societally sanctioned ways. For example the isolation of black dominated central city neighborhoods with their deteriorating housing stock, limited job opportunities, and declining tax base is not an accident of history. It evolves when self-interested bankers, developers, real estate brokers, landlords, and corporate directors do exactly what they are expected to do—act in their own self- interest. The problems of central city residents occur because of and not in spite of the system. Just as the good fortune of the privileged is a function of the dynamics of the system so too is the misery of the dispossessed. Black political participation is becoming a routinized element in this game. Let us elaborate.

On the national level, the Democratic party continues to be the primary political institution through which black interests are articulated and pursued, but among white voters the Democratic party is increasingly a minority party. As black political participation increased, white voters moved to the right and in considerable numbers out of the Democratic party, at least insofar as presidential elections are concerned.

Seeking to remain a viable political force, the national Democratic party has followed its erstwhile white supporters to the political right and, in order to remain within the mainstream of the Democratic party, black political operatives have also moved toward the conservative center, deemphasizing in the process race-specific interests.

Parallel with this shift within the Democratic party has been the rise of support for those who argue that blacks should renounce their loyalty to the liberal wing of the Democratic party and disperse themselves all across the ideological spectrum, from liberal to conservative.

If this advice is followed, black politics becomes not only deracialized but devoid of any particular ideological grounding. Black political participation would become narrowly practical. Capturing public offices and participating in the allocation of services and patronage as determined by existing priorities would become the end objective of black political participation.

As ideologically neutral participants, black political actors may position themselves at any point along the ideological continuum, from radical to reactionary, depending on its impact on their personal political fortunes. An erstwhile black liberal, for example, unable to secure nominations as a liberal, may seek office as a conservative. Indeed, inasmuch as white financial interest will likely continue to have disproportionate influence over electoral outcomes, black aspirants for public office may be inclined to run under whatever label white sponsors are willing to fund. The trend toward deracialization, crossover appeals, and the ideological dispersal of black political actors is already observable. As noted earlier, the only black elected to the governorship in modern times was nominated by the state convention and ran a deracialized campaign. In the 1990 off-year elections, a black conservative was elected from a preponderantly white congressional district in Connecticut and another one was the Republican nominee of Ohio.

In Texas, when the Democratic party nominated a popular black county judge for the state bench, the Republican party, fearing that this might give an edge to other Democratic candidates, quickly followed suit and nominated its own black candidate. The Bush administration raised the deracialization and crossover appeal to a special level in 1991 when it nominated Clarence Thomas, an arch-conservative black, for the U.S. Supreme Court.

There are those who hail deracialization, crossover appeal, and ideological diversification as signs of political maturity and progress. For several reasons, we remain skeptical. These stratagems could serve to diffuse the potential of black political participation as a vehicle for change. Not only might they diminish the weight which comes from numerical strength but they also give credibility and legitimacy to particular ideological positions and policy alternatives no matter what their objective impact on the conditions of the black masses. Moreover, the presence of blacks in the different ideological camps may serve to cancel out each other. Every major white ideological camp will have its black supporters and defenders. There will be no agenda that directly addresses the key issues and concerns of blacks, and no effective structures through which one could be forged. Rather the agenda will be as diverse as there are white factions to rally around. And as the Clarence Thomas episode showed, this could allow malevolent white factions to divide, confuse, and misuse black political actors for their own sinister purposes.

THE CONTINUING PAUCITY OF BLACK POLITICAL INFLUENCE: THE CLARENCE THOMAS APPOINTMENT

The continuing lack of black political clout and influence remains one of the most important yet largely unreported and painful lessons to come out of the raucous controversy over the appointment of Justice Clarence Thomas to the Supreme Court.

This paucity of black political clout and influence is reflected on many fronts and occurs in many subtle and not so subtle ways. It was certainly reflected in President Bush's successful effort to replace Justice Thurgood Marshall, an openly avowed liberal noted for fiercely championing individual and minority rights, with Judge Clarence Thomas, an openly avowed black conservative, whose well-known views on these key issues are clearly opposite those held by Marshall and most African Americans.

In filling the Marshall vacancy, the president faced the challenge of replacing more than a *racial* symbol; he was replacing a *national* symbol. He was replacing the *one* person whose service as director of the NAACP-LDF and as an associate justice on the Court itself steered the *entire* nation toward a new and more just legal order designed to overcome racism and sexism and accord equal justice to all persons.

Thus it was the height of irony and insult that President Bush would appoint an African American (Judge Thomas), whom the president called the "best man for the job," to help undo the historic new legal order which another African American (Marshall) has devoted his entire life to help fashion. Indeed empirical research suggests that based on his record, the new Justice Thomas is likely to spur the development and legitimation of policies that even now are eroding major pillars upon which this new legal order is grounded. In fact, as a relatively young person, Justice Thomas is likely to keep alive certain of Bush's key policy positions, particularly with respect to the role of government in protecting and affirming the rights of women, blacks, and minorities.

In this regard, it was indeed a cruel paradox, even hoax, to witness the sense of racial pride and achievement that flowed from the Thomas nomination as evidenced by the initial strong support Thomas received from the black community. That the Thomas appointment would radiate such racial pride and appeal is clearly due in large measure to the fact that so very *few* African Americans, regardless of party or ideology, hold such high positions in American politics and society. This is a telling commentary on and indictment of *both major parties* and the country generally.

Perhaps the most subtle yet revealing aspects of the Thomas confirmation battle were reflected in the widely acclaimed and dutifully reported role that heretofore largely unknown and unseen black professionals played in the hearings. To be sure, certain of these professionals did indeed exemplify ideological diversity within the black community.

The Second African American on the Court. Appointed by President Bush, the above photo shows Judge Clarence Thomas being sworn in as only the second African American to serve as a member of the U.S. Supreme Court *(AP/Wide World Photos)*

On closer analysis, however, even casual observation suggests that this portrayal of black professionals on nationwide television *conceals* much more than it *reveals* about life in black America. The picture does not begin to portray how race and color still inhibit and stifle the life chances of African Americans, *including black professionals.*

At bottom, this focus on black professionals in the Thomas hearings (as well as in the popular media) obscures and removes from view the dire conditions and problems that continue to characterize most black communities: for example, the fact that about one in every three blacks lives in poverty; that rampant unemployment runs twice as high among blacks than whites, reaching up in the 40 percentile for black youths; that grossly inadequate housing, education, and health systems continue to exist; that crime and drugs constitute serious internal problems; and that the debilitating effects of these and other problems on young black males render them an "endangered species." And we must re-emphasize the subtle and not so subtle forms of discrimination that still confront many of the very black professionals we so proudly extol as evidence of progress.

Moreover, it is misleading and inaccurate to suggest that the Thomas hearings and appointment reflect the "increasing diversity" among African Americans. As with all other groups, there has always been and remains diversity within the black community, but not a diversity over fundamental issues that sharply divide African Americans as much as the Thomas confirmation hearings might suggest. Indeed, empirical research and data show that an overwhelming majority of blacks continue to believe that government *should and must take the lead* in remedying particular problems that over a long tortuous history were officially and unofficially aided and abetted by government at all levels. And these problems continue to disproportionately hurt the life chances and opportunities of African Americans.

It is this question about the role of government that is at the heart of the debate between black conservatives, such as Clarence Thomas, and the more established black political leadership, such as the NAACP and the Congressional Black Caucus. Put very bluntly, there is little or no empirical evidence that there is *increasing* division or diversity in the black community over this fundamental "role of government" question. Rather, the image of this "increasing diversity" reflected in the Thomas hearings and the corresponding credibility and saliency given such developments by the White House, the media, and others, is undoubtedly *far more* than is warranted by the relatively still small minority of African Americans who support conservative candidates in elections (e.g., only about 11 percent of blacks supported Bush in the 1992 presidential race).

Even Judge Thomas's own use of the "Pin Point bootstrap to Supreme Court doorstep" strategy demonstrated vividly the still potent defining power of racism and sexism in our politics and society. Few could listen to Judge Thomas's powerful description of what it was like growing up black in the 1940s in Pin Point, Georgia, without sensing the strength of family and friends and the sheer drive and indomitable courage Thomas needed to overcome the inhuman and despicable roadblocks that stood in his way simply because of race and color.

But neither could one listen to detailed testimony of Judge Thomas concerning his subsequent public record and performance without drawing the belief based on Thomas's own words (e.g., speeches) and actions (as Equal Employment Opportunity Commission director), that no matter the obstacles remaining, the opportunity structure is such in America today that any person—regardless of race, color, or sex—can achieve his or her fullest potential. The Thomas "model" for success suggests that with hard work and purposive goals, one can make it through by pulling up by one's own "bootstraps."

Indeed, prior to and until sexual harassment charges were leveled against him by Professor Anita Hill, an emotional Judge Thomas proudly and repeatedly intoned that "only in America" could a person with his background and life experiences achieve such an enviable opportunity (appointment to the nation's highest court.) But when the judge himself ran into problems from the sexual harassment charges, he did not hesitate to play the "race card," decrying his decreasing confirmation chances as an attempt at "high-tech lynching" due to the racism reflected by the all-white Senate Judiciary Committee that set itself up as both "judge and executioner."

And not surprisingly, the judge's charges echoed sufficient resonance with today's realities and perceptions so as to effectively disarm and silence his chief opposition (e.g., the white Democratic liberals on the committee). At the same time, Thomas's charges of racism served to increase and intensify his support among others, including African Americans. Thus, when the chips were down the judge suddenly discarded the rhetoric of opportunity and ambition and angrily embraced the reality of continuing white racism.

By doing so, Judge Thomas invoked the protective cloak of love and unity that African Americans have long given to their own, especially when that person, whether in fact or by perception, is being hurt by the specter of white racism. This leads to the saddest and most ironic twist of all, that the judge himself—by words and actions throughout his entire public career—has helped to fashion a climate that increasingly discounts racism and sexism as major barriers to opportunity and attainment.

But whether or not Thomas's views are consistent with reality, this is nonetheless the kind of climate that most Americans want to embrace and believe about themselves and their country, since it squares with the symbols and values that are believed or perceived to be associated with constitutionalism and democratic government. And the embrace and belief are even more endearing and creditable when joined by one (Judge Thomas) from the very group that epitomizes most dramatically the nation's struggle for justice and equal opportunity for all.

On the other hand, Thomas's chief backer (President Bush) clearly showed that the "racial card" might also be used to stir fear among whites and hatred against blacks or those who support blacks too strongly. Indeed, who can forget the potentially explosive yet apparently effective "Willie Horton" strategy used by Republican candidate Bush in 1988 to discredit Democratic candidate Michael Dukakis and engender white support for the Republican-Bush cause.

The use of the "racial card" is disturbing on several grounds. Its use by both Thomas and President Bush effectively diverted attention from the major issue in both cases, that is, their respective qualifications for the offices being sought. Further, that both Thomas and Bush gained office suggests the duplicitous and effective use that might be made of the "racial card."

This not so subtle use of racial politics for short-term political gain holds serious long-term implications for our overall politics and society. Consider, for example, how the Thomas nomination was and is being used to forge division and discord among blacks, exemplified during the confirmation battle by open attempts of White House and Republican strategists to undermine and discredit the overwhelming majority not only of *duly* elected black political leaders (e.g., the Congressional Black Caucus) but also the established leadership and organizations in the black community generally (e.g., the NAACP and the black church as exemplified by the National Baptist Association).

That repeated and sundry public opinion polls indicated majority black support for Judge Thomas is *no answer* to this *serious external attack* on the credibility and legitimacy of black leadership generally. Would any other group or community, whose position was so strongly represented through its leadership, be subjected to such open and serious attack from the highest levels of government?

It is one thing that in the course of regular elections and established procedures *blacks themselves* (even with outside help) might wish to turn out such leaders. But it is quite another thing for external forces (the White House, Republicans, or Democrats), seeking short-term partisan gain, *to resort to racial politics to undermine and unravel the duly elected and established leadership fabric providing the fragile thread which holds both a community and democratic society generally together.*

Put very bluntly, sensitive and knowledgeable leaders in public and private sectors must recognize the especial fragility of this thread in a community that erupted in massive protests and disorders in the 1950s, 1960s, and in Los Angeles in the 1990s, the causes of which remain in many ways as stark today as during those times. Under the circumstances, all Americans—including Republicans and Democrats—should work to strengthen, not undermine, the credibility and legitimacy of black leaders who have opted to move from "protest to politics" in attempts to overcome their grievances through "the system." Clearly, of course, in keeping with democratic politics, those who suggest that today's black leaders are out of tune with today's black majority can test this assumption by offering their own candidacies (or slates) through regular elections and established procedures. Unless and until this happens, however, black officials, no less than other officials, deserve the *serious consideration and decent respect* that their *positions* as well as *system integrity and stability* demand.

Of course, an equally and even more serious implication of resorting to "racial politics" is that it spurs increased group division and discord, creating an environment that perpetuates and exacerbates such division and discord. It provides a "model" for those who wish to use the "racial card," no matter what. As mentioned previously, President Bush used it in his 1988 campaign; David Duke followed suit in his 1991 Louisiana gubernatorial campaign; and Patrick Buchanan invoked tinges of biases against particular groups in his 1992 campaign for the Republican presidential nomination.

What can be done? For one thing, it's time to move from a "politics of race and color" to a "politics of policy and performance." As the Thomas confirmation suggests, however, this can prove a very difficult transition given the understandably very strong symbolic ties of race and color. The extent to which this transition can be brought about, both within the black community and in forging meaningful coalitions with others, is directly related to the efficacy and resourcefulness of black leadership and the corresponding desire and commitment of whites to forego racial politics. It is also directly related to the necessity to increase the continued meager representation and influence of blacks and minorities in key socioeconomic sectors whose resources greatly affect the nature of our overall politics and society, for example, business, industry, and the corporate sector; law, medicine, and the professions; science, technology, and engineering; and education and the communications industry.

In the meantime, however, the Thomas confirmation battle and the dire conditions that continue to plague black communities around the nation suggest clearly the pressing need for African Americans to maximize the resources and influence they presently hold in the political sphere. Indeed, to move to a "politics of policy and performance," it is imperative to overcome patterns of withdrawal and alienation and take meaningful steps to increase patterns of registration and participation. And this could well pose a dilemma for established black leadership, especially black elected officials. It is one thing to articulate "civics lesson" theory that decries the evils of withdrawal and alienation and exude the benefits of voter registration and political participation.

But it is quite another thing to *actually work* to overcome citizen withdrawal and alienation and develop strategies to *actually increase* registration and participation. For doing so might require that black leaders forego traditional political wisdom to "play it safe" with known constituencies and rather exhibit uncommon courage and commitment to improve the overall influence and conditions in their communities. But the Thomas hearings, reflective as they were of the continuing pains of racism and sexism in our politics and society, suggest that black leaders might have to do even more.

Indeed, those leaders whose constituents are most directly affected must at least be willing to exhibit uncommon courage and unceasing commitment to causes for which some African Americans, and others as well, have in the past given their very lives. Put even more directly, to really attend to the very dire needs and concerns of their many black constituents and an increasing number of other Americans, it may well be that black leaders today, not unlike their predecessors in past years, might have to take stands and positions that could jeopardize their own futures.

The problems involved should and must be of the highest concern. For at bottom, in one form or another, these serious problems inhibit and stifle the freedom and life chances of *all* Americans, even while disproportionately affecting some more than others. Indeed, the continuing paucity of black political clout and influence, reflected so vividly in the Thomas hearings, is itself reflective of the continuing problems we face as a people and nation.

THE BLACK UNDERCLASS AS A SYSTEMIC PHENOMENON

The notion that the United States is now characterized by an emerging permanent black underclass has been commonplace in both the scholarly and popular literature since the mid-1970s. This "discovery" of the black underclass has been accompanied by foreboding predictions of the dire social consequences which may follow if ameliorative action is not undertaken. As of now, however, no significant national programs have been developed to address the problems of the black underclass. This is so, at least in my opinion, because the presence of the black underclass, to the extent that there is such an empirically identifiable group, is a logical, perhaps even necessary, outgrowth of the American political economy conditioned by white racism. Therefore any real solution would require fundamental changes in the American economic system. By that I mean, the presence of the black underclass is not a result of either the malfunctioning of the American economic system or the pathology of the members of the underclass. Rather, the presence of the underclass is the outcome of routine, systemically prescribed actions of major elements of the political economy.

One of the purposes of this essay, then, is to offer an explanation of the presence of the black underclass as a systemic phenomenon. A second is to assess the implications of the presence of the black underclass for the future of the struggle for racial equality in the United States.

II

We may begin by clarifying who or what is the black underclass and how it came into being before discussing how various constituent institutions of the political economy create and maintain the conditions which give rise to the black underclass. What is the black underclass? In both the popular and scholarly literature the concept remains a bit fuzzy and imprecise. It is generally understood to refer to a growing number of black persons who are uneducated, unskilled, unemployed and often unemployable, or employed in low-paying jobs, living in unrelieved poverty and immersed in a culture conditioned by these abject circumstances, with only limited chances or hope for upward mobility. Harsh as the foregoing recitation of conditions may sound, they are in no way novel or new developments among African Americans for they have dogged the black nation throughout American history. If these conditions have always characterized a sizable proportion of the black population, how do we explain the use of the term "emerging black underclass," implying, as it were, that it is a new phenomenon. The key to understanding this conceptualization is the use of the adjective permanent. The term is used to imply that members of the present underclass differ from earlier editions by the fact that the former and their progeny are destined to remain in the circumstances which characterize the underclass while members of the earlier underclass were more upwardly mobile. Simply put, the argument seems to be that the present underclass is intergenerational and self-perpetuating while its antecedents were more transient.

This perception of the permanent underclass is misleading, in my view, both historically and conceptually, and it leads to misguided and inappropriate public policies. It is misleading historically because it assumes that the underclass is a new development without providing any evidence, either scientific or anecdotal, to support the claim. It is conceptually flawed because by its narrow focus on the characteristics of the members of the underclass, it obscures the symmetrical relationship between the rise of the conditions which entrap the underclass and the routine operations of basic societal forces.

Rather than conceptualizing the current black underclass as a new development, it may be more historically accurate and theoretically insightful to view it as a contemporary manifestation of a long existing problem. I suggest this because if the defining characteristic of the underclass is the absence of realistic chances for upward mobility, there has always been a black underclass.

I am distinguishing here between defining characteristics and accompanying characteristics as the terms are used by George Graham.[1] Defining characteristics are those qualities selected for the purpose of deciding if a thing is a member of a particular category and which distinguish a phenomenon from other phenomena. Accompanying characteristics are attributes that a thing may have but need not have in order to fall in a given category.

Using this terminology, the defining characteristic of the underclass would be the absence of realistic chances for upward mobility while the accompanying characteristics of the underclass would be historically specific functions of the socioeconomic and cultural systems of a given historical period. For example, the accompanying characteristics of those members of the black underclass of the post-Reconstruction era who often wound up in Southern chain gangs were different from those of the levee-camp roustabouts of the 1930s, many of whom ended up in the penitentiary. Thus, attributes such as welfare dependency, female-headed householding, residential isolation, and involvement in the drug culture are merely accompanying characteristics of the contemporary edition of the underclass.

The current edition of the underclass is the residual of a much larger impoverished group of black poor which existed prior to the unprecedented spiral of black upward mobility experienced during the 1960s. Within this larger historically constant collection of black poor, there was always a core of persons for whom there was no realistic chance for being integrated into the socioeconomic system as productive self-sustaining actors. If such was the case historically as one pattern of production and the accompanying socioeconomic and culture systems gave way to the next, it would mean that the presence of the underclass is not to be explained by the particularities of a given historical moment. Rather, the explanation is to be found in forces that transcend the discrete historical periods.

I shall return to this point later, but first, I wish to review and comment on some of the key assumptions about the size, location, and nature of the underclass. This review and commentary will demonstrate that the gap between black and white economic well-being on almost all indicators has been and continues to be constant and symmetrical and therefore systemic. That is to say, the economic conditions of blacks and whites fluctuate in tandem in response to changes in the economy. I will also argue that the constantly high level of black poverty and its three-to-one ratio to white poverty are simply two indicators of the systemic character of black deprivation and that underclass status is simply the lowest point on that continuum of black deprivation.

Most commentators, both scholarly and popular, identify the black underclass as an urban phenomenon and a product of the pathos of the inner city. Typically, studies begin by identifying census tracts with large concentrations of low-income people and labeling them as underclass neighborhoods. Using this method, Sawhill speculated that less than six percent of the black population live in underclass neighborhoods.[2] Gephart and Pearson suggest that the underclass includes approximately one-fifth of the low-income population.[3]

While the literature tells us that underclass persons are to be found in certain neighborhoods and that members of the underclass are likely to have certain accompanying characteristics, it offers no criteria for determining which individuals are in fact part of the underclass. No one claims that all residents of such neighborhoods are members of the underclass. Nor does anyone claim that all of those who share certain accompanying characteristics, for example, teenage-motherhood, are members of the underclass. Some use the idea of "dysfunctional underclass behaviors" to distinguish between the routine (non-system threatening) poor and the underclass. However, this distinction turns out to be more illusory than real because the presence of these behaviors is inferred from aggregate statistics. Thus, we have no empirically useful definition of the underclass. At least not one which would allow us to predict which individuals are members of the underclass.

Finally, as mentioned earlier, the literature conveys the impression that the underclass is a new or emerging and growing problem. This argument is supported primarily by the finding that the number of poor blacks living in poverty-stricken neighborhoods has increased. However, while the residential concentration of the black poor has grown, the proportion of both individuals and families living in poverty has actually decreased over the last three decades. In fact, it is the escape of middle-income and upwardly mobile black poor which isolates and makes the residual underclass more visible.

The systemic character of black poverty is also reflected in its regional and spatial distribution. Historically, for well-known reasons, the poverty rate among southern blacks exceeded that of blacks living elsewhere. However, as noted in Chapter 2, following the dissolution of the racial caste system in the 1970s, conditions in the South began to approximate those in other regions. By 1987, the South had a poverty rate of 34.5 percent, down from the 41 percent which obtained in 1969. In the Midwest in 1987, 36.6 percent of blacks were classified as poor while 28.8 percent of those in the Northeast and 24.3 percent in the West were poor.

Regarding place of residence, in 1987 the poverty rate among black families remained highest in non-metropolitan areas. Within metropolitan areas, the black poverty rate was 30.7 percent inside and 21.1 percent outside central cities. The black-to-white ratio was 3:8 for metropolitan and 3:6 for non-metropolitan areas. Black poverty among persons classified as rural farm was 30 percent in 1980.

What picture can be drawn from the poverty data presented in the preceding paragraphs and what implications are there for our efforts to understand the nature and predicament of the black underclass? Perhaps most significantly, the data show that black poverty is not a localized or particularized phenomenon. It ranges from 30 percent to 35 percent throughout every region of the country except for the West. It is higher among non-metropolitan than metropolitan blacks and the poverty rate among rural farm blacks is greater than the rate among blacks living in the central city.

The data also show that the black poverty rate dropped significantly between 1959 and 1969 but has not changed measurably since that time. As a matter of fact, since 1970 the proportion of black individuals living in poverty has increased in every region of the country except the South. Only the South, the most laggard region in 1970, showed a significant decrease, from 42.6 percent to 34.5 percent in 1987. Also the black-to-white poverty ratio for the country has remained almost unchanged—it was 3:3 in 1969 and 3:1 in 1987, although it went as high as 3:7 in 1972 and 1973.

When figures on black unemployment rates, family income, and labor force participation rates and black-to-white ratios on these indicators are added to the picture, they lend additional credence to the claim that black economic fortunes are systemic. The black unemployment rate is constantly approximately double the white rate while the median income of black families is almost always at least one-third less than that for whites.

Regarding labor force participation, during the period immediately following Emancipation and continuing into the early decades of the twentieth century, the labor-intensive economy needed large numbers of menial workers. During this period when higher participation rates were more of an indicator of relative deprivation than economic well-being, both black men and women had higher participation rates. However, as the socioeconomic system changed and high labor force participation rates became essential for family and community well-being, black access to the labor force was constricted. Black men were pushed out of the labor force and the rate of increase for black women was considerably less than that of white women. For example, in 1930, 80 percent of black males and almost 40 percent of black females were in the labor force compared to only 76 percent and 20 percent of white men and women, respectively. By 1989, the rate for black men had fallen to 69 percent and for black women was up to 58 percent. The 1985 rates for white men and women were 76 percent and 57 percent, respectively.

This shows that the economic fortunes of blacks in comparison to those of whites ebb and flow in a non-random fashion. Black well-being on practically all indicators remains only a predictable fraction of white well-being regardless of historical, geographical, or economic circumstances. The logical conclusion is that they are all driven by some larger force.

Assuming that the black underclass is an unspecified proportion of the black poor, the data discussed above question the popular notion that the underclass is essentially an urban phenomenon sustained by the presumed anomic culture or residential isolation of inner-city blacks. The poverty rate is actually higher among non-metropolitan blacks and the "objective" conditions associated with the underclass, that is, welfare dependency, high unemployment and unemployability, high incidence of criminal activity, and so forth, are as common in the small- and medium-sized towns and rural areas of the South as they are in the megalopoles of the North.

Again, this suggests that one key to understanding the problem of the black underclass is to view it as a systemic development. That is to say that when the U.S. political economy is operating routinely, it routinely creates the conditions which give rise to the underclass. To pursue this argument, let me return to my earlier conceptualization of the permanent underclass as a residual category.

Following the end of slavery and continuing until 1959, the preponderant majority of the black population was classified as poor. However, as the then labor-intensive economy grew and underwent various structural changes, so did the demand for labor, including black labor. This created screens of opportunity and fueled an extended period of upward mobility for the black population. Consequently, the most salient characteristic of the black poor, until the current historical moment, was upward mobility. This fitted nicely with and reinforced the prevailing myth that those who remain in poverty have only themselves to blame.

However, there have always been those among the poor who had no realistic chance for upward mobility. They were simply submerged among the larger number of upwardly mobile poor. In earlier periods, the underclass obviously constituted a smaller proportion of the poor population, but as more and more of the upwardly mobile poor were absorbed into non-poverty position, the underclass became more pronounced among the poor; they were the residuals. Their obvious accompanying characteristics—poorly educated, unskilled, inferior work experience, and so forth—were then used to explain who they were and why they remained mired in poverty. Hence, the now popular thesis that the black underclass is a new emerging phenomenon and that it is self-perpetuating either because of the culture of poverty in which its members live or because of its residential cultural isolation.

III

Rather than beginning with the tautological assumption that the conditions under which the underclass live explain their condition, a more promising approach might be to try to establish the extent to which the conditions are related to other significant societal institutions and practices. I suggest this because it is widely acknowledged that cultures evolve as a result of the efforts of a people to adapt to the environment in which they exist. Thus, the so-called culture of poverty or the Wilsonian cultural isolation substitute thesis[4] may be viewed as the response to certain conditions rather than the reverse. This is not to deny the obvious, that is, that certain behavioral patterns make members of the underclass less attractive to potential employers. Rather it is to sharpen the focus by raising the question of what factors account for the rise of widespread poverty disproportionately among blacks. The answer, I would argue, is to be found in the undeniable laws of American capitalism as conditioned by white supremacy as a dominant American value.

The American political economy routinely creates a sizable number of persons without incomes sufficient to meet their most basic needs. Since production of goods and services in the U.S.political economy responds to effective demand as opposed to need, persons with limited incomes are unable to command access to a reasonable share of available goods and services through socially sanctioned procedures. As a consequence, a whole array of debilities such as poor health care, poor housing, and poor education befall them. Seen in this way, these debilities are routine outgrowths of the U.S. economic process. The fact that they have remained constants in American life in spite of the impressive advances which have been made in science and technology illustrates this point.

Under these circumstances we are justified in assuming that the laws of the economy give rise to the debilities and that institutional practices governed by the principle of white supremacy result in the disproportionate allocation of these debilities among African Americans. As discussed earlier, black poverty remained approximately three times that of whites over the last quarter century and black unemployment is almost always twice that of whites. Comparable differentials exist between blacks and whites on practically every measure of socioeconomic well-being and these differentials exist among all categories of blacks and whites. The white wealthy are wealthier and the black poor are poorer. Race becomes the criterion for allocating to African Americans a disproportionate share of the debilities which are routinely created by the economy.

This argument may be controversial, but I believe that there is sufficient anecdotal evidence available to justify giving it serious attention and rigorous empirical testing. Let me proceed to make the anecdotal case.

Most observers posit that problems of poor education, poor health care, and inferior work experiences are major constituents of the problem of the underclass. My thesis that the presence of the black underclass is a systemic function would be given credence if it could be demonstrated that the above-mentioned problems are created and sustained by the routine activities of legitimate economic and political institutions and actors. For purposes of illustration, let us analyze the problem of education.

Poor education and the lack of skills and satisfactory work experiences derived therefrom are often cited as the major problem of the permanent underclass. To what extent, we may ask, do the structure and function of the American educational system help create and sustain the conditions which give rise to the problems of the underclass. Presently and historically post-secondary educational training has been the major avenue for black upward mobility. However, the post-secondary educational system in the United States is organized and funded in a manner which benefits the more privileged elements at the expense of the poor, and current trends exacerbate rather than relieve the problems of the underclass. This is so, at least partially, because post-secondary educational systems are arranged and funded in a hierarchical fashion which reinforces the current unequal distribution of both competencies and income.

As Alexander Astin has pointed out, in the United States, public post-secondary educational systems are organized in a hierarchical fashion with universities being at the apex, followed by high-selective four-year colleges, medium-selective four-year colleges, low-selective four-year colleges, and two-year colleges. Admission standards and other practices result in a class stratified scholastic population with high-status persons attending the universities and lower-status students in the two-year institutions.

The funding of public post-secondary education reinforces the class hierarchy. The more selective the institution, the greater the per student subsidy provided by the state. Astin's 1975 data is given in Table 11-1. A rational interplanetary visitor might expect to find a direct correlation between the size of the educational subsidy per student and the presumed educational deficiencies of the student body, that is, the greater the educational problems and financial needs of the student, the greater the subsidy. However, as these data show, just the opposite is the case. As Astin asserts,

> Thus the subsidy is smallest in those institutions enrolling the poorest students, and greatest in those institutions enrolling the most well to do. . . . Here again is another important side effect of a hierarchically arranged public system based upon selective admission: students who are denied access to the universities and more selective four-year colleges (including a disproportionate share of the low income and minority students) receive substantially less public subsidy for their

TABLE 11-1 Financial Aid, Tuition, and Student "Subsidy" in Different Types of Public Colleges (Dollars per full-time equivalent student)

TYPE OF INSTITUTION	EXPENDITURES FOR FINANCIAL AID	TUITION	"SUBSIDY" (EDUCATIONAL & GENERAL PLUS AID EXPENDITURES MINUS TUITION)
Two-year colleges	60	385	1,208
Four-year colleges			
Low selectivity	77	358	1,253
Medium selectivity	94	404	1,448
High selectivity	129	473	2,179
Universities			
Low selectivity	133	490	2,744
Medium selectivity	190	564	2,850
High selectivity	316	519	5,205

Source: A. Astin, *The Myth of Equal Access to Higher Education*. Atlanta: Southern Education Foundation, 1975.

post-secondary education than do students who manage to enter the more selective public colleges and universities.[5]

Clearly, the post-secondary educational system reinforces the existing class differences and hardly anyone would dispute the assertion that elementary and secondary school systems operate in a similar manner and have a similar effect. Indeed the current move toward competency tests as prerequisites for a high school diploma will only aggravate the problem. Competency tests superimposed upon the existing educational system only ensure that even larger numbers of poor children will not receive high school diplomas, and inasmuch as the diploma is an arbitrary prerequisite for many entry-level jobs, chances for upward mobility are limited even more.

The winnowing process of the educational system dovetails with the imperatives of the job market. Inasmuch as the economy does not provide a sufficient number of well-paying jobs for the total population, a significant proportion of the workers must be content with jobs paying poverty level wages while still others can find only intermittent work. "Objective" criteria can be used to ration the limited hierarchically arranged work opportunities. The educational system ensures that these "objective" capabilities are distributed among the population in a predictable non-random class and racially biased fashion.

Just as the education system reinforces the conditions which give rise to and sustain the circumstances within which the underclass is trapped, so do the housing and finance systems. Wilson[6] has argued that the isolation of the underclass in inner-city crime-infested neighborhoods is a primary cause of its permanency. To the extent that this is the case, it seems obvious that this isolation is the result of the community-sanctioned behavior of such diverse actors as bankers, real estate brokers, owners of industrial capital and retail outlets, as well as the more prosperous gainfully employed workers.

For example, it is eminently sensible for the owners of industrial capital and the growing service industries to follow their preferred predominantly white labor force to the suburbs. And it is just as sensible for the conglomerate-owned retail and service outlets to follow suit. Similarly, bankers are not being illogical in a capitalist system grounded in white supremacy when they choose to finance white-dominated suburban rather than central city developments. Mayors and city councils, in turn, are doing what they are expected to do when they support tax schemes, transportation systems, and labor force and growth policies which favor the already privileged at the expense of the poor in order to "revitalize" the inner city. And, finally, middle-income blacks who have sufficient wherewithal to allow them to escape the decadence of the central city are also behaving quite rationally when they follow their white compatriots to the suburbs. The outcome, of course, of this confluence of self-interested and community-sanctioned behaviors is the perpetuation of the conditions which entrap the underclass—a deteriorating housing stock, substandard schools, limited job opportunities, welfare dependency, crime, and unrelieved poverty.

If these conditions which entrap the underclass are systemic, the phenomenon itself must be systemically based as well.

Let me conclude this essay with a brief comment on the implication of the conditions which entrap the black underclass for the future of the struggle for racial equality in the United States. As a residual phenomenon, the permanent black underclass is at once a monument to the successful protest activity of the civil rights movement and a reminder of its theoretical barrenness.

The activists and theoreticians of the movement never articulated a full-blown political philosophy which would have allowed them to understand and explain the connection between the economic and political dimensions of the unequal conditions of African Americans. There was, however, an unarticulated but widely shared assumption among them that the end of state-sanctioned segregation and discrimination would set in motion a train of events which would lead to economic parity between whites and African Americans. And it was assumed, at least implicitly, that black economic parity could be achieved without significant material cost to whites and without fundamental changes in the economic system.

The theoretical barrenness of this position became obvious when a combination of slackened economic growth, certain structural changes in the economy, and the accelerated entrance of women in the labor force precipitated circumstances which produced a counter-white movement.

The decline of the industrial sector, especially in the Midwest, eliminated many of the well-paying jobs that provided a comfortable living and upward mobility for working-class black families. At the same time, the newly created service sector jobs paid less than those in the industrial sector and called for skills not found among the majority of the displaced industrial workers. Moreover, inasmuch as more and more women were entering the labor force, the displaced industrial workers had to compete with more, and often better, credentialed workers for the newly created and lower paying service sector jobs.

During this period of economic dislocation and structural change, whites began to interpret black demands as a call for white displacement, reverse racism, as it were. Generally, whites argued that racism and racial discrimination were no longer societal problems and that any remaining differences between the races were functions of objective differences in individual qualifications and hence not amenable to group remedies. Qualifications and competency tests became shibboleths of the white countermovement. Access to educational institutions, attractive job opportunities, and on-the-job promotions would be determined by "objective" criteria as reflected in test scores.

Predictably, these criteria could be satisfied by only a disproportionately small segment of black aspirants. The result, however, has been the intensification of income inequality within the black community. As Swinton noted, between 1978 and 1986 the increase in black families with the lowest incomes was almost five times the increase in the number of families receiving the highest incomes.[7] As the small number of "qualified" blacks prospered, many more slipped into poverty and into the underclass.

The implications of this development for the future of the struggle for racial equality depend to a great extent on the interpretation given to it by black political and intellectual leadership. That leadership in all probability will continue to come from that segment of the community which benefited most from the gains of the civil rights era. They and their progeny will be more able to meet the imposed competency tests and as a result, they will continue to prosper economically. As they continue to prosper, they may justifiably claim that their good fortune is the result of their own hard work. They may argue that they played the meritocracy game and won.

Meanwhile, the underclass will become relatively more impoverished and increasingly wards of the state. Middle-class black professionals will staff the societal institutions which administer to, and manage the lives of, the underclass. And, as middle-class blacks inherit governmental power in more and more of the country's major cities, blacks will man those public outposts responsible for protecting the dominant propertied classes from the rebellious reactions of the underclass.

To date, most of black political leadership has refused to join mainstream white interests who blame the underclass for their own unhappy state. They have insisted that the causes are to be found in more fundamental economic forces conditioned by institutional racism. However, they have shied away from exploring the systemic nature of the underclass phenomenon and as a result, they have no program or plan of action for addressing the problem.

Perhaps surprisingly, black intellectual leadership has been much more inclined to accept the argument that the plight of the underclass is of their own making. A group of strategically placed black intellectuals in prestigious Eastern universities have played a leading role in propagating this thesis. Through their works which are published in influential policy-oriented journals and magazines, they reinforce the conventional claim that the problems of the underclass are primarily problems internal to the black community and evidence of the failure of black leadership and of the selfishness of the black middle class from which that leadership arises. And in turn, these intellectuals help create a climate which allows a hostile or indifferent white leadership to create, cultivate, and elevate to prominence a new reactionary black leadership class. The new black leadership class, as demonstrated by certain black leaders who achieved prominence during the Reagan era, is prepared to join with the most conservative forces in society on matters involving race and public policy. Whether white conservatives are successful in creating a new black leadership class will be a key element in determining how black leadership interprets the problem of the underclass.

If black leadership views the underclass as a systemic problem, it may force a public debate on the dialectical relationship between poverty and wealth, between affluence and decadence, and between privilege and deprivation. Such a point of departure would at least stimulate a national debate on the systemic character of the problem of the underclass. And it could be the first shot in a real war against poverty.

RODNEY KING AND LOS ANGELES: ANOTHER DEFINING OPPORTUNITY

Rodney King and Los Angeles have given us yet another opportunity to define ourselves as a people and as a nation. But what we witnessed in 1992 shows that we have not learned nor profited much from history.

The situation reflects much about our past. It raises the specter of Chief Justice Roger Taney's comments in the infamous 1857 Supreme Court decision in *Dred Scott* where the Chief Justice said that blacks "have no rights which the white man is bound to respect," providing fuel for a climate that led to the Civil War.

In more recent times the King verdict raises specters of the early dark days of the civil rights movement in the 1950s and 1960s when the full fury of law and practices in the South were used to brutally repress (even kill) blacks and their supporters. It also raises the specter of what happened during the urban disorders of the 1960s. How could we so easily forget Watts?

In broader perspective, these historical periods suggest two lessons: (1) Real progress and breakthroughs in dealing with racial problems have come only in the wake of crisis situation; and (2) once the crisis has subsided, promising hopes are dashed by reversion to indifferent/hostile climates where rights and interests of African Americans become prime targets for heartless retrenchments, callous indifference, and woeful neglect.

The King verdict thus adds to an increasingly hostile climate that evidence how once promising civil rights gains of the 1950s and 1960s are obviously now being eroded with more *speed than deliberation*.

It is a climate that has come full circle and has now produced a Supreme Court that is unsympathetic to civil rights and liberties. [Consider, for example, the recent court decision narrowly construing the scope of the Voting Rights Act (*Presley* v. *Etowah County*, 1992); and the even more recent decision that portends to erode the spirit and promise of the 1954 desegregation cases (*Freeman* v. *Pitts*, 1991).]

It is a climate where use of the "racial card" is commonplace in both public and private arenas such as in elections and in the workplace. Consider, for example, the "Willie Horton" strategy used by President Bush in the 1988 election and the "Pin Point/High-tech lynching" strategy used by Justice Clarence Thomas in his fight to win confirmation to the Supreme Court.

It is a climate that reflects in too many ways that rights and interests of blacks and similar groups are not being fairly represented or protected by *either* of the two major parties; nor by the Congress, the president, the justice system, nor any other governing institutions. It is a climate that fosters both the rhetoric and actions of racial bias and hatred. And overall, it is a climate that has become all too accepting and comforting, even supportive of those (e.g., the "David Dukes," the "Patrick Buchanans") who engage in such divisive actions.

Overall, it is a climate of increasing hopelessness and despair where many blacks—irrespective of class—are subject to daily inequities, indignities, and humiliations that are less visible but no less hurtful and damaging to their individual worth and well-being.

There are many "Rodney Kings" in America today. Their plight and treatment remain obscure, not having been captured on video and dramatically televised to the nation and the world. They nonetheless provide a continuous "powder keg" waiting to explode by a Rodney King-type "spark."

Clearly, as the Rodney King situation shows, this type of climate spurs actions that can fracture the kind of trust and confidence people in a democracy must have in the rule of law and their governing institutions.

It is not enough for leaders, especially the president, to sit by and *react* to such situations; thy must show proactive and extraordinary political as well as moral leadership in order to make an extraordinary form of government (democracy) work. The stakes are high, for what we do not only affects our own future but also could well determine the course of the entire world where old and newly emerging states in the international arena are seeking patterns and guidance for their own futures in democratic governance.

Unless elective political leaders deal with such problems and unless the courts, including the Supreme Court, uphold basic constitutional legal rights for *all* persons, the overall racial discord in this country could escalate to levels not seen since the advent of the civil rights movement.

The difficulty and dilemma facing African Americans today is captured well by Benjamin Hooks, who, as executive director of the NAACP, reacted to the Supreme Court's affirmative action decisions in recent years. Hooks said that the Rehnquist Court "is more dangerous to the legitimate hopes and aspirations of black people in this nation than the segregationist foes of the civil rights movement."[8]

And in indicating that blacks will turn to Congress in hopes of overcoming the adverse court decisions, Hooks said that "if, however, it appears that Congress will not do anything to act, then we think the only recourse left to us is civil disobedience, on a scale which has never been seen in this country before." Though made in different context, the relation of Hooks's comments to the situation is obvious.

When courts, which are in a unique position to do so, fail or are perceived to have failed to protect rights, there is a heightening of hopelessness and despair. It strongly suggests that there is *no one* else to turn to and this could lead to breakdowns in law and order, as evidenced by the violent aftermath following the Rodney King verdict.

This suggests that just to shrug one's shoulders and say, "Well, that's the way the system works" *is not enough*, especially when graphic evidence suggests the contrary. Somehow courts, and elective political institutions as well, must provide that *fine line* which differentiates constitutionalism and the rule of law from what otherwise degenerates into tyrannical rule and naked state oppression.

A sad and telling commentary about the Los Angeles situation and our nation generally is how matters being discussed in the 1990s are strikingly similar to those discussed in the Kerner Commission report following the urban disorders of the 1960s, including the Los Angeles Watts riots.

What should be done? Clearly the *leadership impetus should and must come* from President Clinton and the Congress. But it must also come from each of us in our own respective spheres of authority and influence. It is much easier to vent our wrath and offer advice to others, especially from a distance, but much more difficult to apply the same standards to ourselves.

The Los Angeles situation reinforces what we should have learned from history: *The force of arms and no amount of state and military power can stifle for long the deep human yearnings of all persons to have an equal and fair opportunity to develop to their full potential.*

What many white Americans have *never fully understood* and what African Americans can *never fully forget* is that *no one can really and fully be free and secure until all persons are equally free and secure.* Los Angeles has given us another opportunity to learn this lesson!

MATCHING HOPE WITH REALITY: AFRICAN AMERICANS AND THE 1992 PRESIDENTIAL ELECTION

Not since the election of President John F. Kennedy had there been such hope and excitement about the election of a president as there was about the election of President Clinton. That hope and excitement were kindled and nourished by the effective use and power of symbols. As we shall see, the force of Clinton's personality and style served to mute and blur the essential character and substance of his ideological stance and policy proposals. Even more, campaign developments allowed and enhanced the apparent Clinton strategy to position himself as a mainstream middle-of-the-road candidate not obligated to any particular group and faction.

At the same time, however, such campaign developments worked to make Clinton the more attractive and reasonable option among all the candidates, both in his fight for the nomination within his own party and in the end between himself and the Republican incumbent candidate Bush. Thus by the time of the election the choice became so clear to many voters, including most African Americans, that it seemed to stir their hope and excitement about the possibilities of a Clinton presidency more than close analysis would warrant.

Indeed, that hope and excitement must be placed in the context of the reality of American politics and society. More specifically, that hope and excitement must be placed in the context of (1) the nature and dynamics of the 1992 presidential election and the Clinton campaign as related to the interests of African Americans and (2) the structure and operation of American government and politics in terms of dealing with fundamental problems that continue to disproportionately hurt the life chances of African Americans.

The nature and dynamics of a presidential campaign determine in large measure what groups will have access and how they might fare should their side prove successful. Indeed, how the pre-convention stage of the campaign developed, especially the decision of particular candidates to enter the race for the Democratic presidential nomination, had a lot to do with the role and options open to blacks in the subsequent developments in the primaries, the convention, and the presidential campaign and general election. And it is clear that positions taken in these arenas affect who and what kind of access particular persons and interests would have.

Traditionally, of course, the perennial factor facing any potential candidate for the nomination of either of the two major parties is the need to find or cultivate sufficient resources to mount a creditable campaign. This is particularly difficult for those who wish to challenge an incumbent president of their own party. And given the immediate, overwhelming, and strong popularity accruing to President Bush after the Persian Gulf War, it became even more difficult for potential nominees in *either* party to challenge the president. Even so, such decisions must be made quite early in view of the primary election calendar and the requirements needed to campaign for a major party presidential nomination.

As such, in the context of the 1992 race, it became necessary to make such decisions before there were any clear signals that President Bush's popularity would wane in consequence of sharp focus on the continuous and serious economic downturn. In the end, the president was challenged from within his own party by arch-conservative Patrick Buchanan, mainly on the basis of Bush's reneging on his 1988 campaign pledge not to raise taxes, and by former Ku Klux Klan leader David Duke. David Duke dropped from the race early, but Buchanan found sufficient encouragement to stay the course, culminating in a fiery speech at the Republican convention that clearly turned off women, blacks, and minorities. The cumulative effect of these campaigns, particularly that of Buchanan, was to move Bush much farther to the extreme right than he perhaps wanted or needed to be.

Meanwhile, on the Democratic side, the race was joined early by former Senator Paul Tsongas, and later by other principal candidates such as Senator Robert Kerrey of Nebraska, Senator Tom Harkin of Iowa, former Governor Jerry Brown of California, and, of course, Governor Bill Clinton of Arkansas. The race was also initially joined by Governor Douglas Wilder of Virginia, the first black ever elected to a state governorship.

Some other potential candidates—such as House Majority Leader Richard Gephardt, Governor Mario Cuomo of New York, Senator Bill Bradley of New Jersey, and Senator Jay Rockefeller of West Virginia—did not enter the contest. But insofar as African Americans were concerned, the most important person who did not enter the 1992 race was Jesse Jackson. Indeed, despite Wilder's apparent attempt to garner the black vote, it was Jackson on whom major attention was focused. He was the one black candidate who would command attention, and everyone knew it. Jackson had run twice and done quite well, especially in 1988. But several questions caused his pause from making a third try: 1) Could he count on the kind of solid support he received from black leaders in 1988? (2) Would his candidacy, as some party leaders suggested, be likely to cause divisions, thereby lessening Democratic chances to recapture the White House? (3) What affect might a third try have on his future leadership possibilities both in and outside the party? In the end, and to the obvious relief of party and some black leaders, Jackson decided not to try.

To be sure, Doug Wilder had entered the race but had neither the name recognition, oratorical ability, charisma, or standing of Jesse Jackson in the black community or with certain other important interests in Democratic party politics, for example, labor. Wilder apparently wanted to parlay the kind of race-neutral campaign with which he had won the governorship of Virginia into the presidential campaign. But it didn't work in the black community, nor in attracting others, and in the end Wilder withdrew from the campaign.

Overall, Jackson's decision not to enter effectively left the black community and certain other more liberal segments of the party (e.g., labor) without much focus or direction. And as the campaign developed, the downsides of Jackson's decision not to run became increasingly obvious. In contrast to Jackson's 1988 campaign, for example, there was no one who could or would forcefully and clearly articulate policy preferences favored by the black community or provide a rallying point for black delegates and others to bargain for their interests and concerns at the national convention. Moreover, having a black candidate, especially one who articulates policy preferences favored by many in the black community, can energize the black vote. The cumulative effect of Jackson's decision was that it allowed Clinton and the Democrats, unlike Bush and the Republicans, to avoid taking positions that might appeal to black voters but might otherwise alienate other voters within and outside the party. This, of course, made it easier for Clinton (or any other Democratic nominee) to maintain more of a mainstream-centrist image with respect to the volatile issue of race.

In the end, of course, it was Governor Clinton who eventually won the nomination and the ensuing campaign and in the process profited greatly from both Jackson's decision and the black vote. Clinton's widely publicized successful tenure as governor of Arkansas, plus an apparent favorable image and relations he had cultivated over the years with black voters and black leaders in his own state and around the nation, helped commend his candidacy to the black community. Indeed, except perhaps for Jerry Brown, there really was no obvious competition among the candidates to garner the black vote. And clearly President Bush did little, if anything, to attract the black vote. Moreover, of course, it was also apparent that the strongly implied biases against blacks and minorities emanating from the Republican convention also did not help Bush.

But though clearly more preferable than Bush, Governor Clinton too was careful to distance himself from special interests or groups, including blacks. Indeed, Clinton had obviously crafted a very deliberate "centrist-mainstream" strategy, carefully honed and promoted through the Democratic Leadership Council (DLC)—of which Clinton was a key leader. The apparent and open objective of DLC and this strategy was to recapture Reagan Democrats and appeal to the middle class and avoid too much focus on issues of relevance to the poor and underclass, who are disproportionately black, and minorities who live in urban areas. Overall, this "middle-class, centrist" focus fits well with the mainstream tendencies of American politics. After all, Americans seem strongly attached to the view that "the *middle* way is the best *way*," and that "*compromise and consensus* not *conflict and division* is the hallmark of American politics." Further, people like to identify with the middle class, not with the lower class or poorer groups.

Clinton's carefully honed image did not allow him to identify too much with any particular group or faction of party and took special efforts to show this. The apparent distance which he kept from Jesse Jackson throughout the campaign, for example, was illuminated vividly by the well-publicized "Sister Souljah incident." In this instance, Clinton openly criticized the singer (in a speech before Jackson's own Rainbow Convention) for reportedly saying, in wake of the Los Angeles riots, that blacks should stop killing each other and start killing whites. The force and symbolism of Clinton's remarks, whether intended or not, clearly allowed him to enhance his carefully honed "main-stream-centrism." At the same time, however, Clinton's personality and his sheer presence and style evoked such potent and favorable symbols so as not to alienate significant segments of the black community.

As the campaign evolved, developments allowed Clinton to maintain and enhance this centrist image. For example, Perot's quick-fix schemes to address the deficit and Bush's "do-nothing" approach allowed Clinton to take a stance on the economy somewhere in between. And the economy was and is the central issue. In short, once again Clinton came through as the middle-of-the-road, reasonable candidate, avoiding extremes.

The *politics of race,* ever present in American politics and certainly in presidential elections, tended to be obscured in the 1992 campaign by focus on *politics of the economy*. Indeed, continuing downturns in the economy portended to have a devastating effect on all persons and was especially illuminated by the plight of middle-class whites who began to feel the pains of unemployment and insecurity that blacks and minorities have long felt disproportionately over the years.

Thus, as matters turned out, Clinton's new Democratic party could address many issues that have long affected blacks and minorities—housing, education, health care—in terms of what is needed to stabilize the plight of the middle class brought on by a disastrous economy.

Somehow Democrats were able to forge an apparently fragile yet effective coalition in the convention and the campaign. Much credit goes to Clinton and Ron Brown, at the time chair of the Democratic National Committee and also to Jesse Jackson who held an important card in the overall party configuration, whether openly acknowledged or not. Whatever the situation, Jackson did not choose to play that card and in fact did endorse Clinton on the eve of the convention. By this time, however, it was clear to Jackson and others that Clinton not only would win the nomination, but was also obviously being strengthened by *the increasing belief that he could win the election.* This belief was the prime consideration after 12 years of what they considered retrogressive Republican rule. Moreover, it was also increasingly apparent that Clinton's personality and style gave him an almost enviable comfort level with blacks (and many others) that made him an appealing candidate to a diverse range of interests, individuals, and groups. And this appeal became even more apparent and evident when compared with the other viable option, President Bush.

However, this hope and excitement stirred by Clinton's candidacy and eventual election must be viewed in terms of the politics of reality. For example, it was apparent throughout the pre-convention, convention, and presidential campaign and election that there was no obvious black or minority presence or leadership in the Clinton organization. This observation was particularly noticeable with respect to Jesse Jackson whose presence and voice were effectively muted and obscured in the convention and throughout the campaign. Jackson created somewhat of a paradox for Clinton and party leaders. Indeed, it was Jackson's strong appeal to blacks and association with liberal causes that made him especially popular among these groups whose support Clinton and party leaders wanted to keep. On the other hand, it was this very strong appeal of Jackson to these groups that made him unpopular with more moderate-conservative voters such as Reagan Democrats whose support Clinton and party leaders strongly believed they needed to win. As a result, Clinton's more open links to the black community were not through the more historically identified black leaders but rather through more mainstream and more recently emerging black leaders such as Ron Brown (party chair), Mike Espy (D-Mississippi) and John Lewis (D-Georgia).

To be sure, Clinton did endorse certain of Jackson's policy positions such as District of Columbia statehood and a national health care system. However, these positions were taken in a broader context of a clearly apparent mainstream platform and campaign that overall took more moderate centrist and Republican-like positions on such highly salient issues as crime and welfare reform, which in much modern political parlance have become code umbrellas under which to convey particular attitudes about race. At the same time, however, Clinton took strong liberal positions with respect to other volatile issues such as abortion and gay/lesbian rights. But his positions were not that strong or clear with respect to urban problems; instead they were couched in "deracialized" terms, for example, as ways to help the "forgotten" middle class by creating jobs and overcoming unemployment and developing a national system to guarantee adequate health care for all persons. Overall then, the Clinton and Democratic party image was not that clear one way or the other; it was somewhere in between.

Whatever Clinton's stance, however, blacks continued to increasingly and overwhelmingly vote for him. And their support obviously played a key role in certain key states where the black share of the total Clinton vote could be viewed as pivotal, even determinative, in the election outcome, for example, Illinois (26 percent); Michigan (17 percent), Ohio (20 percent); Georgia (40 percent); and Louisiana (50.6 percent) for Clinton. Overall, blacks gave Clinton 82 percent, Bush 11 percent, and Perot 7 percent. What is interesting and instructive is that the black vote was clearly energized and the turnout higher in states where strong black candidates were running, for example, Illinois, Louisiana, and Georgia. This clearly suggests that a live and vigorous campaign of a Jesse Jackson could potentially have made for real differences (perhaps even outcome) in the 1992 presidential election.

Indeed, a three-way race with a Perot was more likely to lead to a Clinton victory than a three-way race with a Jesse Jackson who clearly would have won a sizable black vote. But as the campaign unfurled and developed, it was clear that Clinton and the Democratic party would retain the black vote. For, the reality was that there was no other place for them to go other than to stay at home. And with the increasingly retrogressive policies and actions of the Bush administration, this was neither a viable nor wise option. As a result, there was increasingly real concern, and not without reason, that issues of concern to blacks and minorities were being ignored in the campaign, for example, a lack of concrete attention to urban issues such as those reflected by the Rodney King incident and the subsequent Los Angeles riots in 1991. Indeed, listening to the campaign one might well conclude that the Rodney King incident and Los Angeles riots were almost forgotten, and they were. In general, Clinton was able to forge a winning coalition relatively free of commitments to specific interests or groups, such as labor or blacks and minorities. In a fundamental sense, the African American vote may be viewed as more of a choice itself between hope and reality. It may be conceptualized, for example, that as a vote of hope, Clinton would make good on his broad promises and that these actions (e.g., the substance of these espoused policies) would redound to blacks as well as whites and would consequently be seen as a vote against the deleterious material realities of the Bush administration and campaign.

Unlike in 1984 and 1988, black political leaders did not attempt to use a direct presidential candidate strategy (as done by Jackson) to push their political objectives. Rather they supported Clinton without exacting any obvious or apparent commitments in exchange for their vote, which in any case can be exercised only at election time.

This suggests that black influence in American politics and society continues to be minimized and blunted by the clear continuing lack of black strength and presence of blacks in other major socioeconomic sectors: business and industry; education and communications; and law, science, and the professions. Blacks remain woefully underrepresented in these sectors, and as a result lack the kind of continuous monitoring influence that other interests have in day-to-day policy making or in shaping individual and public attitudes due to the lack of black representation in the media. For this reason, it is instructive to reread the Kerner Commission Report concerning urban riots of the late 1960s and chart the progress or lack thereof in terms of dealing with deficiencies outlined in that report.

Thus, because of their relative lack of continuous leverage in politics, the bottom line with respect to how blacks will fare during the next few years depends in large measure on Clinton and how he sees his role. Some clues as to his views on race can be gleaned from his appointments of blacks to key positions in Arkansas, to his transition team as president-elect, and to his cabinet once having become president. Clearly Clinton's election has brought a sense of excitement and hope to blacks and many other Americans which has not been seen since President John F. Kennedy. But it must be remembered that with respect to matters of importance to blacks, that is, civil rights, Kennedy did not move until faced with mounting demonstrations and protests from blacks and many others.

To be sure the situation is different today, but the life chances and material conditions of blacks continue to be hurt disproportionately by many of the same problems. However, let us assume that Clinton intends to really move and bring about more of a politics of inclusion for women, blacks, and minorities and is really ready to tackle controversial issues. Even if he is so disposed, however, and before we develop too much hope and excitement, it might be useful to once again look at certain fundamentals of American politics; how the nature and structure of the system and rules of the game offer clear advantages to those who want to maintain the status quo; and the obvious roadblocks to those who wish to bring about fundamental change.

Even considering the tremendous powers of the presidency, as well as the addition of more women and minority members elected to Congress and at the state and local levels, one still has to deal with and overcome inherent built-in limitations of federalism—the separation of powers, bicameralism, staggered elections, life-term appointed federal judges, and entrenched bureaucracies. Gridlock, for example, might be overcome in terms of *symbols*, that is, with Democrats now in control of the White House as well as the Congress. But it remains to be seen whether such gridlock will be overcome in terms of *substance*, for example, by enacting effective remedies to overcome gross socioeconomic and other systemic inequities that continue to disproportionately hurt blacks.

Clearly, these limitations can be overcome and fundamental change can occur, but it requires enormous and continuous commitment of leaders and electorate over time. And this can prove very difficult to accomplish. In short, the *reality* of American politics is that those (e.g., entrenched and established interests) who *oppose* fundamental change have a much better chance to prevail than those (e.g., emerging and aspiring interests) who seek to bring about such fundamental change.

Nonetheless, we may have reached a point in our nation's history where politics as usual may no longer be sufficient to deal with the rapidly changing realities of both a new domestic order as well as a new world order. Sheer demographic trends caution that we must begin to make major reforms and readjustments throughout the entire socioeconomic spectrum of our politics and society. Moreover, in order to deal with these changing realities, major reforms and adjustments must also be made in black leadership, in black interest groups, and the black community generally in order to deal with these changing realities, for example, coalition politics and an increase in black elected officials who in the future might come from mixed racial and ethnic contexts where blacks will not be a major voting bloc or force.

Black leaders, for example, must work harder at forming closer connections with all segments of their constituencies if we are to overcome the disaffection and loss of faith that many blacks and minorities have. In a real sense, it could well be that Clinton's election represents perhaps one of the few remaining opportunities to deal peacefully with the serious and divisive problems reflected in the Los Angeles riots of 1992.

Throughout the presidential campaign and election one could not help but be struck by the apparently fragile yet effective coalition that Clinton and the Democrats were able to maintain, at least until now. It is becoming increasingly clear, however, that the overriding challenge today and over the next few years is can or should the coalition be held together. That the coalition *can* be held together was evidenced in part by the generally reinforcing and warm relations that existed between President Clinton and African Americans during the presidential campaign and election. Even during the campaign, however, that relationship appeared at times quite uneasy and under strain. For one thing, as the campaign unfurled, the choice for African Americans between Clinton and President Bush was clear: by its actions the Bush administration had shown little concern or sensitivity toward blacks and minorities.

The coalition also came under strain during the campaign, when as one writer put it, "Mr. Clinton seemed obsessed with proving that he could be stern with black folks."[9] The writer continued:

> To show toughness on crime, he executed Rickey Ray Rector, a brain-damaged black man who seemed unaware that death was permanent. To neutralize the black left, Mr. Clinton scolded Jesse Jackson from Mr. Jackson's own podium at the Rainbow Coalition in Washington. This angered even Mr. Jackson's detractors, who saw it for the spanking-the-blacks routine that it was.[10]

And Mr. Clinton's actions and behavior during the Rodney King incident and subsequent Los Angeles riots were likewise "so feeble" that they indeed "sounded like George Bush." When combined, actions such as these do suggest that blacks were once more being taken for granted by the Democrats and being ignored by the Republicans.

On the other hand,however, Clinton seemed to somehow have or do just enough to keep the support and vote of most African Americans. Undoubtedly, Clinton's image of being sensitive and supportive of black concerns was clearly projected by the obvious easy rapport he developed with black audiences during the campaign and election. This rapport was apparently also bolstered by his having taken certain actions as governor of Arkansas (such as the appointment of several blacks to important state government positions) that also helped him to project a rather favorable civil rights posture. Moreover, Clinton's sharp criticism of the Bush administration policy toward Haitian refugees was also applauded by black leaders.

Overall, when viewed on balance and in broad perspective, the coalition that came to exist between Clinton and African Americans during the 1992 presidential campaign and election was perhaps based more on the *practical* limitations of necessity and choice, than it was on *principled* grounds of policy compatibility and mutual trust. But though more practical and less principled, the coalition nevertheless held together and was clearly effective in winning the crucial black vote for Clinton in the 1992 presidential election.

And after the election, the Clinton/African American relationship was clearly strengthened by his appointment of a record number of African Americans to his cabinet. But as the *symbolism* of campaign rhetoric and cabinet appointments gave way to the *substance* of policy making and implementation, relations between Clinton and African Americans began to cool and come under severe strain. This chilling of relations, as discussed in Chapter 9 of this book, seems to have been brought about by several Clinton actions. These actions included: (1) compromises apparently made by the president to salvage his budget package in the Senate which seemed to severely undercut Clinton's campaign promise to address serious problems affecting blacks, minorities, and the poor (such as job creation); (2) Clinton's decision as president to support the restrictive Bush administration immigration policy toward Haitian refugees, a policy which as a candidate he pledged to reverse; and (3) the president's withdrawal of the nomination for assistant attorney general for civil rights of Lani Guinier, a well-experienced civil rights lawyer and legal scholar.

Taken together, these actions clearly disturbed African Americans and many others. They stirred the Congressional Black Caucus, for example, to warn Clinton that the "caucus can harm as well as help this presidency." The situation led one writer to suggest that such a development might hurt President Clinton, but might well benefit American politics:

> Too long have blacks behaved as the chattel of the Democrats, patronized by the party and written off by Republicans." "A tryst between black Democrats and the Republicans won't change this equation," said the writer, but "[a] movement of black voters to the Republican party most certainly would."[11]

On closer analysis, however, it is not at all clear that such change would make much of a difference in the life of African Americans as might be suggested at first blush. Indeed, the uneasy and uneven relations between Clinton and African Americans reinforce once more how certain basic systemic, structural, and institutional factors serve as powerful influences in shaping the behavior and policies of *both* major parties, especially on an issue as deeply etched and as far-reaching as is the matter of race in American politics and society.

No matter such influences or other barriers, it is becoming increasingly clear that our inability or unwillingness to effectively overcome the problems of race and ethnicity even now pose uncommonly serious threats not only to democratic government, but to the sheer peace and security of our nation and the entire world.

How to include African Americans and other minorities peacefully and fully in democratic governance and society can go far to show the way for others. But it remains to be seen whether President Clinton and our political leadership generally is up to the task.

BLACK LEADERSHIP AND THE CONTINUING STRUGGLE FOR RACIAL JUSTICE

> The dynamics, threats and challenges of today's struggle for unqualified racial justice may well require a new kind of Black leadership. There are serious questions whether the charismatic individual leaders who played so important a role in recent decades are appropriate for the modern era. There are uncertainties as to whether the structure and function of the traditional civil-rights organizations can cope with the problems spawned by their past successes. The types of strategy and action that the present requires may demand a new coalition of political, community, religious and academic leadership among Blacks. The danger is that a vehicle to bring about such a coalition is not currently available, and it needs to be developed and put into use before it is too late.[12]

It is now commonplace to decry the absence or the poor quality of black leadership in the United States. The assertion that we have not had strong leaders since the assassination of Malcolm X and Doctor Martin Luther King, Jr., is often heard as is the counterrefrain that the day of the charismatic national black leader has passed and that what we need presently are pragmatic "nuts and bolts" local leaders capable of developing and executing plans to consolidate the gains, real or imagined, of the 1960s. Frequently heard also is the allegation that black leaders are sellout artists pursuing their individual or class interests at the expense of the black collectivity. Conversely, there are those who argue that black leadership has done and is doing all that it can within the externally imposed constraints under which it is obliged to function.

Assertions such as the foregoing indicate that the question of black leadership is a timely and important one, and the diversity of the perceptions of black leadership attests to the need for serious reflection on the nature of contemporary black leadership and on the kind of leadership appropriate for the immediate future. There is a need for both empirical field studies of existing leadership patterns and practices and for serious interpretive essays which attempt to describe and assess existing leadership patterns. This paper falls into the latter category.

Essentially, I argue in this essay that contemporary black leadership is increasingly irrelevant for the vast majority of blacks in the United States because that leadership has elevated the intermediate objective of the civil rights movement (CRM) of the past quarter century, that is, full legal inclusion of blacks into the political and economic system to the level of ultimate objective. When such inclusion, which was posited as being more or less a necessary and sufficient condition to assure equal status or at least constant movement in that direction, not only proved to be insufficient for black liberation, but the position of the black masses also continued to depreciate, black leadership, because of its self-generated confusion over means and ends, was unable to move to the next logical point. Instead, it floundered and splintered. Some leaders seemed to argue that a more intensified repeat of the 1960s would be sufficient while others argued that the civil rights movement had created the legal and structural conditions requisite for black equality and that the task of contemporary leadership is to convert this potential into reality through pragmatic politics. In my view, both positions are ahistorical and uninformed by a systematic analysis of the contemporary U.S. political economy and the place of blacks in it. Consequently, leadership patterns emanating from these assumptions are increasingly irrelevant.

I attempt to make this argument by offering a way of conceptualizing black leadership in the context of the politics of an oppressed people in a late twentieth-century capital-intensive state in which the notion of white supremacy provides the ideological basis for the cultural system; by commenting briefly on the character and relevance of black leadership during earlier historical periods; by analyzing the leadership forms developed and carried over from the civil rights movement of the 1960s; and by showing the incongruence between the assumptions of these leaders regarding the nature of the black predicament and the current post-civil rights movement reality.

Inasmuch as this essay is being written to, hopefully, help clarify the role played by those who are characterized in popular parlance as black leaders, no fine-tuned operational definition of the term is offered. For the most part, the concept refers to individuals who occupy certain institutional positions and who, because of that fact, are referred to and are perceived as leaders by significant numbers of other black people. Subsumed under the concept are heads of major black institutions such as civil rights organizations, religious, civic, social, and educational institutions, elected and appointed public officials, as well as persons who may not hold such institutional positions but are commonly deferred to as leaders.

CONCEPTUALIZING BLACK LEADERSHIP

Black leaders, as is the case with leadership elsewhere, come to occupy their positions as a result of their own initiatives as well as through the willingness of potential followers to defer to them. That is to say that there is always a certain reciprocity between leadership and followship and that in spite of the sometimes widely accepted notion that black leaders are imposed upon the community by alien elements, the reality is not as straight-forward. To be sure, the political culture which predisposes the community to indulge or reject the initiative of potential leaders is influenced disproportionately by forces alien to the black community. However, political practices in the community defer to and thereby give legitimacy to the institutional forms which are prescribed by the political culture. In this sense, black people voluntarily participate in the process out of which surface those commonly recognized as black leaders. The key, therefore, to developing a useful conceptualization of black leadership is to understand the forces which structure the black political culture, especially those elements which bear most heavily on leadership.

To begin, black political life should be viewed as a subsystem yet also as an integral part of the dominant U.S. politico-economic system. A major attribute of the system is pervasive inequality and immobility of income and wealth and the derivative wide disparities among the population on those indices used to measure comparative well-being. The political culture conditions individuals to believe that such inequality is necessary for societal growth and development; it also creates the erroneous notion that income mobility rather than immobility is the norm. The political culture also fosters the view that the wide disparities on indicators of well-being result from differences in individual capabilities or self-discipline rather than systemic factors.

As far as black people are concerned, perhaps the most important assumption of the U.S. political culture is the racist notion of white supremacy and inherent black inferiority. This notion of inherent inferiority is used not only to allocate disproportionately to blacks the debilities inherent in the U.S. political economy—joblessness, poor health care, and so forth—but to justify the resultant pathology as well. Black leadership arises in this context. The primary concern of race leadership has always been to eliminate the wide disparities which exist between blacks and others in the society. Although only a few of those who aspire to black leadership positions consciously accept and articulate the prescription of white supremacy and black inferiority, much of black leadership and black followship, at least tacitly, defers to the notion that the inequitable material status of blacks is a function of certain inadequacies among blacks themselves. Accordingly, the idea of improvement through individual transformation becomes a dominant theme of black leaders.

Again, as is the case of all oppressed peoples who live among their oppressor, black leadership and followship view their chances of reducing the wide disparities between blacks and whites as contingent to a great extent upon their ability to enlist the support of powerful whites. Thus, the cultivation of white allies becomes another dominant theme of black leadership, as does competition among black leaders for such support.[13]

While there are many identifiable white political tendencies or interests in the U.S. political system, all of those with systemic power are committed to maintaining white domination. Thus, to the extent that black leadership assumes that white allies or support are necessary to achieve its goals, it of necessity brings to the battlefield its own Trojan horse.

The assumption that black advancement requires the support of white forces which possess systemic power leads blacks, quite logically, to attempt to forge alliances with the most powerful white interests since it is the latter whose support can make a difference.

Conversely, the dominant white interests, by dint of the fact that they are dominant, have a compelling interest in minimizing stress and strain in the political system because they stand to lose most during times of social unrest. The dominant white interests,in spite of the fact that they have always been largely responsible for the oppression of blacks or as the political culture puts it euphemistically the state of "race relations," become the logical partner of black leadership. Such asymmetrical partnerships almost always result in the weaker partner being dominated by the stronger.

For the half century prior to the Reagan era, the "liberal" wing of the U.S. ruling class dominated the political system and constituted the primary alliance partner for blacks. Consequently, they influenced significantly the selection of black leaders and the agenda pursued by them. Up until the post-civil rights movement period, the agenda pursued by black leaders was highly moralistic and abstractly political. Although the dire economic conditions of the black nation were duly noted, the agenda was characterized by moralistic preachments against prejudice and exhortations to end racial segregation which was assumed to result from prejudice. One was left to assume that the dire economic conditions had their basis in racial prejudice rather than vice versa.

LEADERSHIP AND THE QUESTION OF RELEVANCE

The argument that black leadership is becoming increasingly irrelevant requires a statement of the criteria used to measure relevance. We assume that at a minimum, the function of leadership is to stimulate thinking and discussion among the followship about the appropriate description of their present predicament, the desired future being sought, and optimum alternative strategies for realizing that future. Leadership should also synthesize and evaluate the views emanating from the followship and seek to marshall support for those alternatives which have the possibility of transforming the status quo in the desired direction. The litmus test for relevance is whether the proposed activity can be shown to have a logical relationship with the factors which give the status quo its essential character and which, if changed in the direction being advocated, would alter those characteristics in a favorable manner. The argument being advanced here is that the initiatives of contemporary black leaders increasingly do not intersect with the essential characteristics of the current black predicament. More about that later.

During antecedent historical periods up to and including the civil rights movement, black leadership passed this test of relevance inasmuch as the accepted description and the debates over optimum strategies were logically related to those societal conditions which framed the black predicament. During the antebellum period, for example, the debate over slavery and colonization, free soil movement, and so forth, all spoke to the essential question. Proposed alternative responses would alter the essential nature of the black predicament.

During the Reconstruction period, the debate over land reform, political participation versus economic development, and liberal arts versus industrial education all flowed quite logically from the objective conditions which characterized the black predicament. Likewise, during the interwar period and the succeeding decade, the efforts of black leaders to end state-sanctioned racial discrimination in political participation, housing and education had the possibility of altering relevant characteristics of the status quo. The same argument can be made for efforts of black leaders during the civil rights period.

CONTEMPORARY LEADERS AND GROWING IRRELEVANCE

An analysis of leadership forms developed during the period of the civil rights movement is a necessary prerequisite for understanding the current black predicament and the practices of contemporary black leadership. The objective conditions which framed the black predicament in the post-World War II period included state-sanctioned racial segregation and discrimination, unabashed exclusion of blacks from many sectors of the economy, and a South Africa-like system of apartheid in the U.S. South, the area in which more than half of all blacks resided. This pattern of oppression was clearly counterproductive to the growth and development of the country and to its role as the leader of the Western world. The Carnegie Foundation's decision to fund the Myrdal study was but one example of the awareness of this fact. Thus, the civil rights movement always had a certain level of support among the dominant white leadership although the level and intensity of that support varied. While the dominant white forces were supportive of black efforts to eliminate the holdover feudal racist conventions of the South, they wished to control the pace of social change and to ensure that the push for legal equality would not alter fundamental economic relations.

Over time, a set of prescriptions and proscriptions evolved within which the black struggle was expected to be confined.

During the civil rights movement, those leaders who conformed to these prescriptions and proscriptions were rewarded by dominant economic and political interests while those who did not incurred the wrath of the state and neglect of private philanthropy. Those strategies which assumed that black economic deprivation could be eliminated through enforcement of civil rights laws in conjunction with black self-improvement schemes funded by government or private philanthropy were favored. Consequently, the leadership which survived the 1960s was overly deferential to these assumptions.

However, a case can still be made that black leadership during the civil rights movement was relevant. The elimination of apartheid in the U.S. South, the establishment of fair employment practices and contract compliance, and the elimination of state-supported segregated education were all essential developments. In a sense, the question as to whether black oppression was/is systemic could not be resolved until this legal underbrush had been cleared.

Unfortunately, the leaders who survived the civil rights movement period as well as new leaders who entered the stage in the 1970s made no effort to place the dual legacy of the civil rights movement—the elimination of state-sanctioned discrimination and the resultant increase in the size and overall well-being of the black middle class on the one hand and the intensified impoverishment of the "black underclass" on the other—in its proper dialectical and systemic context. It is the increasingly permanent character of black poverty and the functional integration of the shrinking black middle class which constitute the essential characteristics of the current black predicament. In the following paragraphs, I will comment upon the response of black leaders to this reality, but first a word or two about what I have referred to as the functional integration of the black leadership into the state apparatus.

The black leaders who survived the civil rights movement were essentially elected and appointed officials—particularly big city mayors, black congresspersons, state and federal bureaucrats, and the heads of civil rights organizations and other institutions. Once the struggle for legal inclusion was successfully culminated, the view that the black struggle was now an economic one became current. Channeling economic resources into the black community was given top priority, at least in rhetoric if not in practice. These leaders controlled the flow of eleemosynary resources designed to bring about social change coming into the communities from governments and private foundations. At the local level, black leaders and organizations were beholden to these national leaders for their survival. This relationship between national black leaders and public and private funding sources integrated them functionally into the state apparatus.

This functional integration was reinforced by changing social practices which brought black leaders into more intimate relations with powerful whites. Black leaders are now routinely appointed as directors of major corporations and some are invited to join exclusive social clubs. Such associations further integrate black leadership into the apparatus.

The upshot of all of this is that what passes for black opposition are black leaders and organizations more or less integrated as functional parts of the very social order which gives rise to the conditions which call forth their need to exist.

Let us see how various types of contemporary black leaders define the current reality and respond to it. Heads of civil rights organizations and civil rights politicians have all recognized the development of the "permanent underclass," but all have failed to raise the question of the systemic nature of these conditions. No effort has been made to stimulate within the black community discussions regarding the limits of the existing political economy. Instead, militant descriptions such as those offered in the Urban League's annual state of black America documents are followed by policy recommendations consistent with the reformist ideology. For example, chronic underemployment and unemployment are to be addressed by job training programs and welfare reform. The fact that after more than two decades of such programs the problem is more severe has not led to a reassessment of their position.

Black public officials continue to take the position that the key to black advancement lies in the electoral arena. While acknowledging the limits of such politics, any effort to build alternative political institutions is perceived to be suicidal. By implication the limitations of electoral politics are accepted as the ceiling on possible black political advancement. Officials are then assessed not so much on the liberating potential of their political practices as on their ability or willingness to facilitate black participation within existing public programs. Thus, the conservative who opposes all civil rights initiatives but who helps arrange, say, a SBA loan for a black constituent, is identified as one who delivers.

Conclusion

Prior to the present era, black leaders for the most part were not integrated into the system. They were outsiders. They viewed the system as outsiders and they offered their critiques as outsiders. Their status as outsiders conditioned how they related to those who actually exercised power. Not unduly constrained by system maintenance concerns, they could act as the radical conscience of society and prod and push the system beyond the then-accepted limits. That was the case before the Civil War when black leadership played a major role in ending slavery. Black leadership was also pivotal in the social transformation that followed the Civil War. It was a major force in the Pan-Africanist movement which nurtured the anti-colonial movements of the interwar years. And, it was the black movement of the 1960s that paved the way for the rise of the movements of Native Americans, women, and other subordinated groups.

Today, the situation has changed dramatically. The black leadership class are no longer outsiders. Though still disproportionately small in number, a critical mass of well-prepared and appropriately credentialed black men and women are integrated into the institutional citadels of power in the United States. They are insiders.

The most important question to raise under these circumstances is: How will this institutionally grounded leadership define the problems of black rank and file? What will they say about the causes of continued deprivation and what will they propose as solutions? Will they dare raise questions about the systemic character of black oppression? Will there be a need for a second tier of black leadership comprised of outsiders who will prod and push the system including its ensconced black leadership?

Notes

1. George Graham, *Methodological Foundations for Political Analysis* (Waltham, MA: Xerox College Publishing, 1971), p. 41.
2. Isabel Sawhill, "An Overview," *Public Interest*, no. 96 (Summer 1989), p. 6.
3. Martha Gephart and Robert Pearson, "Contemporary Research on the Urban Underclass," *Social Science Research Council Items* (June 1981), p. 4.
4. See William J. Wilson, *The Truly Disadvantaged* (Chicago: University of Chicago Press, 1987).
5. Excerpted from Alexander Astin, *The Myth of Equal Access to Higher Education* (Atlanta: Southern Education Foundation, 1975), p. 12.
6. Wilson, *The Disadvantaged*.
7. David Swinton, "The Economic Status of Blacks 1987," *The State of Black America 1988* (New York: National Urban League, 1988), p. 134.
8. *The New York Times*, July 10, 1989, p. 7.
9. Brent Staples, "Wanted: A Million Black Republicans," *The New York Times*, June 21, 1993, p. A14, cols. 1-2.
10. Ibid.
11. Ibid.
12. Kenneth Clark, "The Role of Race, The Black Plight, Race or Class? A Debate between Kenneth B. Clark and Carl Gersham," *The New York Times Magazine*, October 5, 1980, p. 33.
13. For elaboration on this point, see Matthew Holden, *The Politics of the Black Nation* (New York: Chandler, 1973), especially Chapter 2.

INDEX